Released
Samford Univers

D0909861

Southern Negroes, 1861-1865

SOUTHERN NEGROES

1861-1865

BY

BELL IRVIN WILEY, *1906 —*

Foreword by C. Vann Woodward

LOUISIANA STATE UNIVERSITY PRESS
Baton Rouge

Samford University Library

ISBN 0-8071-0090-0 (paper)
Library of Congress Catalog Card Number 38-12709
Copyright 1938 by Yale University Press
Copyright © 1965 by Bell I. Wiley
All rights reserved
Manufactured in the United States of America
Louisiana Paperbacks edition published August, 1974,
by special arrangement with the author.

Annex
973.715

E
185.2
.W65

TO
MY MOTHER AND FATHER

82-03876

FOREWORD

WHILE historians had little trouble agreeing that without the Negro slave there would have been no Civil War, they neglected for a long time the history of this central figure in their voluminous writing about the war. The Negro's role in the Civil War was too important a subject to be neglected by less disinterested observers, and the myth-makers quickly took over. Their myths were of prime importance in vindicating, justifying, and defending all sorts and kinds of interests: dispossessed slave holders, Confederate policy makers, Radical Reconstructionists, federal army officers, philanthropists— every agency or interest, in fact, that had to do with the Southern Negro, before, during, or after the war. The myths they wove left the truth covered in obscurity and confusion.

Bell Irvin Wiley was the first professional historian to wade into this difficult field, restore order, and bring light. After he published this book in 1938 other historians followed up with more detailed studies of aspects he first explored, such as the Negro in the army, in school, and in the Port Royal Experiment. But their findings have supplemented rather than supplanted his work. His book still stands as the best general treatment of this important subject in existence.

The first myth to fall before Wiley's scrutiny was one of the South's most beloved and celebrated — the myth of the loyal slave, faithfully laboring in support of his Confederate master. Wiley does cite instances of touching personal loyalty, but adds that these instances, "in the light of contemporary evidence, must be considered as exceptional," and concludes that "in the invaded areas insubordination seems to have been more common than submission." The slave often proved to be a spy, a collaborationist, and a malingerer. The evidence destroys the legend of the Negro's indifference to freedom.

The myths of the liberators fare little better under the historian's investigation than the myths of the old masters.

The wielders of "the terrible swift sword" often brought woe and tragedy to the liberated, treated them brutally, exploited them shamefully, and neglected them cynically. The agents charged with the freedmen's welfare too often abused their authority and turned over their charges to the mercies of those from whom they were to be protected. The invading enterprisers who equated freedom with the wage system taught the liberated a terrible first lesson in the meaning of free enterprise. The philanthropists who brought their own brand of salvation for the slave are credited with good intentions, but also with a poor record of fulfillment. "Those Negroes who were assembled in contraband camps," writes Wiley, "died by the thousands; those who were employed on plantations received treatment little better than that which they had received under the old regime; those who entered military pursuits were dealt with in a manner more becoming to slaves than to freedmen."

The most heroic role the Negro played, that of soldier, was in fact the most miserably rewarded and disillusioning. In pay and rank, in food and medical care, in assignment and duty the Negro soldier was mistreated and discriminated against from start to finish: "The inconsiderate and discriminatory treatment accorded the Negroes in Federal military pursuits is a regrettable episode in the transition of the colored race in America from slavery to freedom."

To read Professor Wiley's study is to realize what a traumatic experience liberation must have been for the American Negro slave. "In fact," he writes, "the entire experience of Southern Negroes during the War of Secession was discouraging and disillusioning." In the light of this record we can understand why it was that the end of slavery only meant the beginning of the fight for real freedom.

C. VANN WOODWARD

New Haven, Connecticut
September 1964

PREFACE

THE Southern Negro during the War of Secession has been a neglected phase of American History. Studies of the slave era usually end with the outbreak of the war; those which deal with the period since emancipation usually begin with 1865, or treat the war years in sketchy introductory fashion. This monograph is an attempt to fill in the gap.

This study tells of the experience of the Negroes during the most significant period of their history in America. It portrays the relations between the white people and the Negroes during an era crucial for both races.

The subject of this monograph was first suggested to the writer several years ago in a dissertation on the Negro in the Confederacy prepared for the doctor's degree at Yale University. A few of the chapters of that dissertation, completely rewritten from materials enriched by subsequent research, are included in Part One of this study. For the writing of much of Part One, and all of Part Two the author is indebted to Yale University for the award of the Currier Research Fellowship. This stipend made possible an entire year of intensive and uninterrupted research after the conferring of the doctor's degree. The award by the United Daughters of the Confederacy of the Mrs. Simon Baruch Prize of one thousand dollars to this study in the competition of 1935 relieved the author of his share of the expense of publishing the monograph.

During the writer's peregrinations through the country in search of manuscripts and other original materials he has become indebted to many scholars both lay and professional. The limitation of space precludes the possibility of individual mention of all those who have rendered valuable aid. Among those whose advice, counsel, and guidance were exceedingly helpful are the following: the late Professor Ulrich B. Phillips of Yale University, under whose direction the dissertation was written; Professor Ralph Henry Gabriel of Yale University; Dr. T. P. Martin of the Library of Congress; Professor W. K. Boyd of Duke University; the late Dr. Dunbar Rowland of the Department of Archives and History of the State of Mississippi; Miss Ellen Fitzsimmons of the Charleston, South Carolina, Library Society; Professor Charles W. Ramsdell of the University of Texas; Professor Howard K. Beale of the University of North Carolina; Miss Anna M. Roberts of Mississippi State Teachers College; and Professor Thomas S. Staples of Hendrix College. Particular acknowledgement is due Professor Leonard W. Labaree of Yale University. As editor of the Yale Historical Studies, Professor Labaree read the study several times in its various stages of development. His generous criticism has been an invaluable factor in bringing the monograph to completion.

B. I. W.

Hattiesburg, Mississippi,
  February 8, 1938.

CONTENTS

PART I

NEGROES IN THE CONFEDERACY

SOUTHERN NEGROES

I

THE COMING OF THE "YANKEES"

FROM the launching of the first "on to Richmond" drive in July, 1861, until the surrender of Lee at Appomattox, the conflict between North and South was a war of invasion on the one hand and a war of resistance on the other. In 1861 Federal penetration of the Confederacy was limited to a small portion of northern Virginia and seacoast areas of the Carolinas. During that year life for the Negroes in the South went on in much the same manner as before. True, there was a great deal of excitement in the air, much beating of drums, and much waving of flags. "Ole missus' " eyes often betrayed weeping and "ole massa" was exceedingly quiet and thoughtful after "young massa" rode away. But there was a full crop of cotton in the fields; and the fact that a war was under way somewhere in the distance did not retard the growth of grass in the cotton rows or diminish the number of chores around the house. There was much work to be done and all through the South the Negroes went about the performance of their daily tasks. Even after the invasion of northern Virginia, western Tennessee, northern Mississippi, and other peripheral portions of the South, the life of the Negro in the interior was not appreciably altered. The second and third years of the war brought greater impingements on food, clothing, and labor, but the necessary adjustments were made gradually and with very little disturbance.

The coming of the "Yankees," however, whether to northern Virginia in 1861, to western Tennessee in 1862, or to central Georgia in 1864, wrought immediate and radical changes in the life of the slaves; and the effects of invasion on all areas were very much alike. When the Federals approached, many planters removed their Negroes to the interior. If time permitted, they frequently rented plantations and arranged in advance for the transfer of slaves and other movable property. There was a tendency, however, for owners to postpone their departure as long as possible, thinking to get more of their crops gathered before the Federals arrived, or hoping that a turn in the fortunes of war might relieve them of the necessity of removal.[1] In some cases, masters and slaves lingering too long were caught unawares by the cry "Yankees coming"; the result was a disordered flight.

Reluctance of planters to remove their slaves sometimes provoked military authorities to compel them to transfer the able-bodied males to places beyond the reach of the Union army.[2] This was due to the initiation by the Federal government of the policy of employing the Negroes in military pursuits. "Every sound male black left for the enemy," wrote Kirby Smith to Sterling Price, "becomes a soldier whom we have afterward to fight."[3] Facilities for transportation of slaves were provided by the military authorities.[4]

The planter usually selected his more valuable slaves—domestic servants and field hands—for removal and left the old and decrepit ones behind for the "Yankees."[5] Chil-

1. A Virginia lady wrote on July 30, 1862: "Uncle Jourdan was prepared to run this morning with the larger portion of his negroes . . . but has concluded to wait a few days and see if Stonewall Jackson will not whip Pope in that time." Library of Congress, Diary of Betty Herndon Maury.

2. Charleston *Mercury*, Nov. 18, 1861; also Nov. 27, 1862, message of Governor Pickens to the South Carolina legislature.

3. *Official Records of the Union and Confederate Armies*, Ser. 1, XXII, pt. 2, 990, Sept. 4, 1863. The *Official Records* will be cited hereafter as *O. R.*

4. W. W. Scott, ed., *Two Confederate Items*, p. 11.

5. Grant to Halleck, Feb. 18, 1863, *O. R.*, Ser. 1, XXIV, pt. 1, 18; Library of Congress, Journal of Samuel P. Boyer, entry of Nov. 23, 1863. The attitude which hard-pressed planters sometimes had toward a surplusage of non-working slaves is indicated by an entry in the diary of a

dren were taken or left, according to the dictates of sentiment or circumstances. Sometimes when an owner had to
leave members of his family at the plantation in the path
of the enemy, he selected a few of his most faithful slaves
to remain with them to help look after the affairs of the
farm. In some cases, slaves who were suspected of disloyal
designs were removed first. The overseer of Mulberry Hill
Plantation in Virginia wrote the owner: "I . . . sent Dave
to Lynchburg thinken it a safer place than here, for at that
time there were 10,000 Yankeys at Buffaloe."[6]

"Running the negroes," as their movement was generally designated, was a practice much in vogue in the
South, especially after the Federals began their extensive
campaigns of 1862. Travelers on the highways often met
great droves of slaves, moving from the coast to the "up
country" in South Carolina, from Mobile to the environs
of Montgomery, from Mississippi to Alabama, to Louisiana, or even to Texas. It was estimated that two thousand
slaves were removed from Washington and Tyrrell counties to the interior of North Carolina within a ten-day
period in the fall of 1862. A short time later a Texas newspaper reported that trains of from fifty to sixty wagons,
belonging to refugees from Louisiana, were often seen on
the highways.[7] These caravans of refugees were interesting sights—Negro women, their heads wrapped in gaudy
bandanas perched high on wagons loaded with chairs,
tables, and bedding; stalwart Negro men trudging beside
the slow-moving vans; dust-covered, barefooted "picka-
ninnies," to whom the journey was more of a frolic than a
flight, now running along beside the wagons, now stealing

North Alabaman: "John Cockborn attempted to celebrate . . . by running off to the Yankees. The scoundrel leaves here his wife and 6 children
for us to feed. I wish he had them." Diary of J. B. Moore (MS. in private possession), entry of July 21, 1862.

6. Wallace to McDowell, May 8, 1862, Mulberry Hill Plantation Letters
(MSS. in private possession).

7. *The True Issue* (La Grange, Texas), Jan. 1, 1863; A. J. Fremantle,
Three Months in the Confederate States, pp. 82, 86.

a ride on the "perch-pole"—an offense which was apt to
call forth a sharp threat from an observant "mammy"
that "de conjurer 'll git you for sho."

At night the overseer or owner would halt the party
near some convenient creek or spring and unload a few
necessary provisions. The men would build a roaring fire,
while the women busied themselves with the preparation of
supper. After the meal, the Negroes might buoy their
spirits and entertain their master with a few spirituals.
Then to bed, but not, perhaps, without a prayer by the
master for freedom from the "Yankees" accompanied by
audible "Amens!" and "Grant it Massa Jesus!" from the
members of the dark circle whose secret prayer, in some
cases, was for freedom from "massa," whatever that freedom might mean.

Sometimes the planter would move a part of his Negroes
into a nearby wood, swamp, or canebrake to await the
passing of an invading force.[8] If the Federals lingered in
the neighborhood for a long time, or if the invasions became frequent, the party would have to abandon the wood
or swamp for places more remote. Some planters were kept
moving from place to place in quest of a safe retreat from
the seemingly omnipresent "Yankee."

The necessity of "refugeeing" was a hardship for
planters and Negroes alike. It often meant the severance
of family ties.[9] This hardship was sometimes accentuated
by a cold reception in the community chosen for the new
home.[10] In the case of the Negroes, sadness resulting from
the severing of home ties was sometimes tinged with regret
at being farther removed from the "Yankees" and freedom.[11] A Tennessee owner sought to alleviate the unpleas-

8. Susan D. Smedes, *A Southern Planter*, p. 210; Wm. R. Boggs, *Military Reminiscences*, p. 30.

9. U. B. Phillips, *Life and Labor in the Old South*, p. 234.

10. Montgomery *Daily Advertiser and Register*, Feb. 21, 1864.

11. The mixture of the emotions of the Westover Plantation slaves is
commented on by Professor Phillips in his *Life and Labor in the Old
South*, p. 234. When Selden left Westover for the interior, the slaves left

antness incident to removal by calling all his Negroes together and giving them a drink of whiskey immediately
before ordering their departure.[12]

So strong was the aversion of Negroes to "refugeeing,"
that they sometimes openly resisted removal.[13] The announcement by the planter of his intention of moving to
the interior often resulted in a wholesale flight of his slaves
to the Federal lines.[14] When President Davis issued an order for the removal by the military authorities of slaves in
northwestern Mississippi, the State legislature raised a
protest that the execution of such an order would "cause
the larger portion of the slaves to go to the enemy." So
strong was the objection, that the President revoked the
order.[15]

Many masters abandoned their slaves rather than move
them when the "Yankees" arrived. An editorial in the
Charleston *Daily Courier* headed "Onesimus" said that
"masters have deserted their servants under panic and surprise, even after full opportunities of preparations, about
as often in comparison with the numbers, as servants have
designedly left their masters. For such masters, we know or
propose no special recompense or sympathy."[16] These "fu-

behind "wept bitterly." But before he returned five months later, all except five had "gone away with the Yankees."

12. *Diary of Ephraim Shelby Dodd*, p. 28, entry of Nov. 30, 1863.

13. Charleston *Mercury*, Nov. 23, 1861.

14. J. J. B. Hilliard to Mrs. C. C. Clay, Jr., Oct. 21, 1863, Duke University Library, Clay Papers; Diary of Betty Herndon Maury, entry of
July 22, 1862.

15. *Jefferson Davis, Constitutionalist, Letters, Papers and Speeches*,
Dunbar Rowland, ed., VI, 84, 92; *Laws of Mississippi*, 1863, Nov. Sess.,
chap. 140, Resolutions. There were exceptions to the slaves opposing
removal. The father of Frances Fearn, a Louisiana master, offered his
slaves the choice of going with him to Texas or remaining at home until
the "Yankees" came. They begged to be taken with him. *Diary of a Refugee*, p. 28. For a similar case see J. F. H. Claiborne's "Reminiscences of
the Late War," New Orleans *Daily Picayune*, July 5, 1883. Claiborne's
slaves implored him to leave Louisiana and to take them with him. They
were "afraid of the jay hawkers, afraid of being impressed into the Confederate army."

16. Charleston *Daily Courier*, Sept. 17, 1864.

gitive masters," as General Hunter called them, were sometimes held in contempt by their abandoned black subjects;
at least, such seems to be the implication of a song said to
have been sung by them and attributed to a colored author:

> Say darkeys hab you seen de massa,
>   Wid de muffstash on he face,
> Go 'long de road sometime dis mornin'
>   Like he gwine leabe de place.
> He see de smoke way up de river
>   Whar de Lincum gun-boats lay;
> He took he hat, an' leff berry sudden,
>   And I spose he's runned away.
> De massa run, ha, ha!
> De darkey stay, ho, ho!
> It mus' be now de kingdum comin',
>   An' de yar ob jubilo.[17]

When the report "Yankees coming!" reached a community, there were many slaves who chose to expedite the advent of freedom by going to meet their deliverers. The
question as to approximately how many slaves ran away to
the Federals during the war cannot be answered. But it
can be said with safety that the arrival of Union soldiers
in any part of the South marked the beginning of a flow of
black humanity toward the Federal camp; and that, in
many cases, the flow was so great that it carried away the
bulk of the male slave population.[18]

The very close relationship between the approach of the
Federals and the flight of the slaves is illustrated by the
case of Shirley Plantation on the James River in Virginia.
The Federals first came to the vicinity of the plantation on

17. George Cary Eggleston, ed., *American War Ballads*, II, 200. Edmund Kirke (pseudo.), who gives this verse in his *Down in Tennessee*,
p. 125, claims to have heard an old Negro grave-digger singing it in a
Nashville cemetery after Federal occupation of the town.

18. Professor T. S. Staples in his *Reconstruction in Arkansas*, p. 183,
goes so far as to say that "wherever federal forces appeared, most of the
able-bodied adult Negroes left their owners and sought refuge within the
Union lines."

June 30, 1862. There is no evidence in the records of any slaves having run away prior to that time. On July 14, 1862, two weeks after the arrival of the Union force, the journal records that "15 Negro men and boys ran off at different times up to this date." A few days later a woman and two children absconded. In a short time the Federals passed on. On July 13, 1863, the "Yankees" made their second appearance in the vicinity, coming up the river with eight or ten gunboats. In the next three days, fifteen Negro men ran off to them. On April 5, 1864, the Federal fleet again came up the river. This time there were "140 or 150 transports and gunboats." For a while there was no notice of any slaves running away; but evidently preparations were being made. On May 10, the exodus began. From May 10 to May 14, thirty Negroes, principally women and children—most of the men from the place having run away on previous visits of the Federals—went to the fleet. By June 20 seventeen more had departed. This brought the total of the runaways for the three Federal visits to eighty. The records indicate that this was practically the entire slave population of Shirley.[19]

The proportion of slaves running away from Shirley is doubtless exceptional, but an abundance of evidence indicates a close parallel of tendencies in other invaded areas.[20] A Confederate general estimated that a million dollars' worth of Negroes was escaping weekly to the Federals in North Carolina in August, 1862.[21] Frontier counties in Virginia were exempted from the impressment act because they had lost such a large proportion of their slave population.[22] William Butler of the United States Christian

19. Library of Congress, Shirley Plantation Records.
20. The diary of A. Franklin Pugh and the records of LeBlanc Plantation (MSS. in Louisiana State University Library) reveal a course of circumstances on Louisiana places strikingly similar to that at Shirley. Pugh lost most of the able-bodied hands from his four plantations as a result of Federal invasion; LeBlanc had a separate page in the back of his plantation record book on which he recorded the names of the runaways and the time of their departure.
21. O. R., Ser. 1, IX, 477.
22. Acts of Virginia, 1863, Called Session, chap. 6.

Commission wrote from Mississippi that "after Pemberton marched out with his army, Vicksburg was looked upon by the Negroes as the very gate of heaven, and they came trooping to it as pigeons to their roost at night."[23] On April 20, 1862, Mrs. Betty Herndon Maury noted in her diary that the "full band" of the Federal army across the river from Fredericksburg was playing "Yankee Doodle" and the "Star Spangled Banner." The entries after that date contain numerous references to Negroes running away.

The slaves displayed a considerable degree of ingenuity in effecting their escape through the Confederate lines. They frequently deceived the pickets by telling them that they belonged to "de nex' plantation" and were simply on their way home.[24] The problem of obtaining passes was often solved by getting some intelligent slave to write them.[25] This was more easily accomplished in cities than in rural sections. There seems to have been a sort of "bootleg ring" in Richmond devoted to "running negroes" through the lines, with a white man at its head, who prepared all the passes and furnished a four-horse wagon for transportation. The charge was "from two to three hundred dollars according to the number engaging seats in the wagon."[26]

Drastic steps were taken during the war to prevent the escape of slaves to the Federal lines. Picket lines were "doubled" on the York River in February, 1864, in an ef-

23. Mobile *Daily Advertiser and Register*, Nov. 15, 1863, quoting G. W. Elliot. For other Union evidence of the flocking of Negroes to the Federal camps see: Horace James, *Annual Report of the Superintendent of Negro Affairs in N. C.* (1864), p. 57; Thos. W. Conway, *Report on the Condition of the Freedmen in the Department of the Gulf*, p. 4; report of General Butler from Newport News, Va., May 27, 1861, *O. R.*, Ser. 1, II, 53.

24. Charleston *Mercury*, July 4, 1864.

25. Richmond *Enquirer*, Dec. 27, 1864.

26. Richmond *Daily Dispatch*, March 10, 1864. See also Richmond *Enquirer*, Jan. 9, 1864. There are reports of a similar ring operating in Savannah. Fugitives were .charged $50 a family; if they lacked the cash they might pay in kind—pork, bacon, etc. Montgomery *Weekly Mail*, Oct. 28, 1863.

fort to stay the Negro exodus to "Yankeedom."[27] The passport system was rigidly applied in frontier regions.[28] In all the Confederate states there were local organizations formed such as "home guards," "independent scouts," and "mounted pickets" to help preserve order and to prevent the escape of slaves. The Georgia legislature passed an act in March, 1865, requiring the governor to "establish a line of mounted pickets of such numbers and at such points as he may deem sufficient for the purpose of arresting and preventing the escape of slaves."[29] The use of small boats by slaves in the coastal regions was greatly restricted or entirely forbidden.[30] Legislation was enacted to tighten the patrol laws in practically all the Confederate states.

Individuals and local organizations also took steps to prevent the escape of Negroes to the Federals. Citizens assembled in public meeting at Hempstead, Texas, in the fall of 1862 adopted a resolution "that the Legislature be requested at an early day to enact a law making it a capital crime for any slave to desert from his master with the intent of going over to the enemy." That this was not a mere explosive utterance is indicated by the fact that an executive committee was appointed for immediate action, "to try and hang any negro caught in attempting to escape to the enemy." A group of planters in Mississippi petitioned the governor to detail a man conscripted for the Confederate army for special and important service at home; they added the explanation that he was the "owner of a pack of Negro dogs and has devoted a good portion of time to the patrol duty."[31]

27. Richmond *Enquirer,* Feb. 9, 1864.
28. *O. R.,* Ser. 1, XVII, pt. 2, 638.
29. *Acts of Georgia,* 1865, Called Sess., Res., no. 30; Brown to Johnston, March 14, 1865, Georgia Archives, Governor Brown's Letter Book, 1861–1865.
30. *Acts of Virginia,* 1861–1862, Reg. Sess., chap. 86; 1863–1864, Reg. Sess., chap. 36; *O. R.,* Ser. 1, XIV, 744. The flag of truce in the hand of a slave on the shore or off the coast was a sight familiar to the crews of the Federal fleet. See Journal of Samuel P. Boyer, *passim.*
31. Houston *Tri-Weekly Telegraph,* Oct. 31, 1862. Foster to Pettus, Oct. 20, 1862, Miss. Archives, Ser. E, no. 58.

Some of the slaves who ran away returned to their masters after a brief sojourn within the Federal lines. Their return, in some instances, was due to homesickness; in others, it was due to the disillusioning influences of hardship or disease in the Federal camps.[32] The action of three Negroes on Magnolia Plantation in Louisiana is probably typical of that of many in other parts of the South. The Negroes ran away on May 26, 1862. On May 30 they returned. The overseer, in making a record of their return, wrote: "They say they have Seen the Eliphant and are glad to get Home."[33]

The attitude of the slaves toward the invading "Yankee" varied from extreme fear and hostility in some cases to unrestrained veneration in others. Instances of genuine fear were much more numerous in isolated and backward communities, where the slave population greatly exceeded the white element. This fear was sometimes due to the impressions which the Negroes had obtained from stories told them by their white masters and mistresses. When the Federals came to Port Royal, South Carolina, in 1861, the Negroes, instead of running to meet them with open arms, in some cases ran the other way. The Union authorities were much perplexed. On investigation they found that the slaves were under the impression that they were going to be seized and sent away to Cuba. Their masters had told them this. It was with great difficulty that confidence was established by the newcomers.[34]

32. Charles H. Wesley, *Negro Labor in the U. S., 1850–1925*, pp. 88–89.
33. Magnolia Plantation Records (MS. in the custody of Professor J. de Roulhac Hamilton at the University of North Carolina).
34. E. L. Pierce, *The Freedmen of Port Royal, South-Carolina, Official Reports*, pp. 308–309. Contemporary newspaper reports indicate that the masters were not always guilty of wilful misrepresentation when they told their slaves that they would be sent to Cuba by the "Yankees." They believed it would be so. The report of Lincoln's colonization scheme accentuated this belief. Natchez *Daily Courier,* July 3, 1862; Montgomery *Weekly Confederation,* July 21, 1861; J. G. McNeilly, "War and Reconstruction in Mississippi," *Publications* of Miss. Hist. Soc., *Centenary Series,* II, 169. The *Southern Recorder* of June 25, 1861, carried this no-

Southerners were not unaware of the wholesome influence which a fear of the "Yankees" would have on the loyalty of their Negroes.[35] This, coupled with the amusement which they derived from working on the imaginations of their servants, led to the origination and circulation of many stories of the diabolical appearance and the cruel practices of the Federals. Some of these were exaggerated as they were retold by the Negroes. A slave who escaped to the South Atlantic blockading fleet from Georgia in April, 1863, said that his mistress had "told him that as soon as he came to the 'Yankees,' so soon would they put a harness, prepared for the purpose, on him and compel him to drag cannons and wagons about like horses."[36] An old colored woman in Shelby County, Tennessee, said that when she asked her mistress what the "Yankees" looked like, she was told, "They got long horns on their heads and tushes in their mouths and eyes sticking out like a cow. They're mean old things."[37] Georgia owners told their slaves that the Federals threw women and children into the Chattahoochee River, and that when the buildings were burned in Atlanta they filled them with Negroes to be roasted by the flames.[38] With such stories as these in circulation, the observation of one old Negro when he was first told that the newcomers in blue were the "Yankees,"

tice: "*Abolitionists Selling Negroes.* Several hundred Negroes have been stolen from their owners in Virginia by the . . . soldiers of Lincoln who declare their intention to ship them for sale in Cuba to help pay the expenses of the war."

35. *The Southern Churchman,* April, 1864, contained a reprint of the report of President Yeatman of the Western Sanitary Commission, telling of the destitute condition of the slaves who had been freed in the Mississippi Valley. The editor, commenting on the report said: "Let every master or mistress call up the servants and read this account to see who are their friends. O Lord, how long?"

36. Journal of Samuel P. Boyer, entry of April 25, 1863. An item from the Norfolk *Day Book,* copied by the Charleston *Mercury,* Nov. 13, 1861, reported that Negroes at Old Point were "being put into the harness like so many oxen."

37. Orland Kay Armstrong, *Old Massa's People,* p. 301.

38. New Orleans *Times,* Jan. 4, 1865, quoting New York *Post.*

"Why dey's folks," and the exclamation of another, "Great dairdy! So Yankees stan'!" are not surprising.[39]

Among the little Negroes the term "Yankee" was a veritable bugbear.[40] Their elders often used the threat "the Yankees'll git you" to hold them to good behavior. When the dusky urchins happened to be the first ones on the place to see the approaching columns, they would run to their "mammies" "with eyes like a full moon," crying "Yankees coming."[41]

There were instances in which the slaves' attitude toward the Union soldiers was characterized more by hostility or contempt than by fear. The ruthlessness with which cabins were ransacked and personal effects taken was highly offensive to the Negroes.[42] In such cases, the "day of jubilo" was turned into a day of sadness.

Some of the Negroes were apparently indifferent to the approach of the Federals. They regarded the newcomers as neither devils nor deliverers, but simply as another group of masters. This is reflected in the assertion of some Port Royal, South Carolina, slaves to a Union official that "the white man do what he pleases with us; we are yours now, massa"; likewise the statement of an old Virginia Negro that she came to the Federals "because others came."[43]

39. *South Carolina Women in the Confederacy*, I, 220, narrative of Margaret Crawford Adams; Elizabeth W. Pearson, ed., *Letters from Port Royal*, p. 217.

40. Catherine Hopley, in *Life in the South*, I, 288, says that the term was as much a bugbear "as was a Frenchman some years ago to our English nursemaids."

41. Mrs. Rogers, "Reminiscences of a War Time Girl," in M. P. Andrews, ed., *Women of the South in War Times*, p. 300.

42. For instances of theft and spoliation of Negro goods see: "Journal of Mrs. Henry G. Dulaney, 1862–1863," in Marietta Minningerode Andrews, ed., *Scraps of Paper*, p. 67; Library of Congress, Diary of John N. Waddell, entry of Nov. 11, 1862; Mrs. Elizabeth W. Allston Pringle, *Chronicles of Chicora Wood*, p. 233; Mary B. Chesnut, *Diary from Dixie*, p. 397. The forcing of Negroes into the Union army was another factor which aroused their hostility.

43. Pierce, *Freedmen of Port Royal*, p. 308; *Report of a Committee of the Representatives of the New York Yearly Meeting of Friends upon the Condition and Wants of the Colored Refugees*, p. 7.

In the majority of cases, the slaves seem to have received the "Yankees" with enthusiasm. But the expression of their joy was often repressed in the presence of their "white folks." Normally they threw off all restraint and gave themselves to shouting and singing and "bressing de Lawd." By some "Mas Linkum" was venerated as a god and his soldiers as divine emissaries.[44] General Sherman's name was mixed "with that of Moses and Simon and other scriptural ones as well as 'Abraham Linkom,' the Great Messiah of 'Dis Jubilee' " by the praying and shouting black hordes at Savannah.[45] His army entered Covington, Georgia, with flags unfurled and the band playing patriotic airs. "The Negroes were simply frantic with joy," Sherman said. "They clustered about my horse, shouted and prayed. . . . I have witnessed hundreds if not thousands of such scenes; and can now see a poor girl in the very ecstasy of the 'Methodist' shout, hugging the banner of one of the regiments and jumping up to the 'feet of Jesus.' "[46]

Closely related to the Negroes' attitude toward the "Yankees" is their conception of the war and its issues. In some isolated communities the slaves may have known practically nothing of the existence of the conflict, much less its causes. An aged Virginia servant, who remembered the War of 1812, on hearing the distant boom of the cannon of the Federal gunboats on the Rappahannock River, is reported to have said, "Well, I 'clare 'fo' Gawd, dere's dem damn Britishers again."[47] Another Virginia slave explained to a group of his companions that the cause of the war was that "somebody from across the water sont a ship-

44. A gang of Negro workmen on the wharves of Beaufort were conjecturing as to the qualities and characteristics of the President. An aged "praise man" interrupted impatiently, "What do you know 'bout Massa Linkum. Massa Linkum be ebrewhere. He walk de earth like de Lord." *O. R.*, Ser. 3, III, 436.

45. M. A. Howe, ed., *Home Letters of General Sherman*, p. 319, letter of Dec. 25, 1864.

46. W. T. Sherman, *Memoirs*, II, 180.

47. Statement of Joseph Christian Bristow, Urbanna, Virginia, to the author in 1933. The old slave belonged to Bristow's relatives.

load o' money to us cullud folks and somebody stole it; an'
now dey gwine fight it out."[48] The degree of ignorance
manifested by these two Negroes was exceptional. Many of
the slaves knew the issues of the war from its early stages.[49]
The majority of them knew that their freedom was at
stake after the issuance of the Emancipation Proclamation. There were a number of methods by which they might
obtain information. The domestic servants often heard the
topics of the day discussed by the whites. Booker T. Washington listened to the conversations about the war as he
fanned the flies from the table at the "big house."[50] However, the whites usually avoided commenting on prospects
of emancipation in the presence of Negroes. Bishop Isaac
Lane of the African Methodist Episcopal Church satisfied
his curiosity as to what the "white folks" discussed among
themselves by stealing into a closet adjoining the dining
room and listening to the conversation.[51] In other cases,
slaves listened to war-talk from places of concealment under their masters' houses and in the branches of conven-
iently situated trees.[52] Some masters took the slaves into
their confidence, especially their most trusted ones, and

48. Statement of Anderson Brown, Petersburg, Virginia, ex-slave and
ex-Union soldier, to the author in 1933. Brown heard the Negro make
this explanation.

49. A slave belonging to the Reverend John A. Broadus of Virginia
displayed a remarkable knowledge of events preceding the war in a letter
to his master, Nov. 5, 1860. After stating that his health is good, and expressing the hope that the master and his family are feeling well, he
says: "My dear master, I hear much of the coming election. [He was
working on the University campus] I hope that Mr. Lincoln or no such
man may ever take his seat in the Presidential chair. I do most sincerely
hope that the Union may be preserved. I hear, through the white gentlemen here, that South Carolina will leave the Union in case he is elected.
I do hope she wont leave, as that would cause much disturbance and perhaps fighting. . . . Well do I recollect when I drove a wagon in the old
wars . . . but I hope we shall have no more wars, but let peace be in all
the land." Archibald T. Robertson, *Life and Letters of John Albert
Broadus*, p. 177.

50. *Up from Slavery*, p. 10.

51. Statement of Bishop Lane to the writer in 1932.

52. Elizabeth Hyde Botume, *First Days Amongst the Contrabands*,
p. 6.

frankly told them that their freedom was one of the basic issues of the war. Body servants were effective agents among the Negroes in the spreading of news of the war. In 1861 a great many servants accompanied the Confederate soldiers to the army. In the camps they were in the war atmosphere; they heard its issues discussed at the mess and around the campfire; some even talked with prisoners. When rations became short in 1862 and 1863, the majority of these servants were sent home. They were usually not hesitant in imparting to their sable brothers the information which they had gained. Negroes who went to exposed areas to work on defenses also had excellent opportunities to hear about and discuss the issues of the war. One of the chief objections offered by the planters in the interior to sending their slaves to work on fortifications was that they brought dangerous ideas back to the plantations, creating dissatisfaction and unrest.

The slaves were ingenious at passing on from one to another the news which came to them. By the use of "keywords" they were able to carry on conversation about the progress of the war even in the presence of their owners. In a certain section of Virginia "grease" was used as a code word, and, according to Robert Russa Moton, "If a slave coming back from town greeted a fellow-servant with the declaration, 'Good mornin' Sam, yo look mighty greasy this mornin',' that meant that he had picked up some fresh information about the prospects of freedom which would be divulged later on."[53] In another locality Negroes who prayed for Abraham Lincoln referred to him as "Old Ride-Up."[54] While the whites were ignorant of the detailed workings of the "grapevine telegraph," as this secret, informal means of Negro communication was called, they were aware of its existence, and they marveled at its effectiveness.

More than one owner who was complacent in the assur-

53. *What the Negro Thinks,* p. 10.
54. Joseph E. Roy, "Our Indebtedness to the Negroes for their Conduct during the War," *New Englander,* LI (1889), 354.

ance that his "niggers knew nothing about the war and cared less" would have been startled had he known the extent of their knowledge. He would doubtless have been chagrined had he known the aspirations so effectively concealed behind their deferential smiles and obsequious manners. After the close of the war, when the white people of a certain community had passed a resolution expressing appreciation for the loyal conduct of their slaves, an old Negro made the observation: "They needn't have done that for every now and then we were falling behind a stump or into a corner of the fence and praying for the Union soldiers."[55]

It was not an uncommon thing for slaves to obtain knowledge of military events before their masters. Intelligent domestic servants were frequently sent to get the mail. Those who could read would scan the headlines for the news and pass it on to the Negroes whom they encountered on the way to the "big house." Those who could not read would often pick up scraps of information by lingering at the post office after the issuance of the mail and listening to the reading and discussion of the news by the whites. In several instances masters received their first knowledge of the Emancipation Proclamation from their slaves.[56]

After the Federals came into a community, the Negroes sometimes had more complete information about local and remote events than their masters. The "Yankees" would tell the Negroes of their intention of occupying houses of certain citizens, when they intended to leave the vicinity, and what recent victories had been won. This intelligence, when passed on to the masters, was spoken of by them as "nigger news."

Information concerning the progress of the war was

55. Roy, *New Englander,* LI (1889), 354.
56. Bishop Isaac Lane was regularly sent for his master's mail. He knew how to read. When the issue of the paper containing the Emancipation Proclamation came he hid it and told his master that no paper came that day. He later read it secretly to some of the slaves. Loyal Publications Society, *Publications,* no. 28, p. 4.

generally received with great interest by the slaves. While they were usually very proficient at affecting unconcern, there were times when their actions and their looks betrayed them. A Chattanooga editor observed that, "the spirits of the colored citizens rise and fall with the ebb and flow of this tide of blue devils, and when they are glad as larks, the whites are depressed and go about the streets like mourners."[57]

Although numerous instances might be cited of Negroes being indifferent to the success of the Union army and even of their rejecting freedom when it was offered to them, these instances are the exceptions rather than the rule. It is true that many slaves had very imperfect ideas of the meaning of freedom.[58] It is probably just as true that many of them, had they known what freedom entailed, would have recoiled from it. But the sentiment of the spirituals indicates that the slaves had been longing for freedom for many years.[59] They were looking forward to it in 1861. They had no definite idea as to when it would come; but when the marching of troops and the beating of drums announced that a war was in progress, it was natural for them to hope, and even to believe, that it would bring their liberation. This was demonstrated by an old slave woman on a plantation in eastern Virginia. On the Sunday of July 21, 1861, she was in the kitchen cooking dinner. Occasionally the roar of the cannon at Manassas could be heard. The old "mammy" greeted each "boom" which came to her ears with a subdued, "ride on Massa Jesus."[60]

57. Montgomery *Weekly Mail*, Aug. 15, 1863, quoting Chattanooga *Confederate*.

58. Brig. Gen. I. E. Ransome, U. S. A., wrote from Natchez, Mississippi, in 1863, that the Negroes were leaving their masters by the thousands; that they were "all anxious to go" though they did not know "where or what for." *O. R.*, Ser. 1, XXIV, pt. 2, 681. A Louisiana Negro, when asked by a Northerner early in 1861 what he would do if he were free, replied: "Well, I'd go huntin' with massa and take his gun." Another replied that he would "jes roll and holler." *Southern Recorder*, Feb. 26, 1861, quoting Boston *Globe*.

59. Robert Russa Moton, *What the Negro Thinks*, p. 9.

60. Statement of Anderson Brown, Petersburg, Virginia, to the au-

The Negroes' secret longing for freedom during the war is reflected in their surreptitious prayer meetings. Long after the occupants of the "big house" had drowned their cares in sleep, a group of slaves might be assembled in the quarter praying for freedom and the success of the Union cause while one of their number watched for the "patarollers."[61]

Booker T. Washington said that the first knowledge that he had of the fact that he was a slave and that the freedom of the Negroes was being discussed was "early one morning before day when I was awakened by my mother kneeling over her children and fervently praying that Lincoln and his armies might be successful and that one day she and her children might be free." He also said that, though he was just a child during the war, he later recalled "the many late-at-night whispered discussions" in which his mother and the other slaves on the plantation indulged. He expressed the belief that "even the most ignorant members of my race on the remote plantations felt in their hearts that the freedom of the slaves would be the one great result of the war, if the northern armies conquered. . . . I have never seen one who did not want to be free or one who would return to slavery."[62]

The early policy of the Union authorities in freeing the Negroes who came to their lines encouraged the slaves. The issuance of the Emancipation Proclamation lifted their hopes for freedom still higher and made them more concerned than ever for the success of the Union army.

The action of the slaves when freedom was brought to them is another indication that they had been looking for-

thor in 1933; he said that he was in the yard just outside the kitchen window playing marbles and heard the woman's words. Small Negroes in their play sometimes speculated on the changed conditions which freedom would bring and what would be their lot. One would say, "I'se gwine have a carriage an' an' gold watch." Older Negroes would squelch such seditious utterances. Statement to the author by Mrs. Jane Allen, Montgomery, Alabama, in 1932. G. C. Eggleston, in *A Rebel's Recollections,* p. 256, says of the slaves: "Most of them coveted freedom . . . and yet they remained quiet, faithful and diligent."

61. See Chapter VI.   62. *Up from Slavery,* pp. 7–15.

ward to it with more than a passive interest.[63] Even trusted
slaves, those who had helped hide the silver and other valuables, sometimes followed the deliverers when they came.[64]
It was not disloyalty, but the lure of freedom, which im-
pelled them to go. The attraction of freedom is demonstrated by the difficulty with which old domestic servants
sometimes resisted it. One venerable Negro, after the
"Yankees" had passed by the plantation taking most of the
Negroes with them, said to his young master, with a note
of sadness in his voice: "Well I never expected us to hear
freedom come and knock at my door and I refuse it, but
that is what me and my family have done."[65] An old cook
in the service of a South Carolina family was put on a
wage basis in the summer of 1865. After a time, she expressed a desire to go into a town about a mile away to
work. The mistress and her family, being anxious to keep
one who was such a good cook and who had been with them
so long, offered to raise her wages to almost twice the
amount she would receive in town. The old slave, after
offering one evasive excuse after another, finally said, "No,
Miss, I must go. If I stays here I'll never know I'm free."[66]
A similar case was that of an old Georgia Negro who, when
asked why she left the old plantation, responded, "What
fur? 'Joy my freedom."[67]

The ultra-idealistic manner in which the Negroes
thought of freedom is vividly illustrated by an incident

63. An old slave near Covington, Georgia, when asked by Sherman if he
"understood about the war and its progress," replied that "he had been
looking for the angel of the Lord ever since he was knee high," and that
he supposed "our success was to be his freedom." W. T. Sherman, *Memoirs*, II, 180. See also W. T. Sherman's interview with the Negro ministers at Savannah, *O. R.*, Ser. 1, XLVII, pt. 2, 40, 41.

64. Elizabeth Allen Coxe, *Memories of a South Carolina Plantation
during the War*, p. 47.

65. *Ibid.* Stephen Vincent Benét in *John Brown's Body*, pp. 80–82,
gives a graphic portrayal of the emotional struggle experienced during
the war by a well-treated slave. A genuine affection inclined him toward
continued loyalty to his master. But the war so stirred his irrepressible
longing for freedom as to render him sleepless at night.

66. W. W. Ball, *The State That Forgot*, p. 128.

67. Sidney Andrews, *The South Since the War*, p. 353.

which took place in Alabama shortly after the termination
of the war. A white man riding to his work early one morning observed a group of colored children huddled on the
side of the road. Near them in a ditch, he saw a woman
stretched out, quite inert. He asked the children who she
was. The oldest one replied, "Mammy." The man then
asked what her trouble was, adding the remark that she
looked as if she might be dead. To this the child responded,
"Yassah, massah, she is daid, but she's free."[68]

The slaves often showed great elation on the reception
of freedom, even on plantations where their treatment had
been exceptionally good. Booker T. Washington says that
"there was little if any sleep" the night after word was
sent to the slaves' quarters that "something unusual was
going to take place at the 'big house' the next morning."
After the slaves had assembled and had been told that they
were all free, "for some minutes there was great rejoicing
. . . and wild scenes of ecstasy." His mother "leaned over
and kissed her children while tears of joy ran down her
cheeks. She explained to us . . . that this was the day for
which she had been so long praying."[69] Even more demon-
strative was an old Virginia Negro who when informed of
his freedom "went out to the barn and jumped from one
stack of straw to another as fast as he could jump," and
"screamed and screamed!"[70] After Lee's surrender, Mrs.
Roger Pryor, who was staying at her brother's plantation
near Petersburg, Virginia, was waked in the middle of the
night by a shrill scream, " 'Thank Gawd! Thank Gawd
A'Mighty!' Then all was still." The next morning an old
colored man explained that "Sis Winny . . . got happy
in the middle of the night and Gawd knows what she would
have done if Frank hadn't ketched hold of her and pulled
her back in the kitchen."[71]

68. Memoirs of J. R. Webster (MS. in private possession).
69. *Up from Slavery*, pp. 20–21.
70. *Nineteenth Annual Report of the American Missionary Association*
(1865), p. 17.
71. *Reminiscences of Peace and War*, p. 385.

The fact that the slaves' ideas of emancipation had become so exaggerated—a factor in their elation—is suggestive that freedom had long been discussed and idealized. The cases of the Vicksburg Negro who expected his race to assemble in New York after the war and "have white men for niggers,"[72] and the South Carolina Negro who, in answer to his master's inquiry as to where he was going replied, "I dunno, Massa; dey dun gi me dis hoss; I suppose I'se gwine to Heben or a better place,"[73] are doubtless exceptional; but the association of emancipation with "comin' of de Kingdom" and "de day of Jubilo" indicates the existence for a long time of a deep-seated desire for freedom.

While the attitude of the Negroes toward the "Yankees" was characterized by the greatest variations, and while the reactions to freedom ranged from indifference to elation, there can be no doubt that the general effect of Federal invasion upon the institution of slavery was disturbing and disruptive.

72. T. W. Knox, *Camp-Fire and Cotton-Field*, p. 373.
73. Narrative of Nettie P. Evans, Anderson County, South Carolina, in *South Carolina Women in the Confederacy*, II, 159.

II

PRIVATIONS AND PRIVILEGES

BEFORE the war the fare of the plantation slave consisted basically of corn bread and meat; game, sirup, sweet potatoes, peas, and rice were added or substituted "as locality and season might suggest." The usual allowance for each field hand was "a quart of corn meal and a half-pound of salt pork per day." The food might be cooked in a central kitchen or issued to the different families for preparation in their own cabins.[1]

Both black and white inhabitants of the frontier districts began to suffer from a lack of food early in the war; and their suffering increased as the conflict progressed. In most of these areas the slave population was proportionately small; the food supply was taxed by intermittent raids of both armies; productiveness was greatly reduced by the running away or removal of most of the able-bodied male slaves and the absence of the adult male whites in military service. Destitute conditions in northern Mississippi are vividly portrayed in letters written from that section to the governor. A letter from Tishomingo County is typical: "Relief cannot long be delayed without great suffering to the people, many of whom are now on short rations of even bread, while very few have any forage at all, not even fodder or shucks."[2] In some cases the citizens

1. Phillips, *Life and Labor in the Old South*, p. 197; *American Negro Slavery*, pp. 265, 312.
2. G. A. Taylor to Governor Clark, Feb. 15, 1865, Miss. Archives, Ser. E, no. 68. For other examples, see T. E. Peques, Lafayette County, to Governor Clark, March 30, 1865, *ibid.;* and no. 65, A. V. Ventress, Wilkinson County, to Governor Clark, Feb. 6, 1864. For conditions in counties of northern Georgia see *Southern Recorder*, Nov. 10, 1863, speech of Governor Brown to legislature. The Georgia legislature voted 97,500 bushels of corn to needy citizens in sixteen counties of northern Georgia in 1863. *Public Acts of Ga.*, 1863, Reg. Sess., no. 66. The papers of Z. B.

were able to improve their unhappy state by trading cotton to the Federals for food and clothing.[3] Concerning an invaded section in Louisiana a native wrote early in 1865: "Our country is entirely changed. . . . Want and beggary are visible everywhere now. Hundreds of families in this parish are now without bread to eat, whilst but few, even of the wealthier classes can boast of a pound of meat. . . . The Federals on their retreat left the country a waste. The horses and mules are all gone; there is no labor left. . . . Some neighborhoods are without men in them to bury the dead."[4]

In the interior regions of the South, where most of the slaves were located, there seems to have been an abundance of food during the entire period of the war. With the restriction of the acreage devoted to cotton and tobacco, beginning with the crops of 1862, the productive energy of the slave population was diverted primarily to the growth of foodstuffs.[5] While the war brought changes in the type of food received by the Negroes in these regions, only in rare cases did it lessen the quantity.

One of the first noticeable dietary changes was a substitution of other items for meat in the rations. This was due, to some extent, to the scarcity of salt which began to be felt keenly in the fall of 1862.[6] In spite of the adoption of various methods of procuring salt and for preserving meat

Vance, E. J. Hale, and D. L. Swain (MSS. in the Library of the North Carolina Historical Commission), depict the suffering from the shortage of food among the people of western North Carolina. There were few Negroes in that section.

3. For specific examples, see letter of Wm. E. Nugent to Governor Pettus, Sept. 29, 1863, Miss. Archives, Ser. E, no. 61, and communication of Citizens of Bolivar County to Governor Clark, Feb. 20, 1864, *ibid.*, no. 65.

4. E. M. Cullam to O. M. Roberts, April 15, 1865, University of Texas Archives, O. M. Roberts Papers.

5. Parthenia Hague, *A Blockaded Family,* pp. 17 ff.; Walter L. Fleming, *Civil War and Reconstruction in Alabama,* p. 235; Smedes, *A Southern Planter,* p. 226.

6. A Monticello, Mississippi, planter wrote Governor Pettus, Dec. 1, 1862: "We have corn for bread; we have hogs for meat, but no salt to save it." Miss. Archives, Ser. E, no. 58.

with less salt[7] there was a continuous shortage in all except the regions adjacent to the sea coast or salt springs.

From the paucity of available material on the subject, it is difficult to determine to what extent the scarcity of salt affected the Negroes' meat rations during the war period as a whole. It is probable that planters resorted to the expedient of killing hogs only as meat was needed, thus obviating the necessity of trying to preserve it for any great length of time.[8] There are evidences that, in some sections, meat continued to be an important item in the slave diet until late in the war. An editorial in the Richmond *Sentinel* in February, 1864, said that, although farmers knew that the army was "suffering," they had "not been able to reduce their weekly rations of 3½ lbs. of bacon per hand."[9] In some counties of Virginia voluntary meetings were held by planters for the purpose of cutting down the meat rations of slaves to the same amount as that furnished to the soldiers.[10] One reason for the planters' reluctance to reduce the meat ration was that they were afraid that the Negroes would become discontented and go to the "Yankees."[11] Another reason was that meat was considered essential to the diet of working hands; women and children, white and black, did without bacon and pork that the Negro men doing heavy work might have an adequate supply.[12]

There was a general scarcity of tea, sugar,[13] and coffee throughout the South, but slaves felt these privations

7. Pickling processes were used; but they were not very satisfactory for the preservation of meat in hot weather. *Southern Field and Fireside,* May 10, 1862.

8. The Greenwood Plantation (S. C.) Records intimate this practice (MS. in Library of Congress). See entry of Aug. 8, 1862.

9. Quoted by Montgomery *Weekly Mail,* Feb. 16, 1864.

10. *O. R.,* Ser. 4, III, 1113.

11. Montgomery *Weekly Mail,* Feb. 16, 1864, quoting Richmond *Dispatch;* Greenwood Plantation Records, entry of Aug. 8, 1862; letter of E. W. Harris to his son George C. Harris, Oct. 5, 1861, Tennessee Archives, Harris Papers.

12. Fleming, *Civil War and Reconstruction in Alabama,* p. 244.

13. Except in the sugar-growing area.

little for they had seldom tasted these luxuries in previous years.[14]

The war caused an increase in some items of the slaves' food. Notable among these were molasses and sorghum.[15] A Jackson, Mississippi, planter recommended the substitution of two pints of molasses for two pounds of pork in the weekly ration as a satisfactory means of solving the problem of meat shortage. His Negroes were pleased with the change.[16]

The control of the Mississippi River by the Federals and the disorganization of transportation facilities prevented the shipment of molasses from Louisiana in appreciable quantities after 1862. The necessity of some substitute for both molasses and sugar led to the cultivation of sorghum or Chinese sugar cane, on an extensive scale, especially in the upland regions of the South where sugar cane would not grow.[17] The use of sirup from the sorghum cane —it was sometimes called sorghum molasses—was recommended as a partial substitute for meat. "Negroes are amazingly fond of it," wrote one planter, "and nothing could agree with them better."[18] Sugar was said to have been obtained from refining the sirup in some instances.[19]

Sweet potatoes came into more general use during the war.[20] Their consumption was particularly encouraged in

14. Booker T. Washington, *Up from Slavery*, p. 10.
15. The increased use of molasses is indicated by the increased output in Louisiana. In 1861 it was 18,414,550 gallons; in 1862 it was estimated at 36,982,505 gallons. *Confederate States Almanac* (1863), p. 41.
16. *Southern Field and Fireside*, Nov. 9, 1861.
17. Charleston *Daily Courier*, March 2, 1863; Montgomery *Weekly Advertiser*, Feb. 10, 1864, quoting Petersburg *Express;* Kate Cumming, *Hospital Life in the Confederate Army of Tennessee*, p. 151. Texas alone produced 16,000,000 gallons of sorghum sirup in 1862; this was said to be "nearly equal to all the molasses produced in the South the year before the war." The crop of 1865 was more than double that of 1862. *Texas Almanac* for 1872 (Richardson and Co., publishers), p. 49. Molasses and sorghum sirup when used as a substitute for sugar were sometimes spoken of as "long sweetening." Fleming, *Civil War and Reconstruction in Alabama,* p. 235.
18. Charleston *Daily Courier*, March 2, 1863.
19. *Ibid.*, Nov. 3, 1863; July 24, 1864.
20. The Richmond *Whig*, Sept. 14, 1864, commented on the exception-

South Carolina where the Confederate authorities discontinued the tax in kind on them. The rotting of great quantities at the depots made this action advisable.

It is quite possible that the influences of the war, in general, made for an improvement in the fare of the slaves. On account of the restriction of cotton, vegetables were available in greater quantities and varieties. The extension of the plan of cooking in central kitchens under the supervision of the whites or expert Negroes, to save time and prevent waste, was conducive to better preparation of food.[21] Moreover, the absence of effective means of discipline tended toward better feeding as a method of keeping the slaves contented.[22]

The blacks probably experienced more changes and more hardships in the matter of clothing than of food. Spinning and weaving on the plantations had generally ceased before 1861;[23] but, during the war, the growing effectiveness of the blockade and the depletion of the stock of mill-made cloth in the hands of the merchants necessitated the resumption of home manufacture to an increasing extent.[24]

ally fine crop of sweet potatoes in 1864. The Charleston *Daily Courier*, May 4, 1864, reprinted an old pamphlet which explained the use of the sweet potato in making a fermented drink which the Negroes called "mobby." It also spoke of the "excellent bread" being made from the tuber.

21. Fleming, *Civil War and Reconstruction in Alabama*, p. 244; Charleston *Mercury*, Nov. 12, 1862.

22. Montgomery *Weekly Mail*, Feb. 16, 1864. The military authorities complained that the slaves were better fed than the soldiers. *O. R.*, Ser. 4, III, 1113. The Negroes at Magnolia sought to secure an improvement of their rations by working on the fears of their master after the "Yankees" came to the neighborhood; the overseer wrote on Nov. 24, 1862, "Negroes grumbling about food, etc. Wont work they say on Pork and Corn Bread. Must have flour, biscuits, beef, etc., or they will go somewhere else, etc." Magnolia Plantation Records.

23. *Southern Cultivator*, July, 1861. The exceptions to this rule were found mostly in the areas outside the black belt.

24. There were a considerable number of textile mills built in different parts of the South during the war, but these were devoted primarily to the manufacture of cloth for army uses. J. C. Schwab, *The Confederate States of America*, p. 271. Fleming, *Civil War and Reconstruction in Alabama*, pp. 157, 236.

By 1864 most of the clothing worn by slaves was spun, woven, cut, and sewed on the plantations.[25]

Although various restrictions were placed on the growth of cotton, the surplus which remained from the crop of 1861, together with the small amount grown during the war, was far more than enough to meet the needs for home and government use.[26] Great difficulty was often experienced in securing cards for the "combing" of the fibre in preparation for the spinning wheel. Home manufacturing seems, however, generally to have provided a reasonable sufficiency of summer clothing for the Negroes.

While wool was grown on a much more extensive scale during the war than previously, the supply was never adequate to the needs of the people. Some planters sought to meet the deficiency by substituting cow hair, altogether or in part, for the wool filler used in making the heavy jeans cloth for the slaves' winter clothing.[27] The result was said to be "a very even and handsome texture . . . quite strong and serviceable . . . as comfortable and durable for pantaloons as for Negro suits entire."[28]

The shortage of heavy goods became so acute, in some instances, as to cause planters to rip up wool mattresses in order to provide winter garments for their Negroes.[29] On the R. F. W. Allston plantations in South Carolina carpets were cut into large pieces in 1864 so that the Negroes "who were expecting blankets that year should not be disappointed." Thick damask curtains were also cut to make "thickly lined" coats for them.[30]

25. Mrs. N. B. De Saussure, *Old Plantation Days*, pp. 41, 77; Hague, *A Blockaded Family*, pp. 15, 39; Victoria V. Clayton, *White and Black under the Old Regime*, p. 100; Mary J. Welsh, "Makeshifts of the War between the States," *Publications* of Miss. Hist. Soc., VII, 106; Fleming, *Civil War and Reconstruction in Alabama*, p. 236.

26. Schwab, *The Confederate States of America*, p. 278; C. Girard, *Les Etats Confédérés*, p. 15.

27. Fleming, *Civil War and Reconstruction in Alabama*, p. 237, says that cow hair and horse hair could be had at local tanyards.

28. Montgomery *Weekly Advertiser*, March 9, 1864.

29. A. P. Ford, *Life in the Confederate Army*, pp. 78–79.

30. Pringle, *Chronicles of Chicora Wood*, p. 196. The twice-a-year issue

The shortage of buttons made it necessary for every set to be used several times. When they were worn out, or lost, new ones had to be improvised from coarse thread, soft wood, or persimmon seed. Caps were made of scraps of woolen cloth sewed to fit each head. The front piece, or bill, was taken from a wornout head piece, or a new one was shaped from cardboard and covered with cloth.[31] In sections where palmetto was available, it was boiled to make it pliant, cut into strips, and braided into plaits. These were sewed together and shaped into hats.[32]

There were very few factory-made shoes available for the Negroes after the first year of the war. In cases where they were obtainable the price was usually so high as to make their purchase impracticable.[33] Planters attempted to solve the problem by setting up tanneries and making shoes on their own premises. A fair degree of efficiency was attained in tanning leather suitable for uppers, but it was too soft and light for soles,[34] and there was no satisfactory method of attaching it to the uppers. This difficulty led to the adoption of wooden soles.[35] In some cases hickory or dogwood was used because of its wear-resisting qualities,[36] but soles from either of these were exceedingly heavy. The most satisfactory soles were made from some soft, light wood, with iron rims around the edges to receive the brunt of the wear. The wooden bottoms were usually made by the plantation carpenter who "cut out channels" on the edges so that the leather uppers when tacked on would not over-

of clothes continued at Magnolia Plantation through 1862 and 1863. That the overseer was having difficulty is indicated by a notation after an issue on July 22, 1863, "Devil of a Time." Magnolia Plantation Records.

31. Welsh, "Makeshifts of the War between the States," *Publications* of Miss. Hist. Soc., VII, 108.

32. *Ibid.*

33. Hague, *A Blockaded Family,* p. 33; Charleston *Daily Courier,* Sept. 16, 1863.

34. A soldier who attended a wedding in Virginia in 1864 noticed that "nearly all the saddles had been denuded of their skirts to make soles for shoes." Marcus B. Toney, *The Privations of a Private,* p. 67.

35. That is, soles and heels in one solid piece of wood.

36. Toney, *The Privations of a Private,* p. 67.

lap the top of the soles, to be worn or torn by contact with rocks and other hard objects. The iron rims were fashioned and nailed on by the plantation blacksmith.[37]

If leather was unobtainable, canvas, scraps of carpet, or some other heavy cloth might be used for uppers.[38] Sometimes the planter preferred to buy the soles and simply attach the cloth or leather uppers. There were a number of factories in the South engaged in making both soles and uppers. In October, 1862, a Natchez, Mississippi, firm advertised "Wooden soles for making Negro shoes . . . at thirty cents per pair for cash."[39] A Columbia, South Carolina, concern offered cloth top shoes for five dollars, or the wooden soles separately for a dollar and a half per pair, in February, 1863.[40] Some of the shoes made by the factories were entirely of wood, according to the "Dutch" style.[41] Both these and the wooden-sole type were clumsy, noisy, and uncomfortable.[42]

The slaves in the larger towns and cities seem to have suffered much less from shortage of clothing than did those on the plantations. In the matter of Sunday clothing they seem to have fared much better than did their masters and

37. These statements are based on conversations of the author with ex-slaves. Various types of wooden shoes are on display in the Confederate Museum at Richmond and the North Carolina Hall of History at Raleigh.

38. A pair of wooden-soled shoes with uppers of carpet cloth is on exhibition in the Confederate Museum at Richmond.

39. Natchez *Daily Courier,* Oct. 21, 1862.

40. Charleston *Daily Courier,* Feb. 11, 1863.

41. A factory in Raleigh specialized in this type of shoe. On Jan. 2, 1862, it advertised that thirty hands were turning out a hundred pairs of shoes a day and that there were more orders than could be filled. Fayetteville (N. C.) *Observer.* Several pairs of shoes and soles made in Raleigh are on exhibition in the North Carolina Hall of History, Raleigh. One of the "Dutch" type shoes is partially covered with leather, evidently the remnant of a complete leather covering.

42. Washington, *Up from Slavery,* p. 11. A Georgian objected that "A Negro boy might take a notion to light a fire with them which was the fate of a pair presented to us . . . and they are also very unfit to 'trip it on the light fantastic toe' . . . they are by no means light, though fantastic in appearance." Montgomery *Weekly Advertiser,* Dec. 17, 1862, quoting the Augusta *Chronicle.*

mistresses, especially during the first two or three years of
the war. This was due to the fact that it was common for
white people to pass their half-worn garments on to their
Negroes. Although the whites ceased to let the Negroes
have their good clothes after the blockading of Southern
ports, the fact that the whites wore those which remained
every day, while the Negroes wore theirs but once a week,
resulted after six months or a year in the Sunday wearing
apparel of the Negroes having a "decidedly fresher as-
pect";[43] and of course there was little likelihood of a white
person asking a Negro to return a garment which had
once been given him.

The superiority of the Negroes' Sunday dress over that
of the whites was widely commented on, especially by Europeans. Colonel Fremantle, who took a Sunday afternoon
ride with a friend in Houston, Texas, in May, 1863, noticed "innumerable negroes and negresses parading about
the street in the most outrageously grand costumes—silks,
satins, crinolines, hats with feathers, lace, mantles, etc.,
forming an absurd contrast to the simple dresses of their
mistresses."[44]

While food and clothing constituted the basic factors in
the life and happiness of the Negroes during the period of
slavery, amusements and privileges were not without importance. It is true that the amusements were simple and
the privileges were few; but this only caused them to be
cherished the more highly.

Although the limitations placed upon the slaves' activities depended to a considerable extent on the disposition
and indulgence of the individual masters, there were numerous general restrictions imposed by state laws, supplemented in some cases by local ordinances. These laws varied

43. J. B. Jones, *A Rebel War Clerk's Diary at the Confederate States
Capital*, I, 202, entry of Dec. 3, 1863.
44. *Three Months in the Southern States*, p. 75; for similar observations in San Antonio and Charleston, see *ibid.*, pp. 56, 186. For comments on the Sunday finery displayed in small towns in southern Mississippi in the fall of 1862, see *Two Months in the Confederate States* (by
an English Merchant), p. 91; for Americus and Cuthbert, Georgia, see
[Catherine Hopley], *Life in the South*, II, 336.

somewhat in different states and at different times; but, ordinarily, they forbade the slaves to leave the plantations without passes or in groups without white escort, to assemble at night without a white person being present, to be out of the quarter after a certain hour at night, to carry weapons except with the written consent of the master, to own property, and to buy and sell goods without written authorization. White persons were forbidden to sell liquor to slaves and to teach them to read and write. To give force to these laws, citizens were required to apportion among themselves the work of patrolling their respective districts at stipulated intervals.[45]

These laws were framed with the idea of securing the subordination of an inferior race to a superior one. The degree to which they were enforced tended to vary with the white man's feeling of security. If his dominance was threatened by abolitionist propaganda, or rumors of an uprising, the force of the law was fully utilized; in times of long continued tranquillity, there was an increasing relaxation.

John Brown's raid, the election of Lincoln, and the "invasion of the South" tended to make the Southern people apprehensive as to their ability to keep the slaves in proper subjection. Their uneasiness was increased by the departure of a great portion of the white male population for the army. The result was a widespread sentiment in favor of a closer regulation of the slaves' activities.

This sentiment is reflected in the tightening of the state patrol laws at the beginning of the war. A Florida law of December, 1861, provided that the patrols should make their rounds once a week, or "more than once a week when informed by a creditable citizen of evidence of insubordination or threatened outbreak, or insurrection of slaves." The old law had provided for patrol only once every two weeks. The new law also provided that the report of the patrol captain should be made in writing instead of orally

45. Phillips, *American Negro Slavery*, pp. 492 ff.; *Life and Labor in the Old South*, pp. 162-163.

as before.[46] A Georgia law of 1862 canceled exemptions from patrol duty.[47] A Louisiana law of the same year imposed a fine of ten dollars or twenty-four hours' imprisonment for failure to perform patrol duty.[48] In South Carolina, towns of from 500 to 2,500 gross population were declared to constitute separate beats for patrol purposes.[49] The Texas legislature passed a law in January, 1862, providing that beats be patrolled once a week instead of once a month.[50]

This tightening of enforcement machinery was accompanied by a revision of the slave code for the purpose of restraining those activities of slaves which were conducive to escape or disorder. A Virginia law of 1862 gave the courts of the tidewater counties the authority, on application of any three freeholders, to direct all boats to be removed from places where they might be used by runaway slaves. The courts might even order boats to be destroyed and their value to be paid the owners out of the county levy.[51] In 1864 the maximum fine for a boat owner transporting a slave without the consent of the master was increased from fifty to five hundred dollars.[52]

Changes were also made in the laws against slaves being allowed to remain alone on plantations. A Mississippi enactment of 1861 repealed the law permitting as many as five slaves to live apart and provided that no slave was to be quartered more than a mile from the master's residence without some person capable of performing patrol duty having charge of him.[53] The Florida legislature in 1861 increased the fine for permitting a slave to reside alone on plantations from fifty cents to one hundred dollars.[54] In Arkansas, where no law of this nature seems to have been

46. *Laws of Fla.*, 1861, Reg. Sess., chap. 1291, no. 34.
47. *Public Acts of Ga.*, 1862, no. 40, sec. 1.
48. *Acts of La.*, 1861–1862, Reg. Sess., no. 130.
49. *Acts of S. C.*, 1861, Reg. Sess., no. 4568.
50. *General Laws of Texas*, 9th Leg., 1861–1862, chap. 80.
51. *Acts of Va.*, 1861–1862, Reg. Sess., chap. 86.
52. *Acts of Va.*, 1863–1864, Reg. Sess., chap. 36.
53. *Laws of Miss.*, 1861–1862, Reg. Sess., chap. 40, sec. 1.
54. *Laws of Fla.*, 1861, Reg. Sess., no. 34.

in existence prior to the war, an act was passed in the fall of 1861, requiring a white person capable of preserving order to be resident on every plantation.[55]

The apprehension in regard to slaves having weapons was manifested in the revision of the Texas law on that subject in 1863 providing that a white person convicted of selling, giving, or lending dangerous weapons to slaves should be confined at hard labor in the penitentiary from two to five years.[56]

In Alabama the penalty for the violation of the law against furnishing liquor to slaves was changed from a fine of fifty dollars to one of two hundred to five hundred dollars, or imprisonment in the penitentiary from one to five years.

The laws against trading with slaves were also modified with the idea of further restricting the evils accruing from that practice. The Mississippi legislature increased the penalty for permitting slaves to go at large and trade as free men, from fifty dollars to five hundred dollars and sixty days in jail. It provided further that the fact that such a slave was going at large and trading should be sufficient proof that the person in charge of him had given him permission.[57] A Virginia act increased the fine for violation of the law against boat operators permitting slaves to sell articles on their vessels.[58]

The question naturally arises to what extent the revision of the laws and the tightening up of the enforcement machinery actually restricted the activity of the slaves. The answer must come, in part, from inference. It is probable that during the early part of the war the slaves felt the restriction of the laws to a considerable extent. The same sentiment which led to the enactment of the statutes

55. *Acts of Ark.*, 1861, Spec. Sess., no. 41, sec. 1.

56. *General Laws of Texas*, 1863, Extra Sess., chap. 15, sec. 3. An Alabama law granting the right to justices of the peace in certain counties to give slaves permission to bear arms was repealed in 1864. *Laws of Ala.*, 1864, Reg. Sess., no. 121.

57. *Laws of Miss.*, 1861, Called Sess., chap. 38, sec. 1.

58. *Acts of Va.*, 1863–1864, Reg. Sess., chap. 35.

tended to secure their observance. The patrollers probably performed their duties with less nonchalance than before the war. Planters were probably more cautious about issuing passes and permitting their slaves to travel unaccompanied by whites, and allowing them to assemble at churches without whites being in attendance.

As the war continued, however, there was a tendency for the laws to lose their force. Among the factors responsible was the breaking up of the enforcement machinery. The demands of the army gradually reduced the number of men of patrol age in the various communities to such a degree that a regular weekly patrol became a heavy burden, if not an impossibility. In order to make more men available for patrol service, the ages of persons subject to ride the beats were extended to include boys and old men, and exemptions were reduced to a minimum. Since the ages of persons subject to militia and patrol service were the same, the calling away of the militia to perform active military service deprived communities of the old men and boys capable of patrolling the beats. Even the overseers who had been exempted "for additional police" were gradually taken from the communities by revisions of the exemption law.

The disrupting influence which the demands of the army had upon local patrols is indicated by a letter written from Jackson County, Mississippi, in August, 1862, protesting against the removal of the militia. The writer said that he and another man had been compelled to bear the entire responsibility of patrolling "beat no. 1" for the past four months, and "if there is any more men taken out of this county, we may as well give it to the negroes . . . now we have to patrole every night to keep them down."[59] Gov-

59. C. F. Howell to Governor Pettus, Aug. 23, 1862, Miss. Archives, Ser. E, no. 57. In Mississippi the organization and administration of patrols was in the hands of county boards of police. The president of the Yazoo County board wrote Governor Clark in April, 1864, that it was impossible for him to get a meeting of that body though he had used every means in his power. N. G. Nye to Governor Clark, April 18, 1864, Miss. Archives, Ser. E, no. 65.

ernor Pickens, in a message to the legislature in November, 1861, spoke of the patrol system in South Carolina as having been "deranged by the breaking up of the beat companies."[60] The derangement eventually became so serious that the legislature required the governor to claim exemption from Confederate military service of such persons as he thought "indispensable for the government of the slaves" and the protection of the citizens.[61]

The deterioration of the civil machinery for controlling the slaves led to the adoption of various forms of supplementary military control. In Alabama the militia was divided into two parts: boys of sixteen and seventeen years and men from forty-five to sixty constituted the first-class militia, and men from eighteen to forty-five the second class. Persons composing the first class, commonly designated as the county reserves, were required by a law of 1864 to perform patrol duty.[62] In some counties of North Carolina, Mississippi, Georgia, and Alabama, military organizations were formed under such titles as "local guards" and "home guards" to police slaves and to arrest stragglers.[63] In the frontier sections of Mississippi, Louisiana, and Georgia, and in some districts of South Carolina, companies of "independent scouts," or "mounted police," were provided by the military authorities to keep slaves in subjection, to prevent their escape, and to preserve order.[64]

In spite of the general interlocking of civil and military machinery for the regulation of the slaves, enforcement in some cases seems to have been very loose and ineffective.

60. Charleston *Mercury*, Nov. 27, 1861.
61. *Acts of S. C.*, 1864, Dec. Sess., no. 4704.
62. *Acts of Ala.*, 1864, Called Sess., no. 3.
63. E. G. Ashton to Governor Vance, Sept. 27, 1864, Vance Papers; Governor Brown to G. F. Pierce, Aug. 25, 1864, Governor Brown's Letter Book, 1861–1865; Governor Brown to the Militia composing the First Division, Sept. 10, 1864 (MS. in Georgia Archives); *Laws of Miss.*, 1863, Reg. Sess., chap. 1, secs. 7 and 27.
64. *Laws of Miss.*, 1863, Nov. Sess., chap. 1, sec. 27; G. P. Whittington, ed., "Letters from John H. Ransdell to Governor Thomas O. Moore, dated 1863," *Louisiana Historical Quarterly*, XIV (1931), 488; Richmond *Daily Dispatch*, March 30, 1865; Coxe, *Memories of a South Carolina Plantation during the War*, p. 36; O. R., Ser. 1, XVII, pt. 2, 740.

This was especially true in localities near the military lines
where the white population had been greatly reduced by
conscription and by "refugeeing." A citizen of Bolivar
County, Mississippi, wrote in June, 1863, that "the county
is left almost alone and negroes are going whare they
please."[65] A Port Gibson resident had written three months
earlier that "the negroes are under no restraint at night";[66]
in February, 1864, a Perry County resident wrote, "there
has been soldiers sent here . . . but they are doing little or
no good . . . there is no discipline or order among them.
The cavalry have been . . . a riding through the country
afrolicing and stealing. The civil laws have been trampled
under foot."[67]

Another factor in the relaxation of the enforcement of
the slave laws was public sentiment. It is unlikely that the
feeling of uneasiness and uncertainty in regard to the conduct of the slaves which caused the general revision of the
laws at the beginning of the war retained its high pitch for
a great length of time in most sections of the South. The
fact that the Negroes did not rise up and that they went
about their work, effectively concealing any concern which
they felt about the war, tended generally to allay suspi-
cions and fears and led to a corresponding relaxation in
the force of the law.

Recurrent apprehensions at times in different communities, due to the running away of a number of Negroes, to
cases of flagrant insubordination, or to rumors of plots to
rebel, led to temporary resumption of vigilant enforcement. The adoption of the policy of arming the slaves by
Federal generals had disquieting effects in the South, but
the announcement by Lincoln in the fall of 1862 of his in-

65. R. L. Bowles to Governor Pettus, Feb. 23, 1862, Miss. Archives,
Ser. E, no. 61.
66. E. C. Patterson to Governor Pettus, Feb. 23, 1863, Miss. Archives,
Ser. E, no. 59.
67. Sheriff of Perry County to Governor Pettus, Feb. 8, 1864, Miss.
Archives, Ser. E, no. 65. In some counties of Mississippi court sessions
were suspended for long periods of time. Dunbar Rowland, *History of
Mississippi, the Heart of the South*, II, 816.

tention to declare the freedom of the slaves seems to have caused a more general sentiment for scrupulous enforcement of patrol laws. It is true that there were many light statements made concerning Lincoln's *"brutum fulmen"* and many expressions of confidence in the immunity of the slaves to his "fiendish designs," but these were accompanied by measures for protection.[68] Governor Pickens, in a message to the South Carolina legislature in November, 1862, said that "the infamous proclamation" would "produce none of the effects intended by its vulgar author." But, he added, "to protect ourselves from any effort instigated by the deluded or ignorant I would urge the immediate organization of a large State Police Guard under the direct command of the Governor, to be ordered out at such times and in such Districts as he may think proper, to be kept at least for some months in actual daily duty to give a feeling of safety to the helpless."[69] Governor Brown of Georgia spoke of the horrors which might result from a servile insurrection and advocated the extension of the militia ages and the arming of the men brought into militia service with pikes and bowie knives for the performance of patrol service in their respective military districts. "If it were generally known among our slaves," he added, "that these precautions had been used . . . I cannot doubt that a salutary effect would be produced."[70]

That these expressions were not merely the attempts of state governors to arouse a lagging zeal for the conduct of the war is indicated by the attitude taken toward the proclamation and its possible effects by some of the people. The citizens of Hanover County, Virginia, at a mass meeting in October, 1862, appointed a committee to make recom-

68. Montgomery *Weekly Advertiser*, Dec. 9, 1863. This attitude is reflected in a mock dialogue between two Negroes published in the Natchez *Daily Courier*, Nov. 12, 1862: *"Latest From Ethiopia*—Tom: 'Say Pomp a 'liable darkey tell me just now dat Jeff Davis gwine to 'taliate 'bout de President's Proclamation—he gwine to declare all de negroes in de Norf states slaves arter de fust of Janwery next.' Pomp: 'Bress us all.' "

69. Charleston *Mercury*, Nov. 26, 1862.

70. *Southern Recorder*, Nov. 11, 1862.

mendations as to what action they should take. The committee reported, after a recess, that while they did not mean "to attach undue importance to the late proclamation," they felt that prudence required that some precautionary measures be adopted. They submitted resolutions, which were adopted by the meeting, expressing the sentiment that slaves were more likely to remain faithful if they were kept at home and clear of the influence of bad advisers, and pledging themselves not to allow the Negroes to leave their homes, except on the owners' urgent business, or to visit their wives occasionally. They also pledged themselves to permit no slave to leave home without a pass and to coöperate in effective control by requiring every Negro whom they met on the road to show his pass. These resolutions were published by the Richmond *Enquirer* with warm endorsement.[71]

During the last two years of the Confederacy the responsibility of controlling the slaves was left almost entirely to the individual proprietors and to the military authorities. The statement of an old slave that "de patarollers never come around 'case dey wuz all gone to de wah," is probably not far from the truth. In regions along the coast and in the line of Federal invasion military authority was rigorously applied by scouts and pickets; in other sections it was exercised only in unusual circumstances.

The absence of an effective agency of control in the community, such as the patrol or militia company, tended to cause the exercise of less restraint on the plantation. The person in charge, usually an old man, a woman, or a boy, was inclined toward leniency in dealing with the slaves by the knowledge that there was no convenient power to which he or she might appeal in case of insubordination.[72] The fact that a flogging or a threat of a flogging at night sometimes sent a Negro in search of "de Yankees and freedom" before morning was probably not without its effects. Again, the faithfulness and fortitude shown by the Negroes, as well as their apparent sympathy and understand-

71. Issue of Nov. 4, 1862.　　72. Richmond *Whig,* Jan. 1, 1864.

ing in times of sorrow, were conducive to greater indulgence on the part of the owner. The white people of the South were too absorbed in the conduct of the war and the struggle for existence to devote much energy and thought to the control of the Negro when it was possible "just to leave him alone."

Whether the law was rigidly or loosely applied, the Negro was not devoid of amusements and privileges during the war. Diversions were probably reduced when the enemy was near or when the struggle for the necessaries of life became hard as it sometimes did in the frontier and "white" counties. But down in the "black belts" of Texas, Alabama, Mississippi, South Carolina, and Georgia where Negroes and food were as abundant as "Yankees" were scarce, the Negroes enjoyed life. They had their "Sat'day evenins off" for lounging about the quarter, or working in the garden, or going fishing. On "Sat'day night" the fiddle and the banjo might be brought out and tuned up, a roaring bonfire built, and the pleasures of the dance enjoyed until a signal from "the big house" announced the time to retire; or if the Negroes had been taught that such pleasures were incompatible with religion, they might seek a more pious, if not a more orderly, diversion in a cabin prayer meeting. On Sunday the slaves put on their best clothes and went to the white folks' church, or their own plantation chapel.

When a couple became enamored the master was usually favorable to the "tying of the knot" if he thought the match a good one. On some plantations much ado was made over a slave wedding. A sumptuous supper was served in the dining room at the big house or, if the weather would permit, out in the open,[73] though, during the war, the entire assemblage, white and black, were often clad in homespun and the wedding cake sweetened with molasses.

At night the Negroes sometimes went in quest of the 'possums which abounded in the thickets of the hills and

73. Clayton, *White and Black under the Old Regime*, p. 131.

ravines, or of the 'coons which were to be found in the tall
timber.[74] These hunts were not discontinued during the
war. The meat obtained had enhanced value, in some instances, because of the shortage of pork and beef. But the
hunting of 'coons probably declined because of the scarcity of firearms and ammunition and, in some instances,
because of an increased sentiment against slaves carrying
guns. It is possible that hunting was hindered, in some
cases, by a lack of dogs. The impetus given to sheep raising to obtain the much-needed wool led to a sentiment to
get rid of curs; this was accentuated by the increased cost
of feeding them.[75] The loss of his "houn's" must have been
a grievous one to the Negro.

Whiskey was scarce on account of the laws against the
distillation of grain; the penalties for letting slaves have
it without the master's order were heavy. The Negroes
contrived, however, to get it surreptitiously on occasion.[76]
Sometimes the master gave his slaves a "dram" for me-
dicinal purposes,[77] but this practice was probably cur-
tailed during the war.

In Alabama, barbecues continued to be great annual
events for the slaves during the war. These were sometimes
given on the Fourth of July, but that was more or less by
coincidence, since the celebration was for the "laying by"
of the crops rather than for the signing of the Declaration
of Independence. On the night before the day set apart for

74. Fleming, *Civil War and Reconstruction in Alabama*, p. 243.
75. *De Bow's Review*, XXXIII (1862), 33; *Southern Cultivator*, July,
1861. One of the Allston overseers was ordered to kill all dogs belonging
to Negroes. J. B. Jones considered the death of his daughter's favorite
cat near the end of the war as a bit of good fortune for himself, since its
keep was costing him $200 a year. *Rebel War Clerk's Diary*, II, 258.
76. Chesnut, *Diary from Dixie*, p. 288; *Southern Confederacy*, Feb. 6,
1862.
77. Negro women on the Allston plantation, Chicora Wood, had the
idea that "a liberal supply of whiskey" was indispensable to child delivery. Pringle, *Chronicles of Chicora Wood*, p. 223. When the Yankees approached Chicora Wood, a quantity of whiskey was poured in a branch.
Old "Daddy" Aleck who was very fond of "sperrits" went down below,
got down on his all-fours and quenched his thirst from the "passing
stream." *Ibid.*, p. 227.

the barbecue, whole shoats or beeves were slowly roasted over hot coals in open pits while being basted with highly seasoned sauce. About ten o'clock in the morning the sable crowd assembled. Toward noon, the tables were loaded with the savory meat and great quantities of fruit, vegetables, and corn bread. When the groups had been arranged around the tables, some honored old "daddy" would lift his hands and "say de blessin'." After the feast, "fiddlin' and dancin'," singing, and merry-making were in order for the rest of the day.[78] As old slaves tell of these occasions today, their faces beam with the light of pleasant memories.

In the cities and large towns the Negroes sought amusement in parties and balls; and these seem to have been more numerous and more elaborate during the war than before. This may be attributable in part to the fact that the increase in the practice of self-hire[79] gave the slaves better opportunity to make the money necessary for such affairs and gave them more freedom of action;[80] it may also be due, to some extent, to the weakening of the police force by the demands of the army.[81]

Except in invaded regions, and in areas near the Federal lines, the war seems not to have wrought any great changes in the life to which the slave was accustomed. Recurrent revisions of the slave codes prompted by fear of insubordination and insurrection doubtless impinged periodically upon the Negro's freedom of movement, but the disruptive influences of the war tended gradually to render ineffective most of the regulatory measures. Probably the greatest deprivation experienced by the war-time Southern Negro was an insufficiency of winter clothing.

78. Hague, *A Blockaded Family*, pp. 122 ff.; Fleming, *Civil War and Reconstruction in Alabama*, p. 243.

79. Charleston *Daily Courier*, March 4, 1864, Feb. 9, 1865; Richmond *Daily Dispatch*, Jan. 2, 1864; Richmond *Examiner*, Jan. 2, 1865.

80. Many of these slaves lived apart "in their own houses, making their own contracts." P. G. Pillow to Governor Watts, Sept. 22, 1864, Ala. Archives.

81. Mobile *Daily Advertiser and Register*, Dec. 13, 1863.

III

LABOR

IN view of the fact that the crops of 1861 were already under way before the war attained the magnitude of a general conflict, there was very little difference in the acreage devoted to the various agricultural products that year.[1] Before the planting season of 1862 arrived, however, the situation had greatly changed. The Southern ports had been placed under a blockade which prevented cotton from going out, except in comparatively small quantities, and also prevented supplies from coming in.[2] A large portion of the adult white male population had been withdrawn from productive agricultural pursuits and had become a charge upon the remaining community for food and clothing. The great grain and meat producing areas of Kentucky and middle Tennessee had passed under Union control. This situation, coupled with the belief that the best way to end the war was to force a cotton famine in Europe, led to a widespread movement in 1862 and 1863 to reduce the cotton crop and to devote the productive energies of the Confederacy to the growth of foodstuffs.

Early in 1862, editorials began to appear in the newspapers urging a reduction of the cotton acreage.[3] In Georgia, Alabama, and Mississippi, county meetings were held in which planters drew up resolutions pledging themselves to limit their cotton crop to the amount necessary

1. The 1861 cotton crop was estimated at 4,500,000 bales by the British consul at Savannah. *Annual Cyclopedia* for 1862, p. 254. The 1860 crop was approximately 4,700,000 bales.

2. In August, 1862, the British consul at Charleston estimated that 50,000 bales of cotton had been shipped through the blockade, most of which had gone to Nassau. Charleston *Daily Courier,* Dec. 18, 1862.

3. An editorial appeared in the *Southern Recorder,* March 25, 1862, under the heading "All Corn—No Cotton."

for home uses.[4] The farmers of Sumter County, Georgia, resolved that they "would not plant for the present year more than two acres of cotton to the hand unless the blockade be raised before April 1."[5] It was proposed in some sections that a general convention of Southern planters be called to take action restricting cotton production.[6]

These voluntary steps were paralleled by executive and legislative action. The Confederate House of Representatives adopted a resolution on March 3, 1862, advising farmers to refrain from the cultivation of cotton and tobacco and to devote themselves to the raising of provisions and livestock.[7] On March 21, the legislature of Arkansas passed an act declaring unlawful the planting of more than two acres of cotton per Negro working-hand and imposing a fine of from five hundred to five thousand dollars for violations of the law.[8] Governor Pettus of Mississippi issued a proclamation "enjoining all planters to plant not more than one acre to the hand in cotton."[9]

The increasing effectiveness of the blockade and the loss of most of the Mississippi River led to an increasing sentiment to restrict the crop of 1863. In December, 1862, the Alabama legislature levied a tax of ten cents on every pound of seed cotton grown in excess of 2,500 pounds per full hand.[10] About the same time the Georgia legislature restricted planting to three acres per hand;[11] in March, 1863, South Carolina fixed the limit at one per hand.[12]

4. See issues of the *Southern Field and Fireside* and the *Southern Recorder* for February and March, 1862.

5. *Southern Field and Fireside,* March 29, 1862.

6. *Ibid.,* March 1, 1862.

7. Appleton, *Annual Cyclopedia* for 1862, p. 260. A bill providing for the restriction of cotton acreage by Confederate law was introduced in the Senate, but after a lengthy debate as to expediency and constitutionality it was defeated by a vote of 11 to 8. *Ibid.,* pp. 260–262.

8. *Acts of Ark.,* 1862, Spec. Sess., pp. 7–8, secs. 1–5. Negroes under 14 years of age were not to be counted as hands.

9. Natchez *Daily Courier,* May 22, 1862.

10. Montgomery *Weekly Advertiser,* March 18, 1863.

11. *Public Acts of Ga.,* 1862, Reg. Sess., no. 1, secs. 1–2.

12. *Acts of S. C.,* 1862–1863, no. 4620. Florida's limit of one acre per

The Confederate Congress passed a joint resolution in April urging farmers to desist from cotton planting and to increase their food crops.[13]

Virginia matched the restrictive action of the cotton states by limiting the planting of tobacco to 2,500 plants per field hand, and fixing the maximum for any producer at 80,000 plants.[14]

The question naturally rises as to the actual effect which such agitation and legislation had on the production of cotton and tobacco. Indications are that in 1862 the acreage of cotton was reduced to one-third of what it had been in ordinary years,[15] that it was further reduced in 1863, and that by 1864 it was not more than one-fifth of the normal crop.[16]

As the acreage of cotton and tobacco was restricted, the labor of the slaves thus released was turned to the cultivation of food crops. Diversification became the rule throughout the Confederacy.[17] In the "canebrake" region of Ala-

hand was not fixed until December, 1863. Governor Milton was doubtful of the expediency and constitutionality of placing legislative restrictions on the growth of cotton. *Laws of Fla.*, 1863, Reg. Sess., no. 39; *O. R.*, Ser. 4, II, 488.

13. James M. Matthews, ed., *Confederate States of America. . . . The Statutes at Large*, 1st Cong., 3d Sess., Res. no. 2. (Cited hereafter as Matthews, ed., *Statutes at Large*.) A bill introduced in the Texas legislature early in 1863, on recommendation of the governor, to restrict the growth of cotton in that state, was killed in the Senate; the chief objection to it seems to have been that the regulation of crops was not a governmental prerogative. *Texas Republican*, Feb. 19, 1863; *True Issue* (La Grange), Feb. 19, 1863.

14. *Acts of Va.*, 1863, Adjourned Sess., chap. 34.

15. Charleston *Daily Courier*, Dec. 18, 1862. "An English Merchant" estimated the 1862 crop at one-fifth of the usual crop. *Two Months in the Confederate States*, p. 102. See also: *Annual Cyclopedia* for 1862, p. 253; *Hinds County Gazette* (Miss.), Sept. 24, 1862.

16. Schwab, *The Confederate States*, p. 279.

17. There was less change in slave labor in the areas which had been devoted to the raising of sugar and rice before the war because of the great need of these commodities for feeding soldiers and civilians. In 1864, rice planters were compelled to devote more attention to the growth of other articles for their own use because the disorganization of transportation facilities precluded the possibility of getting them elsewhere. See R. F. W. Allston Papers (MSS. in private possession) for 1864, *passim*.

bama, where before the war "plantations were all devoted
to cotton, with enough corn to feed the plantation animals
and bread for the Negroes," cotton fields were "all converted into corn and wheat fields."[18] At Greenwood Plantation in South Carolina, where in 1859 the crop had been
200 acres of cotton, 115 acres of corn, and a few acres of
peas, the proprietor, in 1862, expressed a determination to
plant "50 acres of Cotton and the rest in Corn, Peas, and
Potatoes."[19] The owner of a large Mississippi plantation
reduced his cotton crop from 350 to 38 acres and devoted
the surplus land to the growth of food crops.[20] Abundant
crops of wheat were grown in North and South Carolina.[21]
Proprietors all through the South, whose plantations had
been devoted almost exclusively to the growth of cotton,
began in earnest to grow wheat, rye, oats, rice, corn,
pumpkins, and peanuts.[22]

To this war-imposed diversification the slave laborers
evidently adapted themselves with marked success. The
testimony of the press, of travelers, and of the invading
Federals, indicates that there was a sufficiency, if not a
surplus, of produce, in uninvaded portions of the South
during the entire period of the war.[23] Within three months
of the fall of Richmond, a writer in a journal published in
that city said that the amount of provisions remaining in

18. J. W. Dubose, The Canebrake Negro, 1850–1865, Ala. Archives,
Dubose Papers.

19. Greenwood Plantation Records, entry for Feb. 1862.

20. Louisiana State University Library, Pleasant Hill Plantation
Records.

21. Charleston *Daily Courier*, June 27, 1863. The correspondent reported a 300-acre field of wheat near Concord, N. C.

22. Fleming, *Civil War and Reconstruction in Alabama*, p. 232;
Hague, *Blockaded Family*, p. 17; W. W. Davis, *Civil War and Reconstruction in Florida*, p. 215.

23. W. T. Sherman, *Memoirs*, II, 182; Howe, ed., *Home Letters of
General Sherman*, pp. 314, 316; Charleston *Mercury*, April 7, 1864 (quot-
ing editor of Richmond *Whig*), July 14, 1864 (quoting Memphis *Ap-
peal*), Jan. 24, 1865; O. R., Ser. 4, III, 65–66, 75; Schwab, *Confederate
States*, p. 276; Charlotte R. Holmes, ed., *The Burckmyer Letters*, p. 50;
Charleston *Daily Courier*, Dec. 2, 1863; E. A. Pollard, *Life of Jefferson
Davis*, pp. 251 ff.

the Confederacy was "still very great—enormous—sufficient to support far greater efforts . . . material exhaustion is not yet felt . . . in the slightest or most distant degree."[24] In February, 1865, General Lee wrote that "our
resources fitly and vigorously employed are ample."[25]

That there were areas in the South in which scarcity was
the rule is not to be denied. But these were usually either
districts near the military lines which had been required to
furnish provisions for one or both armies and had been deprived of many of their laborers, or "white areas" in which
the proportion of slaves was comparatively low. It is also
undeniable that there was much suffering in the army due
to scarcity of provisions. But these hardships were due not
so much to the shortage of provisions as to failure of distribution.[26] This failure was attributable to several factors, chief among which was the deterioration and disorganization of railroad facilities. While citizens in the frontier regions and soldiers in the camps were suffering from
hunger, huge quantities of foodstuffs were rotting at depots in the interior because of inability to secure transportation for them.[27] Impressment was also partially responsible for the unavailability of produce. Farmers were hesitant to send their produce to the market for fear that it
would be taken at unremunerative prices by the seemingly
omnipresent "agents."[28] The constant fluctuation of the
currency tended to make growers hold their produce for a
long time in anticipation of a higher price.[29] "Shylocks"
contributed to the creation of an unreal scarcity of goods

24. Quoted by Pollard, *Life of Jefferson Davis*, p. 445.
25. *Ibid.*   26. Schwab, *Confederate States*, p. 276.
27. *Ibid.*, pp. 273, 374; *O. R.*, Ser. 4, II, 483–484, 486–487, 881–883; III,
89; *Southern Recorder*, March 15, 1864; *Journal of the Senate of the
State of Miss.*, Governor Clark's message to the Mississippi Legislature,
Feb. 20, 1865; J. B. McMaster, *History of the People of the U. S. during
Lincoln's Administration*, pp. 585–586.
28. Schwab, *Confederate States*, p. 276; Davis, *Civil War and Reconstruction in Florida*, pp. 190–191; F. L. Owsley, *States Rights in the Confederacy*, pp. 240–241.
29. *O. R.*, Ser. 4, II, 1010. Much of the suffering among soldiers' families was caused by the failure of the small incomes to keep pace with the
soaring prices.

by buying up great quantities of commodities and then withholding them from the market until seeming "starvation" conditions enabled them to sell at exorbitant prices.[30]

The agricultural laborers of the interior regions alone probably produced more than a sufficiency of the necessaries of life for everyone in the Confederacy; but circumstances over which apparently no one had control prevented them from being obtained by the people who had the greatest need of them. J. B. Jones was doubtless expressing a significant fact as well as a widespread sentiment when he wrote in his diary in November, 1863: "We are a shabby looking people now—gaunt. . . . But there is food enough and cloth enough if we had a Roman Dictator to order an equitable distribution."[31]

Labor on the plantations was encumbered with many difficulties during the war. Outstanding among these was the lack of adequate supervision. The Confederate Congress, taking cognizance of the need and value of the proper direction and control of plantation laborers, passed a law in October, 1862, exempting one owner or overseer for every plantation having twenty Negroes.[32] But the storm of protest which this law provoked, coupled with the increasing need of men for the army, led to revisions in May, 1863, and February, 1864, which reduced the overseer exempts to a mere handful.[33] According to the report of the Conscript Bureau in December, 1863, the number in

30. Stephen Elliott, *Gideon's Waterlappers* (pamphlet, sermon), p. 10; Charleston *Mercury*, Jan. 24, 1863; *Southern Confederacy*, April 1, 1863; *Laws of Fla.*, 1861, Reg. Sess., chap. 1258.

31. Jones, *Rebel War Clerk's Diary*, II, 101.

32. Matthews, ed., *Statutes at Large*, First Cong., Sess. 2, chap. 45. This was popularly known as the Twenty-Negro Law. It applied only in cases where there was no state law requiring the residence of an adult male white on each plantation.

33. Rowland, *History of Miss.*, I, 817; *O. R.*, Ser. 4, II, 691; III, 180. A Mississippian deserted after the passage of the exemption law saying that he "did not propose to fight for the rich men while they were at home having a good time." *Publications* of Miss. Hist. Soc., VIII, 14. Another Mississippian, from Hancock County, wrote Governor Pettus, that "owing to . . . the Negro law there is a ginerl Backought [back out] all through this part of the State." Rubin Lee to Governor Pettus, Oct. 28, 1862, Miss. Archives, Ser. E, no. 58.

Samford University Library

Virginia was 200; in North Carolina, 120; in South Carolina, 301; and in Georgia, 201.[34] Sometimes overseers exempted-by Confederate authorities were taken by the state for service in the militia.[35]

The scarcity of overseers, and of men capable of acting as overseers in the various communities, led to the practice of having one man exercise a general supervision over a number of plantations.[36] In some communities cripples rode about from place to place directing the work of the Negroes.[37]

The immediate supervision of the plantation was often discharged by women. A South Carolina widow, forty-two years of age and mother of nine children, managed an estate on which there were about seventy-five slaves. She often rode to the edge of the field and directed the work of the Negroes from her sidesaddle, taking her knitting along in order that two sons in the "Rebel" army might not be sockless.[38]

The women often had able seconds in the colored drivers or some other dependable slaves. Mrs. Victoria Clayton and her colored driver "Joe" directed the activities of a large plantation in Alabama. The two would make occasional inspection trips over the place. At the end of every day's work the Negro would report to his mistress and advise with her as to the best course of procedure for the

34. Charleston *Mercury*, Jan. 1, 1864. There were a few men detailed as overseers by order of President Davis, but these details were revoked in the fall of 1864. *O. R.*, Ser. 4, III, 712.

35. J. T. McPherson to Governor Vance, Dec. 8, 1864, Vance Papers; M. R. C. Clark to Governor Pettus, July 10, 1863, Miss. Archives, Ser. E, no. 61.

36. A Louisiana planter assumed the supervision of five large plantations in addition to his own. His only compensation was "patriotism." The burden of his duties was accentuated by the failure of the owners to coöperate with him in the procurement of the necessary provisions. Letters of E. W. Harris to Geo. C. Harris, May 4, June 30, Oct. 5, Oct. 17, 1861, Harris Papers.

37. E. H. Hicks to Governor Pettus, March 16, 1863, Miss. Archives, Ser. E, no. 60.

38. Ball, *The State that Forgot*, p. 113. This woman was Mr. Ball's grandmother.

work ahead. Mrs. Clayton kept in touch with her husband
in the army by letter and by visits. During her absence
"Joe" was ably assisted by his wife "Nancy" in discharging his supervisory duties.[39] There were a number of cases
in which plantations were placed under the complete control
of the slave drivers. "Uncle Jacob" was placed in charge
of Guendalos and "Daddy Hammedy" of Loch Adele, two
of the R. F. W. Allston plantations. The faithfulness of
"Daddy Hammedy" proved a happy contrast to the per-
fidy of a white man who was supposed to "give an eye to
the place" which the Negro was managing.[40] Negroes
chosen to act as foremen were usually selected on the basis
of trustworthiness and ability to command the respect of
the other slaves.[41]

While instances of effective work done under the direction of women and slave drivers are numerous and often
very striking, there can be no doubt that plantation labor
suffered considerably from the absence of overseers during
the war.[42] Letters from women residents on plantations to
the state governors are replete with complaints of the
slaves' idleness, their neglect of farm equipment, and their
abuse of livestock.[43] The accumulation of this and other

39. Clayton, *White and Black under the Old Regime*, pp. 99, 116.
40. Pringle, *Chronicles of Chicora Wood*, pp. 214–215, 270. An old Negro woman "Tay" supervised the work on a South Carolina plantation
for a season. Ford, *Life in the Confederate Army*, pp. 128 ff.
41. J. W. DuBose says that the Negro foremen in the "canebrake" district carried leather straps which they used at their own discretion. "The
Canebrake Negro, 1850–1865."
42. Davis, *Civil War and Reconstruction in Florida*, p. 212; *O. R.*, Ser.
4, I, 1084; II, 401–402; Library of Congress, Diary of Edmund Ruffin,
V, 870; Mrs. Nannie E. Wright to Governor Murrah, April 21, 1864,
Texas Archives; *The Gazette and Comet* (Baton Rouge), June 5, 1861.
43. Women often found the supervisory duties vexatious, burdensome,
and discouraging. An elderly Mississippi proprietress wrote Governor
Pettus asking for the release of her overseer from militia duty, saying
that her servants "were not doing half-work." Mary B. Carter to Governor Pettus, March 14, 1863, Miss. Archives, Ser. E, no. 60. A Texas
woman who, with the aid of a Negro foreman, attempted to oversee her
husband's place after his departure for the war wrote him at the end of
a year replete with difficulties and worries that she thought it best to hire
out the Negroes for the approaching season. "I do not think it is worth

contemporary evidence forces the conclusion, despite the numerous post-war panegyrics on the diligence and industry of the Negroes during the war, that the Negroes usually became slow and shiftless when left to the supervision of women, boys, and old men. Certainly the best work was done on plantations where there was some adult male to act as overseer and on small farms where the fewness of the Negroes intensified personal relationships and simplified supervisory work.[44]

Another handicap affecting plantation labor was the de-

while," she said, "for me to try to stay here without someone to stay here with me for the negroes will not work." Mrs. W. J. Whatley to her husband, Nov. 23, 1862, University of Texas Archives, transcripts of Whatley Papers. Another Texas woman who attempted a similar undertaking had even greater difficulty. In numerous letters to her husband she complained that the Negroes would not work, that they abused and neglected the stock, tore down the fences, broke the plows, and refused to obey. For a while, a part-time overseer was engaged to assist her, but he proved "no count," according to her statement, spending too little time in the fields and too much time around the cabins with the colored women; he was discharged and another employed, but the change brought little improvement in the state of affairs. The new manager beat the Negroes unmercifully and even shot at them, but these extreme measures weakened rather than strengthened his control. Little wonder is it that his irate employer wrote her husband, "I am getting mighty tired of this old fool Myers," and that she did not intend to have him back another year. In the spring of 1864, after months of unrelieved harassment, she wrote that she was overwhelmed with the "thought of negroes to be clothed and fed, the crop yet to make, the oxen so poor, no corn, and to cap the climax, the black wretches trying all they can, it seems to me, to agrivate me, taking no interest, having no care about the future, neglecting their duty." "With the prospect of another 4 years war," she wrote two days later, "you may give your negroes away if you wont hire them, and I'll move into a white settlement and work with my hands." A week later she said, "The negroes care no more for me than if I was an old free darkey and I get so mad sometimes that I think I don't care sometimes if Myers beats the last one of them to death. I cant stay with them another year alone." Letters of Mrs. W. H. Neblett to her husband, Aug. 5, Aug. 25, Oct. 15, 1863; Feb. 27, March 7, March 18, March 20, March 28, June 5, June 19, 1864, University of Texas Archives, Neblett Papers. Senator Clay's mother had the greatest difficulty, even with resort to cajolery, persuasion, and the withholding of rations, in securing any work from slaves on her husband's Alabama plantation. Letters of Mrs. C. C. Clay, Sr., to C. C. Clay, Jr., especially those of Feb. 28, March 6, March 24, and Sept. 5, 1863, Clay Papers.

44. Davis, *Civil War and Reconstruction in Florida,* p. 215; *O. R.,* Ser. 4, III, 355–356.

terioration of farm tools and machinery. Plows and hoes might be kept in order by the plantation blacksmith, but the repair of reapers and threshers was not so simple. The parts for these were not obtainable in the South and the war prevented them from being secured from the North. The three reapers at Shirley Plantation in Virginia were used through the wheat harvest of 1862, but after that time all the harvesting was done by cradles, presumably because the inadequacy of facilities for repair made the continued operation of the reapers impossible.[45] On account of the lack of threshing machinery some farmers resorted to the crude method of beating the heads of wheat across barrels placed on sheets and then letting the wind fan away the chaff as the grain was poured from containers held high from the ground. It is probable that the shortage of flour in the Confederacy was due, to a great extent, to the lack of harvesting, threshing, and grinding facilities.[46]

That rice growers were also seriously hindered by the deterioration of threshing machinery is indicated by the difficulties experienced on the R. F. W. Allston plantations in South Carolina. The overseer of Nightingale Hall wrote to Mrs. Allston in October, 1864: "I think if I had the mill in order that I would be able to Begin to trash on Monday weeak but I have neither oil or any Packing yarn and the mill Bands is very much out of order as the most of thime is very old and Roten. . . . I have no engine near for gandeolos [another Allston plantation] therefore I can not Begin to trash thare until I get the Engine near home."[47]

The taking of horses and mules for army use also interfered with plantation labor.[48] The impressment of slaves, especially during the planting and harvesting season, greatly inconvenienced planters. James H. Hammond wrote to General Pemberton in April, 1862, that crops

45. Shirley Plantation Records.
46. Hague, *A Blockaded Family*, pp. 22–24.
47. W. Sweet to Mrs. R. F. W. Allston, Oct. 26, 1864, Allston Papers.
48. Owsley, *State Rights in the Confederacy*, p. 238.

would be reduced one-half if the effective male slaves were taken for three weeks at that time.[49]

In the frontier districts the planters' labor problems were multiplied by the running away of the Negroes in great numbers, by the difficulty of keeping them sufficiently fed and adequately clothed, by the more or less recurrent Federal raids which frequently resulted in the removal of provisions, laborers, and livestock and the destruction of machinery, and by the demoralizing influence of the nearness of the "Yankees" on the work of the slaves.

Field labor was heavily drawn on during the war by what may be termed the "home industries." The comparative isolation imposed upon the South resulted in almost every plantation becoming a manufacturing unit in which Negroes were the laborers and women the supervisors.

Making of clothing was the leading home industry. On most plantations the spinning wheel and the loom had fallen into disuse before the outbreak of the war, but not enough time had elapsed to prevent them from being restored to a working condition and to make impossible the recovery of the art of operating them. In some cases, they were dragged forth from the attics and basements before they were needed. The wave of patriotism which caused such extensive volunteering among the men had its counterpart in a "home-spun" craze among the women.[50] Spinning and knitting parties became a fad among the social set. But ere many months had elapsed that which had been a fad became a necessity. Before the year 1862 had passed a writer in De Bow's Review was able to say: "Every household has become a manufacturing establishment; the hum of the spinning wheel may be heard in every hamlet and the rattle of the loom sings the song of better times to our glorious South."[51]

Most of the spinning on the plantations was done by the

49. J. H. Hammond to General Pemberton, April 28, 1862, Library of Congress, Hammond Papers.
50. Elizabeth Saxon, A Southern Woman's War-Time Reminiscences, p. 18.
51. De Bow's Review, XXXII (1862), 833.

Negro women. In some instances they were already familiar with the processes involved; but usually they had to be taught by their white mistresses.[52] Since weaving was heavier work than spinning, Negro men were called on to assist the women in the operation of the looms. The cutting and sewing of the cloth were usually done at the "big house" by the white women, or under their close supervision, since they required a greater degree of skill, and since mistakes in the cutting might be very costly.[53]

The preparation of clothing for a large number of slaves entailed a tremendous amount of work. There were usually two issues a year, one of winter clothing in the fall and the other of summer clothing in the spring. A month or two was required each time to get the new clothes ready.[54]

Some planters were able to avoid the trouble of making the cloth for their slaves at home until the latter part of the war, either by purchasing from local merchants and manufacturers, or by sending cotton or wool to a factory to be made up for them.[55] On the Allston plantations in South Carolina spinning and weaving seem not to have been resorted to until the fall of 1864, and even then part of the material was purchased.[56]

52. *Daily Clarion Ledger* (Jackson, Miss.), April 16, 1908, "Our Women in the War" supplement; Clayton, *White and Black under the Old Regime*, p. 114. Mrs. Clayton, like many other Southern women, had to learn how to spin and weave herself before she could teach her Negroes. There were cases of old Negro "mammies" teaching white women to spin. Constance and Hetty Cary, Richmond society favorites, took their first lessons in spinning and weaving from an old "auntie" in the "quarter." Mrs. Burton Harrison, *Recollections Grave and Gay*, pp. 141–142.

53. Fleming, *Civil War and Reconstruction in Alabama*, p. 243. On large plantations the work of the whites was largely supervisory. On small plantations the more common practice was for whites and blacks to work together in all stages of clothmaking.

54. *Ibid.*

55. [Hopley], *Life in the South*, I, 227–228. Gregory, the owner of Greenwood Plantation, sent 160 pounds of wool to Augusta to be made into cloth in Oct. 1862. Greenwood Plantation Records, entry for Oct. 1862.

56. Allston Papers, *passim.*

The problem of clothmaking was complicated by the scarcity of cotton cards. The Mississippi legislature placed $100,000 at the disposal of Governor Clark in 1863 for the purchase of cards. As large quantities could not be purchased in the Confederacy nor secured from the outside except in exchange for cotton, the governor made a contract for the purchase of 16,000 pairs on condition that Confederate authorities would permit the shipment of 800 bales of cotton through the lines as part payment for them.[57] The Georgia legislature made an appropriation of $100,000 to encourage the manufacture of cotton cards, but production on a large scale was prevented by the impossibility of obtaining the necessary wire in the Confederacy. The scarcity and prohibitive prices of new cards required that the greatest possible service be obtained from old ones. The best parts were taken from the most badly worn cards and used to patch others less worn. When loom sleys wore out or were broken, replacement was very difficult. "Except to replace a few missing reeds," wrote a Mississippi woman, "this difficulty was beyond the housekeepers."[58]

The proficiency of the home craftsmen increased with experience. There were frequent commendations of the quality and even the appearance of the homespun garments in the periodicals of the day. Burckmyer wrote his wife in December, 1863, that he had recently seen a fashionable lady "in a black and white homespun dress, spun and woven by her own servants in her own loom, and it was really very genteel and becoming."[59] The durability of the

57. Governor Clark to J. W. C. Watson, Dec. 2, 1863, and Clark-Edmondson Contract, May 29, 1864, Miss. Archives, Ser. E, no. 65.

58. Welsh, "Makeshifts of the War between the States," *Publications* of Miss. Hist. Soc., VII, 106. A Texas woman became much vexed at one of her slaves for using a pair of cards to comb a "pickanniny's" head. The wires, unaccustomed to this type of wool, were bent beyond repair. Mrs. W. H. Neblett to her husband, April 5, 1864, Neblett Papers. There are indications of a shortage of spinning wheels in Mississippi in the latter part of the war. W. W. Siddell to Governor Clark, Dec. 9, 1864, Miss. Archives, Ser. E, no. 66.

59. Holmes, ed., *The Burckmyer Letters*, p. 233.

home-woven clothing is attested by the fact that when a South Carolina woman visited "the old plantation," fifteen years after Lee's surrender, she saw Negro women still wearing some of the dresses made during the war.[60]

Most of the leather used in the Confederacy was tanned on the plantation or at local tanneries by the slaves. The proper performance of this work required considerable training and exertion. First, the bark had to be cut from the trees—oak bark was preferred because it was richest in tannic acid—and chopped or ground into fine pieces.[61] It was then placed in a large vat, covered with boiling water, and allowed to soak for a week or more while the leather was being made ready for tanning. The first step in preparing the hides was to split them lengthwise into two parts; they were then suspended from beams and the membrane scraped from the flesh sides. After the scraping was finished, the hides were soaked in lime water for several days.[62] As soon as the hair would "slip," they were worked over beams and rinsed. This process removed the hair, but to remove the lime from the tissues of the skins it was necessary to wash them in a hen-dung solution, called "bate." After another rinsing they were placed in the tan ooze—the water in which the bark had been soaking—and permitted to remain there until they became "evenly colored" and showed a "handsome fine grain." During the period in which the skins were soaking in the tan ooze, they had to be raised and lowered two or three times a day. It was important to keep the ooze at a moderately warm temperature and a proper strength.[63]

In order to meet the problem of salt shortage, the slaves were sometimes required to dig up the soil under the smoke-houses and place it in huge vats or hoppers. Hot water was poured over the dirt and then boiled down to obtain a

60. De Saussure, *Old Plantation Days*, p. 41.
61. A Jackson, Mississippi, ex-slave told the author that "white oak tanned leather white and red oak tanned it red."
62. A weak·solution of lye made from ashes was sometimes used instead of lime.
63. *Southern Field and Fireside*, Oct. 19, Nov. 2, and Nov. 30, 1861.

dingy, but highly cherished, salt. A South Carolina farmer obtained a half gallon of salt from two bushels of dirt in this way.[64]

The home manufacturing system produced a number of other articles for plantation uses. Lye obtained from ashes was mixed with refuse grease to make soap. Candles were made by dipping yarn into melted beeswax.[65] Wheat, rye, corn, okra, peanuts, and sweet potato cubes were parched and ground and the beverage resulting from boiling them optimistically spoken of as "coffee"; molasses provided the "long sweetening." "Tea" was made from blackberry, raspberry, crossvine, and sage leaves, and from spicewood and sassafras roots. Dyes were obtained from roots and barks of various sorts, from elderberries, and from walnut hulls.[66]

The development of the "home industries" was paralleled by a marked extension of manufacturing in the villages, towns, and cities. The impetus to industry did not come wholly from the war. Considerable sentiment had been manifested during the two decades before the war, through the press and in various conventions, in favor of making the South more independent industrially. A part of this sentiment was due to the growing prospect of a disruption of the Union.

Though the prevailing opinion in the ante-bellum South was apparently opposed to the wide use of Negroes in industrial pursuits, there seems to have been an increasing interest in the subject during the years immediately preceding the war. Some leaders were of the opinion that the best way to solve the problem of the rapidly increasing slave population—it doubled between 1820 and 1850—was to put the Negroes to work in cotton and wool fac-

64. Charleston *Daily Courier*, April 25, 1863.
65. Andrews, ed., *Women of the South in War Times*, p. 23.
66. Welsh, "Makeshifts of the War between the States," *Publications* of Miss. Hist. Soc., VII, 102 ff.; Andrews, ed., *Women of the South in War Times*, *passim;* Hague, *A Blockaded Family*, pp. 40 ff.; Saxon, *A Southern Woman's War-Time Reminiscences*, p. 38.

tories, in iron furnaces, and in the manufacture of various other articles which were being bought from the North.[67]

The outbreak of the war forced upon the South the industrial transformation for which her thinking economists had been pleading; and the rapidity with which it was effected was remarkable. In the summer and fall of 1861, factories which had been closed were reopened and their machinery set in motion again. Establishments which had been languishing because of lack of patronage were extended and enlarged in an effort to supply the ever-growing demands. New plants came into existence, some to produce articles hitherto not made in the South. The whole country began to hum and stir with a new industrial life.

An idea of the nature and extent of the development which took place may be obtained from the answers to a questionnaire sent out from Richmond in the winter of 1861–1862 to various towns and cities inquiring as to "what branches of manufacture or other industry have sprung up during the existing war." Columbus, Georgia, reported thirteen new establishments; one of them made shoes for the army; another manufactured spinning wheels and shuttles; another was making 1,200 yards of India rubber cloth per week for the army; the Columbus Iron Works manufactured engines and machinery for a gun boat, brass field pieces, shot and shell; the Eagle Manufacturing Company, an old concern, had "added several articles to its list of production." Its weekly output of cassimere had been increased from 2,000 to 12,000 yards.[68] Wilmington, South Carolina, reported that establishments for the manufacture of alcohol, potash, tallow candles, peanut and rosin oils, salt (by evaporating sea water), shoes, sabres, bayonets, and "various kinds of edge tools," had come into existence as a result of the war.[69] Laurens, South Carolina, reported that "all the old manufactures

67. Wesley, *Negro Labor in the U. S., 1850–1925*, pp. 13–17.
68. *De Bow's Review*, XXXIII (1862), 77–78.
69. *Ibid.*, XXXII (1862), 329–330.

which may be gathered from the last census have recurred and have been infused with additional life . . . more particularly the manufacture of shoe leather."[70]

In Norfolk, Virginia, thirteen new branches of manufacture had been established: one made friction matches; another bits, buckles, and singletrees; another drumheads and musical instruments; one "Essence of Coffee"; two made candles; one manufactured brass cocks and engine fixtures. Nineteen factories in existence before the war had since been enlarged. They were devoted to making, among other things, boots, shoes, hats, caps, carts, saddles and harness, pumps, and soap.[71] Reports from the larger cities required more time for preparation, and owing to the suspension of *De Bow's Review*, were not published. But the story was doubtless the same there as in the towns—the establishment of a great number of new enterprises and the enlargement of old ones.

Some of the new manufacturing plants employed Negroes from the beginning. Both old and new depended on colored laborers to an increasing extent as white workmen were called on to go to the ranks.[72]

The iron works in Alabama and Virginia used a great number of slaves during the war. The Tredegar Works advertised for the hire of 1,000 Negroes in January, 1864, to work at its plant in Richmond, at its blast furnaces in Rockbridge and Alleghany counties, and at its collieries in Henrico and Goochland counties.[73] In Alabama the operation of iron works became a common activity among refugees with slaves. The Negroes were employed principally in cutting wood for charcoal and hauling iron to shipping points, but some performed tasks requiring skill.[74] A refu-

---

70. *De Bow's Review*, XXXII (1862), 332.   71. *Ibid.*, p. 158.

72. A South Carolina law of 1863 provided for the exemption of only those railroad employees whose work, in the judgment of the Adjutant and Inspector General, could not be performed by slaves or free Negroes. *Acts of S. C.*, 1863, Sept.–Dec. Sess., no. 4669.

73. Montgomery *Daily Mail*, Jan. 2, 1864. "Remoteness from the enemy's lines" was mentioned as an inducement to hire.

74. Wesley, *Negro Labor in the U. S., 1850–1925*, p. 104.

gee from Tennessee put 200 Negroes to work cutting wood
and hauling iron for the Janney Furnace in Calhoun
County. Another Tennesseean brought several slaves—all
trained smiths—to Jefferson County and set up a "water
blast forge, smith and foundry" with the intention of making farm tools. But they had to shoe so many horses for
the soldiers that little time was left for making tools.[75]

A great number of slaves were employed in coal-mining
projects in different parts of the South. Most of the coal
consumed by the Confederate Government came from Alabama.[76] Early in the war the legislature of that state
passed an act exempting any man from military service
who signed a contract to dig coal with twenty slaves for
the Confederate Government. According to Ethel Armes,
this started an exploration for coal all over the coal-pro-
ducing section. The operation of coal mines, like that of
the iron works, was frequently taken up by refugees from
exposed areas. The Thompson brothers of Hinds County,
Mississippi, moved to Bibb County, Alabama, and opened
up the "Thompson Mines." They put their Negroes to
work loosening the coal with pick and bar and hauling it
to the surface in mule-drawn cabs. Since there were no
pumps to keep the mines dry, water had to be carried out
in buckets.

Salt factories in various parts of the Confederacy also
employed a great number of slave laborers. The Negroes'
work in this connection consisted chiefly in cutting and
hauling the huge quantities of wood required for the
evaporation of salt water obtained in coastal regions and
at salt springs.[77] R. F. W. Allston of South Carolina went
into the salt-making business on an extensive scale after

75. Ethel Armes, *The Story of Coal and Iron in Alabama*, p. 164.

76. *Ibid.*, p. 149. Kate Logan says that slaves were employed in coal
mines operated by her father in Virginia. Kate Logan, *My Confederate
Girlhood*, p. 27.

77. There were 120 salt-making establishments in the Charleston city
limits in December, 1862, manufacturing 1,320 bushels a day and using
about 4,000 cords of wood a week. Charleston *Daily Courier*, Dec. 16,
1862.

the war broke out. He entrusted the work entirely to his slaves. The establishments were set up on the "salt creeks" back from the coast in concealment from the Federal gun boats which were always on the lookout for "Rebel" salt works. The thin curls of smoke from the furnaces were often discerned by the "Yankees," however, and a shot through the trees would send the Negroes "skedaddling" to cover. Interruptions became so frequent that all the boiling had to be done at night to prevent the smoke from being seen.[78]

Though there was widespread and well-founded complaint during the war of the shiftlessness of slave laborers both on the farm and in the factory on account of the absence of masters and overseers, the exigencies of armed conflict tended generally to support a position taken by many leading Southerners before 1861, namely, that Negro labor, properly directed, was adaptable to diversified agriculture and to a varied industrial program.

78. Pringle, *Chronicles of Chicora Wood*, pp. 26–27.

IV

CONDUCT

AN appraisal of the behavior of the slaves during the struggle which involved their freedom is made difficult by the conflicting nature of much of the evidence on the subject. The tenor of statements made during the war is generally in marked contrast with those made afterwards. Contemporary commendations of the slaves' conduct do not harmonize with the steps which were taken to insure a more rigid control.[1] There also is a pronounced difference between the testimony of North and South, both during and after the conflict. This is attributable in part to the close association of the conduct of the slaves with the issues of the war. For the Negroes to show a disposition to resist the authority of their owners, to "throw off the yoke of bondage," and to give secret aid and joyful reception to the Federal armies, supported the claim of the North that the "institution" was irksome, oppressive, and cruel; for them to perform positive acts of loyalty to their masters, to resist the allurements of the "Yankees," or simply to go about their work in a quiet way with evident unconcern, bolstered the Southern contention that the general influences of slavery were wholesome and benevolent, and that the Negroes were content with a servile position in society. This situation tended to make Confederates suppress and minimize reports of misconduct and insubordination—at least to reserve them for "home consumption"; their circulation in the North gave the "Yankees" too much satisfaction. Federals, on the other hand, showed

1. See Chapter II. There was a general tightening of the state patrol laws throughout the Confederacy at the beginning of the war. At various later times, this action was repeated in the different states. W. H. Russell, correspondent of the London *Times,* noticed and commented on this divergence of expression and action. Charleston *Mercury,* June 26, 1861.

a disposition to make the most of instances of the slaves' desertion of their master and their support of the Union cause, as indications of the weakness of the South's system of social and political inequality. The persistence of the tendency of North and South to use the war-time conduct of the Negroes as a justification of their respective positions on the slave question, coupled with the proneness to idealize that part of the past which is pleasant and to forget that which is unpleasant, continued to prejudice thought on the question long after the clash of arms had ended.

There were a number of factors which influenced the slaves' conduct during the war, one of the most pertinent of which was that of personal attachment. Those Negroes who were closely associated with their owners were usually the most loyal under trying circumstances. The body servants of the Confederate soldiers were more intimately associated with their masters than any of the others. In many cases, soldiers and servants had been childhood playmates. Each had a genuine affection for the other, which was cemented by common exposure and hardship in the army. No class of slaves had as good opportunities for desertion and disloyalty as the body servants but none was more faithful. Next in the rank of close association with the whites were the house servants; they were also next in the degree of loyalty. When the young masters left for the war, they sometimes received the embrace as well as the parting blessing of the old kitchen "mammy."[2] When the home was saddened by the news of death, the tears of the black members of the household were often more profuse and just as sincere as those of the whites.[3] When the "Yankees" made their dreaded raids, the uneasiness of the whites was often shared by the black domestics; together they watched through hours of uncertainty until the danger passed.[4] Next to the domestic servants in the degree of in-

2. John Allen Wyeth, *With Sabre and Scalpel,* p. 54.
3. Mrs. Irby Morgan, *How It Was,* p. 90.
4. Dolly Sumner Lunt, *A Woman's War-Time Journal,* p. 32.

timacy and frequency of association with the whites were the drivers or foremen, and, as a general rule, their conduct was much more loyal than that of the rank and file. They were often entrusted with the keys when the approach of the enemy necessitated the masters' flight.

Just as the understanding and affection engendered by close association tended to keep slaves loyal and well-behaved in times of distress, so did remoteness and lack of association make them more susceptible to disorder and disloyalty. On the large plantations the field hands were the first to give trouble. On plantations in the charge of overseers, rarely visited by the owners, there was often very little affection felt by the Negroes for their masters; and they were usually disloyal when the "Yankees" came. On small farms where the master and his Negroes were accustomed to work side by side, instances of unfaithfulness were less common.

The influence of close association on the conduct of the slave was much greater when it was supported by a specific commitment of trust. The body servant was strengthened in his determination to render faithful service by the explicit charge of the mistress to stay with "Mas' Henry" under all circumstances and not to come home without him. The domestic to whom valuables were unreservedly entrusted for safe-keeping rarely failed to return them, even though several years might elapse before safe delivery was possible. The calling together of the slaves by the master on his departure for the war and the commitment of his family to them for safe-keeping seemed to have a salutary effect on their later conduct;[5] but this charge, involving more persons, was less definite and consequently tended to be less effective than the individual commitments mentioned above. Booker T. Washington's statement that a Negro rarely betrays a specific trust has much support in the history of the war between North and South.[6]

Negroes who had been well treated before the outbreak

5. W. W. Malet, *An Errand to the South in the Summer of 1862*, p. 46.
6. *Up from Slavery*, p. 13.

of the war were generally more faithful during the trying days which followed.[7] Slaves of kind and considerate masters who were induced to leave them, or were forced away, sometimes came back after the passing of the Federals, and resumed the discharge of their plantation duties.[8] In cases where the Negroes had been driven and cruelly treated, they were inclined to use the discomfiture of the owners to their own advantage. This is reflected in the action of the slaves at Magnolia after the coming of the Federals to the vicinity gave them an opportunity to assert their wishes. Contrary to general practices, the Negroes on this plantation were not given a Christmas holiday. On December 25, 1862, they went to work as usual, but shortly after breakfast they returned to the "quarter" saying, according to the record of the overseer, "that never having had a chance to keep it [Christmas Day] before, they would avail themselves of the privilege now, they thought."[9] So averse were some Negroes to their masters, on account of treatment accorded them in slavery days, that they refused to work for them after the adoption of the wage basis for labor.[10]

The amount of outside interference was also a very important element in the behavior of the slaves. The mere proximity of Federal soldiers had disquieting effects, but their entry into a town or community, bringing to the Negroes exaggerated ideas of freedom and encouraging them to seize property, and sometimes to commit acts of violence against their masters, was invariably the occasion of disturbance. That the slaves were orderly before the "Yankees" came and that they were disorderly after they came is a general rule that might be applied to almost any invaded portion of the Confederacy.

However, all of the disorder among the Negroes attendant upon Federal invasion cannot be attributed directly to

7. R. H. Williams, *With the Border Ruffians*, p. 441.
8. De Saussure, *Old Plantation Days*, p. 82.
9. Magnolia Plantation Records, entry of Dec. 25, 1862.
10. Williams, *With the Border Ruffians*, p. 440.

the invaders. Their coming was immediately preceded by the exodus of most of the resident whites capable of exercising any effective discipline. Considerable disturbance would have resulted from this withdrawal of accustomed authority had the "Yankees" not come at all.[11] A resident of Port Gibson, Mississippi, wrote to Governor Pettus in February, 1863, that "the Negroes are under no restraint at night . . . nightly depredations are committed on my place. No care and forethought can prevent this unless we have a white man on the place."[12] Another Mississippian wrote from Bolivar County in August, 1864, stating that the recent withdrawal of the military patrol from the vicinity had been followed by manifestations of insubordination and rebellion among the Negroes, and protesting against the removal of any more of the adult males from the county.[13] Communications from other areas tell the same story; where control was lacking disturbances were common.[14]

The infrequency of serious disorders in the interior regions was due, to a considerable extent, to the general adoption of the policy of overlooking minor infractions and administering swift and severe punishment for offenses of an insurrectionary nature. This practice made it possible for a few civilians, aided in some areas by military

11. A. E. Burnside wrote to Secretary Stanton from New Berne, N. C., in March, 1862, "Nine-tenths of the depredations on the 14th after the enemy and citizens fled from the town were committed by the Negroes before our troops reached the city. They seemed to be wild with excitement and delight. . . . The city is being overrun with fugitives from the surrounding towns and plantations." *O. R.*, Ser. 1, IX, 199.

12. E. C. Patterson to Governor Pettus, Feb. 23, 1863, Miss. Archives, Ser. E, no. 59.

13. A. B. Bradford to Governor Clark, Aug. 27, 1864, *ibid.*, no. 66.

14. For example see: Emily Hewitt to Governor Shorter, Aug. 13, 1862; citizens of Lowndes County to Governor Shorter, Sept. 10, 1862; Mrs. S. A. Parsons to Governor Shorter, Nov. 4, 1862; Jane Moore to Governor Shorter, Dec. 21, 1862, Ala. Archives; H. Hines to Governor Pettus, May 14, 1861; J. W. Boyd to Governor Pettus, Aug. 1, 1862, Miss. Archives, Ser. E, no. 57; *Two Diaries* (Misses Susan R. Jervey and Charlotte St. J. Ravenal), *passim; O. R.*, Ser. 1, II, 1010; VI, 78 ff.; XV, 534; Neblett Papers, *passim.*

detachments, to keep the slaves in subjection. The procedure in cases of plots to rebel is illustrated by an instance in Brooks County, Georgia, in August, 1864. On the same day that evidences of the plot were discovered a public meeting was called, an examining committee of twelve appointed, and at six o'clock in the afternoon three Negroes were hanged.[15] In September, 1864, a group of about thirty Amite County, Mississippi, Negroes who had armed themselves with their masters' guns and ridden off toward the river cheering and shouting were overtaken within a few miles of their destination by a group of Confederate scouts and most of them killed.[16]

Severe punishments were administered for other offenses which threatened to subvert authority. Scouts in South Carolina disguised themselves as "Yankees," went to a cabin of a Negro whom they suspected, and offered him a bribe if he would show them to the camp of the "Rebel" troops who were hid in the swamp. The unsuspecting Negro complied with alacrity. When the party came to the hiding place, the Negro was seized by the *pseudo* "Yankees" and "strung up" to a limb.[17] A slave arrested on a suspicion that he had designed "to commit a great crime against the peace of a family" in Blakely, Alabama, was killed when he tried to break away from the patrollers. The man arraigned for firing the fatal shot was acquitted with the explanation that the community was in a state of great uneasiness and alarm at the time.[18]

The effectiveness of stringent measures was increased by giving them a wide publicity. Newspapers gave their ready coöperation by carrying exchanges in order that planters everywhere might be able to inform their slaves what hap-

15. *Southern Recorder*, Aug. 30, 1864. For a similar case in Mississippi early in 1861, see J. D. L. Davenport to Governor Pettus, May 14, 1861, Miss. Archives, Ser. E, no. 52.

16. H. Clessedy to Governor Clark, Sept. 12, 1864, Miss. Archives, Ser. E, no. 66.

17. *Two Diaries*, p. 18 (Diary of Miss Susan R. Jervey).

18. Mobile *Daily Advertiser and Register*, Nov. 15, 1863.

pened to "bad niggers" in other sections and to let them draw their own conclusions.

A factor in the Negro's general good conduct was his habit of non-resistance. A long period of servitude had taught him the discretion of forbearance and caution.[19] He was capable of violence, but he rarely resorted to it unless he was driven by desperation, or unless he was prompted by some outside influence. He desired freedom, and in some instances, the desire was very great, but he chose to wait for its coming rather than to resort to the futile shedding of blood in an attempt at revolution.[20] His reluctance to resort to violence, even when opportunity was afforded, against those for whom respect and obedience had been habitual is well-illustrated by the case of a South Carolina house servant. After the Federals came, he indulged freely in making abusive remarks concerning his master in their presence. An officer who overheard him said: "We have caught him [the master] and now what shall we do with him?" The Negro immediately replied, "Hang him, hang him—hanging is too good for him." "Well," said the officer, "he shall be hung, boy, and since he injured you so much, you shall have a chance to pay him back. You shall hang him yourself, and we'll protect you and see it done." Whereupon the immediate response: "Oh no, cant do it—Cant do it—Cant see Massa suffer—Dont want to see him suffer."[21]

When the good conduct of slaves exceeded a passive submission to authority, there were numerous ways in which they demonstrated their loyalty. They sometimes informed their masters of plans of certain ones of their number to go to the "Yankees."[22] A runaway who took refuge in a

19. Moton, *What the Negro Thinks*, pp. 64–65.
20. Eggleston, *A Rebel's Recollections*, pp. 256–257.
21. R. S. Holland, ed., *Letters and Diary of Laura M. Towne*, p. 35.
22. See: J. Belflowers to Mrs. R. F. W. Allston, Nov. 30, 1864, Allston Papers; Mrs. C. C. Clay, Sr., to C. C. Clay, Jr., Sept. 5, 1863, Clay Papers; Mrs. W. H. Neblett to her husband, Nov. 25, 1863, March 7, 1864, Neblett Papers.

Negro cabin on the Hill Plantation in Louisiana was seized by the black driver with the idea of detaining him until Hill's return. A scuffle followed in which some of Hill's Negroes who came to the driver's rescue were cut. The driver went to the "big house," got his master's gun, and killed the fugitive.[23] Confederate newspapers reported several cases of "Yankee" stragglers being taken into custody by slaves and turned over to their masters.[24]

There are many pieces of silver in Southern homes today which owe their continued presence below the Mason and Dixon line to the fact that they were hidden or kept by faithful slaves, usually the most trusted domestic servants, during the period of invasion. All the valuables on a South Carolina plantation were saved by an old Negro man who sewed them up in the mattress on which he slept every night. He even kept the matter a secret from his wife. When he saw the Federals coming, he went into the dining room, snatched up a few pieces of silver which had been left out because they were indispensable to serving meals, stuffed them in his boots, and pulled his trousers down over the tops. He deceived the soldiers by feigning a hatred for his owner, even to the extent of slapping the white children. He "cried like a child afterwards because he 'had to hit Mas' Horace's children.' "[25] One of the Allston slaves who had been very active in helping his mistress bury the family valuables went to her when the Federals arrived in the neighborhood and asked that she give him

23. Montgomery *Daily Mail*, Oct. 22, 1864, quoting Tuscaloosa *Observer*.

24. A. P. Ford tells of a case of two Federal officers who, having eluded their Confederate captors, went to a Negro cabin to get food. They were promptly seized and turned over to the military authorities. Ford, *Life in the Confederate Army*, p. 34.

25. John B. Irving, *A Day on the Cooper River*, Louisa Cheves Stoney, ed., pp. 92–93. For another case of a slave manifesting insolence toward his owners to deceive the Federals, see Coxe, *Memories of a South Carolina Plantation during the War*, p. 65. The extent to which the domestics sometimes shared the fears of their owners is indicated in the burial by those on a Mississippi plantation of their own "valuables." An old cook insisted on burying her pots and kettles. Smedes, *A Southern Planter*, pp. 207, 210.

some provisions and let him go away for awhile. To her remonstrances that his presence was needed for protection, he replied, "Miss, I know too much, ef dem Yankees was to put a pistol to my head and say, tell what you know, or I'll shoot you, I cudn't trust myself. I dunno what I might do." So she let him go.[26] A North Carolina owner entrusted a bag of gold to one of his Negroes, $8,000 in currency to another, and $7,000 to another. The Negroes kept the treasure until after a Federal raid was over.[27] An old Negro couple on the Butler plantation in Georgia came to their master on his return to the place after the war bringing ten silver half-dollars tied up in a bag. The Negroes had received the money from a "Yankee" captain in exchange for some chickens in the second year of the war, but had refused to spend it during the days of need which followed because the fowls which had been sold were "massa's."[28]

During periods of raid and occupation the slaves sometimes manifested an active interest in their master's welfare and safety. Those belonging to a Tennessee minister brought him the money which they made in the employ of Federal officers who were quartered in the town.[29] During a raid in South Carolina the women domestics on a plantation begged to be allowed to spend the night in the "big house," and the men took it upon themselves to picket the house by turns.[30] A colored maid in another South Carolina household saved a considerable portion of her mistress's wardrobe by telling the Union troops that the trunks of clothing were her own. There were cases of slaves

26. Pringle, *Chronicles of Chicora Wood*, p. 288. An old slave on the Dabney Plantation to whom some valuables had been entrusted for safe keeping, came creeping back with the package shortly after the Federals came. Between sobs she explained that she couldn't keep them any longer because "dey tells me dey has a wand and dat wand will pint to anything they tell it. I gave up all I had . . . but I couldn't give up your things." Smedes, *A Southern Planter*, p. 209.

27. V. T. F. McKesson to Governor Vance, July 4, 1864, Vance Papers.

28. Frances Leigh, *Ten Years on a Georgia Plantation*, p. 23.

29. Diary of John N. Waddell, entries of Nov. 21, and Dec. 15, 1862.

30. Ford, *Life in the Confederate Army*, p. 117; letter of Louise Porcher to Mary Pettigrew, June 28, 1865, Pettigrew Papers.

remonstrating with the Federal soldiers or rebuking them for the treatment accorded their masters' families.[31]

Instances of positive loyalty such as those cited above have remained foremost in the minds of the Southern people and have become the chief cornerstone of the tradition as to the conduct of the slaves during the war. But these acts of loyalty, in the light of contemporary evidence, must be considered as exceptional. They were usually performed by domestic servants, a class constituting a very small minority of the Negro population.

Disloyalty of slaves to their masters has been a neglected phase of Confederate history. Yet in the invaded areas insubordination seems to have been more common than submission; and the latter was not a rule without exception in the interior regions. A common type of misconduct was insolence toward the whites. A Fredericksburg lady, just a few days after the Federals camped on the opposite side of the Rappahannock River and began to play patriotic airs, wrote in her diary: "The Negroes are going off in great numbers and are beginning to be very independent and impudent."[32] A North Carolinian wrote to his governor in August, 1864: "Our Negroes are beginning to show that they understand the state of affairs, and insolence and insubordination are quite common."[33] Even the little Negroes became impudent with the change of conditions. A Savannah, Georgia, woman was awakened one

31. New Orleans *Daily Picayune,* July 5, 1883, letter of J. F. H. Claiborne; Diary of J. B. Moore, entry of April 30, 1862; statement of Mr. J. St. Claire White, Charleston, South Carolina, to the author in 1932; letter of Louise Porcher to Mary Pettigrew, June 28, 1865, Pettigrew Papers. The Porcher slaves not only rebuked the soldiers (Negroes), but referred to them as "wild Africans," and expressed surprise that they spoke the same language as themselves.

32. Diary of Betty Herndon Maury, entry of April 25, 1862. Isaac Applewhite wrote to Governor Pettus from Columbia, Mississippi, on June 6, 1862: "There is greatly needed in this county a company of mounted rangers . . . to keep the Negroes in awe, who are getting quite impudent. Our proximity to the enemy has had a perceptible influence on them." Miss. Archives, Ser. E, no. 57.

33. E. R. Tiles to Governor Vance, Aug. 7, 1864, Vance Papers.

morning early in 1865 by a dusky urchin jumping up and down beneath her window and singing with great gusto,

> All de rebel gone to h———,
> Now Par Sherman come.[34]

That domestic servants, though generally not susceptible to "Yankee" suggestions, were sometimes guilty of impudence is indicated by the action of a Culpeper, Virginia, coachman who, after the Federals told him that he was free, "went straightly to his master's chamber, dressed himself in his best clothes, put on his best watch and chain, took his stick, and returning to the parlor where his master was, insolently informed him that he might for the future drive his own coach."[35]

All cases of insolence are not traceable directly to "Yankee" influence, however. An editorial in the Selma (Alabama) *Morning Reporter*, August 27, 1863, expressed regret at the lack of order resulting from the diminution of the police force, and stated that "the Negroes . . . are becoming so saucy and abusive that a police force has become positively necessary as a check to this continued insolence." A bill was introduced in the Georgia House of Representatives in November, 1862, "to punish slaves and free persons of color for abusive and insulting language to white persons."[36]

Impudence of the slaves was frequently associated with a refusal to work. The owner of Greenwood Plantation in South Carolina wrote in August, 1862: "We have had hard work to get along this season, the Negroes are un-

---

34. Francis Thomas Howard, *In and Out of the Lines,* p. 204.
35. Richmond *Enquirer,* Aug. 6, 1862.
36. *Southern Recorder,* Nov. 25, 1862. Available records do not permit the tracing of this bill. It seems never to have become a law, however. For other evidences on the insolence of slaves, see: J. Belflowers to Mrs. R. F. W. Allston, Oct. 19, 1864, Allston Papers; *O. R.,* Ser. 1, XVII, pt. 2, 201, Sherman to Rawlins; Magnolia Plantation Records, entry of Oct. 2, 1862; Pringle, *Chronicles of Chicora Wood,* pp. 269 ff.; Richmond *Daily Examiner,* Dec. 2, 1864; Elizabeth F. Andrews, *War-Time Journal of a Georgia Girl,* pp. 70, 122.

willing to do any work, no matter what it is."[37] Mrs. C. C.
Clay, Sr., complained that she had to beg the slaves to do
"what little is done" on the Clay Plantation; that the ones
who milked the cows "grumbled and threatened if someone
else did not go get the calves; that the one who built the
fire in the plantation house objected to being ordered to
make fires elsewhere."[38] Negroes on the Crain Plantation
in Louisiana began to refuse to work on Saturday in 1862,
after Farragut's fleet passed up the river. All during the
years 1863 and 1864, the Negroes on this place seem to
have worked or loafed, very much according to their own
inclinations.[39] Shortly after the Federals came into the
vicinity of Magnolia Plantation in 1862, the slaves began
to manifest a more leisurely attitude toward their duties.
The overseer complained in August, 1862, that "the Negros was very slow getting out and some Two or three did
not get out a tall [sic]."[40] Three weeks later he wrote: "negros are moving very slowly. The ring of the Bell no longer
a delightful sound. . . . Many negros continually going
along the road back and fro to the forts . . . great demoralization among the negros."[41] The continued refusal of
the slaves to work with any degree of regularity provoked
the overseer to say in October: "*I wish every negro would
leave the place* as they will do only what pleases them, go out
in the morning when it suits them, come in when they please,
etc."[42]

The refusal to work was sometimes a "strike for wages."
The slaves on Woodland Plantation in Louisiana presented
themselves before the overseer one morning in August,
1862, and said that "they would not work eny moore un-

37. Greenwood Plantation Records, entry of Aug. 8, 1862.
38. Mrs. C. C. Clay, Sr., to C. C. Clay, Jr., Sept. 5, 1863, Clay Papers.
39. Univ. of Texas Archives, A. E. Crain Plantation Account Book,
1861–1867.
40. Magnolia Plantation Records, entry of Aug. 25, 1862.
41. *Ibid.*, entry of Sept. 12, 1862. J. Belflowers wrote to Mrs. R. F. W.
Allston on March 20, 1865: "the People the way that they work will not
make them Bread. go out at 10 Oclock come in at 12 O'clock." Allston
Papers.
42. Magnolia Plantation Records, entry of Oct. 18, 1862.

less they got pay for their work." After a parley they agreed to go on without pay for another week.[43] Within the next few weeks this owner and those of all surrounding plantations had to go over to the wage basis, due largely to Federal influences. Magnolia Plantation was the only exception; here, though work was irregular and demands for pay reiterated, the owner succeeded in holding his Negroes through the season of 1862 by promising them a "handsome present" when the crops were "taken off."[44] A refusal to grant wages often resulted in a wholesale flight of the blacks to the Federal camp.[45]

Another form of irregularity of conduct was the refusal of slaves to submit to punishment for their misdoings. An aged Texas planter tried to whip a recalcitrant hand in the summer of 1863. The Negro, according to the statement of a neighbor, "cursed the old man all to pieces," walked off into the wood, and then sent back word that he would return to his work if a pledge were given that he would not be whipped. The terms were accepted and he came back.[46] Other slaves in this Texas community seem to have been under very little control. They rode their masters' horses at night, took hogs and beeves for their own use, and worked or loafed much as they chose. One of the overseers on the Neblett Plantation, named Myers, attempted to whip a Negro who was reported to have said that "Myers or no white man" would flog him. The Negro walked off saying that he had done nothing deserving punishment. Myers was openly resisted by two other Negroes on the place, one of them holding the overseer off with a stick. The mistress of the plantation finally advised Myers to refrain from the use of severe methods with the slaves as long as they went about their work. On one occasion she wrote to her husband who was absent in the army that it

43. *Ibid.,* entry of Aug. 11, 1862.
44. *Ibid.,* entries of Aug. 25, 1862, and Jan. 25, 1863. The owner's promise was kept; $2,500 was distributed among the slaves.
45. Diary of Betty Herndon Maury, entry of May 13, 1862.
46. Mrs. W. H. Neblett to her husband, Aug. 13, 1863, Neblett Papers.

would make matters no better to have the Negroes whipped, "so I shall say nothing and if they stop work entirely I will try to feel thankful if they let me alone."[47] Planters in this and other communities actually became afraid to punish their slaves. A Tennessee woman wrote to her husband in 1863 that "overseers generally are doing very little good and they complain of the negroes getting so free and idle, but I think it is because most every one is afraid to correct them. I tried to correct our negroes for a thing last summer; it would frighten Mr. Ashford [the overseer] out of his wits almost."[48] Senator Clay's mother wrote him from Alabama, September 5, 1863, that one of her men had told her of the threat of three of the other slaves to kill the overseer if he attempted to punish them. She advised a neighbor who had hired one of her slave women not to punish her because the Negroes had threatened to burn the neighbor's house when the "Yankees" came if he did. Mrs. Clay even went to the colored woman and "begged her to think of the sin" of her proposed crime.[49]

Unfaithfulness of slaves was also demonstrated by the fact that wherever the Federal armies penetrated they received abundant aid from the Negroes in the way of information and guidance.[50] This was given secretly until the actual appearance of the soldiers and then it was often given openly and unreservedly. The prevalence of the practice of Negroes acting as guides to the Federals is indicated by the letter of a Confederate States district attorney to General Winder in 1864 urging severe punishment for a Negro, Heath, who had been found guilty of that offense, on the ground that "the crime with which he is

47. Mrs. W. H. Neblett to her husband, Aug. 13, Nov. 23, Nov. 29, 1863, and March 7, March 12, March 18, April 6, 1864, Neblett Papers.
48. Mrs. James Abernethy to her husband, Jan. 11, 1863, Abernethy Papers (MSS. in private possession).
49. Mrs. C. C. Clay, Sr., to C. C. Clay, Jr., Sept. 5, 1863, Clay Papers.
50. *O. R.*, Ser. 1, X, pt. 2, 162; Charleston *Mercury*, Jan. 11, 1862; Cumming, *Hospital Life in the Confederate Army of Tennessee*, p. 159; *New Englander*, LI (1889), 355.

charged is one of such frequent occurrence that an example should be made of Heath. It is a matter of notoriety in the sections of the Confederacy where raids are frequent that the guides of the enemy are nearly always free Negroes and slaves."[51]

Slaves, more particularly field hands, often aided the Federal soldiers in their search for valuables. Shortly after a "Yankee" raid, a South Carolinian wrote that "the people about here would not have suffered near as much if it had not been for these Negroes; in every case they have told where things have been hidden and they did most of the stealing."[52] A soldier who marched with the Union Army through Louisiana in 1863 said that all along the road the Negroes stood at the gates ready to tell the whereabouts of their masters' saddles and horses. "Many a man," he added, "who has boasted that all his slaves could be trusted . . . had his eyes opened on those days of our advance." He ventured the conjecture that "nearly half our cavalry horses were changed in the Teche country, and in the vast majority of cases, it was the favorite servants who pointed out the hiding place and said, 'you gives us free, and we helps you all we can.' " Such cases, he said, were "innumerable."[53]

Misconduct among the slaves during a period of invasion usually took the form of seizure and distribution of property, and a general celebration of the advent of freedom. A plantation owner in Rapides Parish, Louisiana, gave a vivid description of the general disorder which prevailed among the slaves in his community in letters written to his neighbor, Governor Thomas O. Moore, just after a Federal raid. The overseer on the governor's plantation, forced to flee before the approaching raiders, turned the keys over to the slaves. The "Yanks coming directly afterwards and telling them everything was theirs and that they were free to do as they pleased, they turned out and I

51. *O. R.*, Ser. 2, VI, 1053.
52. *Two Diaries*, p. 35 (Diary of Charlotte St. J. Ravenel).
53. George H. Hepworth, *The Whip, Hoe, and Sword*, pp. 142–144.

assure you that for the space of a week they had a perfect
jubilee—Every morning I could see beeves being driven
up from the woods to the quarters—and the number they
killed of them . . . it is impossible to tell." Two of the
Negroes put a Confederate soldier in the stocks and
"abused him very much." The furniture was taken from
the governor's house and distributed among the Negro
cabins. When the raiders passed on, most of the adult Negroes followed them, taking as much of their master's
property as they could and regretfully leaving that which
they could not carry. Most of those who remained, and
those who came back after a few days, were whipped and
put to work again. The example and the suggestion of the
raiders was responsible, to a great extent, for the misconduct of the slaves; but it was against the latter that the
governor's correspondent brought the greater degree of
censure. Their conduct had convinced him, he wrote, that
Negroes were the "greatest hypocrites and liars that God
ever made." He added that his feelings toward them had
"entirely changed," and that he cared nothing for them
"save for their work."[54]

The conduct of the slaves in Rapides Parish was very
similar to that of the Negroes in the vicinity of Magnolia
Plantation during the raid in 1862. There the Negroes
quit work and gave themselves to riotous celebration. On
one plantation they drove off the overseer and immediately
"Rose and Destroyed everything they could get hold of.
Pictures, Portraits and Furniture were all smashed up
with Crockery and everything in the House." On a neighboring place they erected a gallows in the quarter for the
purpose of hanging their master. Some of them marched
around through the neighborhood, "with flags and drums,
shouting 'Abe Lincoln and Freedom.' "[55]

There were similar disorders in South Carolina. At Poo-
shee Plantation, the slaves, on the suggestion of the Negro

54. G. P. Whittington, ed., "Letters from John H. Ransdell to Gov.
Thomas O. Moore, dated 1863," *La. Hist. Quarterly*, XIV (Oct. 1931),
491–502.
55. Magnolia Plantation Records, entries of Oct. 19 and 21, 1862.

soldiers, "cleaned out the storeroom and the meat room."[56]
On Whitehall Plantation, after the "Yankees" told the
Negroes to help themselves, "they rushed into the house
and took beds, carpets and everything."[57] At Nightingale
Hall, one of the Allston plantations, the slaves locked the
overseer in the house and posted a Negro with a shotgun
outside the door with instructions to shoot him if he tried to
go out.[58] From another Allston plantation the overseer
wrote to his employer that the slaves had "Puld down the
mantle Pieces taken off all the doors and windows Cut the
banisters and sawed out all such as they wanted and have
taken a way the fenceing a Round the yeard brok down the
old Stabel and Carpenter Shop." About two weeks later he
wrote that the Negroes were continuing "puling the building to pieces," that they had even "broke into the Brick
Church and taken out all the board that was left in it."
His postscript gives a suggestion as to the completeness of
the change which had taken place: "it looks verry hard to
pull ones hat to a negro."[59]

When the report came to Mrs. R. F. W. Allston that
the Union soldiers had given the barn key to the Negroes
at Guendalos, a plantation belonging to her brother-in-
law, and that the provisions were to be distributed among
them, she went to an officer, obtained an order for the delivery of the key, and with her daughter set out to investigate. On her arrival at the plantation she was surrounded
by a crowd of several hundred angry, sullen Negroes. Instead of the usual smiles and curtsies there was an ominous
silence. The blacks crowded closer and closer around the
carriage. Mrs. Allston got out, called for the head man,
inquired about the crops, and then said to him, "and now
Jacob I want the keys." He refused, but after she showed
him the order of the Federal officer, he was about to hand

56. *Two Diaries,* p. 22 (Diary of Charlotte St. J. Ravenel).
57. Letter of Eliza C. Palmer to Dr. R. Y. Dwight, March 30, 1865
(MS. in private possession).
58. Pringle, *Chronicles of Chicora Wood,* pp. 264 ff.
59. Letters of J. Belflowers to Mrs. R. F. W. Allston, March 18 and
April 2, 1865, Allston Papers.

them to her when a huge man sprang forward and shouted, "Ef you gie up de key, blood'll flow," emphasizing his threat by shaking his fist in the old slave's face. The shout rose up among the pressing, clamoring, gesticulating crowd, "Yes, blood'll flow for true."

At Mrs. Allston's request the coachman drove off to try to find her son. The scene which followed, graphically depicted by the daughter, suggests how near to the jungle was the reversion of the slaves when accustomed authority had been dissipated by "Yankee" interposition:

The crowd continued to clamor and yell first one thing and then another but the predominant cry was "Go for de officer, fetch de Yankee." . . . They sang, sometimes in unison, sometimes in parts, strange words, which we did not understand, followed by a much repeated chorus:

> I free, I free,
> I free as a frog
> I free till I fool,
> Glory Alleluia!

They revolved around us holding out their skirts and dancing now with slow swinging movements, now with rapid jig motions, but always with weird chants and wild gestures. When the men sent for the officer reached the gate, they turned and shouted "Dont let no white man e'en dat gate," which was answered by many voices, "no, no, we wont let no white pusson e'en—we'll chop um down wid hoe—we'll chop um to pieces sho"—and they brandished their large sharp gleaming rice field hoes. . . . Those who had not hoes were armed with pitchforks and hickory sticks and some had guns.

The composure of the women kept them from suffering bodily injury. After a few hours the coachman returned without having found his young master, and the two ladies returned home. Early in the morning there was a knock at the door; but before any one had time to answer, a black hand thrust the keys to the Guendalos storehouses inside.[60]

60. Pringle, *Chronicles of Chicora Wood*, pp. 269 ff.

In a few cases the misconduct of the Negroes reached the point of personal violence and attempts at insurrection. Two slaves, one under the guise of a Federal soldier, caught and "mercilessly whipped" an aged lady in Madison County, Mississippi.[61] Policemen who returned a fugitive in Louisiana were fired at from ambush as they rode away from the plantation and one of them was mortally wounded.[62] Colored laborers on the David Pugh Plantation in the same state attacked the owner and overseer and injured them severely.[63] A Natchez resident traveling in Louisiana in 1863 was assailed, robbed, and "brutally murdered" by Negroes.[64] In a number of cases Confederate pickets were fired upon by slaves.[65]

Assaults upon women were not unheard of. The postwar statement of an ex-slaveowner that "no woman in the whole South was ever molested by a negro during the Civil War"[66] and many other similar testimonials are not substantiated by the evidence. A Texas newspaper reported the hanging of a Negro for attempted rape of a white woman in Fayette County, Texas, in 1863.[67] A colored man of Ware County, Georgia, attacked the lone feminine resident of a farm at night in 1864, violated her, and then choked her into insensibility.[68] A Negro in Virginia was reported to have "abused a lady and threatened her husband."[69] A Mississippian wrote to Governor Clark in August, 1864, that a Negro, whose master was away from home, "went into the bedroom of a couple of young ladies,

61. R. Winter to Governor Pettus, Sept. 24, 1863, Miss. Archives, Ser. E, no. 61.
62. Magnolia Plantation Records, entry of Aug. 13, 1862.
63. *O. R.*, Ser. 1, XV, 172.
64. New Orleans *Daily True Delta*, Nov. 11, 1863, quoting Natchez *Courier*.
65. *O. R.*, Ser. 1, VI, 78 ff.; XXIV, pt. 2, 468.
66. Robert Bingham, *An Ex-Slaveholder's View of the Negro Question in the South*, p. 13 (reprint from European Edition of *Harper's Monthly*, July, 1900).
67. *The True Issue* (La Grange, Texas), Jan. 1, 1863.
68. Savannah *Republican*, Jan. 27, 1864.
69. *O. R.*, Ser. 1, II, 1010.

and when he laid his hands on one of them, she screamed out, and he slapped her over." The correspondent added that "this is not the first case of this kind for it is very common. I have heard of some six or eight cases of it recently."[70]

Although rumors of insurrections among the slaves were numerous during the war, only a few plots were detected; actual outbreaks were fewer still, and these were immediately suppressed. In May, 1861, a Louisiana owner, being suspicious of disloyalty among his Negroes, crawled under a cabin one night and overheard the discussion of a plot of the slaves to rise up against their master. The date set was July 4, 1861, at which time they had been induced to believe that Federal troops would be near. They planned to kill the white men, take the white women and the fine horses, and "march up the River to meet Mr. Linkum." White men were suspected of being involved in the scheme.[71]

Eighteen Negroes were committed to jail for attempting to excite an insurrection in Hancock County, Georgia, in October, 1863.[72] Three Negroes and a white man were hanged in Brooks County in August, 1864, for plotting a "large work of destruction" among the slaves.[73] Plans for an extensive insurrection on Christmas Eve, 1864, near Troy, Alabama, were revealed a short time before the "rising" was to take place. "Deserters and escaped Yankee Prisoners" were accused of being the chief instigators by some of the Negroes in their confessions.[74] There were two minor outbreaks among the Negroes in Mississippi in July, 1862; one of these resulted in the cutting of an overseer's throat.[75] Plans for a general insurrection throughout the South were outlined in a letter found in the mail of

70. O. F. M. Holladay to Governor Clark, Aug. 19, 1864, Miss. Archives, Ser. E, no. 66.

71. H. Hines to Governor Pettus, May 14, 1861; J. D. Davenport to Governor Pettus, same date, Miss. Archives, Ser. E, no. 52.

72. *Southern Recorder*, Oct. 6, 1863.

73. *Ibid.*, Aug. 30, 1864.   74. *Ibid.*, Dec. 27, 1864.

75. *O. R.*, Ser. 1, XV, 534; J. W. Boyd to Governor Pettus, Aug. 1, 1862, Miss. Archives, Ser. E, no. 57.

a Federal steamer captured off the coast of North Carolina in May, 1863. The letter, signed "Augustus S. Montgomery" and bearing the endorsement of "C. Marshall, Major and Aide-de-camp, Department of North Carolina," was to be circulated throughout the various military departments of the South. It provided that officers at different posts were to promote plans among the Negroes for a general and simultaneous movement on the night of August 1, 1863. The slaves were to arm themselves "with any and every kind of weapon," to burn all the bridges, to destroy railroads and telegraph lines, and then take to the swamps or mountains. No blood was to be shed except in self-defense. A copy of the letter was sent to President Davis and General Lee by Governor Vance and measures taken to prevent any outbreak. Nothing seems to have developed from the plan.[76]

A survey of the evidence of the period makes inescapable the conclusion that disorder and unfaithfulness on the part of the Negroes were far more common than post-war commentators have usually admitted. A correspondent of Senator Clay's wife wrote in 1863 from Selma, Alabama, where he had been in a position to observe the doings of Negroes in an exposed locality, that "the 'faithful slave' is about played out. They are the most treacherous, brutal, and ungrateful race on the globe."[77] This statement is doubtless extreme, but it is no farther from the truth than the encomiums of the slaves' loyalty and devotion which have been so universally circulated and accepted in the South.

The majority of Negroes in the Confederacy, however, were neither loyal nor disloyal in a positive way. They simply waited to see what would happen. Their situation is reflected, though not with entire correctness, in the answer which one of them is said to have given when asked by a fellow slave if he thought that the issuance of the Eman-

76. *O. R.*, Ser. 1, XVIII, 1068, 1069, 1077.
77. John F. Andrews to Mrs. C. C. Clay, Jr., July 10, 1863, Clay Papers.

cipation Proclamation meant a general arming of the Negroes: "Yo' talkin' fool talk nigger! Ain' yo' nebber seen
two dogs fighten ober bone 'fo' now . . . well den, yo' ain
nebber seen de bone fight none is you?"[78]

When the Federals came, the Negroes usually welcomed
them. But if a change in the fortune of war restored the
control of their masters, they made the best of the situation. A Negro soldier captured by "Rebel" cavalrymen in
1864 was brought to Libby Prison in Richmond. Like
most of the ex-slave prisoners, he said that he had been
forced into the Union army against his will. When asked
if he was willing to take the oath of allegiance to the Confederacy, he replied, "Yes, Massa, I takes anything I can
get my hands on."[79]

As a general rule, unfaithfulness and disorder were
common in the invaded areas and rare in the interior. Most
of the serious disturbances were attributable to Federal influences, but some of them were due as much to the withdrawal of accustomed authority as to outside suggestion.
That the slaves in the interior did not "rise up" against
their masters is not surprising when one takes into consideration their lack of facilities for rapid communication
and concerted action, the affection which the most intelligent ones had for their master's families, the fear inspired
by the summary execution of those whose plots to rebel
were detected, and the tremendous advantage which the
whites had over them in every respect, save that of numbers.

78. Allen C. Redwood, "The Cook of the Confederate Army," *Scribner's
Monthly*, XVIII (1879), 560.
79. Richmond *Enquirer*, March 10, 1864.

V

THE SLAVE TRADE

ARTICLE I, section 9, of the Confederate Constitution forbade the "importation of Negroes of the African race from any foreign country other than the slaveholding states or territories of the United States of America" and required Congress to pass such laws as would "effectually prevent the same."

The adoption of this provision was not secured without much opposition. Some contended that while it might be expedient to prevent the importation of African slaves, the prohibition should be statutory, not constitutional. Others, including Toombs, Stephens, and Jefferson Davis, held that the closing of the trade by any means was unwise.[1] When the permanent Constitution was brought before Congress for adoption in March, 1861, the prohibitory clause was approved by a vote of four states to two; Georgia, Louisiana, Alabama, and Mississippi supported it, while South Carolina and Florida voted against it.[2]

In the meantime, Congress, in pursuance of a mandate in the provisional Constitution, had passed a bill making the importation of slaves from any country except the United States a felony punishable with heavy penalties. The sixth section of this act specified that Negroes illegally imported should be transferred to the custody of "foreign States or societies upon condition of deportation and future freedom,"[3] but if such delivery should not be feasible, the President was to cause them to be sold at pub-

1. J. T. Carpenter, *The South as a Conscious Minority*, p. 250, quoting A. M. Hull, "The Making of the Confederate Constitution," *Southern Historical Society Publications*, IX, 284–285; *Southern Recorder*, Feb. 19 and 26, 1861.

2. *Annual Cyclopedia* for 1861, p. 161.

3. *Journals of the Confederate Congress*, I, 95.

lic auction in any state where the sale was not unlawful.
President Davis, considering this an evasion of the policy
declared in the Constitution, vetoed the bill. An attempt to
pass it without his approval failed by a vote of 15 to 24.[4]
Congress seems never to have taken up the question again.

While the African slave trade was being discussed, there
was considerable agitation in favor of preventing or restricting the importation of Negroes from the slave states
of the Federal Union. One argument was that these states
should be made to feel some inconvenience for not having
availed themselves of the opportunity of uniting with the
Confederacy. Another, more generally used, was that if
the trade was not restricted, the states which were still under the abolition government, feeling their property in
slaves insecure, would dispose of it entirely and "thus
bring the Black Republican territory to the border of the
Confederacy."[5] But sentiment on this subject was never
strong enough to procure an enactment.

Concerning the slave trade within the Confederacy the
records are scant. Bills of sale for the period are seldom to
be found. Newspaper advertisements throw less light on
the volume of trade during the war period than before because their number was affected by the scarcity of paper.
The most satisfactory sources are the reports of sales
found in the local news columns. These are very meagre—
almost completely lacking in some newspapers—but by
combining the information which they contain with occasional comments of diarists, the general trend of the slave
market may be followed.

Slave prices during the war were influenced by a number of factors, one of which was the relation between the

---

4. *Journals of the Confederate Congress*, I, 98.
5. There were some who regarded the failure of the border slave states
to enter the Confederacy as an advantage; they would act as a "moral
breakwater against the current of fanaticism and hate setting towards
the South," and by their position in the Federal Government would "compel it to hold hands off from the Southern Confederacy." *Southern Recorder*, March 5 and 12, 1861.

supply and demand of laborers. The restriction of the acreage devoted to cotton caused an apparent surplus of field hands in the early part of 1862. Although the cultivation of food crops was substituted for that of the fibre to a considerable extent, the demand for the new produce did not seem great enough in 1862 to require all of the labor which had been released from the growth of cotton. The result was a depression of slave prices. Later in the war, as more whites were drawn into the ranks and as the effectiveness of the blockade increased, the surplus of Negro workers was largely absorbed in meeting the increased demand for food and clothing.

The movement of slaves from regions threatened with invasion caused a depreciation of values in the interior sections to which they were carried. Many of the refugee owners placed their Negroes on the market because they could not make satisfactory provision for taking care of them. The effects on the local trade were immediately felt. The situation in Richmond as pictured by the editor of the *Enquirer* in October, 1862, is doubtless typical of many other towns not far removed from areas threatened with invasion. "The market for the sale of slaves has within the past week been subject to a decided depression and the prices will continue downward, doubtless for some time," he said. "Bidders are few and the market is stocked—overstocked we might more properly say—owing to the large number of slaves brought from the upper counties of Virginia. Parties having slaves in such localities and wishing to obtain high prices for them would do better to take them farther South, for the present at least."[6]

The most pertinent factor influencing prices was the depreciation of Confederate currency. As money became cheaper, market values soared. In the early part of the war, however, prices did not respond immediately to inflation; and when they did begin to rise in the latter half of

6. Richmond *Enquirer*, Oct. 18, 1862.

1862, there seems to have been a failure to understand the real cause of the increase. Newspaper comments on "good prices" were numerous, but no reference was made to the fact that they were due to the depreciation of currency; instead they were generally attributed to confidence in the success of the movement for independence and an indication of the futility of Lincoln's emancipatory scheme.[7] But the failure to associate "high niggers" and cheap money could not continue long. After the setbacks at Gettysburg and Vicksburg the boost in prices naturally was not to be attributed primarily to confidence in Confederate success. In September, 1863, a contributor to the Columbus, Georgia, *Sun* wrote: "Why should Negroes bring from $1000 to $1500 more in Confederate money than in any other when the value of both depends entirely upon our success in the war? The solvency of one cannot fail without entailing the loss of the right of property in the other." "If the cause fails," he added, "our right to property in slaves fails simultaneously. Confederate notes, bonds, stocks, and negroes will all go together."[8]

At Charleston, mainly from sales reports in the *Mercury*, local prices of slaves may be gathered for nearly every quarter of each Confederate year. Typical items concerning young adult males are given in the accompanying table. From July, 1863, to January, 1864, and from January, 1865, to the end of the war, no prices are reported in the Charleston papers.[9] For these periods, quotations from the Richmond and Augusta markets are tabu-

7. An editorial in the *Hinds County Gazette* (Miss.), Sept. 24, 1862, on "The Value of Negro Property," after the quotation of a few high prices, closed with the remark, "Pretty fair prices considering the assurances from Washington that the institution shall be wiped out."

8. Quoted by *Southern Recorder,* Sept. 1, 1863.

9. It may be that the Federal bombardment which began in July, 1863, caused a suspension of the Charleston market for a time. After January, 1864, reports of sales were resumed and a comparison of the prices with those of Richmond and Augusta indicate that the slave market was not appreciably affected by the continued shelling of the lower part of the city during the months following.

lated. Each price in currency is accompanied by its equivalent in gold.

Year	Quarter	Age	Price in Currency	Corresponding Value in Gold	Average Quarterly Value of Gold Dollar
1861	4	20	$1,160	$1,050	1.2
1862	1	28	895	746	1.2
	2	18	850	570	1.5
	3	23	1,100	647	1.7
	4	21	1,230	473	2.6
1863	1	20	1,450	410	3.5
	2	20	1,630	291	5.6
	3				11.0
	4*	20	2,300	144	16.0
1864	1	20	5,850	266	22.0
	2				19.0
	3	Adult males	4,140	190	21.7
	4	22			31.3
1865†	Feb. 11	Adult males	5,000	100	
	Mar. 22	Adult males	10,000	100	

* Figures for fourth quarter are taken from the Augusta market as reported by the Augusta *Chronicle and Sentinel.*

† From the Richmond market as reported by J. B. Jones in his *Diary.* Both the currency prices and the gold values for 1865 are from the *Diary.*

The Charleston prices seem to correspond rather closely to those of Richmond, Savannah, and Augusta. They are a little lower than those of the interior cities such as Raleigh and Montgomery; this is probably due to the greater security of the latter cities from attack and invasion; for the same reason, Texas prices tend to run higher than those of regions east of the Mississippi.

The table shows a general upward trend of the price of slaves in currency and a general decline of their value in gold throughout the war period. It is interesting to observe the tendency of slave values (in gold) to vary with the fluctuation in the state of military affairs. Throughout 1861 the level of values prevailing at the beginning of that year was generally maintained.[10] In the early part of 1862 military reverses in Tennessee and the Federal occupation of strategic points on the North Carolina coast, followed in April by the capture of New Orleans, together with the movement to restrict cotton acreage, caused a marked decline. The downward trend was stayed somewhat in the fall by the brightening of the horizon occasioned by Bragg's movement into Kentucky and the failure of McClellan's peninsula campaign. During the half-year following the loss of Vicksburg and the failure at Gettysburg, slave values seem to have suffered a depression more pronounced than that of any other six months of the war. There was a temporary revival early in 1864, due probably to the hopes created by the passage of the Conscription, Taxation, and Funding Acts on February 17, 1864, and the thwarting of the efforts of the Federals to make rapid advances in Virginia and Georgia. The next and last sharp decline was occasioned by the march of Sherman through Georgia and South Carolina and the closing in of Grant's army around Richmond. In February and March, 1865, able-bodied male slaves were selling in Richmond for five thousand to ten thousand dollars, but these extravagant figures represent a gold value of not more than one hundred dollars.

The volume of the trade in slaves in 1861 seems not to have been far below normal. Sales probably fell off with the decline in prices which came in the spring of 1862, but by fall they were increasing. Trade was brisk during the first months of 1863. Newspapers frequently commented on the good prices and large sales. The rising prices doubtless encouraged speculation.[11] Fremantle, an English artil-

10. *Hinds County Gazette* (Miss.), Jan. 8, 1862.
11. This is indicated by unusually high prices at some of the auctions. A "likely waiter" sold for $8,000, and a nine-year old boy for $2,120 in

lery officer who made a trip through the South in April, May, and June, 1863, said that the value of Negroes who were seen working in the fields "was constantly appraised" by his fellow travelers. In Louisiana he became acquainted with an old man who had come from Texas for the specific purpose "of buying slaves cheap." Many owners, driven from their places in Louisiana by Federal invasion, were naturally inclined to sell their Negroes at a greatly reduced figure because of inability to take care of them; and persons growing cotton in Texas for export through Mexico were not indisposed to take advantage of the bargains. When Fremantle reached Charleston in June he was impressed by the volume of business "in buying and selling negroes," and by the fact that the papers were "full of advertisements of slave auctions."[12]

The military reverses of July, 1863, caused a great decline in sales, but during the spring of 1864 the trade began to recover. A new slave brokerage firm was established at Montgomery in April of that year. Advertisements in the local papers indicate that it anticipated an extensive business. New quarters had been fitted up "to receive and accommodate . . . all negroes" which might be consigned to the new dealers. They were to "keep constantly on hand a large and well selected stock such as families, house servants, gentlemen's body servants, seamstresses, boys and girls of all descriptions, blacksmiths, field hands." Instructions were given to daily newspapers at Savannah, Mobile, Atlanta, and Columbia to carry the advertisement for one month and forward the bills to Montgomery.[13]

The Charleston market, which seems to have been very

Atlanta in April, 1863. The reporter remarked that these were "steep prices," but that they would probably become "steeper." Montgomery *Weekly Mail*, April 29, 1863, quoting Atlanta *Intelligencer*.

12. Fremantle, *Three Months in the Southern States*, pp. 62, 85, 179.

13. Montgomery *Weekly Mail*, April 19, 1864. About the same time that this firm was preparing for such an extensive business in Montgomery a correspondent of the Charleston *Mercury* wrote from Richmond that there was "little disposition to buy Negroes" there. Charleston *Mercury*, April 5, 1864.

quiet during the last six months of 1863, showed a renewed briskness in the early part of 1864. On January 28, the firm of Alonzo J. White sold a parcel of ninety-three Negroes of all ages for an average price of $2,636.[14] Sales seem to have fallen off during the spring and summer, but in the fall they were increasing. On November 1, a cook and washer with her five-year-old child sold for $8,500, a nineteen-year-old seamstress for $7,600, and an eighteen-year-old cook and laundress for $5,000.[15] Advertisements of Negroes were more frequent than they had been earlier in the year.

Trade in Georgia seems to have been brisk in the fall of 1864. On September 6, eighteen slaves were sold in Augusta for an aggregate price of $34,975. On the same day, six slaves were sold at Columbus and five at Savannah. A twenty-four-year-old Negro boy brought $7,000 at Savannah.[16] On December 30, 1864, nineteen Negroes belonging to an estate in Moore County, North Carolina, were sold at Raleigh. The paper reporting the sale said that there were a number of persons "anxious to buy." The prices were characterized as ridiculously high and the editor suggested to the purchasers "that it would have been wiser to give a third as much for the Negroes and to invest the remaining two-thirds in Confederate bonds to help the government to protect them in the enjoyment of their property."[17]

The sale of slaves continued in some localities until the end of the war. On March 22, 1865, J. B. Jones of Richmond wrote in his *Diary* that "buying and selling for what they call 'dollars' are still extensively indulged; and although the insecurity of slave property is so manifest yet a Negro man will bring $10,000 at auction." It is not unlikely that some Negroes were sold after Lee's surrender. The Augusta *Tri-Weekly Constitutionalist* on April 14,

14. Charleston *Mercury,* Jan. 29, 1864.
15. *Ibid.,* Nov. 2, 1864.
16. *Southern Recorder,* Sept. 13, 1864.
17. Fayetteville *Observer,* Jan. 5, 1865.

1865, reported the sale of a Negro woman and four children for $5,500 at Columbus. The date of the sale is not given; if it was after April 9, news of Lee's surrender had probably not reached that place.[18] From April 14 to May 5, 1865, a Texas newspaper carried an advertisement offering a farm in exchange for Negro property. The same paper contained notices of large rewards for the return of fugitive slaves as late as May 19.[19]

It is not reasonable to suppose, however, that the trade in slaves ever again approached the volume which it had before the reverses of July, 1863. That the buying of Negroes continued to the extent which it did in the latter part of 1864 and in 1865 is remarkable. It can be attributed in part to blind patriotism. There were some people who would not permit themselves to believe that the Confederacy was doomed as long as there was an army on the field. They hoped that the North would lose heart, or that Europe, having waited until both sides were exhausted, would step in and prevent a restoration of the Union. Such persons, according to one contemporary, continued late in the war to add to their slaves, "firm in the belief of the ultimate success of the South."[20] An Alabama planter who paid $6,500 each for two slaves in the latter part of the war, on being reproached by his wife for investing in such uncertain property, retorted, "Wait till you get to the bridge before you cross the river." When the Federals arrived a short time later, and the report came to him one morning at breakfast that his ebony acquisitions had yielded to the lure of freedom, he remarked, "Humph, that's the dearest nigger hire that I ever paid," and continued sipping his coffee.[21]

18. Advertisements for fugitive slaves continued in the *Mercury* and *Daily Courier* until Federal soldiers occupied Charleston in February, 1865. The transfer of the papers to Union control brought an abrupt end to these. In February, 1865, an Augusta firm in the slave-insurance business was still advertising in the *Daily Chronicle and Sentinel*.
19. *Texas Republican* (Marshall, Texas), April 14–May 19, 1865.
20. Saxon, *A Southern Woman's War-Time Reminiscences*, p. 33.
21. Hague, *A Blockaded Family*, pp. 160–161.

But there were other planters whose patriotism did not becloud their sense of business. When they began to feel that the Confederacy had little chance of success, or that, even in the event of independence, "slavery would be difficult to enforce," they sought to dispose of their Negroes.[22] The patriotic zeal of Edmund Ruffin did not prevent the sale of his slaves at an opportune time. On December 2, 1864, his son wrote to Thomas Ruffin: "I sold at the last Amelia Court fifteen Negroes belonging to our Marlbourne property—all that we saved except one man—they were women and children, and brought an average of $2,500." He added the significant comment that "these were all consumers and likely to be for some time and were sold on account of the expense of keeping and the doubtful tenure of the property."[23]

Many of the slaves who worked in the towns and cities as domestics, mechanics, or ordinary laborers were hired by their employers. This practice of hiring, though largely confined to urban communities, was not unknown in rural sections. The period of hire in the case of domestics and laborers was usually a year. The contracts were made in the last days of December and the first part of January. At the time of hire, the employer gave a bond payable at the end of the year for the amount agreed upon. Clothing and food were usually provided by the hirer. Slaves were often permitted to seek their own employers, but much of the placement was done through regular hiring agencies.

Practically all contracts of hire for 1861 were made before the outbreak of the war at rates not affected by it. The volume of hires in 1862 was about the same as for 1861.[24] The rates, however, seem to have been lower. Reports from Mississippi and North Carolina indicate a 30 to 40 per cent reduction from the $100–$150 average paid

22. Saxon, *A Southern Woman's War-Time Reminiscences*, p. 33.

23. J. de Roulhac Hamilton, ed., *The Papers of Thomas Ruffin*, III, 434. Many of Edmund Ruffin's male slaves ran away during the war.

24. Salisbury, North Carolina, reported an increase in the number of Negroes hired, but this seems to have been an exceptional case. Fayetteville *Observer*, Jan. 9, 1862.

as unskilled adult male wages in 1861.[25] This reduction
cannot be attributed to the currency, because the slight
depreciation would have tended to raise instead of lower
the rates.[26] It was probably due to the fact that a surplus
of laborers was expected to result from the restriction of
cotton culture.

In 1863, slave wages were much higher. Employers of
unskilled adult laborers in Virginia and South Carolina
paid from $200 to $300 a year. The continued depreciation of currency caused the general rate to rise in 1864 to
a range of $300–$600 and in 1865 to $1,000 and $1,200.[27]
These rates, characterized as "exorbitant" by the newspapers, caused a noticeable sluggishness in the hiring market.
Early in January, 1864, the Richmond *Whig* reported
that "Negroes hire slowly in Petersburg. Four-fifths are
estimated to be without homes the present year, whereas,
heretofore, the great majority of servants for hire have
been disposed of by the 31st of December. The cause is the
extraordinary and unreasonable prices demanded."[28] Late
in the same month the *Enquirer* commenting on Richmond
hires said: "There is a decided lull in the market for the
irrepressible Negro and the stock on hand at the various
agencies is yet superfluously large. The eye wearies with
looking at Negroes waiting to be hired. The grand rush
for high prices made in the beginning of the year backed
by the fact that there are more Negroes concentrated in
Richmond than belong here is the occasion of this overstocked condition." The high prices were said to have
caused many small families to "manage *ex necessitate* to
do without the assistance of Cuffie," while large families,

25. *Hinds County Gazette* (Miss.), Jan. 8, 1862; Fayetteville *Observer*,
Jan. 6 and 9.
26. A gold dollar was worth 1.2 in currency in January, 1862. Schwab,
The Confederate States, p. 167.
27. Charleston *Mercury*, April 5, 1864; Richmond *Enquirer*, Jan. 5,
1864, Jan. 6, 1865. The editor of the *Enquirer* was of the opinion that
Congress should conscript for army work all Negroes for whom hires of
$1,000 were asked.
28. Issue of Jan. 4, 1864.

for the same reason, had to reduce their force of domestics.[29]

When the gold value of the currency is taken into consideration, however, the "exorbitant" prices of 1864 and 1865 were very low. The gold equivalent of the $600 in currency which an employer promised in January, 1864, to pay for the year's hire of a slave was only $28.57;[30] and of the $1,200 which he promised in January, 1865, the equivalent was even less, being only $22.64. On the basis of gold value he was agreeing to pay only one-fifth or one-sixth of what he paid in 1861.[31] The questions naturally rise, why the widespread protest against unreasonable prices and why the reluctance to hire?

One reason was that the expense of "keeping" the slave, which ordinarily fell upon the employer, was greatly enhanced by the depreciation of currency. The gold value of foodstuffs in the South as a whole was continually rising, at least until the first half of 1864. The scarcity in cities, due to lack of transportation facilities, often made prices of commodities higher there. The gold value of clothing was naturally boosted because of the difficulties of its manufacture. This increase in the expense of keeping the hireling tended to offset the real reduction in the rate of hire. Rather than bear the burden of supporting their Negroes, many owners, unable to hire them out at prices originally asked, offered them at greatly reduced figures and in some cases for their keep alone.[32] William S. Pettigrew of North Carolina, after unsuccessful efforts to hire some of his slaves in 1865, paid as high as $500 each to secure their keep.[33]

Another factor which caused a reluctance to pay the

29. Richmond *Enquirer*, Jan. 28, 1864.
30. By December, 1864, the time when he actually paid the hire, the gold value of the $600 was only about $15.80.
31. Schwab, *The Confederate States*, pp. 173 ff.
32. Richmond *Enquirer*, Jan. 28, 1864; Charleston *Mercury*, April 5, 1864.
33. Letters of Wm. S. Pettigrew's agent to Wm. S. Pettigrew, Jan. 24 and Feb. 14, 1865, Pettigrew Papers.

high rates of hire was the belief that the value of currency might change before the year was out to the disadvantage of the employer. This was especially true for 1864. During the hiring season of that year Congress was working on measures calculated to increase the gold value of the currency. An employer was naturally reluctant to give a bond for $600 in January, 1864, which, before it came due in December, might "be worth ten or twenty times" the value it then had.[34] This situation caused a change to hiring of slaves by the month in Virginia, and doubtless, to some extent, in other parts of the country.[35] Such a practice involved less risk of loss for either the employer or owner on account of the changes in the value of currency.

While the slave trade during the war was marked by many fluctuations resulting from changes in the value of Confederate money, variations in the fortunes of war, and shifting of population in anticipation of Federal invasion, the general tendency from the beginning to the end of the conflict was toward an increase in the current prices of Negroes, a decrease in their real value, and a shrinkage in the volume of trade.

34. Richmond *Daily Dispatch*, Jan. 1, 1864.
35. Charleston *Mercury*, Jan. 4, 1864.

VI

RELIGIOUS LIFE

RELIGIOUS practices in the ante-bellum South varied with different sections and churches. The usual custom, however, was for whites and Negroes to attend morning services together, the latter taking seats in the rear or in the balcony. In many churches, special meetings for the slaves were held in the afternoon. Simple messages, particularly adapted to their capacities and needs, were given by white ministers. Occasionally the blacks were favored with sermons by exhorters of their own color.

Secession and the war tended to cause an increase of interest in the religious training of the slaves. Political union with states hostile to slavery had kept the Southern churches more or less on the defensive. The fear of providing material for abolitionist propaganda had made them hesitate to admit shortcomings in the discharge of spiritual obligations to the slaves. But the feeling of unanimity and security engendered by the creation of a government pledged to protect the "institution" caused the churches to abandon their defensive positions and to devote greater attention to the correction of deficiencies in their religious programs.[1]

Another factor which promoted interest in the spiritual welfare of the slaves was the realization of the value of religious training in preserving submissiveness and loyalty amid the disturbing influences of the war. The South Carolina Conference of the Methodist Church, in a plea for the support of slave missions in November, 1861, called attention to their enhanced value in "securing the quiet

---

1. *Southwestern Baptist,* Sept. 18, 1862; *Southern Churchman,* Jan. 31 and Nov. 21, 1862, Feb. 20, 1863; Charleston *Mercury,* Nov. 29, 1862; Joseph Blount Cheshire, *The Church in the Confederate States,* p. 116.

and peaceful subordination of these people."[2] When a declaration of martial law was anticipated in Charleston, the pastor of Trinity Church requested that special services for the colored people which were being held in three churches be not interfered with. It cannot be said definitely that these revival services were inaugurated primarily for the sake of preparing the Negroes for the expected attack on the city, but that the minister was not unmindful of the wholesome tendencies which would result is indicated by his statement that "so long as . . . the subduing restraints of Christianity are kept vigorously at play among the colored people, we may expect to check the insubordination that must ensue should they be thrown on the community inflamed with false hopes of liberation."[3] The complete loyalty of four hundred slaves on a North Carolina plantation was attributed by a correspondent of the *Countryman* to the fact that the owner had provided regular instruction for his slaves. "Among other lessons taught them," he said, "we know this to have been one,— to be contented and satisfied with the condition in which God, who allots to all the place and position in this world, has fixed them. . . . 'Brethren, let every man wherein he is called abide therein with God.' "[4] In 1863, a contributor to the *Religious Herald,* commenting on the value of church work among the Richmond Negroes, said: "May we not hope and pray that large numbers will be savingly converted to Christ, thus becoming better earthly servants while they wear with meekness the yoke of their master in heaven."[5]

The effort to carry on and extend the program of religious training during the war was beset with many difficulties. Notable among these was the diminution of the number of ministers. During the summer of 1861, when

2. Charleston *Mercury,* Nov. 8, 1861.
3. *O. R.,* Ser. 1, XIV, 489–490.
4. Quoted by Charleston *Mercury,* March 27, 1863.
5. *Religious Herald* (Richmond, Baptist organ for Virginia), July 2, 1863. See also B. F. Riley, *History of the Baptists of Alabama,* p. 298.

the zeal for the war was at its highest point, a great number of pastors left their congregations to enter the army as soldiers or chaplains.[6] Later on, many preachers had to abandon their charges because the salaries which they received were not sufficient to support their families.[7] The fact that candidates for the ministry were not exempt from military service made it difficult to replenish the supply of clergymen.[8] This is reflected in the decrease in the number of preachers entering the Georgia Conference of the Methodist Church. In 1858, twenty-seven were admitted; in 1861 (December), ten; in 1862, six—the smallest number in the history of the Conference up to that time. The 1864 Conference did not meet until January, 1865; at that session only three were admitted.

The decrease of contributions was also a great handicap to the churches. People were deprived of their chief source of income through the restriction of the growth and sale of cotton. Lack of marketing facilities, heavy taxes, and impressment reduced the returns from produce. As a result of these circumstances, "many of the most liberal supporters of the church and its institutions were reduced to abject want."[9] Plantation mission work among the Negroes suffered greatly from the lack of funds in spite of denial and sacrifice on the part of the workers.[10]

In frontier districts difficulties were multiplied. Churches were destroyed by fire, damaged by shells, or dismantled by use as hospitals, warehouses, and even stables. Local conferences or associations met irregularly or in fragments. Congregations were broken up by the "refugeeing"

6. George C. Smith, *Life and Letters of James Osgood Andrew*, p. 438.
7. *Ibid.*, p. 457.
8. *Journal of the Proceedings of the Thirty Second Annual Council of the Protestant Episcopal Church in the Diocese of Alabama*, 1863, address of Bishop Wilmer.
9. H. N. McTyeire, *History of Methodism*, p. 664.
10. W. P. Harrison, *The Gospel Among the Slaves*, pp. 384 ff. Available records indicate little decrease in the number of dollars contributed to missions but when the depreciation of their value is considered, the reduction was great.

of pastors and members.[11] The disorganization wrought by invasion is graphically depicted in the minutes of some of the Baptist Associations of Virginia. Those for Dover Association are typical:

1862 Scarcely any portion of the Confederacy has suffered so much from the ravages of war as that over which our churches extend. Some of them are dispersed, while others are enfeebled and destitute of the regular preaching of the word.

1863 As letters from 23 churches have been sent up to this meeting, leaving 25 unheard from, we shall make a very brief report.

1864 The commodious edifice of one of our largest churches is now a heap of ruins. Another building pierced by the cannon balls of our invaders shows ghastly rents . . . seven of our churches are within the enemy's lines . . . their members refugees. The absence of members battling for the rights and freedom of the Southern Confederacy has caused a large decrease in the attendance of our churches and Sunday Schools.[12]

Some of the frontier churches were deprived of a large portion of their black constituents by the irresistible urge to "go to the Yankees." Those who ran away frequently had the doors of the church closed behind them. The Record Book of a Virginia church contains the following entry: "Church Meeting, Sept. 17, '64 . . . Martha . . . was excluded from the fellowship of the Church for fornication . . . church lists revised. Forty-one excluded who have gone off to the enemy."[13] But expulsions and excom-

11. A Georgia woman wrote in her diary on Sunday, July 24, 1864: "No church. Our preacher's horse has been stolen by the Yankees." Lunt, *A Woman's War-Time Journal*, p. 8.

12. *Dover Baptist Association Minutes*, 1862, 1863, and 1864 (all published together in 1866), pp. 8, 12–14, 20.

13. Library of the University of Richmond, Church Book of Upper King and Queen Baptist Church. There are numerous other instances of slaves being disciplined by the church for going to the Federals. See, for examples: Ala. Archives, Records of the Bethel Baptist Church, entries

munications seemed ineffective deterrents. The anticipated privileges of the new "fellowship" evidently more than offset the loss of the old. The Committee on the Colored Population of Virginia reported in 1863 that "hundreds" of slave members had run away;[14] in 1864 it reported that "many of this class of our membership have been excommunicated from the churches, and others will be, for joining our enemies, and in some instances entire congregations have been broken up." Attributing this wholesale exodus, in part, to the lack of proper teaching, the committee recommended that "special instruction should be given them relative to the Christian obligation of faithfulness to their masters under existing circumstances."[15]

A Mississippi Synod while lamenting the fact that so many Christian servants "deluded by evil men and seducers" had left their homes, urged the members "to pray that their eyes may be opened, and, as to those who return, to remember that scripture which commands us to restore such in the spirit of meekness."[16]

In spite of difficulties the Southern churches worked diligently to carry on the religious training of their black members. Missions were consolidated, pastoral circuits enlarged, and Negro congregations united to white ones that greater numbers might be served by the available preachers.[17] White congregations sometimes went without pastors in order that the plantation missions might be supplied. In the absence of a white minister, some respected old Negro

of October and November, 1865; *Minutes of Appomatox Baptist Association for 1864* (Virginia), p. 11; Z. T. Leavell and T. J. Bailey, *Complete History of Mississippi Baptists,* I, 99.

14. *Minutes of the Rappahannock Baptist Association for 1863,* p. 23.

15. *Ibid.,* for 1864, p. 10. The minutes for 1860 indicate that two-thirds of the 14,000 constituents of this Association were Negroes.

16. *Minutes of the Synod of Mississippi* from 1861 to 1867, p. 34 (report for 1863).

17. *Journal of the Proceedings of the Thirty Second Annual Council of the Protestant Episcopal Church in the Diocese of Alabama, 1863, passim;* Cheshire, *The Church in the Confederate States,* p. 122; Harrison, *The Gospel Among the Slaves,* pp. 313–315; Fleming, *Civil War and Reconstruction in Alabama,* p. 226.

might exhort the mixed congregation.[18] In 1863, the Georgia legislature repealed the act which forbade the licensing of slaves and free Negroes to preach.[19] In some cases the slaves themselves assisted materially in the financial support of the church.[20]

The embarrassment of the churches because of lack of ministers and shortage of funds caused much of their work to be taken over by white women. In some instances, they conducted Sunday schools in the churches for both whites and blacks of the neighborhood.[21] A more common practice was for the mistresses of the plantations to call the slaves together on Sunday afternoons or evenings and read and comment on the scriptures.[22] On the Allston Plantation, the mistress had all the Negro children assemble every Sunday afternoon in the little chapel in the "quarter" where she "taught them what she could of the great mercy of God and what he expected of his children." This service, designated as the "Katekism" by the dusky children, was well-attended. The great attraction, however, was probably not the scriptural instruction, but the issuance of the liberal cuts of cake which followed the service.[23]

In some cases the Negroes took the initiative, assembled themselves with the consent of the whites, and conducted their own religious exercises.[24] There they rocked, and reeled, and shouted according to "de movin' o' de sperrit." Eliza Andrews wrote down some of the songs which she

18. Hague, *A Blockaded Family*, p. 11.

19. *Public Acts at Ga.*, 1863, Called Sess., no. 116.

20. *Minutes of the Montgomery Conference of the M. E. Church, South,* for 1864, *passim*. Negroes of the "Big Swamp Colored Mission" paid $150 toward its support in 1864.

21. Andrews, ed., *Women of the South in War Times*, p. 174 (Diary of Mrs. McQuire, Hanover County, Va.).

22. Charlotte *Daily Observer* (N. C.), Aug. 17, 1905, "Our Women in the War Supplement," narrative of Mrs. F. C. Roberts.

23. Pringle, *Chronicles of Chicora Wood*, pp. 92–93.

24. The Dabney slaves, who were moved by their owner from Macon, Georgia, back to their Mississippi home by train in October, 1864, kept up religious services *in transitu* in the cars. Smedes, *A Southern Planter*, p. 222.

heard Negroes singing in a "praise house" on a plantation in Southwestern Georgia early in 1865. One of the "little sperituals" began:

> Mary and Marthy feed my lambs,
> Feed my lambs, feed my lambs:
> Mary and Marthy feed my lambs,
> Settin' on de golden altar
> I weep, I moan; what mek I moan so slow
> I won'er ef a Zion traveller have gone along befo'.
> Mary and Marthy feed my lambs, etc.
> Paul de 'Postle feed my lambs, etc.

and continued on through as many Biblical names as the Negroes could recall. Another song illustrates the incoherence of the Negroes' conception of Bible themes:

> I meet my soul at de bar of God,
> I heerd a mighty lumber.
> Hit was my sin fell down to Hell,
> Jes' like a clap er thunder.
> Mary she coming running by,
> Tell how she weep and wonder,
> Mary washin' up Jesus' feet,
> De angel walkin' up de golden street,
> Run home believer; oh run home believer,
> Run home believer, run home.

Another one began:

> King Jesus, he tell you
> Fur to ketch 'im a hoss an' a mule
> He tek up Mary behine 'im
> King Jesus he went marchin' befo'.

The chorus of a favorite was:

> I knowed it was a angel
> I knowed it by de groanin'.[25]

25. Elizabeth Andrews, *War-Time Journal of a Georgia Girl*, pp. 89–91, 101.

An ordinary church service could be conducted without the aid of a minister. A slave wedding might be dispensed with; the ceremony could at least be postponed until a convenient time.[26] A baptising was considered very important, but that too could await the coming of a preacher to the neighborhood.[27] A funeral, however, was not amenable to such simple adjustment. It was something regarded by the Negro as a sort of grand finale to his earthly sojourn and an appropriate, if not an essential, introduction to the life to come. An "impressive" ceremony was highly desirable,[28] but a "reg'lar preacher" was usually considered indispensable. In order to get around the difficulty presented by the scarcity of ministers, slaves in South Carolina resorted to a practice which they designated as "funeralising." At the time the body was buried a service was held by the Negroes. At some later time, when a preacher came to the community, the grave was "funeralised"; the minister read the regular funeral service substituting the past for the present tense. When the special words, "earth to earth, ashes to ashes, and dust to dust" were uttered a Negro threw earth and dust on the grave.[29] The Reverend W. W. Malet told of "funeralising" a body before the burial. On the last night of his visit to a plantation a slave girl died. As he had made arrangements to leave before daybreak the

26. Sometimes a marriage ceremony was performed by some old slave "preacher." Frequently the union was accomplished by what the Negroes referred to as the "ober de broom and under de blanket" method. "Yer see," one old man explained, "Dey all 'sembles in de quarters, and a man takes hole of one en' of de broom and a 'oman takes hole of tudder en' an' dey holes up de broom, an' de man an' de 'oman dats gwine to get married jumps ober an' den slips under a blanket, dey puts out de light an' all goes out an' leabs em dar." William Wells Brown, *My Southern Home*, pp. 176–177.

27. Baptismal functions were sometimes performed by slave preachers. Harrison, *Recollections Grave and Gay*, p. 145.

28. "Wakes" were sometimes held over bodies the night before burial. Richmond officers arrested about one hundred Negro "wake" participants in 1863 for being unlawfully assembled. They were reported as being engaged in "the most unchristianlike singing and yelling." Richmond *Enquirer*, Oct. 14, 1863.

29. Malet, *An Errand to the South in the Summer of 1862*, p. 201.

next morning and could not wait for the burial, the Negroes said that it would suffice if he would "funeralise" her body. At eleven o'clock he went to the cottage where singing and praying were in progress, and read the burial ceremony. When he came to the words "We commit her body to the ground," one of the slaves presented some earth, dust, and ashes for him to touch with his hand; these were then laid aside, to be taken to the grave and thrown on the coffin.[30]

The interest of the slaves in the war was often reflected in their religious services. They sometimes prayed for the members of their masters' families engaged in the conflict, much to the gratification of the whites. An English clergyman who visited the South in 1862 was impressed by the plea of an old Negro refugee that God would "help us in this time of trial and need." "Protect our massa far away," he prayed, "protect our brothers 'Hector' and 'Caesar' [body servants] with him; defend us now we are away from home; defend our friends and relatives at home."[31] An old Negro who was called on to lead a prayer in a church audience composed of slaves and whites went so far as to pray for the discomfiture of the "Yankees." "Mars Lord," he said, "be pleased to blow wid dy bref an' sink de ships of de wicked enemy. Our boys, good marster, will drive 'em from de lan' but thou alone can reach de gunboats."[32]

It is probable that the slaves' tendency toward opportunism frequently inclined them to phrase their prayers to conform to the wishes of their white auditors. This idea is supported by an incident related by Robert Russa Moton. Shortly after the reverses of Vicksburg and Gettysburg, a group of whites and slaves assembled at the old Guinea

30. Malet, *An Errand to the South in the Summer of 1862*, p. 205.
31. *Ibid.*, p. 50. Mrs. Burton Harrison who attended a Negro cabin prayer meeting was surprised to hear an old Negro pray for "our pore suffering soldiers in the camps and on the march." *Recollections Grave and Gay*, p. 144.
32. *Southern Field and Fireside*, Jan. 8, 1862.

Church in Cumberland County, Virginia, to spend the day designated by President Davis in fasting and prayer for the aid of God in repelling the tide of defeat.[33] After the whites had prayed, an old colored deacon was called on. He responded with the simple prayer that "the Lord's will be done," leaving to God the responsibility as to which side should be victorious. But when old Brother Armstead Berkeley, the pastor of the Negro Baptist Church, was asked to lead in prayer, he was guilty of no such evasion; instead he lifted up his voice and prayed directly, "O Lord, point the bullets of the Confederate guns right straight at the hearts of the Yankees; make our men victorious on the battlefield and send them home in health and strength to join their people in peace and prosperity." On being reproached by his deacons after the meeting for betraying the cause of the slaves by such a prayer he replied instantly and with seriousness: "Don't worry children; the Lord knew what I was talking about." They all were satisfied with this explanation.[34]

The slaves sometimes had opportunities to express their real sentiments toward the war in secret religious meetings. A South Carolina lady who watched a surreptitious church service through a window one night was reminded of "the howling Dervishes" by the "barbaric frenzy" of the participants. "The men," she said, "sat around clapping and singing deep monotonous notes, but the women were shuffling and leaping in a circle, clapping their hands high in the air, their heads thrown back so that some of their turbans had fallen off, singing in high shrill tones . . . the sweat pouring down their faces and eyes glittering." The songs which they sang were strange to the white listener, though she had attended many Negro meetings. Phrases such as "I'll pick up my work and I'll lay um

33. During the war Negroes were frequently required to observe days of fasting and prayer decreed by the Confederate Government along with their white masters. Charleston *Mercury*, June 10, 29, 1861.

34. Moton, *What the Negro Thinks*, p. 11. Dr. Moton gave additional details of this incident to the writer in a personal interview.

down and no man can hinder me"[35] suggest that the Negroes had the "Yankees" as much in mind as "Jehovah."

Because of greater security from detection by the "patarollers" and owners, the slaves held most of their secret meetings in the cabins late at night. As a preliminary to the service, a large kettle—"the kind you scald shoats in," according to an ex-slave—might be turned bottom side up close to the door and its inner edge slightly raised by placing a cob or chip underneath. The Negroes thought that the sound of singing and praying would pass up under the kettle and thus not be heard at the "big house." Sometimes a cat was put under the kettle and when the cat "got to mewing and scratching," the Negroes, thinking this an indication that the "patarollers" were coming, would disperse.[36] Not infrequently a slave was sent to the back door of the white residence to listen and report if he could hear sounds emanating from the "quarter." The almost unanimous testimony of old slaves is that their secret prayers were for the success of the Union cause.

In the last days of the war, slaves, evidently because of the growing certainty of Federal victory, abandoned their secrecy to some extent. The note of freedom in their songs became more pronounced. Booker T. Washington says: "As the great day drew nearer, there was more singing in the slave quarters than usual. It was bolder, had more ring, and lasted later into the night. Most of the verses of the plantation songs had some reference to freedom. True, they had sung those same verses before but they had been careful to explain that the 'freedom' in these songs referred to the next world . . . now they gradually threw

35. Coxe, *Memories of a South Carolina Plantation during the War*, p. 55.

36. This account of the use of a kettle to catch the sound in secret prayer meetings is based on the author's conversations in 1932–1933 with four ex-slaves, "Uncle" Jeff Mason of Jackson, Mississippi; Bishop Isaac Lane of the Colored M. E. Church, Jackson, Tennessee; "Aunt" Julia Boyd, Jackson, Mississippi; and Anderson Brown of Petersburg, Virginia. The story told by "Uncle" Jeff Mason differs from that told by the others in the detail concerning the cat.

off the mask and were not afraid to let it be known that the freedom in their songs meant freedom of the body in this world."[37] Even in the isolated "black belt" of Alabama, a change in the note of the slaves' songs was noticeable as the end of the war drew near. A white resident of that area wrote many years after the war that she could remember vividly one service which she overheard in a Negro church just before Lee's surrender.

> Where oh where is the good old Daniel,
> Where oh where is the good old Daniel,
> Who was cast in the lions den?
> Safe now in the promised land;
> By and by we'll go home to meet him,
> By and by we'll go home to meet him,
> Way over in the promised land.

She "could almost imagine they were on wing for 'the promised land' as they seemed to throw all the passion of their souls into the refrain"; she added: "I . . . seemed to see the mantle of our lost cause descending."[38]

Throughout the war, despite the difficulties accruing from scarcity of ministers, shrinkage of church income, and deterioration of ecclesiastical property, the Negroes found abundant opportunity to indulge their characteristic inclination toward worship; and in the pursuit of their spiritual activities the Negroes received greater encouragement from the whites during the war than they had received while the Southern states were a part of the Union.

37. *Up from Slavery*, p. 19.
38. Hague, *A Blockaded Family*, pp. 126–127.

VII

MILITARY LABORERS

MUCH of the hard work entailed by the military activities of the Confederacy was performed by Negroes. The aversion of the white soldier to menial tasks was one reason for this, but it was not the only one. Conservation of white man-power for fighting purposes was an appreciable factor. Every "Sambo" wielding a shovel released a "Johnny" for the ranks. Then, there were some types of work which the Negro could perform more satisfactorily than the white.

There were many Negroes engaged in the preparation of food for the army, and they seem to have been more proficient than the whites in this type of work. A Southern journalist wrote that he had heard of biscuits made by Confederate soldiers "which if hurled against the side of a house or tree would stick there through a heavy rain storm."[1] In April, 1862, the editor of the Charleston *Daily Courier* in an article captioned "The Health of Our Soldiers," advocated that experienced Negro cooks should be substituted for white ones. He attributed much of the sickness in the army to the "half done victuals" prepared by the untrained white cooks. But better-prepared food was not this editor's only reason for advocating Negro cooks. He considered that "the menial and unpleasant work of cleaning pots and preparing food" was "miserably out of

1. *Southern Cultivator*, May–June issue, 1862. For an interesting account of the experiences of two Negro cooks see an article by A. C. Redwood, "The Cook of the Confederate Army," *Scribner's Monthly*, XVIII (1879), 560–568. One of the Negroes was called "Bill Doins" because he spoke of his cooking utensils as his "doins." He was ingenious in contriving means of preparing food under all circumstances. At one time he cooked a large quantity of bread on a river bank, using the barrels in which the flour was packed as mixing basins. The heads were knocked off the barrels and water added from the river as it was needed. The other Negro was called "General Boeyguard."

keeping" with the soldiers' "previous manner of life and with the exalted nature of the cause" for which they were fighting.[2] Soon afterward, Congress passed an act authorizing the use of four Negro cooks to each company.[3] They were to receive fifteen dollars a month and clothing. Slaves might be employed with their master's consent.[4] Previous to the passage of this act colored cooks were sometimes hired by the soldiers; members of a Texas unit contributed one dollar each to raise the required wages.[5]

The Quartermaster's Department used Negroes as teamsters, many of whom were expert from prior plantation experience. The satisfaction which they gave is indicated by the statement of a Texas quartermaster that he would rather have one Negro teamster than two conscripts to drive a team.[6] General Forrest used Negroes from his own plantation to drive the wagons attached to his command.[7] "Joe" Johnston, on the other hand, would not have Negro teamsters for his transports because he did not trust them.[8]

Slaves and free Negroes were employed as hospital attendants, ambulance drivers, and stretcher bearers. Their duties in hospitals were the cleaning of the wards, cooking, serving, washing, and, sometimes, attending the patients. In some hospitals all this work was done by convalescent soldiers. As the need of men became more acute in the latter part of the war, Negroes were used more extensively, that the white men, convalescents included, might be available for fighting.[9] Hospital authorities regretted this change, for the Negroes required closer supervision. "A ne-

2. Charleston *Daily Courier*, April 10, 1862.
3. These cooks were reported on the company rosters as "laundresses." *O. R.*, Ser. 1, XXXII, pt. 2, 683.
4. Matthews, ed., *Statutes at Large*, First Congress, 1st sess., chap. 64.
5. George Lee Robertson to his mother, Sept. 25, 1861, Univ. of Texas Archives, transcripts of Robertson Papers.
6. *O. R.*, Ser. 1, XXVI, pt. 2, 154; see also McFarlane to Governor Clark, Sept. 23, 1863, Miss. Archives, Ser. E, no. 66.
7. Dabney H. Maury, *Recollections of a Virginian*, p. 221.
8. *O. R.*, Ser. 1, XXXI, pt. 3, 691.
9. Cumming, *Hospital Life in the Confederate Army of Tennessee*, p. 78.

gro is a negro at best," wrote a female hospital official.
"They have to be told the same thing every day and
watched to see if they do it then."[10] The compensation
allowed for each colored hospital worker was four hundred
dollars a year (in 1864). Clothing was furnished by the
Negroes or their owners. Masters were not allowed to feed
their slaves and draw a cash commutation, as in the case of
the fortification laborers. The objection to this was that
such a policy resulted in the Negroes' stealing supplies
from the hospital.[11]

Negroes were employed in great numbers on railroads in
the Confederacy. The extraordinary demands of the war
called for frequent replacement of rails, repair of bridges,
and restoration of road-beds. The advance and retreat of
armies, exhaustion of the food supply in one area, shifting
of the base of operations from one point to another—all
might necessitate rebuilding of old roads or the construction of new ones. The problem of the maintenance of railways was complicated by the shortage of iron. Many more
laborers were required than would have been the case had
there been a sufficiency of this commodity. The scarcity of
rails became so acute that the authorities had to resort to
the expedient of removing rails from one road to another
as exigencies demanded. Lines in remote areas were torn
up to provide iron for roads which were more urgently
needed because of their location in relation to the army.[12]
Details of white men were made early in the war to do
much of this work; but as the need of fighting men increased, slaves and free Negroes were hired; when hiring
failed to provide a sufficient number, impressments were
made.[13]

Slave labor was also used extensively in the manufacture of powder and arms. In February, 1865, 310 of the
400 workmen employed in the naval works at Selma, Ala-

10. Cumming, *Hospital Life in the Confederate Army of Tennessee,* p. 78.
11. *O. R.,* Ser. 4, III, 516.
12. The shortage of iron also made it difficult for the railroad authorities to keep a sufficiency of tools for the workers. *Ibid.,* p. 478.
13. *Ibid.,* II, 358.

bama, were Negroes.[14] In September, 1864, there were
4,301 Negroes and 2,518 whites employed in the iron mines
in all the Confederate States east of the Mississippi.[15] The
proportion of Negroes employed in the niter mines in these
same states was less,[16] because of the exposed location of
the mines and because the nature of the work required a
greater proportion of experts.[17]

The military activity employing the greatest number of
Negroes was the construction of defense works. While the
white armies were being mustered for the field, a host of
blacks was being marshalled for the erection of defenses.
The roar of cannon, the rattle of muskets, and the clatter
of the sword in the hand of the white was accompanied by
the thud of the sledge hammer, the ring of the axe, and the
clank of the shovel wielded by the strong ebon arm of the
field hand as he worked to make impregnable the endan-
gered positions of the Confederacy. Together they worked,
white and black, through the halcyon days of '61 and '62
and the dark periods of '64 and '65, an army of soldiers
and an army of laborers.

One type of defense work done by Negroes was the
throwing up of foundations of dirt or sand for the planting of batteries In a swampy country, such as that around
Charleston, the erection of a battery was a very difficult
task. The foundations had to be largely of timber. Bags
of earth, reinforced by wooden beams might be piled on
sunken timber for a mounting.[18] Obstruction of rivers was
another important phase of defense work. This was sometimes accomplished by felling or laying huge piles of trees

14. Bishop C. F. Quintard, *Personal Narrative,* p. 13. Up to Feb. 1865,
190 guns had been turned out by this establishment.
15. Figures compiled from the report of the Chief of the Niter and
Mining Bureau, *O. R.,* Ser. 4, III, 696.
16. *Ibid.;* 1,888 whites and 1,404 Negroes were employed. In July, August, and September, 1864, the output (deliveries) of the niter mines was
146,883 pounds.
17. *Ibid.*
18. The fact that cannon and mortars of that time were lacking in re-
coil facilities required an undue amount of labor in the preparation of
the foundations.

across the stream.[19] A method more commonly used was the anchoring of a raft across a narrow place in the river.[20] Batteries were usually placed near the rafts to thwart any attempts of the Federals to destroy them.

Negroes were used extensively to build and repair forts or enclosures, such as Henry and Donelson in Tennessee, and Wagner in South Carolina. Negroes also dug canals. Great numbers of them were occupied in throwing up breastworks and in digging trenches for the protection of the soldiers in line. Work of this type, when performed by slaves, was usually done in the Confederate rear, beyond the range of Federal guns. General Magruder wrote General Lee in April, 1862, requesting one thousand Negroes from Richmond "to erect works in the rear which may enable me to save this army in case of being . . . forced to retreat from my present position."[21] The white soldiers usually did their own "digging in" when there was any to be done under fire.

Various methods were used during the war to obtain the slave laborers needed for military purposes. But in the early part of the conflict zeal for the Southern cause was so great that Confederate and state authorities had little difficulty in obtaining a sufficiency of Negro workers. Citizens of Southeastern Texas had local organizations in 1862 which called upon the neighboring planters to furnish laborers in anticipation of the needs of the military authorities; a central committee at Houston acted as a coordinating unit for their activities.[22] Farmers in other localities held meetings in which they voted to lend their slaves without wages;[23] the government was to furnish quarters and rations; planters in some cases even provided the necessary tools and overseers at their own expense.[24]

19. *O. R.*, Ser. 1, XIV, 522.
20. This method was used to obstruct the Alabama, Yazoo, and Red rivers.
21. *O. R.*, Ser. 1, XI, pt. 3, 430.
22. Univ. of Texas Archives, printed circular in John Adriance Papers.
23. Pierce, *Freedmen of Port Royal*, p. 304.
24. *O. R.*, Ser. 1, IV, 140; Fremantle, *Three Months in the Southern States*, p. 72.

A scheme more generally used for securing laborers during the first year of the war was by voluntary contract between the owners—or the Negroes themselves, if they were free—and the military authorities. Newspapers carried numerous advertisements for the hire of Negroes for various defense projects. The terms of hire were usually published in detail.[25] As Confederate money depreciated in value, wages naturally had to be raised. In 1861–1862, fifteen dollars a month with rations and medical attention was the standard compensation. In the fall of 1864, a Georgia engineer offered forty dollars a month, rations, and medical attention.[26]

The policy of hiring Negroes by voluntary contract did not prove a permanent success because of the growing aversion of the planter to having his Negroes employed in military pursuits.[27] Hiring of laborers continued throughout the war, but it had to be supplemented by impressment before the end of the first year of the conflict.

Impressment was first practiced by military officers in the field. They justified their action solely on the ground of exigencies imposed by the war.[28] When an exposed area was threatened with invasion, an officer in charge might not hesitate to call on the planters in the vicinity for a large proportion of their slaves.[29] Cavalrymen were sometimes sent out to bring them in.[30] In cases of absolute necessity, these impressments were approved by Secretary Walker.[31] The action of the military officers seems to have met no serious objection at first. Even when Colonel Ma-

25. For an advertisement prepared by Confederate authorities for the Richmond newspapers in January, 1862, see O. R., Ser. 1, LI, pt. 2, 458.
26. Augusta *Chronicle and Sentinel*, Oct. 14, 1864.
27. See O. R., Ser. 1, XXVIII, pt. 2, 215; Ser. 4, II, 106; III, 478, for evidences of failure of the policy of hiring laborers.
28. *Ibid.*, Ser. 1, LI, pt. 2, 252.   29. *Ibid.*, II, 1007.
30. *Ibid.*, XVII, pt. 2, 756. In July, 1863, the mayor of Charleston on being informed by Beauregard that the completion of the work on Morris Island was essential to the defense of the city, ordered the police to "arrest every able-bodied male slave and take him to the police station to be subject to the order of General Beauregard." Charleston *Mercury*, July 10, 1863.
31. O. R., Ser. 1, LI, pt. 2, 252.

gruder called for one-half of the able-bodied slaves in certain counties of Virginia, his demand was promptly complied with. But when he failed to return the slaves after six weeks, the people began to manifest discontent and to question the legality of the impressment.[32]

Military impressment eventually became so unpopular and its legality so widely questioned that it had to be given up as a general policy. It was superseded by impressment from another source. The new coercing agent was the state governor. In the fall of 1862 most of the Confederate states passed laws bestowing upon their respective governors the authority to impress Negroes in numbers sufficient for the adequate defense of those states, if they could not be secured by voluntary hire. Most of these laws provided that impressment be in uniform proportion to the number of able-bodied male slaves owned, fixed the rate of compensation, and prescribed the age limits within which slaves were subject to impressment.[33] While these state enactments made impressment legal, they did not, as a rule, provide adequate machinery to make it effective. Diversities and inequalities in rate of compensation, period of labor, method of enrolment and appraisal of slaves, existed throughout the South.

Under this gubernatorial system of impressment the military authorities were supposed to make requisitions upon the governors, either directly or through the War Department, for the laborers which were needed. Only a small proportion of those requested were secured. The chief engineer at Charleston made requisitions for an average of 2,500 slaves a month from November, 1862, to February, 1863. The average number received by him for each of these four months was 755;[34] and South Carolina had

32. *O. R.*, Ser. 1, LI, pt. 2, 636, 697.
33. See *Acts of Fla.*, 1862, 1st Sess., no. 62; *Public Laws of N. C.*, 1862–1863, Regular Sess., chap. 16; *Acts of Ala.*, 1862, Called Sess., no. 22.
34. *O. R.*, Ser. 1, XIV, 827.

better impressing machinery than did some of the other states.[35]

In order to correct this ineffective system, a section was included in the general impressment law passed by the Confederate Congress on March 25, 1863, specifically legalizing the impressment of Negroes by the Confederate authorities. The impressment was to be made "according to the rules and regulations provided in the laws of the state wherein they are impressed."[36] In the absence of a state law, the impressment was to be made according to rules prescribed by the Secretary of War. This general law was supplemented by an amendatory act of February 17, 1864, the purpose of which was further to increase the effectiveness of the original act by making the portion dealing with Negroes clearer and more specific.[37] It authorized the Secretary of War to impress slaves up to the number of 20,000 when conditions should require. Impressment of slaves was to be made only after the impressment of free Negroes had failed to meet the needs of the government. If the owner had but one male slave between the ages of ten and fifty that slave was not to be taken without the permission of the owner. Not more than one-fifth of the male slaves between eighteen and forty-five were to be demanded. Credit was to be given for slaves already impressed under authority of the Confederate Government. Full compensation was to be made for slaves lost through death or escape to the enemy while in government employ.

The impressment of slaves and other property by the Confederate authorities caused a serious controversy between the Confederate and state authorities. Some of the states had passed laws regulating impressments for their defense before March 26, 1863. When Congress passed the first general impressment act it sought to obviate conflict with the state laws by providing that slaves should be im-

35. See *Acts of S. C.*, 1862, Dec. Sess., no. 4614, sec. 3.
36. Matthews, ed., *Statutes at Large*, First Congress, 3d Sess., chap. 10.
37. *Ibid.*, 4th Sess., chap. 79; *O. R.*, Ser. 4, III, 208.

pressed according to the laws of the state in which the impressments were made, provided that state had laws on the subject. The parallel system worked smoothly as long as the Confederate officials impressed strictly according to state law. The state governments were evidently willing to let the Confederate authorities go ahead with impressment as long as they conformed to local regulations. They were glad to be rid of the obnoxious task. Governor Brown of Georgia went so far as to refuse to impress slaves through the state machinery to fill a requisition of General Mercer in April, 1863, on the ground that the Confederate Government now had full authority to take slaves and should not call on the state authorities to perform this task.[38]

Such harmony as this was too good to last. The Confederate Government found itself seriously hampered in trying to conform to all the details of the various state regulations. The situation in South Carolina illustrates the difficulty.[39] Confederate regulations provided for the conscription of slaves to be used anywhere in the Confederacy; South Carolina's laws restricted the use of her slaves to the limits of the state. While the Confederate law contemplated the use of slaves in a number of capacities, "in connection with the military defenses of the country"; the state laws required that slaves be detailed for only such work as was "intimately connected with the defense of the state." The Confederate regulations required impressment for twelve months; the state laws provided that a slave engaged in military labor could be withdrawn every four months and a new one substituted in his place. The Confederate regulations contemplated that control of slaves impressed should be taken over by Confederate authorities; the state laws provided for state control through a state agent.[40]

The Confederate authorities, realizing the impossibility

38. *O. R.*, Ser. 1, XIV, 915.
39. See *ibid.*, Ser. 4, III, 1018 ff. Frank L. Owsley gives a good brief discussion of the conflict between state and Confederate authority over impressment in his *State Rights in the Confederacy*, chap. V.
40. See *Acts of S. C.*, 1864, Dec. Sess., no. 4703, for the duties of the state agent.

of securing an effective force of Negro laborers in conformity with state regulations, sought to evade those which were in the way. Attention was called to the fact that, while one section of the law of March 26, 1863, provided that impressments should be according to state law, another section of that same law gave army officers the right to impress forage, articles of subsistence, "or other property whenever the exigencies . . . are such as to make impressments absolutely necessary." Supported by this "other property" phrase, military authorities resorted to impressments of slaves, in some instances in violation of state laws. This procedure was challenged by state authorities. In July, 1864, a Virginia congressman wrote to Secretary Seddon protesting against the recent impressments of slaves in that state. He questioned the existence of "any law authorizing a draft of slaves in Virginia except according to state law and through the governor and the county courts."[41] Seddon's answer was interesting in that it presented a view of the relationship between Confederate and state laws quite different from that expressed in the Confederate law of March 26, 1863: "It seems to me clear," he said, "to prevent the operation of the Confederate law it would be necessary the states [sic] should have provided laws of impressment co-extensive with the necessity intended to be met. As such is confessedly not the legislation of Virginia, the Confederate law in regard to impressment must, on just principles of construction, be held applicable to the slaves of that State."[42]

This elastic reasoning may have been convincing to the Secretary of War; but it tended only to stiffen opposition on the part of state authorities to what they considered encroachment on state prerogatives. Already this opposition had approached the point of open resistance to Confederate impressment measures. Governor "Joe" Brown of Georgia, to whom General Mercer alluded as "our dispu-

---

41. *O. R.*, Ser. 4, III, 547.
42. *Ibid.*, pp. 563–564. For further argument of Seddon on this point, see *ibid.*, pp. 851 ff.

tatious Governor," sought to obstruct military impressment in his state by "delays and points of etiquette between military commanders."[43] The governor of North
Carolina twice refused to impress slaves to fill a requisition
of the War Department to build a much-needed railway
between Greensboro, North Carolina, and Danville, Virginia.[44] The legislature of North Carolina in February,
1865, asked the governor to return slaves who had already
been collected at Wilmington, because the passage of the
Confederate impressment law rendered the state law by
which they had been impressed "inoperative and unnecessary."[45] The Florida legislature passed an act in December, 1864, which stated that "no demand, or impressment
of slaves or free Negroes in this state shall be made except
in conformity with the provisions of this law; and if any
shall be made in violation thereof, it is hereby declared unlawful and void."[46]

The conflict between state and Confederate authority
was most acute in South Carolina. Brigadier General John
Preston wrote to Secretary Seddon from Columbia in
January, 1865, that impressment was being impeded "by
the Legislature of the State, . . . the temper of the executive, and the people. . . . A regiment of cavalry with
bloodhounds in every county in the Confederacy would not
obtain the slaves unless by . . . use of state laws and state
authority."[47]

Confederate officials, convinced that impressment could
not have any appreciable degree of success without the co-
operation of the local and state authorities, sought to avoid
collision with them. Confederate drafting of slave laborers
was generally not resorted to in states having impressment
laws, until after requisitions had proved altogether insufficient.[48] Various other expedients were proposed to obviate

43. *O. R.*, Ser. 1, XIV, 8361.　　　44. *Ibid.*, Ser. 4, II, 385.
45. *Public Laws of N. C.*, 1864–1865, Reg. Sess., Resolutions, p. 35.
46. *Acts of Fla.*, 1864, First Sess., no. 27, sec. 3.
47. *O. R.*, Ser. 4, III, 1019.
48. See *ibid.*, Ser. 1, XXIX, pt. 2, 630, 636, 646; XXVIII, pt. 2, 216.

the necessity of Confederate impressment. A committee of the South Carolina House of Representatives suggested that "poor white" troops from the "up-country" would cheerfully volunteer to do the work being done by the Negroes if they were given extra pay.[49] Governor Brown thought it would be better to use soldiers to perform the necessary labor, even if they had to be paid forty dollars per month extra.[50] Details of white soldiers were used for labor on defenses. But to dispense with Negro labor completely was generally considered impracticable.

Late in 1864, when the conflict between state and Confederate authorities over impressments was at a high pitch, President Davis made a proposal, one of the aims of which was to obviate the necessity of periodic impressment.[51] He recommended that the Confederate Government buy forty thousand slaves, train them as teamsters and pioneers, and retain them as a sort of subsidiary labor corps. He also suggested the expediency of offering freedom to those who should render loyal service to the end of the war. Had his government been able to effect the recommendation of the President, further impressment of slaves might have been avoided. The source of a chronic and increasingly bitter controversy might have been removed. But his proposal, especially that part of it suggesting the emancipation of slaves as a reward for faithful service, provoked a controversy even more bitter than that caused by impressment itself.

The results of impressment, whether by state or Confederate authority, or both, were meagre. In South Carolina, Florida, and Georgia during 1863, Confederate and

49. *Ibid.*, XXVIII, pt. 2, 532. J. H. Hammond was of the opinion that the soldiers could do the work more satisfactorily and economically than the slaves. Hammond to Pemberton, April 28, 1862, Hammond Papers.

50. *O. R.*, Ser. 1, XIV, 916.

51. Periodic impressment was inefficient from the military standpoint. By the time slaves were well-organized they had to be sent home. Joseph E. Johnston was in favor of conferring on the Confederate Government the power to make wholesale, permanent impressment of slaves. Mrs. D. Giraud Wright, *A Southern Girl in '61*, pp. 168–169.

state agents together secured no more than a monthly average of one-fifth of the slaves requisitioned by the engineers.[52] In the latter part of 1863 and 1864, as the need for white men in the ranks became more acute, efforts to make the impressment laws effective were redoubled. The Conscript Bureau was entrusted with the work of impressing Negroes because it was the "most diffused agency" under the War Department. Editorials appeared urging planters to send their slaves to the defenses. Urgent requests of military officers were published in the newspapers. In South Carolina an act was passed declaring the refusal or neglect to send slaves required by the impressment law for work on fortifications to be a misdemeanor punishable by a fine of $200 for each slave withheld.[53] Yet impressment became more and more a futility. General Bragg wrote from Wilmington in January, 1865, that the laboring force of his department, "heretofore large . . . has now dwindled down to a handful."[54]

As the Union army was preparing to close in upon the diminishing forces about Richmond in February, 1865, Lee wrote a letter to Governor Smith of Virginia pleading for more laborers. He said that there was no prospect of having his exterior lines in a suitable condition unless he could get a strong force of workers at once; and that of the five thousand Negroes he had requested two months before he had received only five hundred.[55]

The increasing reluctance of slave owners to respond to the calls of the military authorities for their Negroes seems paradoxical. After the Emancipation Proclamation it was generally understood that the overthrow of the Confederacy meant the end of slavery; yet as defeat became more imminent, as the stability of the "institution" became more

52. *O. R.*, Ser. 1, XXVIII, pt. 2, 533, report of the chief engineer of the department.

53. Charleston *Mercury,* Oct. 12, 1863.

54. *O. R.*, Ser. 1, XLVI, pt. 2, 1036.

55. General Lee to Governor Smith, Feb. 9, 1865, *Calendar of Virginia State Papers,* XI, 261.

precarious, owners became less willing to send their Negroes to help stay the tide of invasion. The situation in Virginia affords a striking example; Governor Smith said in February, 1865: "I issued my requisition. . . . I was overwhelmed with claims set up by the different counties, some insisting they had already furnished more than their quota . . . ; some that they had furnished more than their neighbor counties; some that they were exempt by reason of the heavy losses sustained . . . ; some upon the ground of agricultural necessity, etc."[56] As slave property became more uncertain, there was an apparent tendency to hold to it more tenaciously, as with a death grip.

The failure of the planters to lend the labor of their slaves cannot be attributed primarily to a lack of patriotism. There were many planters "who had encouraged their sons to enlist" and yet who were very slow "to answer the call for their Negro men to defend the towns"; and, in some cases, those who sent Negroes to the fortifications made preparations for their maintenance and care "that were not observed for the soldiers sent out from the hearth stone."[57]

There were several reasons for the planter's recalcitrancy in yielding his slaves to military uses. Outstanding among these was his opposition to the methods by which they were taken. Impressment was particularly odious to him; it was an unwarrantable interference with his individual rights and property. Then there were many planters who felt that the burden of supplying slave labor was unequally distributed. The small slaveholders thought that partiality was shown to the large slave owners.[58] Planters

56. In January, 1865, he had written to the city court clerk of Lynchburg: "That there should not be more than 101 slaves between the ages of 18 and 55 years in your large and crowded city is difficult to believe, and of which not more than thirty are capable of difficult labor." *Ibid.,* XI, 259–260.

57. J. W. Dubose, The Canebrake Negro, 1850–1865, Dubose Papers.

58. D. A. Holman to Governor Pettus, Oct. 27, 1862, Miss. Archives, Ser. E, no. 58; Petition of Holmes County Planters to Governor Pettus, Mar. 23, 1862, *ibid.,* no. 60.

in one locality felt that they were being called on for more laborers than those in another. In some cases impressing agents were suspected of fraudulent dealings. "Those planters who had a good stock of fat fowls, and plenty of good liquors stored away in their cellars," wrote a Texas journalist, "were always the favored parties. That was all the protection they needed."[59]

Some planters objected to the impressment of their slaves because of the pecuniary loss involved. They were promised compensation by the government, but the amount was usually far less than the actual value of the labor;[60] and the owners did not always receive the full amount promised.[61] The pecuniary loss was multiplied if the slaves were taken during a crop season. J. H. Hammond wrote to General Pemberton in April, 1862, that crops would be reduced one-half if the effective male slaves were taken for three weeks at that season.[62] Then, the fact that most of the farmers in the South were engaged primarily in the growing of food crops after 1862 inclined them to feel that their slaves were as advantageously employed on the plantations as on the fortifications; and even more so during the growing and harvesting seasons.

Contributing to the opposition to impressment was a prevalent feeling among slave owners that military labor was detrimental to the Negroes. Planters complained that such work was injurious to health; the slaves were not properly fed; they were subjected to exposure, to cold and rain; they were neglected when ill; their work was unduly heavy or strenuous; they were brutally punished; opportunities to escape were frequent, and the slaves were more apt to take advantage of them than when on the plantation because of their dislike of the unduly hard

---

59. *The Freeman's Champion* (Houston), April 10, 1865.

60. Hammond to Pemberton, May 29, 1862, Hammond Papers.

61. D. A. Holman wrote to Governor Pettus, Oct. 22, 1862, "Some slaves were pressed to work at Grenada under promise of $25 and only got about $12.50 which operates against us now," Miss. Archives, Ser. E, no. 58.

62. Hammond to Pemberton, April 28, 1862, Hammond Papers.

work, and the intoxicating effect of the proximity of the
enemy; the environment of the camp was not wholesome
for the slaves' morals; fighting and gambling were indulged
in; the Negroes had opportunities to learn the best methods
of running away; discussing among themselves, as they
did, the issues of the war, they returned to the plantation
with new and dangerous ideas which they imparted to the
other slaves, thus complicating the problem of control and
discipline at home.[63] Hammond was probably expressing a
sentiment which was widespread—and one which was not
lacking in patriotism—when he wrote to Pemberton: "I
must frankly say that I do not wish to send *my* Negroes."[64]
Instead of sending *his* Negroes he hired free Negroes to fill
the requisitions made on him.[65]

So great was the objection to impressment in the latter
part of the war that planters openly resisted it. A Texan
wrote to his governor in 1864 that he had told the people
of his district to disregard a call made by General Magruder for slave laborers. Another citizen wrote that this
call "would not be obeyed except at the point of the bayonet."[66] Planters even went so far as to tell their slaves to
hide on the approach of the impressing agents and to encourage those at work on the fortifications to return
home.[67]

The slaves were strongly inclined to coöperate with their
masters in evasion of impressment laws. Life for the Negroes
who worked on the Confederate defenses was devoid of the
freedom of movement and the opportunities for relaxation

63. Hammond to James H. Chestnut, April 28, 1862; to Pemberton,
May 29, 1862, Hammond Papers; Richmond *Whig,* Jan. 20, 1864, editorial.

64. Hammond to Pemberton, May 29, 1862, Hammond Papers.

65. Hammond to William Gilmore Simms, April 15, 1863, *ibid.* Hammond's patriotism is attested by the fact that he sent 28 Negroes while
the requisition was for only 16. Twenty of them were hired and the other
8 were his own slaves.

66. Letters of Durant and Haynes to Governor Murrah, April 11, and
Jan. 5, 1864, Texas Archives.

67. Mrs. W. H. Neblett to her husband, Aug. 5, 1862, Neblett Papers;
Tri-Weekly Telegraph (Houston), July 22, 1863.

which ordinarily characterized life on the plantations. There were no "Sat'd'y ev'nin's off" when the enemy was threatening. The endless miles of breastworks could not be "laid by" with the same facility as corn and cotton. The laborers were closely supervised from the time they left the plantation until they returned home or until they ran off to the "Yanks."

When the military officers made a demand upon an owner for a certain portion of his male slaves between certain ages, he made the choice of the ones whom he wanted to go, and sent them to a place designated by the authorities. They were usually accompanied to the rendezvous by the owner or his overseer. There they were met by the sheriff, or some other official, who took charge of them. They were then examined to see if they were "able-bodied," and an appraisal of their value was made and recorded so that just compensation might be made to their owners if they died, ran off, or were captured. After their examination and appraisal, they were conducted by the impressment officer to the scene of their labor where they were committed to the charge of the military authorities.

The laborer seems to have suffered from "over-supervision" during his sojourn at the fortifications. His work involved three different interests and each sought a voice in its control. The case of a Negro working on the Charleston defenses in December, 1864, might be taken as an illustration. The Confederate Government exercised supervision over him through a series of officials. The lowest in rank was the Negro foreman, or driver (one for every 25 slaves); the foreman was responsible to a white overseer (one for every 50 slaves); the overseer was subject to the orders of a manager (one for every 100 slaves); over the manager was a superintendent (one for every 800 slaves), who took his orders from a director (one for every 2,400 slaves). The director was responsible to the chief engineer of the Department of South Carolina, Georgia, and Florida, who received orders from the Secretary of War, directly, or through General Beauregard, commander of the department.[68] The state exercised its control largely through a state agent who was responsible to the governor.[69] This official was required to visit all the camps for laborers to examine their condition, to observe their treatment, their discipline, their food, their clothing, and their medical attendance. He was to make reports to the governor after each round of visits. The owner sought to exercise authority over the slaves through an overseer. Any owner had a right to send an overseer to look after his slaves.[70]

It is not surprising that there were many complaints resulting from this system of supervision. Confederate authorities complained of lack of coöperation from state agents. The latter resented the officiousness of Confederate authorities. Owners railed against both. Confederate officials objected to the overseers sent by the planters;[71] the latter complained that their Negroes were brutally treated by the military supervisors.[72] Meanwhile, the bewildered Negroes, with characteristic patience, sought to satisfy all parties—with as little work as possible.

The laborers' food was furnished by the Confederate Government, or by the state, if they were in state employ. In some cases, owners were allowed to feed their slaves and to receive compensation in cash equal to the commutation allowed soldiers in the service. The regular ration for slaves on the Confederate works in South Carolina in 1863 was "¼ pounds of meal, ½ pound of rice, 1 pound of beef, or ⅓ of a pound of bacon, per day; and 4½ pounds of salt and 4 pounds of soap . . . to 100 hands per week."[73]

68. *O. R.*, Ser. 4, III, 898.

69. *Acts of S. C.*, 1864, Dec. Sess., no. 4703.

70. This may not have been true for South Carolina. The laws of Alabama, Louisiana, Mississippi, and Virginia permitted any owner, or any group of owners, who sent 30 slaves to the works to send an overseer to look after them, his salary to be paid by the Confederate Government.

71. A. J. Livermore to F. S. Blount, April 28, 1864, Miss. Archives, Ser. E, no. 65.

72. Petition of Holmes County Planters to Governor Pettus, March 23, 1863, *ibid.*, no. 69.

73. *O. R.*, Ser. 1, XXVIII, pt. 2, 534, 536. The workers on Sullivan's Island were given a special consideration of two rations of whiskey each day when they had to work in mud or water. *Ibid.*, p. 534.

There were many complaints made by slave owners concerning the feeding of their Negroes in government employ. Doubtless much of this was occasioned by the natural aversion which the owner had to having his slaves impressed. But there were just grounds of complaint. General Bragg wrote President Davis in February, 1865, that there had been "much suffering . . . from the insufficient quantity of food." He stated that soldiers' rations had been issued to the slaves, but that it was altogether insufficient for a laboring man employed in heavy work.[74]

The Negroes suffered more from lack of meat than from anything else, especially during the latter part of the war when the issue of meat to soldiers had to be cut down drastically because there was not a sufficient supply to be had at the commissariat. In such instances, the laborers were introduced to meatless days.[75] Sometimes the meat which they received was "more bone than meat."[76]

It was not unusual for the owners to supplement the government rations with supplies from the plantation when the Negroes were not too far away. William H. Ott, sent by a group of Virginia planters to look after their slaves on the Richmond defenses, wrote to one of the owners that he had "written to several persons in regard to the Rations which the Negroes get which is certainly too light for them to work on. I hope that all the men who have sent their Negroes in my Charge will Endeavor to send them some Extra provisions so that they may have something in addition."[77] The slaves of William Massie sent word themselves that their rations were insufficient and requested their master to send additional food from the plantation.[78]

74. *O. R.*, Ser. 1, XLVII, pt. 2, 1138.   75. Jones, *Diary,* I, 385.
76. Letter of Wm. H. Ott to J. D. Davidson, Feb. 15, 1863, McCormick Agricultural Library, Chicago, Davidson Papers.
77. *Ibid.*
78. M. H. Fitzpatrick to Mrs. Wm. Massie, Oct. 4, 1863, Univ. of Texas Archives, Massie Papers. One of the Massie Negroes employed as a government teamster wrote his mistress a long letter in Feb., 1865, asking her for money, saying that "It would be very useful to me," but adding, "I would not ask you for money but rations are so short." The letter was replete with "respects" to the white members of the Massie household,

Provisions were not sent directly to the Negroes but to the overseers to be given out when needed.[79]

Clothing was generally provided by the owners when the slaves were impressed for short periods of time. If the impressment was for several months, part of it might be furnished by the government.[80] When "Pete" and "Sandy" were sent from Mulberry Hill Plantation near Lexington, Virginia, to the Richmond defenses in January, 1863, to be held for a sixty-day period, the overseer "had them well-clothed and an extra pair of shoes made to take with them." These and two others were impressed in June, 1863, for the same length of time. They had "new clothes and hats and a plenty of bed clothes." They were instructed to "bed together" by twos, "not to separate and to be careful not to let their clothes be stolen."[81] That all the planters were not as generous as the owner of Mulberry is indicated by the report of a South Carolina labor superintendent to his superior in 1863 that "much neglect and indifference is exhibited on the part of the owners in sending their slaves badly clothed and shoed." In the latter part of the war, the scarcity of clothing made it difficult for masters to equip adequately the Negroes whom they sent to the works.[82]

The military authorities sometimes became responsible

and with "how-dye's" for the Negroes. He enclosed a ring for "Lucinda's daughter, Sallie," stating that "I expect its father to contrive it to her." "Matthew" to Mrs. Wm. Massie, Feb. 16, 1865, *ibid.*

79. Letter of Wallace, an overseer, to J. McDowell Reid, a slave owner, June 10, 1863, Mulberry Hill Plantation Letters (MSS. in private possession).

80. The laws of Alabama, Florida, Georgia, North Carolina, and Virginia do not mention clothing. The South Carolina law provided that the government furnish two suits of clothes a year, or one suit every six months, including two pairs of shoes and one hat for the year. *Acts of S. C.*, 1864, Dec. Sess., no. 4703. The Confederate Government took the responsibility for the clothing of the slaves impressed under the act of Feb. 17, 1864. The impressment was for a twelve-month period. *O. R.*, Ser. 4, III, 716.

81. Wallace to Reid, Jan. 10, June 27, 1863, Mulberry Hill Plantation Letters.

82. See *O. R.*, Ser. 1, XXVIII, pt. 2, 535; XLVI, pt. 2, 1014.

for the laborers not having sufficient clothing by holding them longer than the term specified by the state law. A number of slaves sent to the Charleston works in August, 1863, presumably for the thirty-day period specified by the state law, were kept until late in October. The owners sent summer clothing sufficient for the thirty-day period. They did not send any more after the expiration of that period because they were expecting the return of their slaves every day.[83]

Illness was very prevalent among the laborers. The nature of the work was not conducive to good health. Frequently the laborers had to stand in water as they dug the trenches or threw up the breastworks.[84] The heavy and seemingly incessant rains which proved such an impediment to McClellan in his movement against Richmond in 1862 took a heavy toll from the Negroes who were rushed there in great numbers to strengthen the fortifications. Of the 400 Negroes at work on Morris Island in the summer of 1863, as many as 150 were ill at one time. In March, 1865, one out of every ten Negroes at work on the Mobile fortifications was confined to his quarters, or in the hospital, from illness.[85]

The labor camps around Richmond and Charleston were supposed to be visited every day by a physician.[86] The more seriously ill were sent by the visiting doctor to hospitals in the city for treatment. Still, the medical care rendered the Negroes was not beyond criticism. A Charleston engineer reported that the sick laborers were cruelly neglected.[87] The reputation of the Richmond hospitals for laborers was not such as to inspire confidence in all.[88]

83. *O. R.*, Ser. 1, XIV, 974.   84. *Ibid.*, XLVII, pt. 2, 1138.
85. *Ibid.*, XI, pt. 3, 475; XIV, 974; XLIX, pt. 1, 1056.
86. Ott to Davidson, Feb. 15, 1863, Davidson Papers; Wallace to Reid, Feb. 1, 1863, Mulberry Hill Plantation Letters.
87. *O. R.*, Ser. 1, XIV, 974.
88. The overseer of Mulberry Hill wrote to his employer: "I understand that Lewis is in the Hospittal. . . . Please say to him [the overseer at the works] not to let another one of yours be taken there again for he ought . . . if they are very sick to call a p[h]y[si]cian of his own

Some of the sickness of the Negroes was doubtless feigned. The proximity to the enemy's lines proved deleterious to health; this seems to be the import of a letter from D. H. Hill to "Joe" Johnston: "Some 300 Negroes were sent up to fix up the outworks 10 or 15 days ago. A large portion of these have reported sick and left."[89]

The general policy of the military authorities was to use only white soldiers on work within the range of the Federal guns. There were instances, however, when Negroes became exposed to the "Yankee" fire. Their exposure was usually of short duration. When the Federal boats fired on the Mobile works in 1863 all the Negro employees disappeared with the first shot and were not seen again until the firing had ceased. It was later learned that they had been digging bomb-proofs called "gopher-holes" and provisioning them for "just such occasions." Negro workmen at Fort Sumter, after the successful evasion of a Federal shell, would laugh and congratulate each other "dat de Yankees didn't catch dat nigger dat time."[90]

The colored laborers were subjected to a rigid control and allowed few privileges. One reason for this was that the military authorities felt a necessity of extracting a maximum of labor from them during the comparatively short time that they were at their disposal. A more pertinent reason was to prevent the slaves from running away. The Federal camp had a strong attraction for them, its drawing force increasing, magnet-like, with its growing nearness. Joseph E. Johnston wrote to Senator Wigfall in January, 1864, that he had "never been able to keep the impressed Negroes with an army near the enemy. They desert."[91] Stringent measures were taken to prevent the running away of the defense workers. A Texas officer re-

c[h]oice." Wallace to Reid, Feb. 11, 1863, Mulberry Hill Plantation Letters.

89. *O. R.*, Ser. 1, XI, pt. 3, 465, April 26, 1862.

90. W. R. Boggs, *Military Reminiscences*, p. 18; Holmes, ed., *The Burckmyer Letters*, p. 350.

91. Wright, *A Southern Girl in '61*, p. 169.

sorted to the expedient of shutting them up under heavy guard at night.[92] The Secretary of War organized a force of cavalry in November, 1862, to patrol the territory between the Federal lines and the slaves at work on a railroad from Greensboro to Danville.[93]

Another factor tending to necessitate the exercise of a strict discipline on the defense work was the type of Negroes employed there. The impressment laws called for a certain proportion of the able-bodied males on a plantation. The owner could fill the quota with any male slaves within the prescribed ages. There was an inclination for him to keep his more desirable Negroes at home and send the less desirable ones to the fortifications.[94] Unruly slaves within the age limits were the first ones selected for the impressing agent. The owners of some insubordinate Negroes near Lake Washington, Mississippi, went so far as to "earnestly request" a Confederate officer "to bring out a lot of the most unruly and place them at work."[95]

The heaviness and the regularity of the work, the close supervision, the scarcity of food and clothing, the severe discipline—all combined to make life as a fortification worker very unattractive to the Negro. A North Carolina slave is said to have told his master on his return from the fortifications "that they might kill him if they wanted to but that he would never go back to that work." One of R. F. W. Allston's Negroes, at work on South Carolina defenses, replied to his master's statement that the slaves could not come home until the work was done: "My Maussa, dis wuck'll never dun. We'll dun but de wuck won't dun. We's all sick."[96]

Negroes resorted to all kinds of ingenious devices to

92. Wm. Christian to Ashabel Smith, March 6, 1864, Univ. of Texas Archives, Ashabel Smith Papers.
93. *O. R.*, Ser. 4, II, 176.
94. Phillips, *Life and Labor in the Old South*, p. 316; Wallace to Reid, Jan. 10, 1863, Mulberry Hill Plantation Letters.
95. *O. R.*, Ser. 1, XXIV, pt. 3, 701.
96. Fayetteville *Weekly Observer* (N. C.), Dec. 29, 1864, editorial; Pringle, *Chronicles of Chicora Wood*, p. 357.

escape impressment. In Augusta, Georgia, they hid in the
day time. White people had great difficulty in getting
hands to work because they could not find them. The ruse
was successful for a time, but in the summer a revival
meeting began in one of the Negro churches. It was the
"protracted" type of meeting—the kind that ran for
months. The temptation was too great for the Negro men.
They began to flock to the night services—or rather, that
part of the service which took place after dark. The impressing officers heard about the excellent attendance and
made a raid one night on the male portion of the congregation, much to the benefit of the Augusta defenses.[97] Joe,
the servant of Mrs. Julia Morgan, deceived the impressing
agent for a long time by bandaging his arm and leaning
heavily on his cane when he made a public appearance.
One day, as the Negro was limping along the street, he saw
a group of "persons of color" gathered around a platform.
Feeling a sudden impulse to display his unusual prowess as
a singer and dancer, he leaped to the platform and began
a lively jig singing lustily, " 'Carve dat 'possum to de
heart.' " An impressment officer, attracted by his agile
performance, immediately nabbed him for the Confederate
defenses.[98]

Little wonder is it, indeed, in view of the many hardships incident to military labor, that the " 'pressin' agents"
or "conscrip's" as impressment officers were commonly
called by the victims, were dreaded creatures among the
Negroes of the Confederacy.

97. Morgan, *How It Was,* p. 120.   98. *Ibid.*

VIII

BODY SERVANTS

THE aristocracy of all those Southern Negroes who engaged in military activities were the personal attendants of the white soldiers. During the early days of the war the number of these attendants, or body servants as they were generally called, was considerable. A large proportion of the early volunteers belonged to the gentry class.[1] On the plantation the young gentlemen had been attended, in most cases, by personal servants who looked after their clothing, groomed their horses, and cared for their hounds. When they volunteered for military service, these scions of aristocratic families naturally took their servants along with them to look after their needs in camp and on the field.

During the first part of the war, many private soldiers were attended by servants. In one South Carolina company, there were twenty-five men with servants.[2] But as the service became harder and rations became shorter in 1862 and 1863, many of the Negroes were sent home to assist in the raising of foodstuffs. As a rule, only commissioned officers retained servants after the first year of the war. The diminution of the servant corps is well illustrated by the case of the Third Alabama Regiment. It left Alabama "a thousand strong in rank and file and several hundred strong in Negro servants." Two years later there were no Negro servants except a few in the service of the higher officers.[3]

1. Eggleston, *A Rebel's Recollections*, p. 21.
2. Ford, *Life in the Confederate Army*, p. 11.
3. Fleming, *Civil War and Reconstruction in Alabama*, p. 207. In some instances, a few Negroes were retained as company servants "instead of private institutions." Carlton McCarthy, *Soldier Life in the Army of Northern Virginia*, p. 25.

The duties of the body servants varied greatly. In the early part of the war some of the volunteers seemed to have the idea that they might call on their black helpers to perform duties assigned to them which were not to their liking. Eggleston, speaking of Virginia volunteers, said that whenever a detail was made for the purpose of cleaning the camp ground, the soldiers regarded themselves as *only responsible for seeing that the work was done;* so they "uncomplainingly took upon themselves the duty of sitting on the fence and superintending the work" of their Negroes.[4]

The ordinary responsibilities of the servant of an officer were to keep the quarters clean, to wash clothes, shine shoes, brush uniforms, polish swords, buckles, and spurs, to run errands, to go to the commissary and get rations, and to prepare them for the master's table.[5] In some cases the servant acted as his master's barber.[6] If the commissary was too far removed to permit the drawing of rations, or if it was not functioning satisfactorily, the body servant would resort to other expedients for procuring food. Kent, servant of Harry Porcher, boasted to his master's mother of his ability as a "perwider." Porcher corroborated this claim. After a battle he always found the Negro looking for him with something nice to eat, "for his conscience was an elastic one as to the rights of property in food."[7] Von Borcke's servant, William, was noted for his ingenuity in acquiring chickens, turkeys, and various other delicacies for his master's mess.[8]

4. Eggleston, *A Rebel's Recollections,* pp. 36–37.

5. Statement to the author in 1932 of "Ten-Cent Bill" Yopp, Atlanta, Georgia, Negro body servant of Captain Thomas Yopp, Fourteenth Georgia Regiment; statement to the author in 1932 of Judge J. P. Young, Memphis, Tennessee, who served with General Forrest; Mary Ann Webster Loughborough, *My Cave Life in Vicksburg,* p. 62; Armstrong, *Old Massa's People,* p. 283.

6. New Orleans *Daily True Delta,* Aug. 8, 1863, extract from the diary of a Confederate officer.

7. Ford, *Life in the Confederate Army,* p. 78.

8. Heros von Borcke, *Memoirs of the Confederate War,* II, 55, and *passim.*

The Negroes were proud of their ability as foragers. The Reverend "Uncle" Steve Eberhardt of Rome, Georgia, who was for many years a familiar figure at Confederate reunions—the bosom of his "Confederate Gray" coat was almost completely covered with reunion badges—styled himself "the biggest chicken thief in the Confederacy." On special occasion he was accustomed to wear a copious collection of chicken tail feathers in his wide-brimmed hat as a memento of his numerous incursions upon the chicken roost.[9]

The servant was supposed to look after his master's horse, to see that it was well-fed and well-groomed. Sometimes he might have the great privilege of riding the charger about the camp to exercise it. He was supposed to have the horse ready in the morning at his master's order. In unusual circumstances the good servant acted without waiting for orders. On the night before the battle of Fredericksburg Von Borcke attended a party which lasted until the gray of dawn. Just after he fell asleep, he was awakened by his servant, Henry, calling, "Major, de Yankees is shelling Fredericksburg. I done saddled your hoss and de General is ready for to start."[10]

A few of the body servants were sometimes called on to act as musicians for the units to which their masters were attached.[11] Josephus Blake, servant of General John B. Gordon, said that he and two other servants provided the music to which Gordon's regiment marched. One played the fife and one beat the drum. Blake, who beat the snare drum, said that he acquired the art of "drumming" by imitating on the bottom of a tin pan the beats of the white

9. Birmingham *News*, June 7, 1931. Chicken stealing seems to have been a very prevalent practice among body servants. For other instances see Armstrong, *Old Massa's People*, pp. 283, 285–286.

10. Von Borcke, *Memoirs of the Confederate War*, II, 94.

11. This may have been the exception rather than the rule. Congress, by an early statute, provided for regular colored musicians to receive the same pay as regularly enlisted white musicians. Matthews, ed., *Statutes at Large*, First Congress, 1862, 1st Sess., chap. 29.

drummer of a regiment which drilled for a time near his master's plantation.[12]

The servants had opportunities to earn money "on the side" by various methods. They made small charges for washing socks and shirts for members of the company and for running errands. Bill Yopp, servant of Captain Yopp, Fourteenth Georgia Regiment, made a standard charge of ten cents for every task which he performed for a soldier, whether it was washing a pair of socks without soap, or running a five-mile errand. His consistency in making this charge won for him the sobriquet of "Ten-Cent Bill," which followed him till his death in 1936.[13] Primus, servant of John Underwood of Alabama, did a lucrative business in trading horses. Cavalrymen were willing to sell for a trifle mounts which they had worn out with hard usage. One of these "Uncle" Primus would buy for a few dollars, doctor it, and feed it well—from government supplies, of course—until the old horse would spruce up and look "almost as good as new." Then he would sell for a fat profit, invest in another, and repeat the process.[14]

The Negroes also made money by a perversion of their foraging prerogatives. This matter was brought up by one of the officers in an informal campfire discussion in Virginia shortly after the battle of Seven Pines. One officer told the other members of the group that "the Negro servants scour the country far and wide for chickens, milk, butter, eggs, and bread, for which they pay little or nothing, always stoutly swearing that they have expended all massa gave them, and then unblushingly ask for more." "I am positive," he continued, "that Nick and our other boys

12. Blake, when interviewed by the author in 1932, was selling papers and candy on the docks at Vicksburg.

13. Statement to the author in 1932 of "Ten-Cent Bill" Yopp, and some of his white acquaintances. Prior to his death he stayed for several years in the Confederate Soldiers' Home, Atlanta, Georgia, by special permission of the board of trustees of that institution.

14. Memoirs of Private J. T. Webster of Alabama (MS. in private possession).

beg or steal half they pretend to purchase, and yet do not
fail to charge us, the 'cruel masters,' five times the ordinary value of the articles. . . . The other day I gave
Andy $10 for market money, and the wretch brought me
back two antiquated hens and a pound of fresh butter,
'without a cent to spare,' as he solemnly swore, . . . and
if you preach economy, the villains grumble and . . .
whisper that 'massa's getting like de Yankees now he's up
norf.' "[15] He also said that the Negroes had, for two
months, been going out begging milk and butter for "the
wounded" and coming back and selling the milk for one
dollar and fifty cents a gallon and the butter for one dollar
a pound.[16] The Negroes had also been buying whiskey at
five dollars per gallon and then selling it to the soldiers for
fifty cents for a drink of one-eighth of a pint. "They are
making lots of money, and frequently loan it out at heavy
interest."[17] These practices seem to have been winked at or
only mildly condemned by the officers.

The life of the body servant was, generally, not a hard
one. He had ample opportunity to loaf around the camp
with the other Negroes. He had the best of food obtainable
in the army. He might play at cards or, much more to his
liking, sneak away to some obscure nook and roll the dice.
He occasionally obtained whiskey from his master or from
his "foraging."[18] Camp life was all too frequently deleterious to the Negro's morals. Harry Porcher told his mother
that he doubted if his servant, Kent, could stand the restraints of civilization again as his was such a "demoralizing life."[19]

The joviality and light heartedness of the Negroes were
important factors in keeping up the spirit of the camp.

15. *Battle Fields of the South*, II, 63.
16. *Ibid.*   17. *Ibid.*, p. 64.
18. Ford, *Life in the Confederate Army*, p. 85. Kent, servant of Harry
Porcher, was captured by the Federals and made the servant of a Union
officer. When he escaped a short time afterwards, he stole enough whiskey
from his "Yankee" master to treat "Mas' Harry's Mess" on his return
to the Southern army.
19. *Ibid.*, p. 82.

When life became sad or monotonous for "Jeb" Stuart's officers, they frequently built a roaring fire, formed a large circle, and had the servants dance and sing to the music of Sweeney's banjo.[20]

The Negroes were not often under fire, and when they were it was usually of their own choice.[21] They seemed to have conducted themselves creditably when they fell within the line of attack. One Negro, when asked by his master if he were frightened by the bullets, responded: "No, Sah, but I was terribly demoralized." The correspondent of the Memphis *Daily Appeal* in an interesting account of the conduct of some servants who were in a locality being shelled by a Federal battery at Lookout Mountain said that "the principle commotion was caused among the negroes. . . . Which way to retreat, they didn't know, and making the best of their situation, they concealed themselves behind trees and stumps; but which made the most noise, the shells or the negroes, it was difficult to tell. At each diabolical missile that came screaming through the air, you would hear exclamations issuing from between chattering teeth. 'Heyer she comes—get out de way, boys, —look out all you t'ree thousand dollah niggers . . . ain't she got a noisy tail,' etc."[22]

The body servants sometimes took part in the fighting. A newspaper correspondent reporting one of the early engagements of the war said that a servant named Levin Graham refused to stay in camp during the fight, but obtained a musket, "fought manfully," and "killed four of the Yankees."[23] A Negro aide is reported, on having encountered a Union soldier leading two horses, to have shot the soldier and to have led the horses back into the Confederate camp. Captain George Baylor related that two body servants, Tom and Overton, who had previously supplied themselves with arms left on the field by the Federals at

20. Von Borcke, *Memoirs of the Confederate War*, II, 89, and *passim*.
21. Ford, *Life in the Confederate Army*, p. 11.
22. Memphis *Daily Appeal*, Nov. 2, 1863.
23. New Orleans *Daily Crescent*, Nov. 15, 1861.

the battle of Brandy Station "joined in the company charges and succeeded in capturing a Yankee Negro who had ventured too far in front of the Union column, and brought him safely into camp. They were highly delighted with their trophy and retained him a prisoner for several months, compelling him to rub down their [master's] horses, bring water and wood, and do other chores about camp. At night he was required to sleep with them and was threatened with instant death if he attempted to escape."[24]

The body servants imbibed much of the martial spirit which pervaded their environment. A Confederate officer, describing the military tenor of the activities of the Negroes attached to his brigade, said: "Soon as the word 'march' is whispered abroad . . . the cooks shoulder some large bundle of curiosities of their own, and with a saucepan, skillet, or frying pan, all march some fifty yards in front of the band, whistling and singing, forming in regular or irregular files, commanded by some big black rogue, who with a stick and a loud voice enforces discipline among his heavy-heeled corps." "And thus they proceed," he added, "far ahead, monopolizing all attention as we pass through towns and villages . . . frequently dressed up in the full regimentals of some unfortunate Yankee."[25]

Servants in Forrest's cavalry recognized rank among themselves. The one in attendance upon Forrest himself was referred to by the others as the "Gin'ral." One black subaltern, when rebuked by his master for waking him at a very early hour one morning, replied, "The Gin'ral gived us orders that no horns would be sounded dis mornin' and dat ever' body was to be up at four o'clock."[26]

The servants absorbed some of the Confederate soldiers' contempt for the fighting ability of the "Yankees." An Englishman overheard one servant say to another: "Talk of dem Yanks coming down to whip us! Day must be sick!

24. Southern Historical Society *Papers*. XXXI (1903), 366, article from New Orleans *Daily Picayune*, Sept. 6, 1903.
25. *Battle Fields of the South*, II, 62.
26. G. A. Hanson, *Minor Incidents in the Late War*, p. 59.

Why massa can whale a dozen of 'em, 'fore coffee is hot, fair fight."[27]

The servants were sometimes better "Rebels" than the whites. The height to which their patriotism might rise is well exemplified in the statement of a servant, Robin, who was captured with his master on Morgan's raid into Ohio. He was imprisoned for a time apart from his master and then offered his liberty on condition of taking the oath of allegiance to the United States. His response to the offer was: "I will never disgrace my family by such an oath."[28] An English officer who served with the Confederate army told of a Negro body servant running away to the Federals just before the first battle of Manassas and giving a full description of the number and location of certain Confederate batteries. He was recaptured a short time afterwards. Two patriotic Confederate servants of the brigade were of the opinion that he should be shot or hanged as a traitor. He was turned over to them "and met a death at their hands more violent than any white person's anger could have suggested."[29] A number of servants who surrendered with their masters at Vicksburg and who could have had their freedom, with Federal protection, for the asking, chose rather to share the hardships of a Northern prison with those whom they had served in the "Rebel" ranks.[30]

The enjoyment which the Negro derived from his army activities is indicated in a letter said to have been written by the servant of General Bates to his sister in South Carolina:

I've bin havin' a good time ginerally—see a heap of fine country and a plenty of purty gals. . . . I have also bin on the battle fields and heard the bullets whiz. When the Yankees run I . . . got more clothes, blankets, overcoats, and razors

27. *Battle Fields of the South*, I, 158. See also, Fremantle, *Three Months in the Southern States*, p. 281.
28. Richmond *Whig*, Jan. 27, 1864.
29. *Battle Fields of the South*, II, 60.
30. *O. R.*, Ser. 2, VI, 397–398.

than I could tote. I've got an injun rubber cloke with two
brass eyes keeps the rain off like a meetin' house. Ime a made
man since the battle and cockt and primed to try it again. If
I kin kill a Yankee and git a gold watch, and a pair of boots,
my trip will be made. How other niggers do to stay at home,
while we soldiers are havin' such a good time is more than I
can tell.[31]

The relations between the master and his body servant
were usually characterized by mutual affection. The personal servant was frequently chosen from a line of Negroes
which had been associated with the family for a long time.
They felt a responsibility for the protection of their master. Martha, the mother of Kent, Harry Porcher's servant
—she boasted of her family having been slaves of the Por-
chers for five generations—told her son that "he need not
come home if he let anything hu't Mas' Harry . . . an' I
tells Affy, de gal he's courtin', it's no use fur she to fret,
fur 'less Kent brings Mas' Harry back, dere won't be no
weddin' fur him." Kent did not betray his trust. He was
captured by the Federals, but escaped, married Affy, re-
joined his master, and served him till the end of the war.[32]

The servants shared their masters' joys and sorrows,
their successes, and their reverses. Dabney H. Maury, a
Virginian, said of his Negro servant, Jem: "He used to
brag over the other niggers because he was a 'Virginny
nigger' and had been in the terrible battle of the first Bull
Run. In his opinion 'thar is no soldiers like them we left in
Virginny. The privates dar was better den some of dese
yer kurnels.' "[33] In the winter of 1862–1863, Maury was
promoted to the rank of major general. "Jem was much
elated," he said, "at this increase of rank, and swaggered
over the other headquarters darkies accordingly. . . . I
said, 'Jem, you must tuck in those blankets better at the

81. Charleston *Daily Courier*, May 29, 1863. For a letter of similar
tone, dictated to an officer, and addressed to a body servant's wife, see
Battle Fields of the South, II, 67.
82. Ford, *Life in the Confederate Army*, pp. 77 ff.
83. Maury, *Recollections of a Virginian*, p. 163.

foot of the cot. My feet stuck out last night and were almost frozen!' With an indescribable air of humorous impudence, he turned towards me and said, 'Why, you aint growed no longer en what you was, sir, is yer since yer been promoted?' "[34]

There were a number of instances of servants absconding to the "Yankees." Newspaper advertisements for fugitives indicate that most of the body servants who deserted their masters were those who had been hired. In the case of the hired servants the sense of family attachment and the feeling of personal affection engendered by years of association on the plantation, factors powerful in the preservation of the slaves' loyalty amid the tempting influences of the war, were lacking.[35]

Instances of disloyal or traitorous conduct on the part of body servants, however, were comparatively rare. There are numerous testimonies to their firm devotion. One of the most striking cases of courage and fidelity is that of Robert, servant of Percival Porcher of Pinopolis, South Carolina. When the report reached Pinopolis that Porcher lay seriously wounded a few miles out of Richmond, not a white man could be secured to go nurse him. A journey to Richmond was an impossibility for Porcher's wife. She decided to send to attend him, Robert, his body servant, who had been sent home earlier in the war to raise provisions for the family. When the Negro reached his destination, he learned that his master had died. He tried in vain to secure a means of conveying the body to Richmond. He ob-

34. *Ibid.*
35. Sometimes the "lure of freedom" proved more powerful than personal and family attachment, however. A member of the Alabama legislature argued that slaves, as soldiers, could not be trusted, citing the example of his body servant "who had grown up with him from boyhood, who had gone with him to the army and had shared with him, share and share alike, every article of food and clothing," and yet "had seized the first opportunity which presented of deserting him and joining the Yankees." Montgomery *Weekly Mail*, Sept. 2, 1863. Another Confederate soldier told of a servant at the battle of Sharpsburg who, after securing a horse and carrying his wounded master to safety at considerable risk, remounted the horse and rode to the "Yankees." James Dinkins, *Personal Recollections and Experiences in the Confederate Army*, p. 63.

tained permission from the officers, however, to keep the remains unburied for three days. He then walked five miles to the city and tried without success to secure a cart to go for his master's body. He was in despair. "As a last resort he began to walk up and down the principal streets of the city calling out loudly, 'My young master, Mr. Percival Porcher of South Carolina, lies dead in a hospital and I want help to carry him back to his young wife!' An officer heard him, questioned him, took him to General Lee's head-quarters, and there procured an order for artillery horses to be sent out for the remains and for a guard of honor to escort the body in."[36]

When the remains of Governor Allen of Louisiana were interred in the State House grounds in 1885, a letter which he had written to his body servant, Vallery, just a year after the close of the war was read as a part of the cere-mony. In this missive, significant for the light which it throws on the affection engendered by the soldier-servant relation, the governor, after expressing satisfaction with good reports of Vallery, said: "I am also glad to hear that you have not forgotten me, for I think of you very often, not only as my faithful servant in former days, but as my companion in arms and on the battle-field. God bless you, Vallery. I don't know that I shall ever see you again, for . . . I am now starting on a long and painful journey to Paris to see if I can't get well. I would like so much to have you go along to assist me and cheer me up in my exile, but I have not the means to pay your expenses. You must be temperate and prudent, and industrious and save your money. If I am ever a rich man again, I will help you and make you comfortable for life. . . . Goodbye Vallery. . . . You were ever true to me, and I will never, never, forget your services."[37]

The owners of body servants were not unappreciative of the loyalty and devotion of their black attendants. They frequently made provision for their freedom. One of the

36. Henry Edmund Ravenel, *Ravenel Records*, pp. 67–68.
37. New Orleans *Daily Picayune*, July 4, 1885.

last acts of the Mississippi "Rebel" legislature was the authorization of the emancipation of Lloyd, a Negro servant who risked his life to recover the body of his fallen master. Even now gray-haired Negroes, dressed in "Confederate Gray," are among the most honored veterans in attendance at soldiers' reunions. For more than twenty years Confederate body servants of Mississippi have received pensions from the state.

IX

SOLDIERS

DURING the period of the Confederacy the question of making a soldier out of the Negro received considerable attention. In several instances, free Negroes were actually armed and received into state service. Provision was ultimately made for the enlistment of slaves.[1]

It might be supposed from the bitter discussion which he occasioned that the Negro soldier in the South was a Confederate innovation. But this is not the case. An act passed by the assembly of the colony of South Carolina December 23, 1703, made it "lawfull for any master or owner of any slave, in actual invasion, to arme and equipe any slave or slaves, with such armes and ammunition as any other person by the act of the militia are appointed to appear at muster or alarums."[2] This act also provided "that if any slave shall in actual invasion kill or take one or more of our enemies, and the same shall prove by any white person to be done by him . . . he shall have and enjoy his freedom." The master of a slave thus freed was to be compensated by the "publick."[3] An act of the next year went further; it provided for commissioners who should

1. Good papers have been written on the subject of arming the slaves by N. W. Stephenson, *Amer. Hist. Rev.*, XVIII (Jan., 1913); Charles H. Wesley, *Journal of Negro History*, IV (July, 1919); and by Thomas R. Hay, *Miss. Valley Hist. Rev.*, VI (June, 1919). Stephenson's article is devoted primarily to the Congressional battle on the question. Hay emphasizes the Cleburne memorial and the attitude of the army in general. Wesley is more concerned with the sentiment favorable to the proposal and to the racial significance of its final enactment.

2. D. J. McCord, ed., *Statutes at Large of S. C.*, VII, no. 219, sec. xxv.

3. *Ibid.*, sec. xxiii. It is interesting to compare this act with the proposal which President Davis made in November, 1864, to emancipate the army laborers for loyal service. His proposal aroused a storm of protest.

"direct and require said masters . . . on time of alarm
. . . that they cause their slaves, so enlisted and armed,
either with a serviceable lance, hatchet or gun, with sufficient ammunition . . . according to conveniency of said
owners, to appear under the colors of their respective captains, in their several divisions."[4] The slaves served along-
side white men in various divisions. A law of 1708 provided
that "the number of such slaves should not exceed the
number of white persons under each captain."[5]

Negroes served as soldiers under Washington in the
Revolution and under Jackson at New Orleans.[6] But the
increasing number of Negroes in the South, fear inspired
by the Nat Turner insurrection and similar episodes, and
the abolitionist crusade tended to make the Southerners
less and less inclined to entrust arms to the hands of the
blacks.

There seems to have been a disposition in some quarters,
however, to use free Negroes as soldiers in the early part
of the War of Secession. The Tennessee legislature passed
an act in June, 1861, authorizing the governor, "at his
discretion to receive into the military service of the State
all male free persons of color, between the ages of 15 and
50, or such numbers as may be necessary who may be . . .
capable of actual service." If a number sufficient for the
wants of the state did not offer their services voluntarily,
the governor was authorized to press them into service.[7] In
Mobile a group of Negroes was organized for service as
soldiers in the autumn of 1861.[8]

In April, 1861, the free colored population of New Orleans held a meeting and resolved to offer their services to
the governor for the defense of the state.[9] They were permitted to organize. A regiment of 1,400 paraded with white

4. *Ibid.*, no. 277.   5. *Ibid.*, no. 278, sec. i.
6. G. W. Williams, *History of Negro Troops in the War of the Rebellion,* pp. 31, 57.
7. *O. R.,* Ser. 4, I, 409.
8. Horace Greeley, *American Conflict,* II, 522.
9. Charleston *Tri-Weekly Mercury,* April 23, 1861.

soldiers in November, 1861.[10] A *Daily Picayune* reporter, after witnessing a review of troops early in 1862, complimented "the companies of free men of color, all well-dressed, well-drilled and comfortably uniformed." Most of these companies had provided themselves with arms unaided by the administration.[11] A regiment of such Negroes, organized for state service in Louisiana and known as the "Native Guards," retained its organization after the occupation of New Orleans by the Federals and was mustered into Union service in September, 1862. Several companies of free Negroes offered their services to the Confederate Government early in the war. But the War Department deemed it best not to accept them.[12] Such companies were uniformly declined until after the passage of the Negro soldier bill of March, 1865.

The use of slaves as soldiers did not receive widespread attention in the Confederacy until 1863. There were some, however, who advocated steps in that direction much earlier.[13] In January, 1861, a planter on the Mississippi River wrote Governor Pettus that "the hostile feeling now existing between our state and the Federal Government is rapidly extending itself to the lower classes . . . of the

10. Greeley, *American Conflict*, II, 522. The patriotism of the free Negroes may be attributed, in some cases, to the fact that their interests were closely associated with those of the whites. Many of them owned slaves and were staunch defenders of the "peculiar institution." See Calvin D. Wilson, "Negroes Who Owned Slaves," *The Popular Science Monthly*, LXXXI (Nov., 1912). That their show of patriotism was to some degree tactfulness is indicated by the facility with which they changed their allegiance when Butler arrived in New Orleans.

11. Henry Clay Warmoth, *War Politics and Reconstruction in Louisiana*, p. 57. Some of these soldiers told Butler in 1862 that the Confederates had never trusted them with arms. New Orleans *Daily Picayune*, May 27, 1863.

12. *O. R.*, Ser. 4, II, 941. A company of sixty free Negroes presented themselves for service in Richmond in April, 1861, bearing the Confederate flag. They were complimented for their patriotism and sent home. Charleston *Mercury*, April 26, 1861.

13. Stephenson, in his article, "The Question of Arming the Slaves," *Amer. Hist. Rev.*, XVIII (Jan., 1913), is evidently mistaken in his statement that apparently "the earliest proposition" to arm the slaves "was made in the summer of 1863."

Northwestern States who usually constitute the crews of flat-boats." He asked permission to arm his Negroes to protect his plantation from depredations by the flatboaters. He also suggested the expediency of permitting other Mississippi planters to arm and drill their slaves. In July, 1861, W. S. Turner wrote the Secretary of War from Helena, Arkansas, to ascertain if he and "many others" in that vicinity might get the government to receive regiments of slaves officered by white men.[14] A group of planters from Sunflower County, Mississippi, petitioned their governor in April, 1862, to consider the use of slaves as soldiers.[15] A short time before this, a writer in a Louisiana journal had recommended the enlistment of one hundred thousand Negroes as soldiers in the Confederate army.[16]

In the autumn of 1863 the question of arming the slaves received a considerable amount of favorable attention. This was especially true in Mississippi and Alabama, where the pressure of Federal forces was being felt.[17] Newspapers in those states carried editorials on the subject.[18] The Alabama legislature, after a lively debate, petitioned President Davis recommending the consideration of the employment of slaves as soldiers.[19] These and other early proposals to enlist the slaves received the polite but definite disapproval of the Confederate authorities.[20]

There seems to have been a temporary lapse of interest in the question of Negro enlistment for a time in the fall of

14. C. B. New to Governor Pettus, Jan. 14, 1861, Miss. Archives, Ser. E, no. 56; *O. R.*, Ser. 4, I, 482.

15. Miss. Archives, Ser. E, no. 56.

16. New Orleans *Daily True Delta*, April 3, 1862.

17. Montgomery *Weekly Mail*, Sept. 2, 1863.

18. One of these editorials went so far as to advocate the emancipation of those who should be placed in the ranks. *Ibid.*, Sept. 9, 1863, quoting *The Mississippian*.

19. Montgomery *Weekly Mail*, Sept. 2, 1863; Hay, "The Question of Arming the Slaves," *Miss. Valley Hist. Rev.*, VI, 38.

20. The reply to Turner's proposal in 1861 was that "the supply of white men was already in excess of the arms on hand." *O. R.*, Ser. 4, I, 529. In Nov., 1863, Secretary Seddon said: "Our position with the North and before the world will not allow the employment, as armed soldiers, of negroes." *Ibid.*, II, 941.

1863. But General Patrick Cleburne, a division commander of the Army of Tennessee, provoked a sudden renewal
of discussion.[21] After a period of reflection on the discouraging military situation and the other factors involved,
Cleburne became convinced of the expediency of employing slaves as soldiers. He prepared a paper on the subject
and presented it at a meeting of the officers in the Army of
Tennessee in January, 1864. He proposed, with great
earnestness, that a large force of slaves be organized at
once, and that they be promised their freedom as a reward
for faithful service. When news of this meeting reached
Richmond it caused a considerable flurry in official circles.
President Davis requested that Cleburne's paper be suppressed.[22]

A matter of such grave moment, however, could not be
suppressed. As news of the proposal filtered through the
army and the country it aroused a lively controversy. Some
of the soldiers threatened to leave the army if "niggers"
were placed in the ranks.[23] But many soldiers were already
leaving the army for other reasons. The ranks were becoming sadly depleted in the summer of 1864. Men were deserting by the hundreds, some to return to their homes to
look after their destitute families; others to seek the protecting forests of the mountains of Virginia, North Carolina, and Tennessee, where they organized themselves into
armed bands to resist conscription officers. The state governors, especially those of North Carolina and Georgia,
were thwarting Confederate efforts to replenish the ranks
by insisting on the exemption of petty officials.[24]

The ever recurrent problem of "man-power" for the
armies was accentuated by Sherman's steady march

21. Hay gives a good discussion of Cleburne's proposal in "The Question of Arming the Slaves," *Miss. Valley Hist. Rev.*, VI, 40 ff. For Cleburne's memorial and events leading up to its presentation, see Southern
Hist. Soc. *Papers*, XXXI, 215 ff.

22. *O. R.*, Ser. 1, LII, pt. 2, 596.

23. Hay, "The Question of Arming the Slaves," *Miss. Valley Hist.
Rev.*, VI, 50.

24. *O. R.*, Ser. 4, III, 356.

through the heart of the South and Grant's hammering drive against Richmond. This situation, coupled with the growing belief that slavery was the basic deterrent to European recognition, helped to abate opposition to enlistment of Negroes. In October, 1864, the governors of North Carolina, South Carolina, Georgia, Alabama, and Mississippi met at Augusta to discuss problems confronting the country. They passed a series of resolutions, one of which suggested the use of slaves as soldiers.[25]

The Confederate Government was not yet willing to approve a plan to enlist the slaves. President Davis, in his message of November 7, 1864, said that "he must dissent from those who advised a general levy and arming of slaves as soldiers." But there are evidences that the President's opposition was softening. In this same speech he advocated the purchase of forty thousand laborers by the government to be trained and permanently attached to the army. He went so far as to suggest the expediency of freeing those who should render faithful service to the end of the war.[26] In his statement against the use of slaves as soldiers, he made ample provision for a future change of attitude. He said: "But should the alternative ever be presented of subjugation or of the employment of the slave as a soldier, there seems no reason to doubt what should then be our decision."[27]

On the same day that this message from the President was read, the question of enlisting slaves made its first formal entrance into Congress. Two resolutions were introduced in the House, one by Swan of Virginia, the other by Chambers of Mississippi, to the effect that a proper utilization of the white soldiery would make the enlistment

25. *Journals of the Confed. Cong.*, VII, 258; *Journal of the Senate of Miss.*, Feb., 1865, Called Sess., speech of Gov. Clark.

26. In some quarters this was regarded as a "feeler" to ascertain the sense of the country with the idea of following it with a proposal to enlist and free Negro soldiers. Stephenson, "The Question of Arming the Slaves," *Amer. Hist. Rev.*, XVIII, 297.

27. *Journals of the Confed. Cong.*, IV, 258; VII, 255.

of Negroes unnecessary.[28] Both of the resolutions were postponed until November tenth.[29] On that day Chambers called up his resolution. The intense repugnance to the idea of a Negro soldiery which persisted in the minds of some Southerners is reflected in Chambers' statement that he was "ashamed to debate the question"; that "all nature cries out against it. . . . God forbid·that this Trojan horse should be introduced among us."[30]

The debate in Congress was matched by an increasingly intense discussion on the part of the general public. An argument commonly used by those who advocated the enlistment of Negroes was that they were being used as soldiers by the Federals. "Let the negroes fight negroes," wrote "A Native Georgian" to Secretary Seddon in September, 1864.[31] Secretary Benjamin wrote to Fred Porcher in December, 1864, asking him to agitate for action in favor of arming the slaves through the newspapers, "always urging this point as the true issue, *viz.*, is it better for the negro to fight for us or against us." There can be no doubt that this line of reasoning converted many from the opposition.[32] President Davis was apparently among the number influenced by the argument advanced by the wily Secretary of State. In February, 1865, he wrote to John Forsyth of Mobile: "It is now becoming daily more evident to all reflecting persons that we are reduced to choosing whether the negroes shall fight for or against us."[33]

Another argument in favor of making a soldier out of the Negro was that he would make a good fighting man. This contention derived considerable support from the seemingly successful use of colored soldiers by the North.

28. *Journals of the Confed. Cong.*, VII, 247.
29. From the meagre records of the *Journals* it seems that Swan's resolution was not again considered.
30. *Annual Cyclopedia* for 1864, p. 217.
31. *O. R.*, Ser. 4, III, 693.
32. See Montgomery *Weekly Mail*, Sept. 9, 1863; also Richmond *Dispatch*, Feb. 20, 1865.
33. *O. R.*, Ser. 4, III, 1110.

Samuel Clayton wrote to President Davis in January, 1865: "Some people say negroes will not fight. I say they will fight. They fought at Ocean Pond, Honey Hill, and other places."[34] There were many who were convinced that the slave would make a better Confederate than a Union soldier, because he was accustomed to obeying Southern masters; and Southern officers knew better how to handle the Negro than did the "Yankees."[35]

Proponents of recruiting slaves also held that such a step was rendered absolutely necessary by the depletion of the Confederate ranks; that it was the only available means left for infusing new strength into the dwindling armies. In Samuel Clayton's letter to President Davis in January, 1865, he said that the Confederate and state governments had put into service "all white men between the ages of 16 and 60. . . . The recruits must come from our negroes, nowhere else."[36] About the same time General Lee expressed the opinion that the white population was being over-taxed and that Negroes should be placed in the army.[37]

It was argued by some that the placing of a great number of Negroes in the ranks by the wealthy slaveholders would have a salutary effect on the poor whites, many of whom were losing their zeal for what they considered a "rich man's war and a poor man's fight."[38]

The majority of those who advocated enlisting the slaves were of the opinion that such a step entailed giving them their freedom. But this, they said, should not be a deterring factor, in view of the fact that slavery was already "in an expiring condition in the South"; that emancipation was already an accomplished fact if the Federals succeeded; that the situation was such that a choice had to be made between the loss of independence and the loss of

---

34. *Ibid.*, p. 1010.   35. *Ibid.*, Ser. 1, LII, pt. 2, 591.
36. *Ibid.*, Ser. 4, III, 1010.
37. Lee to Hunter, Jan. 11, 1865, *ibid.*, p. 1012. An anonymous writer wrote to Howell Cobb: "I see but one alternative left us and that to fill up our army with Negroes." U. B. Phillips, ed., *The Correspondence of Toombs, Stephens, and Cobb*, p. 656.
38. *O. R.*, Ser. 4, III, 915; Richmond *Enquirer*, Dec. 5, 1864.

property in slaves; that it was better for the Southerner to give up the Negro slave than be a slave himself.[39]

The proposal to enlist the slaves became closely connected with a plan for general emancipation in the last months of the war. The two-fold plan was urged to secure European recognition, and "to neutralize that large party in the North whose sympathy and interests were mainly employed with the Negro."[40] Judah P. Benjamin was a leader in promoting this scheme. In his letter to Fred Porcher in December, 1864, he said that "the action of our people on this point will be of more value to us abroad than any diplomacy or treaty making."[41]

Those who opposed the enlistment of slaves as soldiers supported their position with an array of impressive arguments, one of the most common being that the scarcity of men in the Confederate ranks could best be met by an increased use of Negroes in those military pursuits which did not entail actual fighting; that this increased use would release white soldiers detailed for those purposes for service on the firing line.[42] Closely related to this argument was the contention that Negroes were more needed on the plantations than they were in the ranks; that the raising of food, the making of salt, and the performance of other work in connection with the provisioning of the armies were just as essential to the conduct of the war as service on the battlefield; that if the Negroes were removed in great numbers from the plantation to serve in the army, white men would have to be detailed to do the work which slaves had formerly done, or else both civilians and soldiers would suffer from a shortage of provisions.

A frequently reiterated argument was that the Negro would not make an effective soldier; that his innate tim-

39. Pollard, *Life of Jefferson Davis*, p. 449; *O. R.*, Ser. 1, 1.II, pt. 2, 589.

40. Richmond *Enquirer*, Dec. 16, 1864, editorial. See also N. W. Stephenson, *The Day of the Confederacy*, pp. 197–198; Pollard, *Life of Jefferson Davis*, p. 449.

41. *O. R.*, Ser. 4, III, 959.

42. See Charleston *Mercury*, Nov. 3, 1864, editorial.

orousness and his lack of initiative, accentuated by years
of dependency and subserviency had rendered him devoid
of the essential qualities of a fighter.[43] The slave's inex-
perience in the use of firearms was cited as a pronounced
handicap; some people argued that he had an inborn aversion to the handling of guns and other weapons of warfare.[44] The feeling was widespread that the Negro could
not "stand the gaff" of a battle.

There was apprehension in some quarters that a movement to put Negroes in the army would cause them to run
away in great numbers.[45] Governor Clark of Mississippi
was of this opinion. In February, 1865, he telegraphed
President Davis that "nothing keeps the Negroes from going to the enemy but fear of being put in the Federal
army, and if it be attempted to put them in ours, all will
run away."[46]

Anxiety was expressed also as to the effect which the
arming of the slaves would have on the white soldiers. General Howell Cobb thought that the consequences would be
disastrous. "The moment you resort to Negro soldiers," he
wrote Secretary Seddon, "your white soldiers will be lost
to you . . . you cannot keep black and white soldiers together and you cannot trust Negroes by themselves."[47]

Perhaps the most effective argument against putting
the Negro in the ranks was that it laid the South open to
a charge of gross inconsistency; that it weakened her position before the world. It was pointed out that the institution of slavery was one of the basic principles of the Confederacy. The primary justification for the "peculiar institution" had always been that slavery was for the best

43. *Daily Examiner* (Richmond), Nov. 8, 1864.
44. Laws of the Southern states prohibited or greatly restricted the
use of firearms by slaves.
45. See the *Alabama Beacon* (Greensboro, Ala.), Nov. 4, 1864.
46. Jones, *Rebel War Clerk's Diary*, II, 428.
47. *O. R.*, Ser. 4, III, 1009. The editor of the Charleston *Mercury* wrote
in January, 1865: "The soldiers of South Carolina will not fight beside a
nigger. . . . We are free men and we choose to fight for ourselves. It is
the man who won't fight for himself who wants his niggers to fight for
him." Issue of Jan. 13, 1865.

interests of both whites and blacks because of the latter's inferiority and his incapability to care for himself. For the South to arm the Negro, to call him into the ranks as a full-fledged soldier, would be for her to reverse her position completely. How could one be deemed inferior and fit only for slavery, and at the same time be called on to fulfil one of the highest of duties associated with free citizenship?[48]

Then, if the slaves were freed by the Confederate Government—and it was generally felt that arming the slaves entailed freeing them—another basic principle was thrown overboard. One of the prime reasons for the secession of the Southern states from the Union was their firm belief in the right of property in slaves and the continual threat of the North to interfere with that right. If the Confederate Government stepped in and freed the slaves for faithful service, as was being proposed, she would be guilty of the same offense as "Abe Lincoln and his crowd of Abolitionists."[49]

The arguments against a policy considered so revolutionary were advanced with intense feeling, and in some cases, with obvious bitterness. Howell Cobb spoke of the proposal as the "most pernicious idea that has been suggested since the war began."[50] The Charleston *Mercury* was most outspoken in its opposition. In January, 1865, it carried three editorials on the subject, headed "Whom the Gods Would Destroy They First Make Mad," "Lunacy," and "Men Run Mad."[51] These bristled with such statements as "The proposition . . . is . . . desperate in its absurdity." "Incompetency and mismanagement are riding us down to ruin." "We want no slaves to fight for us." "The poor man . . . is reduced to the level of a nigger, his

48. *O. R.,* Ser. 4, III, 1009.
49. J. J. Seibels wrote to the Montgomery *Daily Mail:* "What a figure do we cut before the world . . . in proposing . . . to do just what we accused the North [of] *intending* to do and for that intention broke up the Union." Issue of March 1, 1865.
50. *O. R.,* Ser. 4, III, 1009.
51. Issues of Jan. 3, 13, and 26, respectively.

wife and his daughter are to be hustled on the street by black wenches, their equals. Swaggering buck niggers are to ogle them and elbow them. . . . Gracious God, is this what our brave soldiery are fighting for?"[52] The irate editor was finally provoked to the extent of saying that "if the slaves were armed, South Carolina would no longer have an interest in prosecuting the war."[53]

The general hostility of the Confederate Congress to the proposition of enlisting slaves which had manifested itself in the discussion of the Chambers resolution on November 10, 1864, continued through December and January. During that period several resolutions were adopted expressive of Congressional antipathy to the proposal. But a growing public sentiment in favor of calling the slaves to the ranks was bringing pressure on the legislators. Judah P. Benjamin instituted a propagandizing campaign through the newspapers. Governor Smith advocated the policy to the Virginia legislature in December, 1864. Lee gave his sanction to it in a letter to one of the Virginia legislators in January, 1865.[54]

Cautiously yielding to the growing pressure of public opinion, the Confederate House of Representatives considered a motion on February 6, 1865, "to inquire into the expediency of calling into military service . . . ablebodied Negro men." On the next day a bill was introduced into the Senate providing for the enlistment of 200,000 Negro soldiers and their emancipation if they remained loyal until the end of the war. The House resolution was committed;[55] the Senate bill was defeated by a vote of thirteen to three.[56]

The friends of the proposal now realized that a tremendous influence would be required to break down Congressional opposition. Conscious of the very great confidence which the country reposed in General Lee, they decided to

52. Issue of Jan. 26.   53. Pollard, *Life of Jefferson Davis*, p. 452.
54. *O. R.*, Ser. 4, III, 915, 959, 1012.
55. *Journals of the Confed. Cong.*, VII, 542.
56. *Ibid.*, IV, 526, 528.

capitalize on his influence. Secretary Benjamin and Senator Barksdale wrote him letters asking an expression of his opinion. Lee wrote Barksdale that he thought the measure not only expedient, but necessary; that he thought the Negro would make an efficient soldier; that the slaves employed as soldiers should be freed.[57]

Lee's expression of approval proved the stroke which broke the back of Congressional opposition.[58] Two days after he wrote his letter to Barksdale the House passed a bill authorizing the President to accept the services of such a number of slaves in the army as he thought expedient. It left the matter of freeing the slaves enlisted to the states in which they resided. On March 8 the Senate took up the House bill, which was preferable to its own because it avoided the constitutional question of freeing the slaves enlisted. After adding an amendment providing that no more than 25 per cent of the slaves from any state should be recruited, it passed the House measure by a vote of nine to eight.[59] With the President's approval on March 13, the

57. J. D. McCabe, *Life of Lee,* pp. 574–575. Lee had committed himself as in favor of arming the slaves previous to this time (Jan. 11). But his commitment was to Andrew Hunter, a Virginia state legislator, and for the guidance of that body. Barksdale and Benjamin wrote him with the idea of bringing the pressure of his opinion, which they knew to be favorable, against the recalcitrant Congress.

58. Lee's stand was skilfully utilized by the administration organ, the Richmond *Enquirer,* to win support for the proposal. "General Lee . . . urges his country's authorities to conscript the negroes" its editor wrote, Jan. 12, 1865; "What man will put himself in the scales against General Lee?" The tremendous influence exerted by Lee is indicated in the action of the Richmond *Examiner.* It was strongly opposed to the policy of enlisting the Negroes until Lee's opinion was expressed. On Feb. 15, 1865, its editor wrote: "General Lee urgently calls for a large force of negroes. . . . The country will not deny to General Lee . . . *anything* he may ask for." The Charleston *Mercury,* however, was unmoved, even by the mighty Lee. A long editorial captioned "General Robert E. Lee— Federalism" even went so far as to question his orthodoxy on the matter of slavery: "General Lee, the advocate, if not the author of this scheme, of nigger soldiers and emancipation is said by those who are acquainted with the families . . . in Virginia to be an hereditary Federalist and a disbeliever in the institution of slavery." Issue of Feb. 3, 1865.

59. *Journals of Confed. Cong.,* IV, 670.

bill became a law. It authorized the President, when he thought it expedient, to call on each state for her quota of 300,000 additional troops "irrespective of color," provided the number of slaves called for from any state should not exceed 25 per cent of her able-bodied male slave population between the ages of eighteen and forty-five.[60]

Steps were immediately taken toward recruiting and organizing the slaves and free Negroes. The Virginia legislature had anticipated Confederate action by passing laws on March 4 and March 6 authorizing the recruiting of slaves and free Negroes within the state and repealing the law forbidding them to bear arms. On March 24 General Lee requisitioned Governor Smith for one-fourth of Virginia's able-bodied male slaves between eighteen and forty-five years.[61] Circular letters were addressed by President Davis to the governors of the other states requesting their coöperation in recruiting Negroes.[62]

Slaves were not drafted even though General Lee expressed the opinion that some form of compulsion was desirable.[63] President Davis thought that the policy of asking owners to volunteer their slaves was preferable. Recruiting was entrusted in many cases to officers of the reserves of the several states. If owners expressed a desire that their slaves be placed under some particular officer, an effort was made to comply with that request. There was no difficulty in finding men who were willing to recruit and command the Negroes; some of this willingness was doubtlessly inspired by the leave of absence from the ranks which an order to recruit entailed.[64]

The enlistment of Negroes seems to have been slow in the West. A Mississippian wrote his governor on April 4, 1865, that the Negroes in Jefferson County were "stam-

60. *O. R.*, Ser. 4, III, 1161.
61. *Ibid.*, Ser. 1, LI, pt. 2, 1068; XLVI, pt. 3, 1315, 1339.
62. *Ibid.*, XLVI, pt. 3, 1370.   63. *Ibid.*, pp. 1349, 1370.
64. *Ibid.*, XLVI, pt. 3, 1367; Jones, *Rebel War Clerk's Diary*, II, 450, 461.

peding" to avoid conscription.[65] In Richmond recruiting
was more lively. This was due, to some extent, to the ingenuity with which the enrolling officers played on the Negroes' love of pomp and ostentation. Flashy parades, well
advertised ahead of time, were held on Capitol Square.[66]
On one occasion the Negroes were permitted to have a ball
after public drill.[67] Ebon soldiers in shiny new uniforms
sent out among their friends made "very good recruiting
officers."[68] The parades of the black soldiers were events of
much curiosity to the white population. Eight or ten thousand people witnessed one held on March 23. Considerable
enthusiasm was aroused by the proficiency shown by the
recruits in drill and manipulation of arms.[69]

There seems to be no evidence that the Negro soldiers
authorized by the Confederate Government ever went into
battle. This gives rise to the question as to whether or not
any Negroes ever fought in the Confederate ranks. It is
possible that some of the free Negro companies organized
in Louisiana and Tennessee in the early part of the war
took part in local engagements; but evidence seems to the
contrary.[70] A company of "Creoles," some of whom had
Negro blood, may have been accepted in the Confederate
service at Mobile. Secretary Seddon conditioned his authorization of the acceptance of the company on the ability
of those "Creoles" to be naturally and properly distin-
guished from Negroes.[71] If persons with Negro blood served

65. P. K. Montgomery to Governor Clark. Miss. Archives, Ser. E, no.
68.

66. *Daily Examiner* (Richmond), March 22 and 23, 1865.

67. *Ibid.*, March 22, 1865.

68. One company which contained thirty-five members on March 27,
was composed of twelve free Negroes and twenty-three slaves. *Ibid.*,
March 27, 1865.

69. *Ibid.*; Montgomery *Daily Mail*, April 24, 1865. Pollard, in his *Life
of Jefferson Davis*, p. 456, leaves the impression that the recruits were
held in contempt. He says that little boys "pelted the fine uniforms with
mud."

70. If they did, their action was not authorized by the Confederate
Government.

71. *O. R.*, Ser. 4, II, 941.

in Confederate ranks as full-fledged soldiers, the per cent of Negro blood was sufficiently low for them to pass as whites.[72]

There were rumors in the North of the use of Negroes in the Confederate army. A Vermont colonel reported in August, 1861, that "the Richmond Howitzer Battery" which had withdrawn before his attack near Newport News "was manned in part by negroes."[73] Ludlow, the Federal agent for the exchange of prisoners, wrote Ould, the Confederate agent, that the South had used Negro soldiers in Louisiana before the North had a single one in the ranks; that Negroes were captured on the battlefield at Antietam and later received by the Confederate authorities in exchange as prisoners of war. Ould denied this statement.[74] Perhaps many of the reports of Negroes fighting in the Confederate army originated from the close attendance of the body servants on their masters during battles. Body servants occasionally took "pot-shots" at the "Yankees."[75]

In this connection it is interesting to speculate, from the Negroes' viewpoint, on what might have been the conduct of slaves fighting for the Confederacy. One of the colored workers on Confederate fortifications at Mobile asked General Richard Taylor in 1864: "Massa Gen'l, . . . how you like our work?" Taylor replied that the Negroes had worked very well. The slave responded: "If you will give us guns we will fight for these works too. We would rather fight for our own white folks than for strangers."[76] The spokesman for a group of prominent Negro ministers and laymen, in an interview with Secretary Stanton, Adjutant

---

72. Henry Clay Warmoth said that many Louisiana mulattoes were in Confederate service but they were "not registered as Negroes." *War Politics and Reconstruction*, p. 56.

73. *O. R.*, Ser. 1, IV, 569.   74. *Ibid.*, Ser. 2, VI, 17, 47.

75. A Confederate officer is quoted as saying at a campfire meeting shortly after the battle of Seven Pines: "Although I lectured my boy about it, I was surprised to find him behind me at Manassas, rifle in hand, shouting out, 'Go in Massa! Give it to 'em, boys! . . . Give 'em h'll.'" *Battle Fields of the South*, II, 64.

76. Richard Taylor, *Destruction and Reconstruction*, p. 210.

General Townsend, and General Sherman in Savannah, January 12, 1865, was asked the specific question: "If the rebel leaders were to arm the slaves what would be its effect?" He replied: "I think they would fight as long as they were before the bayonet, and just as soon as they could get away, they would desert."[77]

The already strife-torn Confederacy might well have spared itself the acrimonious controversy over the arming of slaves. Even if the advocates of such a policy had secured its adoption in time to permit the placing of Negro soldiers on the battlefield in considerable numbers, the tangible results doubtless would have been meagre. In spite of the imposing arguments of those who pleaded for the enlistment of the blacks, it hardly seems likely that slaves who greeted the "Yankees" and grasped freedom with such alacrity under ordinary circumstances, would by the mere donning of Confederate uniforms have been transformed into loyal and enthusiastic fighters for the establishment of a Southern Confederacy and the perpetuation of the institution of slavery.

77. *O. R.*, Ser. 1, XLVII, pt. 2, 40. It must be taken into consideration that the Negro is a genius at anticipating what a white person would like to hear and saying it in a way pleasing to the white. In this connection see Moton, *What the Negro Thinks*, p. 9.

X

A DYING INSTITUTION

WHEN the severance of the Southern States from the Federal Union had been accomplished, there was a wide-spread feeling throughout the seceded section that the position of the "peculiar institution" had been greatly strengthened. No longer would it be exposed to the abusive knocks of "Yankee" statesmen and to the malicious machinations of Northern abolitionists; but, basking in the light of a warming Southern sun, hedged about by a circle of admiring and reassuring friends, it could recover from the accumulated bruises of eight decades of unhappy association with cruel and misunderstanding partners, and attain a strength and a prestige hitherto unknown.

This feeling of satisfaction was enhanced by the adoption of a Constitution which boldly recognized and sought to protect the "institution." There was no awkward side-stepping of terms as in the old Constitution; that of the Confederate Government referred to Negro bondsmen as *slaves*, with a noticeable repetition of the word. This fundamental law made specific guarantees of the protection of slave property within the states, in transit from one state to another, and in any territories which might be acquired. It also provided for the return of fugitives to their masters.

The popular attitude toward these provisions was epitomized by "Little Aleck" Stephens a short time after their adoption in his famous "corner stone" speech at Savannah. The Federal Government, he said, had been built upon the idea of the equality of races, that slavery was wrong in principle, and that it would pass away. The Confederate Government was founded upon exactly the opposite idea, that the Negro was not the equal of the white man, but "that slavery—subordination to the superior race—is his natural and normal condition." This "stone" which had been rejected by the first builders had "become the chief stone of the corner" of the Confederate edifice.[1]

In spite of the apparent security of slavery at the inception of the Confederacy, there were factors which threatened its destruction. Potential dangers lay even in the Constitution, and these did not escape the notice of critical observers of the time. The clause providing for the admission of "other states" by a two-thirds vote of Congress aroused the greatest fear, because this made possible the entrance of *free* states into the *"slave* Republic." The editor of the Montgomery *Post* expressed regret that all states whose constitutions and laws did not recognize and protect slavery had not been definitely barred from the Confederacy. "We of the South," he said, "believing slavery to be a just and lawful institution determined to erect for ourselves a government that would foster and protect it, but in this provision . . . the germ of antislavery has again been planted."[2] The leader most alarmed by this provision, however, was R. B. Rhett of South Carolina. In a series of articles in the Charleston *Mercury* entitled "The Admission of Northern States into the Southern Confederacy,"[3] he fulminated against the people of the Northwest. They were "fundamentally unsound on the question of slavery." They universally regarded slaveholding as "immoral and sinful." "Generation after generation," anti-slavery had "been taken in with their mothers' milk." It could not be eradicated over night. They should be definitely barred from the Confederacy. In September, 1862, he made a long speech in the South Carolina state convention in which he attempted to point out the danger of non-slaveholding states being admitted under the two-thirds clause. All frontier states, he said, would vote for the admission of new states in order to place the

1. *Southern Recorder,* April 12, 1861.
2. Quoted by the Charleston *Mercury,* March 16, 1861.
3. See the daily issues of the *Mercury* of March 25, 26, 27, 28, and April 1, and the tri-weekly issues of March 26, 28, and April 2.

frontier beyond their borders. "Suppose tomorrow Illinois
or Indiana should apply for admission . . . will not Kentucky, Missouri, and other States in the valley of the Mississippi (if in our Confederacy) support the proposition?
Add Tennessee, Virginia, and Maryland and the two-thirds
. . . will be obtained. How long will our Confederacy last
with such associates?"[4]

Furthermore, the provision which fixed representation
on the basis of the white population and three-fifths of the
slaves was regarded as a threat to slavery.[5] In the event of
the admission of states from the Northwest with their
overwhelming white majority, they would have the same
advantage over the slave states that those of the North had
had under the old Union.[6] This clause was viewed by the
editor of the Yorksville *Enquirer* as a gesture toward reunion with some of the free states. "The reproach of weak
and spiritless vassalage should be fully ours should we return to the vomit of Union," he said. "God has delivered
us through the Red Sea of Secession. . . . The people of
the South must rise and resist the very shadow of reconstruction."[7]

The Constitutional prohibition of the foreign slave trade
also occasioned expressions of great apprehension. Many
Southerners believed that importation of slaves was necessary to the preservation of the "institution" throughout
the South. If the traffic were restricted to North America,
the states of Maryland, Kentucky, Missouri, North Carolina, and Tennessee, attracted by the high prices in the
cotton states proper, would gradually sell their slaves. The
result would be a reduction in the number of persons interested in slavery in these states; democracy and free labor
would prevail, and they would be lost to the slave-holding

4. *Southern Recorder*, Oct. 29, 1862.
5. Charleston *Tri-Weekly Mercury*, March 16, 1861. The editor of the
Mercury asked: "Why should there not be representation of all slaves as
well as of only three-fifths of them. Are not slaves persons as well as
women and children?"
6. *Ibid.*, April 2, 1861.
7. Quoted by the Charleston *Tri-Weekly Mercury*, April 11, 1861.

section. Some felt that it was the suppression of the foreign slave trade which had led to the ascendancy of the anti-slavery element in the old Union, because Northern states, induced by the resulting high prices to sell their Negroes, lost their interest in perpetuating the institution; now, the Confederacy was exposed to the danger of a repetition of the same process.

The existence of the war precluded the possibility of these Constitutional dangers developing beyond the potential stage. But in 1863 and 1864 a real threat to slavery became apparent in the agitation to make soldiers out of the Negroes. Much of the bitter opposition which that proposal aroused was based on the disruptive effects which it would have on the "peculiar institution."[8]

But even while the battle over the question of a Negro soldiery was being waged, another serious menace to slavery appeared on the horizon. This was the proposal to make radical changes in the "institution" for the purpose of humanizing or reforming it. The movement had its origin in religious circles and received its greatest impetus from the church, but, ere the close of the war, it had a wide following among the laity. The idea of humanizing slavery was not altogether new at the outbreak of the war. At various previous times proposals had been made to repeal state laws prohibiting the education of Negroes. In 1855 a memorial was circulated in North Carolina asking the legislature to enact laws establishing the institution of marriage among slaves, protecting parent-child relationships, and repealing the statutes prohibiting the instruction of Negroes.[9] These and other similar movements made comparatively little headway, however, the chief obstacle being the fear that Northern abolitionists would use admission of abuses in slavery to the detriment of the "institution." The severance of the political relationship with the enemies

8. See Chapter IX.
9. *De Bow's Review*, XIX (1855), 130; R. H. Taylor, "Humanizing the Slave Code of North Carolina," *North Car. Hist. Rev.*, II (1925), 323–331.

of slavery and the establishment of a government pledged to its protection gave rise to a renewal of the agitation for reform. There was a widespread feeling that the South need no longer adhere to a strictly defensive policy in matters pertaining to slavery, but that she should admit certain patent abuses, seek to discover others, and openly devote herself to the correction of all.

The program of reform as advocated in 1861 and 1862 was limited largely to the enactment of measures recognizing and protecting slave marriages and the repeal of laws which forbade teaching slaves to read.[10] But in 1863 it was extended to include: first, the passage of laws prohibiting the separation of mothers from their children by sales; second, the admission of the testimony of slaves in court as equivalent to circumstantial evidence in order to afford them better protection against cruel masters; third, a restriction of the practice among absentee owners of entrusting the control of their slaves to overseers;[11] and fourth, the repeal of laws prohibiting slaves from assembling and exhorting one another in religious meetings.[12]

The reform movement was aided greatly in the second and third years of the war by the growing feeling that the

10. *Southern Recorder,* Nov. 4, 1862, quoting the *Confederate Union; Southwestern Baptist,* Sept. 18, 1862; *Christian Index,* Sept. 2, 1862; *Southern Churchman,* Jan. 31, 1862.

11. These three items were proposed to the Presbyterian General Assembly at Columbia, South Carolina, in May, 1863, in the form of a pastoral address drawn up at the request of a previous assembly by a committee headed by James A. Lyon, prominent churchman of Mississippi. For the complete text of the proposal, see the *Southern Presbyterian,* XVI (July, 1863). Lyon said that while some of the lay members were "startled at the high ground taken by the address" and were evidently "afraid of outside political sentiment," the majority of the assembly was favorable to it. A motion was adopted ordering the publication of the address, and its recommitment for further consideration. It was reported again to the assembly of 1864 in a slightly revised form and again recommitted. Journal of James A. Lyon, *passim* (MS. in possession of Dr. Robert H. White of Nashville, Tennessee). See also Lyon to Governor Clark, Feb. 10, 1865, Miss. Archives, Ser. E, no. 68, Mobile *Daily Advertiser and Register,* May 22, 1864, and the *Southern Presbyterian,* May 13, 1864, for comment on this address.

12. *Southwestern Baptist,* Sept. 8, 1862.

reverses which the Confederacy was suffering were punishments inflicted by the Almighty for spiritual delinquencies, especially those in connection with the "peculiar institution." In the early fall of 1862, a preacher declared in a meeting of the Central Baptist Association of Georgia that he believed God had brought the "present troubles" upon the South partly because of the legal restrictions upon the teaching of his Word to the slaves.[13] About the same time, a writer in the *Confederate Union*, in an article advocating the repeal of the laws against prohibiting the teaching of slaves to read the Bible, said: "I am not sure but this very law is one of the many reasons why God is withholding, in a degree, his smiles from the righteous struggles we are waging with our cruel foes."[14] The outstanding exponent of this idea, however, was Calvin H. Wiley, a prominent North Carolina educator and religious leader. In 1863 he published a book entitled *Scriptural Views of National Trials* in which he upheld the theory that the war was an affliction sent by the Almighty upon the South to punish her for her sins and shortcomings and to cause her to reform her society. In a chapter devoted to evils in the administration of the "institution," he said: "It is extremely probable that God is now chastising the country for its sins in connection with the subject of slavery." He then proceeded to enumerate these sins as: first, the undue emphasis on establishing the lawfulness of slavery according to the Scriptures to the neglect of ascertaining "what the infallible Word teaches in regard to the obligations of masters and servants"; second, failure to respect the sacredness of the marriage relation; third, disregard of the ties binding parents and children together; and fourth, lack of insistence upon the observance of the Sabbath by slaves as well as masters.[15]

In the last year of the war, as defeat seemed to be overtaking the South, reformists preached with great earnest-

13. *Southern Recorder*, March 31, 1863.
14. Quoted by *Southern Recorder*, Nov. 4, 1862.
15. Calvin H. Wiley, *Scriptural Views of National Trials*, pp. 187 ff.

ness the doctrine that God would permit neither the Confederacy nor slavery to stand unless the "institution" was purged of its patent abuses. A correspondent of the Charleston *Daily Courier*, in August, 1864, said: "The main question at issue in this war, and which it must answer temporarily or finally, is whether God will permit an institution which has hitherto been inseparable from such unmentionable abuses to continue, or whether he will chasten or afflict us into satisfactorily adjusting and amending it."[16] Early in 1865, Bishop Verot, of Savannah, expressed the opinion that "slavery to become a permanent institution of the South must be made to conform to the law of God. A Southern Confederacy will never thrive unless it rests on morality and order."[17] This view was given the clearest and most forceful expression, however, by James A. Lyon and Calvin H. Wiley. The former wrote to Governor Clark of Mississippi, on January 17, 1865, that, while he was convinced that slavery was a biblical institution, he was equally certain that it was not being administered in full accordance with the word of God. "Let us reform those confessed abuses," he continued, "and raise it up to the Bible standard and then we may expect the favor of God and defy the opposition of the world."[18] About a month later he wrote to the governor again stating that he was "clearly satisfied that *Reformation* and not *Emancipation*" was the duty of the South.[19]

On January 24, 1865, Wiley wrote an eleven-page let-

16. Charleston *Daily Courier*, Aug. 6, 1864. This article signed "Dartmouth" was one of several occasioned by a sermon preached in Charleston by the Reverend W. B. W. Howe touching upon the subject of reform. "Gideon" wrote in May, 1864, that he disagreed with Howe in the idea that reforms should be postponed until after the war. "The reforming of our errors is an essential part of self-preservation," he wrote. "Now is the appointed time. God's end when he uses war in his dealings with man is to punish the good and to cause them to repent and abandon their sins." *Ibid.*, May 4, 1864. For another article by "Gideon," see *ibid.*, June 30, 1864.

17. *Ibid.*, Feb. 6, 1865; Richmond *Daily Dispatch*, Jan. 30, 1865.

18. Lyon to Clark, Jan. 17, 1865, Miss. Archives, Ser. E, no. 68.

19. *Ibid.*, Feb. 10, 1865.

ter to his friend Governor Vance of North Carolina in which he said that the South had grievously offended God, first, in endorsing "the separation of mothers and their young children";[20] second, in permitting individuals to dissolve at will the married state; third, in forbidding Negroes to be taught to read; fourth, "in degrading the law by putting the authority of the master above it." "I have never doubted," he continued, "that God in our trials was calling on us to reform the institution of slavery and that if we did not he would abolish it, and that in a way greatly to afflict and degrade us. . . . I hope it is not yet too late . . . but . . . the forbearance of God seems nearly exhausted."[21]

Though the movement for humanitarian reform was viewed with increasing favor by both clergymen and laymen during the last two years of the war, very little was accomplished in the way of remedial legislation. The repeal by the Georgia legislature on April 18, 1863, of the law forbidding the licensing of Negroes to preach may be attributed in part, at least, to the exceptionally strong sentiment for reform in that state.[22] It is possible that the passage of the act by the Alabama legislature in December, 1863, requiring the owner to provide counsel when a slave was indicted "for any offense" and to see that he had a "fair and impartial trial" was a result of the general agitation for reform.[23] James A. Lyon said that he drew up a bill providing for the correction of the most patent abuses of the institution, showed it to the governor of Mississippi, secured his approval of it, and then placed it in the hands of three of the most influential members of the

20. "And now," he added parenthetically, "when God's judgments are heavy on us, there are almost daily auctions in Fayetteville St., Raleigh, where the best and most sacred . . . feelings and instincts of nature are violated . . . and this in the midst of daily prayer meetings and displays of piety."

21. Wiley to Vance, Jan. 24, 1865, Vance Papers.

22. *Public Acts of Ga.*, 1863, Called Sess., no. 116.

23. *Laws of Ala.*, 1863, Reg. Sess., no. 59. The law which this act superseded had required counsel only in cases of capital offenses.

legislature with the request that they commence agitation for its passage. He said further that it was introduced in the Senate early in 1865 and referred to the Judicial Committee, "who reported favorably as to the subject, but unfavorably as to the present being the most opportune time to legislate on the subject; one of the members promised to call the bill up for consideration in the fall session."[24] In the closing days of the war, Mississippi legislators, as well as those of other states, were evidently too much harassed by the pressing problem of maintaining resistance to "abolitionist" invasion to give serious consideration to reform measures.

Leaders who advanced the plea that the only way to save slavery was to reform it were without a doubt sincere in their argument. But a number of considerations indicate that the adoption of their proposals would have led to slavery's ultimate extinction. The education of the Negroes would have made their continued enslavement more difficult. Then, the admission of slaves into courts as witnesses would have had a tendency to cause them to be regarded more as persons and less as property; the legal recognition of marriage and the family relation would have tended toward the same result. The legalizing of slave marriages would have necessitated some provision for divorce. The state would doubtlessly have been called on to bear this responsibility.[25] Increased governmental regulation of slavery would have been deleterious to both the idea and the practice of a domestic and patriarchal institution.

The movement for reform was strong, however. It had the active support of such prominent men, in addition to those already mentioned, as the Reverend W. B. W. Howe of South Carolina,[26] Bishop Elliott of Georgia,[27] and Ed-

24. Journal of James A. Lyon, pp. 112 ff.
25. "A Slave Marriage Law," *Southern Presbyterian*, XVI (Oct., 1863).
26. Charleston *Daily Courier*, April 20, 1864.
27. See pamphlet sermons of Bishop Elliott, entitled *A Sermon Preached in Christ's Church Savannah on Thursday Sept. 18, 1862, Being*

ward A. Pollard of Virginia,[28] though some of the advocates of reform were in favor of postponing the adoption of corrective measures until the fight for independence was won. The reform impulse did not rest on an ephemeral, wartime emotion, but it had been smouldering for many years beneath a silence imposed by the fear of the abolitionists.[29] There can be no doubt that it would have been revived and pushed with renewed zeal in an independent South; and, had the "peculiar institution" survived the dangers which lay in the Constitution and those emanating from a slave soldiery, it is not altogether unlikely that ultimately it would have been "reformed to death" by its friends.

. . . *A Day of Prayer and Thanksgiving,* and *Samson's Riddle,* preached in the same church March 27, 1863; see also a pastoral letter in Thos. M. Hanckel, *Sermons by the Right Rev. Stephen Elliott, D.D.,* pp. 576–577.

28. Edward A. Pollard, "The Anti-Slavery Men of the South," *The Galaxy* (New York), XXVI (Sept., 1873), 329–341.

29. For a list of Southerners who indorsed a remedial code, and their statements, see the appendix of the sixth edition of Samuel Nott's, *Slavery and the Remedy: or, Principles and Suggestions for a Remedial Code.*

PART II
NEGROES UNDER FEDERAL CONTROL

XI

THE BEGINNING OF FEDERAL GUARDIANSHIP

THE problem of the disposition of Southern Negroes within Federal military lines was first forced upon the attention of the Union authorities by an incident which took place in Virginia in the spring of 1861. On May 22 of that year General Benjamin F. Butler arrived at Fortress Monroe and assumed command of the Military Department of Virginia. The next day a reconnoitering party was sent out to Hampton. That night several Negroes escaped from their owners in Hampton and took refuge within the Federal lines. On questioning them the next morning, Butler found that they had been employed in erecting Confederate defenses in the vicinity. He immediately declared that they were "contraband of war" and as such should not be returned to their owners but should be retained in the Federal camp.[1] The term "contraband" which Butler applied to these fugitives, much to their perplexity, became the generally accepted designation for Negroes who had been used by the Confederates in military pursuits for purposes deemed hostile to the United States; it later was applied to all who had been slaves of disloyal owners. By the use of this term Butler implied his acceptance of the slaveholders' claim that Negroes were property.

For the sake of expediency he also utilized another Southern contention. His reply to a Confederate colonel who asked him if he did not feel himself bound by Constitutional obligations to deliver up the slaves under the Fugitive Slave Law was that this act did not affect a foreign country which Virginia claimed to be.

1. *O. R.*, Ser. 1, II, 649; E. L. Pierce, "The Contrabands at Fortress Monroe," *Atlantic Monthly*, VIII (1861), 630–636.

Butler immediately placed these fugitives at work under the supervision of the quartermaster's department on a bakehouse which was being constructed in the fort. On May 25 he wrote General Winfield Scott giving him a full explanation of the matter and asking his approval for what had been done. Both Scott and the Secretary of War, Simon Cameron, gave their indorsement to the general's action.[2]

But when news spread among the slaves of Hampton by "grapevine telegraph" that some of their fellows had been received and protected by the Federals, great numbers flocked to the camp—not only men, but women and children as well. Butler obviously could not apply his contraband theory to all these, for not all of them had been used on Confederate defenses. On the other hand, he was reluctant to receive the men and turn their families away. So he received them all, put the able-bodied ones to work, charging the upkeep of the dependents against their labor, and kept strict account of everything. He reported this action to Scott in a letter of May 27, asking his approval, but apparently he received no answer.[3]

Throughout the month of June, Negroes continued to come to Fortress Monroe; and as they came, those who were needed were put to work by the quartermaster's department unloading vessels, storing provisions, and performing other tasks. Food and shelter were provided for all. These Negroes at Fortress Monroe—they numbered nine hundred before the end of July—constituted the first "contraband camp"—a prototype for many others.

Early in July it was decided that the erection of a line of breastworks was essential to the permanent occupation of Hampton. But the white troops, whose term of enlistment had almost expired, were disinclined to undertake such an unpleasant task. An officer suggested that the contrabands be called upon to perform the labor. Butler's approval having been obtained, steps were immediately taken

2. *O. R.*, Ser. 1, II, 649–652.   3. *Ibid.*, pp. 52–53, 649–650.

to put the Negroes to work. Edward L. Pierce, a Massachusetts private, was detailed to collect and register the Negroes, to provide them with tools, to superintend their labor, and to procure rations for them and their dependents. On July 8 through the assiduous efforts of Pierce, aided by some fellow privates, fifty or sixty Negroes were provided with tools and put to work throwing up embankments. When Pierce and his companions left a week later, their terms of enlistment having expired, the Negroes were still at work and giving a good account of themselves. This was the first instance of the use of Negroes on fortifications by the Federals.[4]

Butler had doubtful authority for his disposition of the Negroes coming to his line. The War Department had approved his retention of slaves who had been used on Confederate defenses; and Congress on August 6 passed an act declaring that owners who had permitted their slaves to be used for such work had thereby forfeited their claim to them. Butler wrote for more definite authority concerning the reception and disposition of the Negroes who were coming in increasing numbers into his line. The reply of the War Department was evasive. It left him uninstructed as to all slaves whose labor had not been used for purposes hostile to the United States.[5]

Federal control over the Sea Island district of South Carolina was inaugurated by Commodore Dupont's capture of two Confederate forts at Hilton Head and Bay Point on November 7, 1861. As the Union forces took possession of the various islands during the days which followed, they found that the fleeing planters had left at their disposal a considerable portion of their worldly goods, the two chief items being several thousand slaves and one of the largest cotton crops which had ever been produced.

4. Pierce, "The Contrabands at Fortress Monroe," *Atlantic Monthly,* VIII (1861), 630–636.

5. *Ibid.* In the fall of 1861 General Wool succeeded Butler as commander of the Department of Virginia. Under his jurisdiction the work of the Negroes was systematized and extended to non-military pursuits.

Some of the cotton had been picked and ginned; but much of it was still in the fields.

The Negroes, for the most part, were very young or very old, the planters having taken the best ones to the mainland with them. After the flight of the whites the abandoned Negroes remained quietly on the plantations, the Negro foremen or drivers retaining a semblance of their old authority and, in many instances, issuing rations from the storehouses. But provisions were scarce and the Negroes destitute. The problem of their sustenance was accentuated by the daily arrival of fugitives from "Rebeldom."

In the early days of Federal occupation the Treasury Department sent agents to the islands to prepare the cotton for shipment, as it was much in demand at the North. These agents employed many of the Negroes in collecting the cotton and loading it on the boats. This marked the beginning of the solution of the problem of the disposition of the Negroes. But it was only the beginning. The great mass of Negroes on the islands remained destitute and without direction.[6]

While the cotton agents were still engaged in their work the Secretary of the Treasury sent down Edward L. Pierce of Milton, Massachusetts, as a special agent to take charge of the Negroes and to start a cotton crop for the next year. Pierce had revealed considerable ability in the management of the contrabands at Fortress Monroe the previous summer. He applied himself to his new task with energy and zeal. One of his first steps was an appeal to interested people in the East for assistance in the form of teachers and provisions. The response to his request was substantial. In February and March, 1862, "Freedmen's Aid" societies were organized in Boston, New York, and Philadelphia.[7] These organizations collected money, cloth-

6. "Letter of the Secretary of the Treasury Relative to the Employment and Sustenance of Slaves," *House Ex. Docs.*, 37th Congress, 3rd Sess., VII, no. 72, 1–6; Pearson, *Letters from Port Royal*, Introduction, pp. v–ix.
7. See reports of these organizations. The Boston Society was organ-

ing, and books on behalf of the Negroes and purchased and forwarded provisions to the South. They also commissioned a number of persons to act as teachers and superintendents.

The first group of those so commissioned, thirty-one in number, set sail from New York on March 3, 1862. The government made them an allowance of transportation, food, and quarters. Their respective societies paid them salaries of from twenty-five to fifty dollars a month, with the exception of a very few who paid their own expenses. These teachers and superintendents had been carefully selected on the basis of their "enthusiasm and good sense." Most of them were young men just out of Eastern colleges. The outstanding member of the group, however, was an older person, E..S. Philbrick, a successful business man of Brookline, Massachusetts. He had contributed one thousand dollars to the enterprise and volunteered his services.

On their arrival at Port Royal the Easterners were distributed on the plantations of the islands. Some were designated as teachers, but as the most immediate need was for the superintendence of the labor of the blacks, most of them were assigned to that work. Both teachers and superintendents acted as distributors of supplies to the needy. Each superintendent was responsible for the oversight of one or more plantations. Philbrick was given the superintendence of three places, among them Coffin's Point, the finest plantation on St. Helena Island. He was assisted by one of the younger men of the group.

When Philbrick and his party arrived on the islands, they found that the planting of corn had already been started on some of the plantations under the direction of the Treasury Department's "cotton agents." This work was encouraged and continued under the new superintendents. But the government was also very desirous of secur-

ized February 7, 1862, under the name of the Educational Commission for Freedmen. It later became the New England Freedmen's Aid Society. The National Freedmen's Relief Association of New York was organized on February 22 and the Port Royal Relief Committee, of Philadelphia—later the Pennsylvania Freedmen's Relief Association—on March 5.

ing a cotton crop from this fertile territory. Though the
season was far advanced by the time Philbrick and his associates were established on the plantations, they immediately organized the laborers into gangs for the purpose of
planting and cultivating cotton.

During the spring other superintendents and teachers
came from the East. At the beginning of the summer a total of ninety-three—seventy-four men and nineteen women
—had assumed their duties as representatives of Eastern
benevolent societies on the islands of South Carolina. Under their charge there were about "3,800 laborers at
steady work on 15,000 acres of corn, potatoes, and cotton."[8]

On the first of July, 1862, as a result of the transfer of
the administration of affairs in South Carolina from the
Treasury to the War Department, the management of
plantations and the control of the Negroes passed into the
hands of Brigadier General Rufus Saxton.[9] Under this
arrangement the superintendents commissioned by the
benevolent societies were placed on the government payroll
and made responsible to the military authorities. But, as a
rule, they remained on the same plantations with their du-

8. Pearson, *Letters from Port Royal*, Intro., p. vii. Following is a list
of the plantations under Treasury control, their location, and the number
of Negroes on them as reported by Pierce on June 2, 1862:

Islands	Number of Plantations	Population
Port Royal	56	1,909
St. Helena (including Dathaw and Morgan) . .	53	2,721
Ladies' (including Waasa, Coosaw, Cat, and Cane)	31	1,259
Hilton Head	15	943
Pinckney	2	423
Daufuskie	3	69
Paris	5	274
Edisto	21	1,278
Hutchinson, Beef, and Ashe	3	174

E. L. Pierce, *The Freedmen of Port Royal, South Carolina, Official Reports*, p. 316.

9. E. L. Pierce, "The Freedmen at Port Royal," *Atlantic Monthly*, XII
(1863), 300.

ties unchanged. The status of teachers was not affected by
this transfer.

Military leaders in the West, particularly those in Missouri, Kentucky, Tennessee, and Louisiana, were confronted with a situation greatly different in respect to Negroes from that in Virginia and South Carolina. In the
two eastern states the Negroes who came under Federal
control were largely those belonging to fugitive and disloyal masters, citizens of states in open rebellion against
the United States. There was obviously nothing else to do
but accept the responsibility for the care of such Negroes
and to put the able-bodied ones to work. In the districts
first occupied by Federal troops in the West, however, a
large proportion of the population was professedly loyal,
and in the case of Missouri and Kentucky the inhabitants
were citizens of loyal states, where Federal laws were still
in force. On the approach of Union troops, the owners of
slaves did not take to precipitate and wholesale flight as
they did in the East, but remained quietly on the plantations. Many planters in "Rebel" states took the oath of
allegiance. These, and the masters in the loyal states, looked
to the Federal authorities to protect them in the possession
of their slave property. But the Negroes usually held a
different view of the matter. They regarded the Union soldiers as deliverers from bondage—an attitude not always
discouraged by the Federals—and in every locality where
the "Yankees" made their appearance the Negroes flocked
to their camps in quest of freedom.

In the early months of the war the authorities at Washington were somewhat evasive and non-committal in regard
to the vexatious question of Negroes. As a consequence,
there was a great divergence in the policies pursued by the
different military authorities. In Missouri and Kentucky
some of the officers excluded all Negroes from their lines;
others admitted all who came; still others sought to admit
only those of disloyal masters.[10] In some cases officers went

10. *O. R.*, Ser. 2, I, 778, 808, 809, 812.

so far as to order soldiers under their command to return fugitives to their masters.[11]

In November, 1861, General Halleck, Commander of the Military Department of the West, sought to secure uniformity of policy within the limits of his command by the issuance of General Order Number 3. By the provision of this order, no more fugitives were to be admitted within the military lines, and those who were already in the camps, not employed by the army, were to be turned out. The reason given for this action was that fugitive slaves had been carrying information concerning the numbers and conditions of Federal forces to the enemy.[12] This order caused a storm of protest especially in anti-slavery circles. On December 9, 1861, a resolution was introduced in the House of Representatives asking that the President "direct General Halleck to recall the said order or to cause it to conform with the practice of other departments of the army." The resolution was laid on the table by a vote of seventy-eight to sixty-four.[13] General Order Number 3 was never fully respected by Halleck's subordinates, though its observance was insisted upon by the department commander until the passage of the Congressional act confiscating slaves of disloyal owners in July, 1862. Grant and Sherman supported Halleck in the enforcement of this order,[14] but in some cases it was openly disobeyed. When a copy of it came to General Mitchell's brigade, it was read at dress parade by Lieutenant Colonel Anthony, Mitchell being absent at the time, and then Anthony read one of his own, in which he threatened punishment to any officer or soldier who should dare to obey Halleck's order; Mitchell did not revoke his subaltern's action when he returned.[15] Colonel "Jim" Lane's propensity for harboring fugitives in Missouri elicited a sharp reprimand from Brigadier General

11. A law of Congress of March 13, 1862, ordered the cessation of this practice.
12. *O. R.*, Ser. 2, I, 778.   13. *Ibid.*, p. 784.
14. *Ibid.*, p. 808; Ser. 1, XVII, pt. 2, 15.
15. *Ibid.*, p. 54.

Merrill. "If you will give more attention to your legitimate business and less to runaway Negroes," Merrill wrote, "you will gain more reputation as a military man than you now enjoy."[16] The Governor of Iowa wrote to the Secretary of War asking that Iowa's troops be not required to serve under Missouri officers as "our troops are not willing . . . that they shall be compelled to drive away from our lines . . . slaves who are willing to render service to the country."[17]

General Halleck's insistence on the observance of General Order Number 3 in the face of so much opposition was doubtless attributable to the practical difficulties which resulted from receiving Negroes into military lines. Not least among these was the conflict with civil authorities who insisted on entering the camps to search for fugitives and force their return to the owners according to the provisions of civil law. Then, the presence of Negroes in the camps was conducive to disease, theft, disorder, and immorality among both whites and Negroes.

The law of Congress of July 17, 1862, necessitated a change of the policy pursued by Halleck in regard to Negroes already within his lines. By section 9 of that act, no military officer was to surrender a slave to any "Rebel" claimant on pain of being dismissed from service nor was he to pass on the validity of the claim of any owner to a slave. This law also declared slaves of disloyal masters who came within Federal lines to be captives of war and, as such, forever free.[18]

In October, 1862, General Grant was placed at the head of the Thirteenth Army Corps which included all the forces in West Tennessee. He immediately began to push preparations for a forward movement into the Confederacy. Previous to this time the Negroes who came into the Union lines were employed only at government work, usually under direction of the quartermaster's department.

---

16. *Ibid.,* XIII, 767.   17. *Ibid.,* p. 643.
18. *Ibid.,* Ser. 3, II, 275–276.

They threw up fortifications, unloaded boats, and did such other work as was required. But Negroes began to flock to Grant's camps in West Tennessee in such great numbers in November, 1862 that his quartermasters and other officers could not provide labor for them.[19] In view of his anticipation of a greater influx of Negroes with the beginning of his southward movement, Grant, by orders issued on November 11 and 14, appointed John Eaton, chaplain of the 27th Ohio Volunteers, to take charge of all the fugitive slaves who were at that time within his lines and all who should enter in the future, except those employed in military pursuits. He also directed Eaton to establish a camp for the Negroes at Grand Junction, Tennessee, where they were to be cared for and set to work picking and ginning the cotton in the surrounding fields. Officers were instructed to send all fugitives to Eaton with such teams, utensils, and other baggage as they brought with them. A regiment of infantry was detailed to guard the Negroes against Confederate raids. Commissaries of subsistence were ordered to issue rations for them on Eaton's requisition.[20]

After an interview with Grant, Eaton entered upon his duties of establishing a "contraband camp" at Grand Junction. When all the abandoned houses had been filled, the Negroes were assigned to cast-off army tents. Provision was also made for the care of the sick. Clothing and tools were provided by the chief quartermaster.[21] The Negroes were put to work in gangs picking cotton for the government, repairing railroads, and unloading steamboats. Their earnings were turned over to Eaton to be used as a fund for the maintenance of the camp. Private individuals were also permitted to hire the fugitives for wages under the direction of the superintendent.[22]

During the early period of his superintendency, Eaton

19. *O. R.*, Ser. 1, XVII, pt. 1, 470.
20. *Ibid.*, LII, pt. 1, 301–302; John Eaton, *Grant, Lincoln, and the Freedmen*, pp. 5, 20.
21. Eaton, *Grant, Lincoln, and the Freedmen*, pp. 18, 21.
22. *Ibid.*, p. 27.

had considerable difficulty in securing the coöperation of the soldiers and officers. Many of them looked with contempt upon all service on behalf of the blacks. They sometimes placed obstacles in the way of the execution of his orders. Capable men were reluctant to act as his assistants. Grant aided in the solution of these and other problems by extending Eaton's authority from time to time.

On account of Federal military reverses at Holly Springs, the Negroes at Grand Junction had to be moved to Memphis early in 1863. The transfer was not effected without great suffering from hunger, cold, and exposure.[23] As employment could be found for only a few of the newcomers within the city, most of them were provided for in camps beyond its limits. Chaplain A. S. Fiske was made an assistant to Eaton in January and to him was assigned the superintendence of the Negroes in Memphis and immediate environs. The largest of the contraband camps, located on a bluff overlooking the river two and one-half miles below the city, was named Camp Fiske in his honor. During the remaining part of the winter many of the Negroes were put to work along the Mississippi cutting wood for the steamboats. With the coming of spring most of them were employed on plantations adjacent to the camps under the general supervision of Eaton and his assistants.[24] Those who were unable to work were subsisted by the government.

When Grant began his operations against Vicksburg from the south, a great many Negroes on abandoned plantations in the vicinity of Milliken's Bend and Young's Point came under Federal control. To prevent them from becoming charges upon the government, Adjutant General Lorenzo Thomas, who came to the Mississippi Valley in April to inspect military conditions and to raise Negro troops, drew up a plan for their employment by civilians "of proper character and qualifications."[25] A commission

23. *Ibid.*, p. 31. 24. *Ibid.*, p. 59.
25. *Ibid.*; Knox, *Camp-Fire and Cotton-Field*, p. 311.

of three was appointed to superintend the leasing of abandoned plantations. Lessees were to pay a tax at the rate of two dollars for each four-hundred-pound bale of cotton produced.[26] They also agreed to employ all Negroes who were hired and turned over to them by the commission until February 1, 1864, to treat them humanely, and to provide them with food and clothing, the cost of the clothing to be deducted from their wages. The rates of compensation were very low: able-bodied men over fifteen years of age received seven dollars per month; women of the same age, five dollars per month; children between twelve and fifteen received half rates. Contrabands under twelve were not permitted to work in the fields.[27]

General Thomas's plan, especially the low scale of wages, was severely criticised and not without reason.[28] There was small likelihood that a Negro would have any money left after the deduction for clothing. Thomas's justification of the system was that it was the best which could be devised, in view of the disturbed state of affairs, for making the recently freed Negroes self supporting.[29]

While Grant and his associates were seeking a practicable solution of the contraband question in Tennessee and Mississippi, General Benjamin F. Butler was confronting a similar problem in Louisiana. A short time after his arrival in New Orleans in the spring of 1862, Butler wrote the Secretary of War a long letter in regard to the Negroes. The situation in Louisiana, he said, was very different from that which he had faced at Fortress Monroe the previous summer. There the Negroes within his lines had been, for the most part, abandoned slaves of disloyal

26. This tax was to be collected by agents of the Treasury.
27. *Annual Cyclopedia* for 1863, pp. 428–429.
28. See James E. Yeatman, *A Report on the Condition of the Freedmen of the Mississippi*, Dec. 17, 1863, p. 4, and *passim*.
29. Eaton said in his *Grant, Lincoln, and the Freedmen*, p. 60, that while the plan was "without doubt faulty in many particulars, its aim certainly was to benefit the Negroes, and in cases where the lessees proved wise, humane, or even manageable, it fulfilled in practice the hopes of its originators."

owners. In Louisiana, a considerable portion of the country had submitted to Federal authority and the white inhabitants were attempting to live quietly under the laws of the United States. Many slaves, both of loyal and disloyal owners, had come to his lines. He had employed as many of these as he had use for in the quartermaster's department; the others he had directed to be sent out of his lines "leaving them subject to the ordinary laws of the community in that behalf." This had seemed to him the only practicable thing to do, as he could not feed all the slaves; and if he permitted them to remain in the camps, the work of the plantations would be disrupted and the growing crops would be lost. He asked the advice of the Secretary of War in regard to his disposition of the Negro question.[30]

A few days before writing this letter Butler had issued a proclamation to the people of New Orleans and environs in which he had promised that "all persons well-disposed toward the Government of the United States who shall renew their oath of allegiance will receive the safeguard and protection of the armies" and that "all rights of property of whatever kind will be held inviolate, subject only to the laws of the United States."[31]

That property in slaves was included in this proclamation is indicated by Butler's subsequent actions as reported in the newspapers. An item in the *Daily Picayune* of May 29, headed "Return of Slaves to their Owners," related that "within the last day or two General Butler has ordered the return of quite a number of slaves who were in the customhouse to their owners and their homes. Among others we hear that six slaves were sent by General Butler's order, in irons, to their owner across the lake. We are glad to hear of this very proper action on the part of the Commanding General." Other news items and advertisements during the months which followed indicate that the buying and selling of slaves and the arrest of runaways

30. *O. R.*, Ser. 1, XV, 439–442.
31. New Orleans *Daily Picayune*, May 5, 1862.

continued throughout the period of Butler's command in
the Department of the Gulf.

The attempt of the commanding general to exclude fugitives from his lines did not meet with the approval of
some of his subordinates. It gave rise to a rather sharp
controversy with Brigadier General John W. Phelps. The
thought of turning away fugitives "of all ages and physical condition . . . infants in arms, many young children
. . . a large number of lame, old, and infirm of both
sexes" who were all "quite destitute of provisions, many
having eaten nothing for days except what our soldiers
have given them from their own rations," could not be en-
dured by Phelps.[32] He protested against the commanding
general's order to exclude the Negroes from his lines. Butler forwarded Phelps's letter to Washington in June. Secretary Stanton seemed to be inclined to support Butler in
his policy of exclusion. But when the correspondence was
shown to Lincoln he expressed the opinion that the laws of
humanity required that fugitives who came to the Federal
camps should not be permitted to suffer for want of food
and shelter, but that they should be provided for by the
quartermaster and commissary departments and the able-
bodied ones put to work.[33] Butler evidently modified his
policy to conform to the President's opinion, and to meet
the requirements of the law of July 17, 1862, which declared fugitives of disloyal masters to be captives of war.

In the latter part of the summer Butler drew up a plan
for the employment of Negroes by the loyal planters of

32. *O. R.*, Ser. 1, XV, 491. Phelps's solicitude for the Negro seems to
have gone beyond the bounds of discretion on more than one occasion.
Captain Edward Page wrote Butler on May 28, 1862, from Kenner, Louisiana: "If on any of the plantations here a Negro is punished when he
most deserves it, the fact becoming known at General Phelps' camp, a
party of soldiers are sent immediately to liberate them [*sic*] and with orders to bring them to camp." *Ibid.*, p. 446. Phelps later raised companies
of Negro soldiers without Butler's authority and then sent in his resigna-
tion when the commanding general ordered that they be put to work on
the levees.

33. *O. R.*, Ser. 3, II, 200.

Plaquemines and St. Bernard parishes. In November it was extended to apply to other parishes which had come under Union control, and to disloyal as well as to loyal planters, provided they remained quietly at home. This arrangement waived the question of the Negroes' freedom. Planters were to pay all able-bodied adult Negroes ten dollars a month for their labor. Of this amount three dollars might be expended for necessary clothing. Children above ten years of age were to receive compensation but their wages were not prescribed by this order. Ten hours were to constitute a day's labor and twenty-six days of ten hours each were to be considered a month's work. Planters were to furnish suitable food for the laborers and proper medicines for those who were sick. They were also to provide for all dependents who bore the relation of parent, child, or wife to their laborers. Planters and overseers were forbidden to inflict any "cruel or corporeal punishment"; but that the realistic Butler felt no qualms concerning severe punishment of recalcitrant Negroes is evident in the provision that "any insubordination or refusal to perform suitable labor or other crime or offense shall be at once reported to the provost marshal for the district, and punishment suitable for the offense shall be inflicted under his orders, preferably imprisonment in darkness on bread and water." Provision was made for the appointment of a commission to assume general direction of affairs connected with plantations.[34]

Throughout the entire period of his command of the Department of the Gulf the disposition of the Negroes was one of the most perplexing problems with which Butler had to deal.[35] And he seems never to have handled it with as much satisfaction as did his successors, Generals Banks and Hurlbut. The Freedmen's Inquiry Commission reported that he was issuing rations to ten thousand Negroes in November, 1862.[36] Many were subsisted by the

34. *Ibid.*, Ser. 1, XV; 162, 593–595.   35. *Ibid.*, p. 162.
36. *Ibid.*, Ser. 3, III, 430.

government unnecessarily on account of the laxity and excessive generosity of the subordinates who had charge of them. One of Butler's last official pronouncements in Louisiana was the promulgation of an order calling attention to the great waste in the issuance of rations to the contrabands. The consumption of provisions had been far in excess of the amount needed; numbers of Negroes had been made dependent upon the military commissariat which "by the exercise of a little judgment and reflection might have been avoided."[37]

The problem of caring for contrabands in the Department of the Gulf, as in all other portions of the South controlled by the Federals, was complicated during the first year of the war by the failure of the administration to formulate definite and uniform policies in regard to the Negro question. In the absence of explicit instructions from Washington, each general in the field was forced to make such disposition of refugee and abandoned slaves as seemed most practicable to him. The result, naturally, was a great diversity of practice in the various military departments.

37. New Orleans *Daily Picayune*, Dec. 6, 1862.

XII

CONTROVERSY AND CHANGE, 1862–1865

THE avowed attitude of Congress at the outbreak of the war was that it had no constitutional right to legislate upon or interfere with slavery in any slaveholding state of the Union. As late as February 11, 1861, the House of Representatives adopted a resolution to this effect by unanimous vote. But during the months which followed, this attitude was to be radically changed by circumstances growing out of the conduct of the war.

The first definite action taken by Congress during the war in relation to the matter of slavery was the passage of an act on August 6, 1861, providing that any property used by the owner's consent and knowledge in aiding or abetting insurrection against the United States was the lawful subject of prize and capture wherever found. When such property consisted of slaves they were to be forever free. The passage of this law was provoked by the "Rebels' " use of slaves in the construction of military defenses, and by the unfounded belief that Negroes had been used as soldiers by the Confederates in the first battle of Bull Run.[1] The measure was sponsored by the anti-slavery element in Congress and was strongly opposed by members from the border states. Mr. Breckenridge of Kentucky, in voicing his opposition to the bill, predicted with remarkable prescience that this act would be one of a series which "will amount before we are done with it, if unhappily we have no settlement or adjustment soon, to a general confiscation of all property and a loosing of all bonds."[2] The antithetical positions of the pro-slavery border-state element on the one hand and the anti-slavery eastern element

1. Henry Wilson, *The Rise and Fall of the Slave Power in America,* III, 238–239, 244.
2. *Ibid.,* p. 238.

on the other, with a group of moderates influenced by the President in between attempting to reconcile both interests for the promotion of the cause of the Union, was a characteristic feature of every Congressional debate on a measure involving slavery.

Congress did not take action again on the harassing slave question until March, 1862. On the thirtieth of that month an act was approved prohibiting officers upon pain of dismissal from service from using any of the forces under their command for returning fugitive slaves. The enactment of this measure was not secured without bitter debate. Border-state members, regarding it as a thrust at the Fugitive Slave Law, sought to attach an amendment exempting the states of Delaware, Maryland, Missouri, and Kentucky.[3] They also attempted to include a provision prohibiting soldiers and officers under like penalty from enticing or detaining slaves of loyal masters. But these amendments were defeated and the original bill was adopted in the House by a vote of eighty-three to forty-two and in the Senate by a vote of twenty-nine to nine.[4]

This law did not secure uniformity, however, in the matter of rendition of fugitives. Some officers interpreted it as forbidding them to surrender slaves under any circumstances; others permitted citizens to come within the lines and take their Negroes away provided they did not resort to force or violence.

On June 19, 1862, a Congressional act abolishing slavery in the territories was approved by the President. In the meantime a proposal to confiscate all slaves of "Rebel" owners who were then or in the future should come within Federal lines, had been introduced and acrimoniously debated in Congress. Although this bill was sponsored by the anti-slavery element and opposed principally by the border-state members, the line of cleavage between North and South was not as distinct as it had been on previous proposals dealing with slavery. The chief argument in favor

3. Wilson, *The Rise and Fall of the Slave Power in America*, III, 297.
4. *Ibid.*, pp. 292–297.

of its adoption was that slavery was proving to be the strength of the rebellion and that the most effective way of crushing it was to strike a blow at the supporting institution. Those who opposed the measure argued that it was unconstitutional, that it was unnecessary, and that it would alienate the Southern friends of the Union.[5] After five months of debate and amendment the bill became a law on July 17, 1862. By its provisions, all slaves of those in rebellion against the United States coming into the possession or under the protection of the government of the United States should be deemed captives of war and made free; the President was authorized to take steps for the colonization of Negroes made free by this act, provided they were willing to emigrate, and provided permission could be secured from tropical countries to receive them; fugitive slaves were not to be surrendered; and no person engaged in the military or naval service was to render fugitives on pain of being dismissed from service.[6]

While Congress was enacting these anti-slavery measures, the President had had more than one occasion to take action on matters pertaining to Negroes. In some respects his attitude had been more conservative than that of the legislative branch of the government. He had signed the bill confiscating slaves used on Confederate defenses with reluctance.[7] On August 8, 1861, Cameron had written Butler that "it is the desire of the President that all existing rights in all the states be fully respected and maintained"; that, in cases of the fugitives from the loyal states, the enforcement of the Fugitive Slave Law "by the ordinary forms of Judicial proceedings must be respected by the military authorities."[8] This policy of returning fugitives was very distasteful to the anti-slavery element; and it was not followed by some of the officers of the army. One of them, General John C. Frémont, commander of the Department of the Missouri, went so far as to set up a

5. *Ibid.*, pp. 332–345.   6. *O. R.*, Ser. 3, II, 275–276.
7. James Ford Rhodes, *History of the United States*, III, 467.
8. Frank Moore, ed., *Rebellion Record*, II, 493, documents.

contrary policy of his own. On August 30, 1861, he issued a proclamation confiscating the property of all disloyal persons in Missouri and declaring their slaves free.[9] When Lincoln learned of this proclamation he wrote its author, the "pet and protégé" of the Blairs, a very moderately-toned letter pointing out the danger of alarming Southern Unionists, and perhaps of driving Kentucky out of the Union by the adoption of the policy set forth in his pronouncement. He requested that Frémont, as of his own motion, modify the proclamation so as to conform to the Confiscation Act of Congress.[10] The general, however, seeking to make an issue out of the matter, refused to modify his action unless openly directed to do so by the President. Whereupon, Lincoln, on September 11, explicitly ordered him to make the proclamation conform to the law of Congress.[11] A storm of protest arose in anti-slavery circles but Northern public sentiment seems to have been with the President.[12]

In his message to Congress of December 3, 1861, Lincoln called attention to the fact that a large number of persons formerly held as slaves had been liberated as a consequence of the war and that others would probably be freed by the voluntary action of the loyal slave states. He suggested that Congress adopt some plan of compensation for such cases of voluntary emancipation, and that steps be taken toward the colonization of the freed Negroes in some place with a climate congenial to them.[13] In his message to Congress a year later, the President renewed this suggestion as to colonization. He also revealed that several countries located in the tropics, or having colonies there, had been approached on the question of receiving American freedmen, and that Liberia and Haiti were "as yet the only countries to which colonists of African descent from here could go with certainty of being received and adopted

9. *O. R.*, Ser. 1, III, 467.   10. *Ibid.*, p. 469.
11. *Ibid.*, p. 485.
12. Rhodes, *History of the United States*, III, 472.
13. *O. R.*, Ser. 3, I, 717.

as citizens." The President added that he regretted to say that "such persons contemplating colonization do not seem so willing to migrate to those countries as to some others, nor so willing as I think their interest demands."[14] He expressed the belief, however, that opinion among the Negroes on this subject was improving and that in the near future there would be "an augmented and considerable migration to both these countries from the United States." He proposed three amendments to the Constitution: the first providing compensation in United States bonds to every state which should emancipate its slaves, either immediately or gradually, before the year 1900; the second allowing the same rate of compensation to loyal owners whose slaves were freed by the chances of war; the third authorizing Congress to appropriate money and otherwise to provide for colonizing free colored persons with their consent at any place outside the United States. He supported his suggestions with a lengthy argument as to their soundness and expediency.[15]

In the meantime the President had found it necessary to restrain another forward general. On May 9, 1862, David Hunter, commander of the Department of the South, issued a proclamation declaring that all persons who had been held as slaves in Georgia, Florida, and South Carolina were forever free. Ten days later Lincoln, having seen a copy of Hunter's order in the newspapers, issued a proclamation nullifying it. In this proclamation Lincoln also appealed to the border states to take advantage of the joint resolution which he had proposed to Congress on March 6, and which that body had adopted by a large majority, providing "that the United States ought to cooperate with any State which may adopt a gradual abolishment of slavery, giving to such State pecuniary aid, . . . to compensate for the inconveniences, public and private, produced by such a change of system."[16]

In the summer of 1862 Lincoln became convinced that a

14. *Ibid.,* II, 885.   15. *Ibid.,* pp. 892–897.
16. *Ibid.,* pp. 42–43.

declaration of emancipation of slaves in disloyal states was essential to the success of Federal arms.[17] He feared, however, the effect of such a step on the attitude of the border states. On July 12 he called the representatives of those states to the White House and tried unsuccessfully to persuade them to adopt his policy of compensated emancipation. Ten days later the President read to his cabinet a proclamation of emancipation which he proposed to issue. Seward objected to the issuance of the proclamation at the time on account of the depression of the public mind consequent upon repeated military reverses; it would seem as if the government were "stretching forth its hands to Ethiopia."[18] Lincoln, impressed with the wisdom of Seward's objections, withheld the proclamation until September 22, five days after the battle of Antietam. In this preliminary proclamation he stated his purpose to recommend again to Congress at the next session the adoption of a practical measure tendering pecuniary aid to loyal slave states which should abolish slavery. He further stated that on January 1, 1863, he would designate the states and parts of states in rebellion against the United States, and that the slaves in those designated areas would be declared forever free.[19] On January 1, 1863, he issued the final proclamation designating as the states in rebellion, Arkansas, Texas, Louisiana (except certain parishes occupied by the Union army), Mississippi, Alabama, Florida, Georgia, South Carolina, North Carolina, and Virginia (except "West Virginia," and certain counties under Federal control). The excepted areas were "left precisely as if this proclamation were not issued." The Negroes declared free were advised to abstain from all violence "unless in necessary self-defense," and to work faithfully in cases where reasonable wages were offered.[20]

A little less than a year after the President issued the final proclamation, a movement was begun in Congress to

17. Rhodes, *History of the United States,* IV, 69.
18. *Ibid.,* pp. 68, 72.
19. *O. R.,* Ser. 3, II, 584–585.   20. *Ibid.,* III, 2–3.

secure the adoption of a constitutional amendment abolishing slavery throughout the United States. On December 14, 1863, a representative from Ohio and one from Iowa each introduced such an amendment into the House. A little later similar proposals were introduced into the Senate and referred to the Judiciary Committee. On reporting the resolution which was to become the Thirteenth Amendment, on March 28, 1864, Senator Trumbull, chairman of that committee, gave some arguments in favor of the adoption of such an amendment. The Congressional legislation on the subject, he said, applied only to Negroes whose owners were engaged in the rebellion. The President's proclamation declared free the slaves of all persons in states designated as being in rebellion, but there were many who held the opinion that the President had no authority to declare the freedom of any slaves except those brought within the Federal lines by the chances of war. Others held a contrary opinion. But regardless of the question of authority, Trumbull argued, the proclamation excepted from its provisions almost half of the slave states; an amendment was the most effective way of securing an unequivocal and everlasting abolishment of slavery throughout the whole country.[21] On April 8 the resolution submitted by Trumbull passed the Senate by a vote of thirty-eight to six. On June 15 it was voted on in the House, but failed of the required two-thirds majority. The amendment was not considered again during that session. On President Lincoln's suggestion it was called up for reconsideration in the House on January 6, 1865; at that time Maryland, Missouri, and Louisiana had already voted to abolish slavery. Nevertheless there was considerable opposition offered to the amendment. When the vote was taken on January 31, 56 members voted against it, 119 for it, and 8 did not vote. This being the necessary two-thirds in favor of the amendment, it was submitted to the states for ratification.[22] Thus was consummated the series of acts

21. Rhodes, *History of the United States,* IV, 473–474.
22. *Ibid.,* V, 48–50.

"loosing all bonds" which Breckenridge had predicted in July, 1861, in his opposition to the bill proposing to emancipate slaves used on Confederate defenses.

While the President and Congress were engaged in determining the status of Southern Negroes, officers in various regions occupied by the Federals were attempting to perfect existing plans for taking care of the hordes of blacks who flocked to the Union lines. In South Carolina, where the control of Negro affairs had been transferred from the Treasury to the War Department in July, 1862, Rufus Saxton, commanding general of the Department of the South, made few changes immediately in the system which had been inaugurated the previous year by Edward L. Pierce. Negroes continued to work plantations in gangs under the direction of plantation superintendents commissioned by benevolent societies. The Negroes received rations and wages from the government. Lack of uniformity of policy on the different plantations, however, caused Saxton in December, 1862, to promulgate a general plan of operations which superintendents throughout the Department of the South were required to follow. According to this plan the Negroes were made responsible for planting and cultivating sufficient corn and potatoes for their own use. To enable them to do this, allotments of land were made to each family at the rate of two acres for each working hand and two-sixteenths of an acre for each child. The plowing of this land was to be done by the plantation plowman under the direction of the superintendent with the stock and implements belonging to the plantation. In exchange for the use of the land, the plantation stock and tools, and the services of the plowman, the Negroes on each place were required to cultivate, in addition to their own allotments, an acreage sufficient to produce corn for the plantation stock, for the plowman, for the superintendent, and for the dependents for whom no other provisions could be made.

Each Negro, or each Negro family, was also to agree to plant and cultivate a certain number of tasks (a task was ordinarily about one-fourth of an acre) of cotton for the government. Negroes were to receive pay for their work in the cotton fields. If any black failed to do the required work on his task within the time specified by the superintendent, the latter was to engage other laborers and pay them instead of the person to whom the tasks were originally allotted.[23]

This plan, the general features of which had been used previously by Philbrick on his three plantations on St. Helena Island, had a tendency to stimulate individual initiative and industry. Each laborer had a definite responsibility and received compensation in proportion to the work which he performed.[24]

In March, 1863, the system set up by General Saxton was disturbed by the sale of 16,000 out of the 76,000 acres of land subject to sale in South Carolina by the government for the non-payment of taxes.[25] Most of the land was bought by Eastern capitalists and philanthropists. Nine choice plantations were purchased by E. S. Philbrick and a group of Massachusetts associates. The superintendents who had been on the plantations during the period of government ownership and control were retained, as a rule, by those who purchased the land.[26] General Saxton, as military governor, had general oversight of the Negroes on the plantations which passed into private hands. The new owners seem to have adhered to the general terms prescribed by Saxton for the government plantations in 1863. Some of them adopted a higher scale of wages. Others followed the share-crop plan of compensation.[27]

In the latter part of 1863 and the early part of 1864,

23. New Orleans *Daily Picayune*, Feb. 1, 1863; Charles Nordhoff, *The Freedmen of South Carolina*, pp. 13–14.
24. *The Williams* [*College*] *Quarterly*, XI (1863), 74–75, Letter of J. H. Goodhue to the editors. Goodhue was the superintendent of a plantation on Ladies Island.
25. *Second Annual Report of the New England Freedmen's Aid Society* (April, 1864), p. 15. Thirty-five hundred acres of this land were purchased by Negroes.
26. Pearson, *Letters from Port Royal*, p. 172.
27. *Ibid.*, p. 191.

most of the land remaining in government possession was sold by the Federal tax commissioners. In April, 1864, General Saxton issued a circular requiring that planters or their superintendents make written contracts with their laborers setting forth the terms by which they were to work.[28] On most plantations the owners, in response to the increased demands of their employees, paid higher wages than those of the previous year.

After Saxton assumed control of affairs under the War Department in July, 1862, the Treasury seems never to have had control of the plantations in South Carolina, except for purposes of sale for the payment of taxes. Treasury regulations governing the shipment of produce and the reception of supplies, however, were considered noxious and excessively rigid by plantation owners.[29]

In 1865 the administration of plantation affairs in the Department of the South seems to have continued along the same lines as during the previous year. The Negroes continued to demand an increase in their wages, but the planters were disinclined to raise them.[30] In January, Saxton was given the title of inspector general and placed in charge of all Negro affairs in the district extending from Key West to Charleston and inland for thirty miles. His responsibility was greatly increased by the arrival in South Carolina of hundreds of Negroes who had been following Sherman's army. While able-bodied men were received into the army as soldiers or put to work in the quartermaster's department, women and children were distributed on the plantations.

In Virginia and North Carolina, the period from 1862 to 1865 was marked by changes in the administration of Negro affairs considerably greater than those taking place in South Carolina during that time. Soon after General

28. Pearson, *Letters from Port Royal*, p. 262. In 1864 about seven thousand acres of land purchased at the sales of 1863 and 1864 were cultivated by Negro owners. *Second Annual Report of the New England Freedmen's Aid Society* (April, 1864), p. 15.

29. Pearson, *Letters from Port Royal*, p. 281.

30. *Ibid.*, p. 295.

Wool succeeded Butler as commander of the Department of Virginia in October, 1861, he issued Special Order Number 72 authorizing the employment of able-bodied contrabands within his lines in military pursuits as servants to officers and as laborers. He justified his action on the ground of military necessity. A low scale of wages was set up but the money, instead of being paid to the employees, was to be set aside as a fund for the support of contrabands unable to work.[31]

This situation naturally proved unsatisfactory, and in November, 1861, Wool issued General Order Number 34, to correct the defects in his previous regulations and to broaden their application. Wages for contraband laborers in the engineer, ordnance, quartermaster, commissary, and medical departments were raised 25 per cent. As an incentive to individual exertion, each laborer was to receive a small portion of his wages to spend as he chose. The remainder, after deductions for clothing, was to be turned over to a fund for the support of non-laborers. Additional pay was to be given for extra work.

The issuance of General Order Number 34 failed to bring the desired improvement in contraband affairs in Virginia. Complaints of fraud, abuse, and suffering were numerous. In March, 1862, in response to a resolution of the House of Representatives, General Wool appointed a committee of three officers to investigate the administration of Negro affairs in his department and to report to him. The findings of this committee, which were transmitted to the House, revealed an unhappy situation. The laborers had received only a very small part of the wages due them. The total amount in arrears was over $10,000. No accounts of the labor performed under Special Order Number 72 had been kept in any of the military departments, though many contrabands "had previously worked months in these departments receiving only subsistence and shelter for their services." In some cases laborers had been defrauded in the

31. *O. R.,* Ser. 2, I, 774.

matter of rations. One officer in charge of dispensing food had cut down the prescribed rations and sold the surplus to sutlers. Sufficient clothing had not been supplied by the employers. Harsh treatment by those in charge of the labor gangs had not been uncommon. The committee recommended that the policy of appropriating the wages of workers to support non-laborers be discontinued because it was unfair to those without dependents and conducive to laziness.

On March 18, 1862, Wool issued General Order Number 22 with the intent of correcting the most patent abuses brought out in the report of the investigating committee. Orders Number 34 and 72 were revoked; wages were to be paid directly to the laborers for their own use; rates of compensation were to be determined by individual industry and ability. On the same day that these changes were ordered the appointment of C. B. Wilder as superintendent of contrabands in Virginia was announced.[32]

The system of administration inaugurated by General Wool, even after these revisions, did not prove satisfactory. It was unduly expensive. It made no adequate provisions for the employment of laborers in civilian pursuits, and the demand for workers in the military departments did not keep pace with the increased supply resulting from the influx of fugitive slaves and the extension of the military lines. As a result, hundreds were thrown upon the charity of the government and benevolent societies. Crowded into camps at Alexandria, Old Point Comfort, and Fortress Monroe, these abject creatures died by the score. Superintendent Wilder secured permission from the War Department to address the governors of various states in regard to sending some of them to the North. The proposal was received with such pronounced disfavor by Governor Andrew of Massachusetts that it was immediately dropped. The suffering would have been alleviated considerably had the government workers received their pay. Many of them

32. *House Ex. Docs.*, 37th Cong., 2nd Sess., VII, no. 85, pp. 1-14.

received no money with which to buy clothing for themselves and their families, even after months of steady employment. In December, 1862, the aggregate amount due contraband laborers in Virginia was reported as $31,-435.95.[33]

In early 1863 the Military Department of Virginia was combined with that of North Carolina, and a short time afterward General Foster assumed command. He immediately ordered changes in the system developed by Wool in Virginia. The oversight of Negro affairs was divided among three superintendents. New contraband camps were established, and stricter regulations governing wages, working conditions, and the distribution of supplies were promulgated. Steps were taken to remove as many as possible of the contrabands to abandoned and confiscated farms to work for their own support. The superintendents were handicapped greatly in the development of this policy by the limited areas available for farming operations and the shortage of implements and livestock.[34]

In the fall of 1863, General Butler succeeded Foster as commander of the Department of Virginia and North Carolina. He immediately issued a General Order dealing *in extenso* with the contraband question. In an effort to remedy the looseness of administration and the divergence of policy which had prevailed under his predecessors he created a department of Negro affairs with a general superintendent at its head responsible directly to him for the care of the contrabands throughout his command. This territory was divided into three districts: that north of the James River was placed under the immediate superintendence of C. B. Wilder, that south of the James River under Orlando Brown, and that in North Carolina under the

<hr/>

33. *O. R.*, Ser. 1, XVIII, 391, 395, 461; *Second Report of a Committee of the Representatives of the New York Yearly Meeting of Friends upon the Condition and Wants of the Colored Refugees* (1863), p. 12; P. S. Peirce, *The Freedmen's Bureau*, pp. 7–8.

34. *Second Report of a Committee of the Representatives of the New York Yearly Meeting of Friends upon the Condition and Wants of the Colored Refugees* (1863), pp. 7 ff.; Peirce, *Freedmen's Bureau*, p. 8.

Reverend Horace James. The duties of these superintendents were prescribed in detail. They were to cause accurate
censuses to be made of all the Negroes, showing their employment. They were to see that all able-bodied Negroes
had something to do, and that they pursued the work assigned to them industriously. Superintendents were to
cause all laborers to be provided with the necessary food,
clothing, and medicine; to examine contracts made between
Negroes and whites in order to see that the terms were fair
and faithfully executed by both parties. They were to take
charge of all lands and property set aside for the Negroes
by the government and by charity, and to see that such
lands and property were used to the best advantage. They
were also to audit all unpaid accounts of the Negroes
against the government and to present them to the proper
department for payment. To facilitate the work of the
superintendents, government employers were ordered to
pay the laborers promptly so that they might provide for
their families. Officers and soldiers were instructed to encourage fugitives to come into the Federal lines; if the
matter of their freedom was brought in question, it was to
be assumed that they were free.

Butler's system had serious defects. It did not provide a
definite scale of wages either for those in government service or for those in private employ. The policy of subsisting
the families of colored soldiers at government expense apparently tended to foster idleness. But, despite these short-
comings, the conditions of the Negroes seem to have been
improved under Butler's administration. Educational activities were systematized, plots of land acquired, cabins
built; order was promoted, and self-respect enhanced.[35]
Few changes seem to have been made by his successors.

The work of the Reverend Horace James as superintendent of contrabands in North Carolina deserves special
mention. Before he assumed this responsible position in the
spring of 1863, Negro affairs had been almost without direction. Soon after the coming of the Federals to North

35. *O. R.*, Ser. 3, III, 1139–1144; Peirce, *Freedmen's Bureau*, p. 12.

Carolina in the spring of 1862, the commanding general, Burnside, had appointed Vincent Colyer of the United States Christian Commission as superintendent of the poor. The jurisdiction of this office was later extended to include a general supervision of colored refugees. Under Colyer's direction many men were hired by the various military departments, dependents were cared for, schools were established, and other steps were taken for the amelioration of the condition of the refugees; but the nature of Colyer's office required that he devote most of his time to the interests of white soldiers and civilians.[36]

When Burnside was transferred to the Army of the Potomac in the fall of 1862, Colyer went with him. The oversight of the Negroes was taken for a time by Chaplain Horace Means. He in turn was succeeded by James. From the early days of the Burnside expedition James had taken active interest in the North Carolina Negroes. Assisted by other chaplains, he had established and conducted evening schools, given religious instruction, and administered to the physical needs of the Negroes. With his appointment to the superintendency of Negro affairs in the spring of 1863, his prerogatives and responsibilities were greatly increased.[37]

The problem of disposing of the Negroes in North Carolina, as in Virginia, was complicated by the fact that such a small amount of land was at the disposal of the Federals. This situation was in marked contrast to that which prevailed in South Carolina, the Gulf section, and the Mississippi Valley. The conditions in North Carolina, and the effect which they had on the disposition of the Negroes, are tersely described by James in his report for 1864: "We control indeed a broad area of navigable waters, and command the approaches from the sea," he said, "but

36. Vincent Colyer, *Report of the Christian Mission to the United States Army*, pp. 4 ff.

37. This summary of James's work in North Carolina is based largely on the *Annual Report of the Superintendent of Negro Affairs in North Carolina* (1864). Quotations, unless otherwise indicated, are from this *Report*.

have scarcely room enough on land to spread our tents
upon. If land had been accessible on which to settle the Negroes, it would have prevented huddling them together in
the fortified towns and in temporary camps. But there was
left us no alternative."

James entered with alacrity upon the task of caring for
the contrabands in North Carolina who in January, 1865,
numbered over seventeen thousand. In all his undertakings
he had the support and coöperation of the commanding
military officers and the representatives of the benevolent
societies. One of his first projects was the establishment of
a colony, or camp, on Roanoke Island. It was his original
intention to furnish the Negroes with implements and livestock and to make them self-supporting; but this design
was thwarted by the enlistment of most of the able-bodied
men in the army. The colony was, of necessity, converted
into "an asylum for the wives and children of soldiers, and
also for the aged and infirm." In the summer of 1863
James went north, raised about nine thousand dollars,
purchased supplies and implements for the enterprise, and
engaged the services of a number of teachers. On his return he took possession of the northern end of the island,
cleared off the timber, laid out the land in one-acre plots,
and assigned these to families. The Negroes, generally enthusiastic at the prospects of owning their own homes and
gardens, entered whole-heartedly into the enterprise. With
the aid of a sawmill purchased by James in the North, the
erection of cabins progressed rapidly. Several schools were
established. Some of the Negroes were taught to support
themselves in part by spinning and weaving. Others engaged in barrel-making, shoe-making, shingle-splitting,
fishing, and military work. For lack of suitable occupa-
tions, many were unemployed. Others were rendered idle
by extreme age or youth. On January 1, 1865, the total
colored population of the island was about three thousand.

Most of the Negroes under Federal control in North
Carolina were congregated in Newbern and vicinity. In
1865 they numbered over ten thousand. About six thou-

sand of these were in the city. Some of them were comparatively well-fixed and profitably engaged as turpentine
farmers, merchants, and craftsmen. Others were employed
by the military authorities as soldiers and laborers. About
one-fourth of the population, however, was dependent
upon the government for support. Almost all those outside
the town were concentrated in a settlement which James
devised for their care and protection.

There were about fifteen hundred Negroes in the vicinity
of Beaufort and Morehead. They were engaged for the most
part in carrying supplies by boat from the railroad termi-
nus at Morehead to Beaufort, two miles away, and in oys-
tering and fishing. Approximately one thousand Negroes
lived along the creeks of Carteret County. Most of them
supported themselves by turpentine farming.

Early in 1865 the military district of North Carolina,
which had been part of the Department of Virginia and
North Carolina under Butler's command, was made a part
of the Department of the South. A short time later it was
declared a separate department with Major General Schofield in command. These changes did not effect James's
administration of Negro affairs to a great extent. One notable alteration was the discontinuance by Schofield of
Butler's policy of issuing rations to soldiers' families without regard to their particular needs.[38]

James's responsibilities and perplexities were greatly increased in 1865 by the influx of thousands of Negroes who
followed Sherman's army from the south. Ten thousand
entered Wilmington and five thousand came into Newbern. The supplies of clothing which the superintendent
had on hand were soon exhausted. Appeals were made to
the North for aid. Responses were generous;[39] but so de-

38. *North Carolina Times* (Newbern), Jan. 21, Jan. 31, March 24,
1865.

39. The benevolent societies most active in the care of the freedmen in
North Carolina and Virginia were the Friends' Associations of Philadelphia and New York, the National Freedmen's Aid Society, and the Rhode
Island Freedmen's Aid Association. James, *Annual Report of the Superintendent of Negro Affairs in North Carolina* (1864), p. 16 and *passim*.

bilitated were these creatures from hunger, exposure, and fatigue that they "melted away almost as rapidly as if they had been swept with grape and cannister."

After the war was over the freedmen in North Carolina and Virginia were urged to return to their former homes, and, if paid wages, to remain with their former masters. The control of Negro affairs was left, as elsewhere, in the hands of the superintendents, treasury agents, and provost marshals until these officers were relieved by officials of the Freedmen's Bureau.[40]

The problems of James, Wilder, and other superintendents acting under military authority in North Carolina and Virginia were complicated by the entrance of Treasury officials into the realm of Negro administration in 1864. On March 12, 1863, Congress authorized the Treasury Department to take control of all abandoned and confiscable lands within the Federal-controlled portion of the South. In compliance with this legislation, the Secretary of War issued an order dated October 9, 1863, requiring military officers to turn over all such lands except that required for military purposes to the properly appointed Treasury agents. On July 2, 1864, Congress passed another law authorizing the Treasury Department through its agents to lease the lands under Treasury control for cultivation, and to provide for the employment and general welfare of the freedmen throughout the South. In accordance with the provisions of this act, the Secretary of the Treasury on July 29, 1864, issued an elaborate set of regulations for the leasing of plantations and the care of freedmen.[41] The insurrectionary states were divided into seven districts, or special agencies; a supervising special agent was placed at the head of each agency. A general

40. James, *Annual Report of the Superintendent of Negro Affairs in North Carolina* (1864), p. 59.

41. These regulations were published and issued as a government document under the title: *Rules and Regulations Concerning Commercial Intercourse with and in States and Parts of States Declared in Insurrection, the Collection, Receipt, and Disposition of Captured, Abandoned, and Confiscable Property, and the Employment and General Welfare of Freedmen.* Hereafter, this will be cited as *Treasury Regulations,* 1864.

agent, responsible to the Secretary of the Treasury, was placed over the whole system. The rules governing the disposition of freedmen provided for the establishment in each special agency of one or more "home colonies" under the direction of a superintendent, where freedmen were to be received and cared for until they were employed on plantations. The superintendents of these home farms were to receive and fill applications for laborers, and to see that written agreements were made between employers and employees. Sufficient contiguous lands were to be reserved for the exclusive use of freedmen capable of cultivating on their own account. These reservations, called "labor colonies," were to be in charge of superintendents who should lease the land to freedmen and supervise their work. Laborers on leased plantations were to receive—in addition to plots of land for garden purposes for each family, fuel, medical attendance, and education for their children— wages ranging from ten dollars to twenty-five dollars per month.

North Carolina and Virginia were included in the Sixth and Seventh Special Agencies defined by these regulations. The system prescribed was not developed as extensively in these agencies as in other parts of the South on account of the limited amount of lands subject to Treasury control. The officials in charge of the agencies, however, exerted themselves assiduously to make the most of the resources and prerogatives at their command. Under Treasury supervision some eighty leases, varying in extent from one-acre plots to large plantations, were made in 1864. Most of the plantations were rented to whites for the cultivation of cotton. The small plots, which far outnumbered the plantations, were taken mostly by colored lessees, who devoted themselves to tar-making and turpentine-farming.[42] In 1865 new leases were made by the Treasury officials under the regulations of July 29, 1864. In spite of reverses during the previous year resulting from disease and the

42. *North Carolina Times,* July 9, Dec. 2, 1864, and Feb. 14, 1865.

ravages of a pest known as the army worm, there was a scramble for renewal of leases.

The control of plantations and freedmen by the Treasury Department seems to have been much more successful in North Carolina and Virginia than in other regions of the South. This was largely owing to the greater efficiency and tactfulness of the Treasury agents in the former districts. The coöperation given these agents by the military authorities was also an appreciable factor.[43] That relations were not always harmonious, however, is indicated by the issuance of a general order from the provost marshal's office in April, 1864, declaring null contracts which the Treasury agents had made at rates of wages higher than those paid to military laborers.[44]

Superintendent James was somewhat irked by the fact that the Treasury agents took the land, the freedmen's chief source of income, without assuming any particular responsibility for the support of dependents. In his report for 1864 he said: "The agents of the Treasury Department had the whole management of these farms. And while they were occupied in many instances by colored lessees, and almost wholly worked by them, the department of Negro affairs was not pecuniarily benefited thereby."[45]

While James and his associates were devising and improving plans for the care of Negroes in Virginia and North Carolina, changes were also being made in the administration of Negro affairs in Louisiana. In the latter part of 1862 slaveholders of Federal-controlled portions of that state were greatly disturbed over the approaching issuance of the Emancipation Proclamation. When Nathaniel P. Banks succeeded Benjamin F. Butler as commander of the Department of the Gulf in December of that year, one of his first official acts was a statement addressed "to the people of Louisiana" to correct public mis-

---

43. *North Carolina Times,* July 9, 1864, Feb. 14 and March 24, 1865.
44. *Ibid.,* April 9 and July 9, 1864.
45. James, *Annual Report of the Superintendent of Negro Affairs in North Carolina* (1864), p. 54.

apprehension. He predicted that "loyal" portions of the state would be excepted from the districts to which the proclamation was to apply. Any unusual public demonstration was prohibited and slaves were advised to remain on the plantations, at least for the time being. Planters were urged to adopt some plan of equitable compensation for labor. No encouragement was to be given to the laborers to desert their employers, but no authority existed to compel them to return. Since slavery existed only by consent and constitutional guarantee, the only possibility of its preservation lay in the cessation of war and the re-establishment of constitutional relations.[46]

The immediate objects of Banks were to relieve the government of the support of the ten thousand Negroes to whom rations were being issued and to find shelter and sustenance for them on plantations. He had found fugitives "herded together" in camps at New Orleans, Carrollton, Donaldsonville, and Baton Rouge, "without regard to sex or age . . . dying in large numbers."[47] In January, 1865, an amount exceeding sixty thousand dollars was spent for the support of these dependent and destitute persons.[48]

In order to promote the resumption of work on the plantations, Banks issued General Order Number 12 on January 29, 1863. By the provisions of this order the Sequestration Commission was directed, upon conference with planters and other parties, to establish a yearly system of Negro labor which should provide for the food, clothing,

---

46. New Orleans *Daily Picayune,* Dec. 25, 1862.

47. Letter (undated) of James Bowen to William Lloyd Garrison in New Orleans *Daily True Delta,* March 19, 1865. Concerning the condition of the fugitives in early 1863, Banks wrote to Garrison in 1865: "Their condition was that of abject misery. I have myself seen at Baton Rouge in one of these Negro quarters, or contraband camps as they were called, one hundred and fifty men, women and children—in every possible condition of misery—cooking, eating, drinking, sleeping, sickening and dying in one room, with a fire built in the center on the floor without chimney, where all phases of this sad history occurred. The same scene was witnessed at every military post." Letter of Banks to Garrison, Jan. 30, 1865, *ibid.*

48. *O. R.,* Ser. 2, V, 279.

proper treatment, and just compensation of the Negroes
at fixed wages or on an equitable share-crop basis. When
the terms prescribed by the commission should be accepted
by the employer, "all the conditions of continuous and
faithful service, respectful deportment, correct discipline
and perfect subordination" were to be "enforced on the
part of the Negroes by the officers of the Government."
The question of the Negroes' freedom was waived by this
order, but the implication was that the law prohibiting
the military authorities from returning fugitives and the
inevitable conditions of a state of war made the slave system unenforceable and ineffective. This order also provided that all persons must maintain themselves by labor,
"Negroes not excepted." Those who left their employers
were to be "compelled to support themselves and families
by labor upon the public works."[49]

In accordance with the provisions of this order, the Sequestration Commission drew up a form of contract for
labor, the general conditions of which were the preservation of the unity of families, the freedom of laborers to
choose their employers for the year, equitable compensation for labor, the limitation of the hours of work, exemption from all forms of corporal punishment, the education
of the laborers' children, and the right of the Negroes to
cultivate land on their own account.[50] The provost marshals of the various districts were charged with the responsibility of seeing that the conditions of the contract were
respected by the employers and laborers.[51] After these
terms for the employment of labor had been drawn up by
the Sequestration Commission, the planters met in convention and voted to accept them.

This system of labor was severely criticized in the North.

49. *Daily Picayune,* Jan. 30, 1863.
50. N. P. Banks, *Emancipated Labor in Louisiana,* p. 7. Placing of re-
calcitrants in the stocks was permitted. *Annual Cyclopedia* for 1863, p.
594.
51. New Orleans *Tribune,* Sept. 24, 1864; Letter (undated) of James
Bowen to William Lloyd Garrison in *Daily True Delta,* March 19, 1865.

General Banks was repeatedly charged with returning the Negroes to slavery.[52] But in spite of opposition, both of Northerners and native Louisianians, the plan was quietly put into operation. That the system was often abused by the planters, that the lash was used, that the extremely low wages were often withheld—and all this with the assent of the provost marshals—is incontrovertible.[53] But the plan did achieve Banks's immediate objective; it made possible the transfer of the hordes of Negroes from the contraband camps to plantations and relieved the government of their support.[54]

In the fall of 1863, as a consequence of the Act of Congress of March 12, 1863, making provision for the control of abandoned and confiscable property by the Treasury Department, agents of the Treasury began to lease the plantations which Banks had turned over to them. The lessees began to sift out the able-bodied Negroes on their plantations and to place the disabled and infirm on unoccupied farms with the expectation that the military authorities would support them. Banks wrote to Halleck in October protesting against this procedure. He contended that since the Treasury had taken over the abandoned

52. The New Orleans *Era*, March 23, 1864. One of the criticisms brought against the system was that only the planters were consulted in the fixing of its terms. Banks, in a denial of this in 1865, said that the only voice which the planters had in the matter was the acceptance or rejection of the plan after it was drawn up. On the other hand twenty intelligent Negroes were sent out to question the slaves as to what they desired in a plan of free labor. *"Their suggestions were implicitly followed."* Letter of Banks to Garrison, Jan. 30, 1865 in *Daily True Delta*, March 19, 1865.

53. Banks to Garrison, Jan. 30, 1865, *Daily True Delta*, March 19, 1865; Report of George H. Hanks, Superintendent of Negro Labor, to General Banks, New Orleans *Era*, March 23, 1864; A. J. H. Duganne, *Twenty Months in the Department of the Gulf*, p. 42. In its issue of Sept. 24, 1864, the New Orleans *Tribune*, organ of the free Negroes of Louisiana, characterized the wages under Banks's system in 1863 as "unreasonably and unjustly low; so low as not to be wages at all." Wages ranged from $3 to $10 a month. *Annual Cyclopedia* for 1863, p. 594.

54. *Daily True Delta*, March 19, 1865; the New Orleans *Era*, March 23, 1864.

plantations, the only source of income, it was only right that it should also assume the responsibility of supporting the dependent Negroes. Halleck's answer left the solution of this problem up to Banks. The latter issued an order on October 27, requiring that all Negroes coming within the Federal lines should be received and provided for by the provost marshals.[55] This order indicates that the army retained complete responsibility for the care of Negroes not employed on plantations by lessees or owners.

The taking over and leasing of abandoned and confiscable plantations by the Treasury Department had many unhappy consequences in the Department of the Gulf as elsewhere. It created a division of authority which was productive of strife and detrimental to the efficient administration of Negro affairs.

The reception and the disposition of fugitives and captured slaves, and the regulation of labor on plantations worked by loyal owners remained in the hands of General Banks in 1864. He also had a quasi-control over Negroes employed on places leased by the Treasury Department. On February 3, 1864, Banks issued General Order Number 23 setting forth general regulations for plantation labor for the ensuing year. They were characterized by him as "a continuation of the system established January 30, 1863." But the provisions were much more extensive. Provost marshals were to provide for the division of the parishes into police and school districts and to organize a competent police force from invalid soldiers. At least one school was to be established in each district for children under twelve years of age. The lash and other cruel punishments were forbidden. Provost marshals were to settle all disputes between employers and Negroes. Sick and disabled persons were to be provided for on the plantations to which they belonged, except those who were received on places to be provided for them at Baton Rouge and Algiers. A working day was defined as nine hours in winter and ten

55. *O. R.*, Ser. 1, XXVI, pt. 1, 764, 775-777.

hours in summer. Laborers were to receive as compensation —in addition to suitable rations, clothing, quarters, medical attendance, and instruction for their children—wages ranging from three to eight dollars per month. At least one-half of the wages was to be reserved until the end of the year. Wages might be commuted for one-fourteenth of the net proceeds of the crop by the consent of both parties. Pay was to be deducted in case of sickness, and rations also when the illness was feigned. "Indolence, insolence, disobedience of orders, and crime" were to be suppressed by forfeiture of pay and such punishments as were provided "for similar offenses by Army Regulations." Laborers had the free choice of employers, but once having chosen an employer they were required to remain with him for the entire year. Those who feigned sickness or stubbornly refused to work were to be turned over to the provost marshals for labor on the public works without pay. Each laborer was to be allowed a small plot of ground for cultivation on his own account. Overseers who insisted on mistreating Negroes were to be punished with reduced wages and diminished rations. In cases where owners or overseers used undue influence to move the provost marshals from their just balance, a change of officers was to be made.[56]

During the year covered by these regulations the administration of Negro affairs was directed by a Bureau of Free Labor headed by a superintendent who acted under the authority of the commanding general of the department. The bureau was the outgrowth of a commission of three appointed by Banks in August, 1863, to assume general charge of the labor, education, and enlistment of Negroes.[57] One of the commissioners, George H. Hanks, later became superintendent of the Bureau of Free Labor. He held this position until August, 1864, when he was succeeded by Thomas W. Conway.

56. *Ibid.*, XXXIV, pt. 2, 227–231.
57. *Ibid.*, XXVI, pt. 1, 704. The commissioners were Col. John S. Clark, B. Rush Plumly, and George H. Hanks.

The system promulgated in February, 1864, by General Banks received criticism from both planters and Northerners hardly less severe than that of the previous year. Wendell Phillips thought that the Negroes were held in a state of "serfdom."[58] The radical Eastern press saw nothing but evil in the plan. The free Negro element of Louisiana added its protests through the columns of its organ, the New Orleans *Tribune*. The editor said that Banks in his General Order Number 23 "used language that even the most tyrannical monarchs of Spain, when she was *the* power on land and sea, never made use of . . . using the word insolence in a public order . . . is a clear proof that he is not a republican. . . . It is useless to discuss here the merits of the different orders issued by that officer, for all know that they have failed to be of any benefit to the colored laborers."[59]

The Banks program was not without friends, however, even in the East. The New York *Times* of July 23, 1864, carried an article in answer to a charge of Greeley's *Tribune* that the wages paid the Negroes were too low. The writer made a detailed analysis of compensation to show that when all factors were considered—fuel, shelter, clothing, food, free education, and medical treatment—the Louisiana Negroes were better paid than Eastern laborers.[60]

The report of Thomas Conway, Superintendent of Negro Labor, for the year ending February 1, 1865, indicates the degree of success achieved under General Order Number 23 in making the Negroes self-supporting. Of the ninety thousand freedmen under the care of the Bureau of Free Labor during the year, only one thousand, on the average, were supported by the government. The amount spent for their subsistence and care was $113,426.40—an

58. Letter of Col. B. Rush Plumly to William Lloyd Garrison in New Orleans *Era*, Oct. 13, 1864. Banks and his friends worked diligently to convince Garrison of the "anti-slavery orthodoxy" of the labor system. *Daily True Delta*, Feb. 23, 1865.

59. Issue of Oct. 12, 1864.

60. New York *Times*, July 23, 1864, quoted by the New Orleans *Era*, Aug. 2, 1864.

average of $9,452.20 per month. In January, 1863, $60,-000 had been spent for the support of Negroes by the government. The number of freedmen on plantations which were managed by the bureau during the year was fifty thousand, distributed on fifteen hundred farms. "Though the year was marked by unparallelled disaster to agricultural interests," according to Conway, there would "not be more than one per-cent of the plantations where payment will not be secured to the freedmen." Planters were not allowed to sell their crops until they gave satisfactory evidence that they had paid their laborers.[61]

The status of the Negroes in the loyal districts of Louisiana was changed in September, 1864, by the adoption of a new Constitution which declared slavery to be abolished throughout the State. Banks had anticipated this action in January by the issuance of a proclamation in which he declared the laws recognizing and regulating slavery to be inoperative and void.[62] Attorney General B. L. Lynch recognized the validity of this action. The courts, as a rule, adopted the attitude that the slaves were free, but this opinion was not unanimous. They were "in much confusion" on the subject until the adoption of the new Constitution.[63]

The latter part of 1864 witnessed a renewal of the conflict between the Treasury and War Departments in regard to Negro affairs. Since the placing in their hands of the control of abandoned and confiscated plantations, in March, 1863, Treasury officials had been insistent that they should also be given the direction of freedmen. On July 2, 1864, Congress gave the Treasury Department authority to assume this direction, and on July 29, the Secretary of the Treasury issued an order setting up a system of administration and prescribing regulations for the control of contrabands.[64]

No steps were taken immediately for the transfer of the

61. *O. R.*, Ser. 1, XLVIII, pt. 1, 703–710.
62. The New Orleans *Era*, Jan. 12, 1864.
63. *Ibid.*, July 8, 1865.   64. *Treasury Regulations*, 1864.

care of the freedmen to the Treasury in the Department of the Gulf. But in September or October, General Hurlbut, commanding the department during the absence of Banks, in obedience to orders from his superior, General Canby, notified B. F. Flanders, the newly appointed special supervising agent of the First Special Agency, to take charge of the Negroes in the Department of the Gulf.[65] On October 26, Flanders wrote Hurlbut that he was ready to take over control of the freedmen in accordance with the Treasury regulations of July 29.[66] On October 28, Hurlbut issued General Order Number 156 providing for the transfer of authority and of all property used for the care of freedmen as rapidly as unfinished business of the Bureau of Free Labor for the current year could be concluded.[67] Flanders wrote the Secretary of the Treasury on October 28 stating that, in his opinion, the rates of compensation prescribed in the regulations of July 29, 1864, were improperly fixed and asking that he be given authority to change them. His letter remained unanswered until November 26, when the Assistant Secretary wrote that "the Treasury Department has not yet assumed charge of the Freedmen. When it does your suggestion will receive consideration." General Canby, to whom Flanders sent a copy of this letter on January 6, 1865, wrote the Secretary of War that he had already transferred the freedmen to Flanders' care, but that he considered the Assistant Secretary's letter a repudiation by the Treasury not only of that transfer, but also of the law of July 2 and of the regulations of July 29.[68] The Treasury agents evidently did not take this view of the matter. Flanders sent two men to Washington to ascertain the exact status of affairs. In the meantime plans were pushed forward to develop Treasury control.

On February 1, 1865, W. P. Mellen, general agent of

65. *O. R.,* Ser. 1, XLVIII, pt. 1, 1049.
66. *Ibid.,* p. 492.
67. New Orleans *Times,* Oct. 30, 1864.
68. *O. R.,* Ser. 1, XLVIII, pt. 1, 492–493.

the Treasury Department, and Flanders' superior, issued
a pronouncement from his headquarters in New Orleans
declaring the regulations of the Treasury of July 29,
1864, to be in force and prescribing a set of additional
local rules governing the leasing of plantations. Leases of
abandoned and confiscable farms were to be made by proper
Treasury agents to loyal persons. Lessees were to agree to
conform to the regulations of July 29, 1864. All well-
disposed owners residing in Federal lines and employing
freedmen were to register their plantations with the supervising special agents and to file agreements to abide by the
Treasury regulations and local rules. Mellen's regulations
were accompanied by an order of General Canby, bearing
the same date, requiring their observance by military authorities. Officers of the army in control of the freedmen
were to remain at their posts until they were relieved by
agents of the Treasury Department.[69]

The leasing and registration of plantations according
to those regulations went forward through February and
the early days of March. But, for some reason, Mellen's
rules did not receive the approval of the Secretary of the
Treasury. As a consequence they were replaced by rules
promulgated by General Hurlbut in General Order Number 23, dated March 11, 1865.[70] The new regulations were
very similar to the ones prescribed by Banks the previous
year. They differed from those which they replaced chiefly
in the matter of compensation for labor. The scale of wages
set up by the Treasury was for males, $25, $20, and $15
per month, and for females, $18, $14, and $10, classified
according to ages; laborers were to purchase their own
food and clothing from a supply which the employer was
required to keep on hand. The scale of wages substituted
by Hurlbut was for males, $10, $8, and $6 per month, and
for females $8, $6, and $5, classified, not according to age,
but according to merit; employers were to furnish food
and clothing.

69. *Daily True Delta,* Feb. 5, 1865.
70. *O. R.,* Ser. 1, XLVIII, pt. 1, 1146 ff.

The failure of the Secretary of the Treasury to approve Mellen's program for the care of the freedmen in the Department of the Gulf was probably due to several factors. In the first place, he was reluctant for the Treasury to assume the burden of supporting those incapacitated for work on account of age, infirmity, or sickness. The experiences of the Treasury agents with a home farm for dependents in the Department of the Mississippi the previous year had not been encouraging.[71] It is also probable that the secretary was doubtful of the full support of the military authorities in carrying out the Treasury regulations—and success could not be achieved without this support. Few, if any, of the higher officers were in sympathy with Treasury control of either abandoned plantations or freedmen. They were of the opinion that the agents and lessees were unduly influenced by the profit motive.[72] Then, too, it is doubtful if authorities at Washington were satisfied with the plan of control proposed by Mellen. A set of regulations which he had previously drawn up in conjunction with James Yeatman for the control of freedmen in Mississippi had been set aside on Lincoln's recommendation.[73]

Planters and military officers had found much fault with both the terms and the administration of the Treasury plan. Both Hurlbut and Banks thought that the system of compensation, though offering apparently high wages, would reduce the Negroes to a state of peonage on account of the provision requiring them to purchase their food and

71. Eaton, *Grant, Lincoln, and the Freedmen*, p. 162.

72. Letter of Banks to Garrison, Jan. 30, 1865, in *Daily True Delta*, March 19, 1865; Letter of Hurlbut to Christensen, *O. R.*, Ser. 1, XLVIII, pt. 1, 1049.

73. *O. R.*, Ser. 3, IV, 143. Lincoln may have been the cause of the disapproval of these regulations. Christensen, Canby's adjutant general, wrote Hurlbut, March 2, 1865, "The President's orders of February 10, and the instructions of the Secretary of the Treasury of February 3, virtually suspend all the action under the regulation promulgated in G. O. No. 13." G. O. No. 13, was Canby's order of Feb. 1, 1865, accompanying the Treasury regulations and ordering their observance.

clothing from their employers.[74] The planters thought the
wages unreasonable, or unfairly fixed. They feared that
the transfer of authority from the provost marshals would
make necessary discipline impossible.[75] The criticism of the
administration of the Treasury regulations by Flanders
and his assistants was no less severe. Hurlbut wrote Adjutant General Christensen March 1, 1865: "I cannot avoid
stating in the plainest terms that there has been a degree of
trifling and inefficiency on the part of the Treasury Department that is likely to work most serious consequences."[76]
The editor of the New Orleans *Daily True Delta*, upon being informed of the taking of the control of Negro affairs
from the Treasury agents, wrote: "The incompetency of
the special supervising agent of the Treasury in this Department is clearly and forcibly illustrated in his ignomini-
ous failure to manage the system of plantation labor. Incompetency is the most charitable construction that can be
placed upon this failure, for there are not wanting those
who believe it was more the result of vast schemes of speculation for self-enrichment than of paucity of intellect."[77]

There was a marked improvement in plantation affairs
after the issuance of General Hurlbut's regulations and
the resumption of control by the Bureau of Free Labor.
Planters who had given up in despair under the former
arrangement now went ahead with their crops; thousands
of Negroes who had been unemployed were put to work on
the plantations.[78] "Prospects that had been blighted," according to Conway, the Superintendent of Negro Labor,
"began to revive, and now [March 29, 1865] I cannot find
a single laborer whose labor I can secure for any purpose.
. . . There is the most satisfactory state of things in this
branch of the public service."[79]

74. *O. R.*, Ser. 1, XLVIII, pt. 1, 1049; Banks to Garrison, Jan. 30, 1865,
in *Daily True Delta*, March 19, 1865.
75. New Orleans *Times*, Nov. 22, 1864 and March 15, 1865.
76. *O. R.*, Ser. 1, XLVIII, pt. 1, 1049.
77. *Daily True Delta*, March 14, 1865.
78. New Orleans *Times*, March 15, 1865.
79. *O. R.*, Ser. 1, XLVIII, pt. 1, 1290.

Very similar to the difficulties experienced by Banks in the administration of Negro affairs in Louisiana were those met by John Eaton in supervising contraband activities in Mississippi, Tennessee, and Arkansas from 1862 to 1865. Many of Eaton's troubles of 1862 and 1863 grew out of the fact that he had no military standing, that he lacked effective means of enforcing his orders, and that his authority was not defined with sufficient clarity. In the fall of 1863, Adjutant General Lorenzo Thomas, acting under authority of the War Department, issued a series of orders calculated to remedy this situation and to make Eaton's powers as superintendent of freedmen adequate to meet his rapidly increasing responsibilities. His first step was to appoint Eaton colonel of a Negro regiment which was then in process of formation. This regiment and another one of like character which was formed a month later were placed at the disposal of the superintendent for the protection of the freedmen in the camps and on the plantations against Confederate raids. Eaton's chief assistants were given commissions in these two regiments.[80] Thomas's next step was the issuance of a special order on November 5 defining the extent of Eaton's jurisdiction. By the provisions of this order, all the Negroes in the Department of the Tennessee, including Arkansas and Mississippi, were placed under his control as general superintendent of freedmen; he was to provide employment for them in camps or on plantations; rations were to be issued to them on his requisition; he was to have supervision of all permits and contracts for labor with private parties, including lessees and owners of plantations; he was to see that the inviolability of these agreements was respected; all assistant superintendents were to be subject to his order.[81]

Shortly after the issuance of the above order, Eaton divided the territory under his supervision into three units; the District of West Tennessee with office at Memphis; the District of Arkansas with office at Little Rock and sub-

80. Eaton, *Grant, Lincoln, and the Freedmen*, pp. 107–109.
81. *Ibid.*, p. 111.

offices at Helena, Pine Bluff, Duval's Bluff, and Fort Smith; the District of Vicksburg with office at Vicksburg and suboffices at Natchez, Davis Bend, Vidalia, and Goodrich Landing. A superintendent was placed over each one of these districts. Colonel Samuel Thomas, whom Eaton had previously appointed as his first assistant, was placed in charge of the important district of Vicksburg. In addition to making this territorial subdivision of administration, Eaton also appointed three assistants, each of whom was to be responsible for one of the following interests: the control of property, the supply of medicines, and the direction of education.[82] The magnitude of Eaton's responsibility is indicated by the fact that at the beginning of 1864 his supervision extended over a territory along the Mississippi from Cairo to Milliken's Bend, populated according to the census of 1860, by 770,000 Negroes.[83]

Eaton's new system of organization had hardly been set up before complications arose with the Treasury Department which threatened to take control of freedmen out of his hands. In furtherance of an act of March 12, 1863, the Secretary of War issued a general order on October 9 directing that all abandoned property, except that required for strictly military purposes, be turned over to the supervising agents of the Treasury Department. In January 1864, W. P. Mellen, general agent of the Treasury Department, called upon James Yeatman, president of the Western Sanitary Commission, to assist him in drawing up a set of regulations under which the Treasury proposed to take charge of the leasing of plantations and to assume the control of labor thereon.[84] Yeatman's coöperation was asked on the strength of a plan which he had drawn up in December, 1863, for the leasing of plantations

---

82. *Ibid.*, pp. 125–126. As to education, Eaton says that his plans were defeated during nine months by circumstances over which he had no control.

83. John Eaton, *Report of the General Superintendent of Freedmen, Department of the Tennessee and State of Arkansas for 1864*, p. 3. To be cited hereafter as Eaton, *Report for 1864*.

84. Eaton, *Grant, Lincoln, and the Freedmen*, pp. 143, 145.

and the governance of freedmen in the country bordering upon the Mississippi.[85] The basic aim of the Yeatman-Mellen regulations, issued in January over Mellen's signature, seems to have been the correction of the objectionable features of the rules promulgated by General Thomas the previous year, which rules they were to replace.[86] In order to alleviate the injustices and difficulties resulting from the employment of overseers, no person was to be permitted to lease more than one plantation; under Thomas's plan one lessee had been in possession of five plantations.[87] Preference was to be given lessees of small tracts. A scale of wages much higher than those previously paid was prescribed.[88] Employers were required to keep on hand a supply of wholesome food and suitable clothing to be sold to the laborers at wholesale cost price, plus 15 per cent. Freedmen's home colonies were to be established at convenient points as places for the collection, registration, and placement of laborers, and as homes for those unable to work. Superintendents of these home colonies were to have oversight of the making of contracts and responsibility for their fulfilment. To help defray the cost of supporting the nonlaborers, each employer was to pay a tax of one cent on each pound of cotton produced. Lessees were required to pay an additional cent per pound as rent.

These regulations, "theoretically better" according to Eaton, than those they replaced, were in practice subject to serious difficulties.[89] Most of these grew out of a lack of understanding and coöperation between the Treasury and the army. In the words of Eaton, "the army was powerless

85. See James E. Yeatman, *Suggestions of a Plan of Organization for Freed Labor and the Leasing of Plantations along the Mississippi River,* pp. 3–8.

86. *Second Annual Report of the New England Freedmen's Aid Society,* pp. 74–77, Appendix.

87. Knox, *Camp-Fire and Cotton-Field,* p. 318.

88. Wages prescribed by the Mellen-Yeatman regulations were: for first-class male hands, $25 per month; second class, $20; third class, $15; for first-class females, $18; second class, $14; and third class, $10.

89. Eaton, *Grant, Lincoln, and the Freedmen,* p. 147.

to assert authority over affairs controlled by the Treasury; the Treasury had no vehicle at its command whereby to enforce its own authority in a district where martial law was the only law, and the result was that in too many cases no authority was exercised at all."[90] The situation was complicated by the fact that Treasury officials ordered a revocation of all the agreements which Adjutant General Thomas had made with the planters, and required them to secure new leases from the Treasury and subscribe to the Mellen-Yeatman regulations.[91] Many of the planters, regarding the Treasury system as impracticable, refused to comply therewith. A great many of them gave up their leases and turned the Negroes back upon the military authorities for support.

Colonel Eaton made a trip to Chattanooga in February, 1864, to report the disturbed situation to Adjutant General Thomas. The latter, on February 20, wrote Secretary Stanton a long letter warning him that if Mellen were permitted to put aside the system which he and Eaton had set up and which experience had proved practicable, many plantations would be abandoned and thousands of Negroes thrown upon the government for support. "I consider the Negroes under my control," he wrote, "furnishing of course labor under the calls of the Treasury agents; but Mr. Mellen assumes that they are entirely under him, and he desires to issue orders accordingly. The military authorities must have command of the Negroes or there will be an endless confusion. I will keep this control unless ordered to the contrary."[92] On February 27, Thomas sent Stanton a wire from Louisville stating that if the Treasury agent should insist on carrying out his regulations

90. *Ibid.*, p. 149.
91. In the latter part of October Thomas had begun to lease plantations for the coming year, dating the contracts from February 1, 1864. His haste in making these leases might indicate that he was attempting to forestall the Treasury agents who had not yet assumed control. *O. R.*, Ser. 3, III, 939–940; Knox, *Camp-Fire and Cotton-Field*, p. 319; *Daily Picayune*, Dec. 25, 1863, quoting New York *Journal of Commerce*.
92. *O. R.*, Ser. 3, IV, 112.

none of the blacks would be provided for, but that if military control be continued there was "yet time to lease
plantations by the Treasury agent and provide for a vast
amount of labor." The next day President Lincoln saw
this dispatch. He immediately wired Thomas as follows: "I
wish you would go to the Mississippi River at once and
take hold of and be master in the contraband and leasing
business. . . . Mr. Mellen's system doubtless is well intended, but from what I hear, I fear that if persisted in it
would fall dead within its own entangling details. Go there
and be the judge."[93]

In obedience to this order Thomas went immediately to
Vicksburg. After a series of interviews with Mellen he issued General Order Number 9 on March 11 in which he
promulgated a series of regulations based on those issued
by General Banks the previous month for the Department
of the Gulf in General Order Number 23. Mellen and his assistants retained control of the leasing of abandoned plantations, but all the Negroes, including those on plantations
leased from the Treasury, were placed under the supervision of Eaton and other military authorities to be governed by the regulations prescribed in General Order
Number 9. The chief difference of the new regulations
from those issued by Mellen was in the matter of the compensation of laborers and the enforcement of justice. The
minimum wage for males over fourteen was reduced to ten
dollars a month and for women of the same age to seven
dollars a month. Employers were to furnish food and clothing.[94] Provost marshals were to be distributed at convenient
points to perform police duties and to decide all questions
between employers and Negroes.[95] Leases which had been
made by the Treasury Department of lands in exposed
districts were not revoked, but instead, an attempt was

93. *O. R.*, Ser. 3, IV, 143.
94. Thomas thought that Mellen's plan to have the Negroes feed themselves "was simply a license to run all over the country stealing." *Ibid.*,
p. 235.
95. *Ibid.*, pp. 166 ff.

made to extend military protection to them. In many instances this proved unsuccessful, especially after the removal of a great number of troops to take part in operations in the East, and, as a result, the Negroes were forced
to take refuge in freedmen's camps.[96]

With the exception of these disturbances in peripheral
areas, plantation affairs, after a period of confusion resulting from the transfer of authority, returned to nor-
malcy under military supervision in the Mississippi Valley.[97] In July, 1864, Eaton reported 113,650 freedmen
under his supervision. Of these, 41,150 were in military
service as soldiers, laundresses, cooks, officers' servants,
and laborers in various staff departments. Those working
in towns and on plantations as planters, mechanics, bar-
bers, draymen, hackmen, conducting enterprises on their
own responsibility, or working as hired laborers numbered
62,300. These were all self-supporting. The remaining
10,200 received subsistence from the government; of these,
3,000 were members of families whose heads were cultivating plantations on which some 4,000 acres of cotton were
planted; they were to pay the government for supporting
them from their first sale of cotton. The other 7,200 were
paupers—those too old or too young to work, the crippled,
and the sick—who had no self-supporting near relatives
to provide for them.[98] Most of these were cared for in contraband camps or freedmen's villages at Columbus (Kentucky), Helena, Memphis, Shipwell's Landing, Goodrich's
Landing, Milliken's Bend, Paw Paw Island, Young's
Point, Vicksburg, Davis Bend—the plantations of Joe
Davis, Jefferson Davis, Turner, and Quitman were confiscated and set aside for the exclusive benefit of the Negroes
—Natchez, and Vidalia; others were provided for on in-
firmary farms, several of which were located in the vicinity
of Goodrich's Landing.[99] Not all the 10,200 Negroes for

96. Eaton, *Grant, Lincoln, and the Freedmen,* p. 155.
97. *Ibid.*   98. *Ibid.,* p. 134.
99. Yeatman, *Report on the Condition of the Freedmen of the Mississippi,* Dec. 17, 1863, pp. 1–13. To be cited hereafter as Yeatman, *Report.*

whom the government provided subsistence were unproductive; in July, 1864, this class had under cultivation 500 acres of corn, 790 acres of vegetables, and 1,500 acres of cotton, besides working at wood-chopping and other pursuits.[100] Seven thousand acres of cotton were cultivated by colored lessees in 1864, some of them managing as high as three or four hundred acres. Most of this cotton was marketed for the Negroes by H. B. Spelman, father-in-law of John D. Rockefeller and president of the Cleveland Freedmen Aid Commission.[101]

In the support of dependents Eaton received much valuable assistance, especially in the provision of clothing, from the Freedmen's Aid Societies. The Western Sanitary Commission was the most active of these operating in the Mississippi Valley. The clothing of deceased soldiers was also turned over to Eaton for the use of destitute freedmen by order of the War Department.[102] A tax was levied for a time on the wages of the able-bodied Negroes for the support of dependents. A large sum of money was realized from this tax, which the freedmen paid with evident willingness.[103]

A resurgence of the controversy with the Treasury Department seemed inevitable as a result of the act of July 2, 1864, extending the jurisdiction of the Treasury over freedmen and the issuance of regulations to that effect on July 29 by Secretary Fessenden. In August Eaton went to Washington to present the conflicting state of affairs regarding the control of Negroes in the Mississippi Valley to the President. After listening to his story Lincoln sent him to the Secretary of the Treasury. Fessenden being out of the city at the time, Eaton secured an audience with Assistant Secretary Harrington and pointed out to him "the harm and confusion sure to result from a transfer so untimely and so unprovided for."[104] A short time afterward,

100. Eaton, *Grant, Lincoln, and the Freedmen*, p. 134.
101. *Ibid.*, pp. 129–130.   102. Eaton, *Report for 1864*, p. 12.
103. Eaton, *Grant, Lincoln, and the Freedmen*, pp. 127–128.
104. *Ibid.*, p. 169.

partly as a result of Eaton's representation, and partly as a consequence of reports made to Washington by Senator Washburne and General Wadsworth, both of whom had inspected affairs in Eaton's department, Harrington addressed an order to Mellen suspending all action under the regulations of July 29.[105] On August 23, the Assistant Secretary wrote Eaton that Fessenden had approved "the suspension of the Regulations whereby this Department contemplated taking immediate control of the Freedmen. . . . In directing such suspension, it was the expectation and desire of the Department that the system and arrangements . . . now being prosecuted under you should be continued without interruption until the crops now in are gathered and the present season closed, and until this Department is prepared in all respects to assume such control under the law."[106] The Treasury regulations of July 29, 1864, never went into effect in the districts under Eaton's superintendence. The situation in respect to the control of freedmen remained as it had been fixed by Thomas's General Order Number 9 until the Freedmen's Bureau assumed authority in 1865.[107]

The difficulty and dissatisfaction accruing from attempts of the Treasury Department to acquire jurisdiction over contrabands, whether in North Carolina and Virginia, in South Carolina, or in the Mississippi Valley, make inescapable the conclusion that freedmen's affairs would have been much more successfully administered if they had been left entirely in the hands of the military authorities.

105. *Ibid.*, p. 170.   106. *Ibid.*, p. 171.
107. *Ibid.*, p. 172.

XIII

WORKING FOR WAGES

THE great majority of Negroes who came under Federal control during the war were plantation laborers. The disturbance and disorder incident to invasion and occupation released many of them for a time from both plantations and labor. But the respite was, as a rule, not of long duration. While freedom was yet in its infancy most of the Negroes found themselves back at work in the fields. Coercion by military authorities was usually not lacking in cases where Negroes were reluctant to resume their agrarian tasks. If "Yankee" soldiers were voluble as to the joys of freedom, the orders issued by their generals were irrefutable evidence that leisure was not among the attributive blessings.

The treatment of the laborers under Federal administration, however, whether under old or new masters, was not the same as before, though the differences were often more apparent than real. One of the most immediate, and certainly in the eyes of the blacks, one of the most significant changes was the payment of wages for labor. The first Negroes to receive money as a result of the war for work done on plantations seem to have been the abandoned slaves in the vicinity of Port Royal, South Carolina, who were put to work picking cotton by agents of the Treasury Department in the latter part of 1861. In the summer of 1862 Butler set up a wage system for plantations in Louisiana. As the war progressed, the ideas of freedom and wages became so closely associated in the minds of the Negroes that planters in regions threatened with Federal invasion were forced to begin payment for labor to prevent their workers from running away.

The rate of compensation for plantation labor varied greatly at different times and in different sections. As a rule, minimum wages, effective for a year or a season, were prescribed by commanders of the various military departments or their representatives. In most cases a specified share of the crop might be substituted for money payments by the mutual agreement of employer and employees. There was a tendency toward a higher minimum wage after the first year of the war, partly as a result of rising prices and partly on account of the demands of the Negroes and their friends at the North.

The lowest minimum scale was that established by General Thomas for Grant's department in 1863. Those wages —$7 a month for men and $5 a month for women, less the cost of clothing—were pitiably low; so low in fact as not to constitute real wages. According to the average planter's interpretation of Thomas's order, he was required to pay the Negro only for the actual days' work done at the rate of $7 for a month's work of twenty-six days or 27 cents a day. If a laborer, on account of disability, or, on account of the failure of the planter to provide something for him to do, worked but ten days during the month, he received but $2.70 for his month's labor.[1] This amount might be further diminished by deductions for clothing, and for the support of dependents. In more than one instance the year ended with a balance against the laborers. A planter near Vicksburg told Fiske at the end of the 1864 season that he did not know what to do about discharging his hands, they were so much in debt to him; yet he "had not paid them a dime of money."[2]

The situation in the Vicksburg district was possibly worse than it was in other sections. The country was more exposed to Confederate raids. Sickness seems to have been more prevalent than elsewhere. The time lost on account of both sickness and invasion was usually borne by the laborers. A great proportion of the Negroes came to the plantations in destitution, therefore requiring the expenditure of a portion of their earnings for food, clothing, uten-

1. Yeatman, *Report*, p. 8.   2. Eaton, *Report for 1864*, p. 35.

sils, and other articles, in addition to the supplies furnished by the planters. Then, too, the fact that supervision of plantation affairs in that area was not as close as it was in some other localities made the Negroes more liable to injustices.

The compensation received by the Negroes depended more upon the spirit in which the regulations were carried out than upon the regulations themselves. In cases where both the planters and the subordinate officers appointed to see that justice was enforced placed liberal interpretations upon the requirements, the blacks received wages not incommensurate with their labor. General Banks, in answer to criticism brought against the scale prescribed by him, pointed out that the common laborer in the Department of the Gulf would receive in rations, clothing, medicine, quarters, fuel, and education for his children the equivalent of more than $300 a year. When the amount of his money wages and the value of the products raised on his garden allotment were added to this, his compensation for the year's labor amounted to a sum ranging from $400 to $500. "It is doubtful," he said, "if unskilled labor is more liberally compensated in this or any other country."[3] Banks's testimony is corroborated by that of others who were familiar with the provisions of his Louisiana system.[4]

But there was sometimes a marked difference between compensation as prescribed in regulations and that actually received by the Negroes on plantations. Employers whose sole concern was to make money were ingenious at finding ways to reduce payments, and this wholly within the prescribed rules, according to their interpretation. Provost marshals, whose function was to see that regulations were complied with, were often won over to the planters' view-

3. Banks, *Emancipated Labor in Louisiana*, pp. 14–15.
4. See the New Orleans *Era*, Sept. 11, 1864. An article in the New York *Times* of July 23, 1864, contained a detailed analysis of Banks's plan of compensation. The contributor concluded that the amount paid the average Negro laborer was in excess of the average received not only by New York's white laborers, but even by her rural school teachers. Quoted by the *Era*, Aug. 2, 1864.

point by personal favors and other considerations.⁵ The situation is well illustrated by a case in Louisiana as described by a New York cavalryman who was quartered for a time on Manning's Plantation, Ascension Parish. "The provost marshals and lessees," he said, "are linked together in the scheme to defraud the Negro. . . . The manager of this plantation agreed to pay the Negroes under him $5 per month, and give them abundant allowances of corn meal and bacon with other articles of food. When paying them off the other day, he would say to this one that he had not hoed his cotton well, and to another that he was not quick enough in getting out in the morning, and to another that his or her mules were not promptly on the spot when the sun rose in the east, and so on through the whole list of three or four hundred hands, giving to some 50 cents, to others $1, and so on up to $3, and very seldom indeed overrunning the last amount."⁶

There were some employers, however, who exceeded the conditions prescribed in government regulations in the matter of compensation of their hands. Among these was E. S. Philbrick, a Massachusetts business man who went to South Carolina as a plantation superintendent in 1862 and who, with a group of associates, bought nine plantations in 1863. The pay specified by General Saxton in 1863 was 25 cents a task for hoeing and planting; Philbrick paid 35 cents. In 1864 the government's requirement was 30 cents a task, and Philbrick paid 40 cents. In addition, premiums amounting to 15 cents a pound were paid for harvesting the cotton. Many Negroes made considerable extra money by the sale of hogs, chickens, and eggs. The average family

5. James McKaye, *The Emancipated Slave Face to Face with His Old Master*, p. 26; Duganne, *Twenty Months in the Department of the Gulf*, pp. 42–43, 51. Duganne denounced the delinquent provost marshals severely, referring to them as "overseers in pay of the Federal Treasury." So prevalent did the use of bribery and cajolery on the part of the overseers become that an article was inserted in Banks's General Order No. 23 providing for the removal of the provost marshal in cases where "undue influence" was used to move him from his "just balance" between capital and labor. *O. R.*, Ser. 1, XXXIV, pt. 2, 230.

6. New Orleans *Tribune*, Oct. 22, 1864, quoting New York *Tribune*.

of a man, wife, and two children twelve and fifteen years of age who worked for him in 1864 would earn, according to Philbrick, the equivalent of $380.[7]

When they first began to receive payment for their work, the Negroes had little idea of the meaning and value of money. A plantation superintendent in South Carolina, on beginning the fall payment of his hands for cotton picking, asked "Old Nancy," as he placed $40 in her hands, how much she thought it was. "Me dunno, massa;" she replied, "you knows." "As much as ten dollars?" "Oh yes, massa;" she answered, "I tink you give me more nor dat." A smile spread over her face as he counted out the money for her. She received it quietly. Others were more demonstrative than "Nancy." When "Sinnit" was paid she lifted up her hands and eyes and said, "Tank de Lord; I must go praise." "Old Grace," on being informed that the pay received by her was for the cultivation and picking of an entire bale, exclaimed, "Good God, me lib to raise bale o' cotton! Come along, Tim, less get some vittle."[8] An octogenarian Negro when handed a small bill by a South Carolina superintendent asked, "Dem figures on dare, dey Uncle Sam's wife?"[9]

The Negroes' possession of their newly acquired money was of short duration. Those on Philbrick's plantations spent fifteen hundred dollars in three days at his store immediately after the reception of a new stock of goods in the fall of 1863. One woman spent forty dollars at a single visit to the store. Gaudy bandanas and flashy calicoes were purchased in great quantities. Domestic wares were also eagerly sought after; and among these, trunks were in greatest demand.[10]

"Sharpers" were not lacking to take advantage of the Negroes' ignorance of financial matters. A group of Fed-

7. Letter of Philbrick to editors of the New York *Evening Post*, Feb. 24, 1864, in *Second Annual Report of the New England Freedmen's Aid Society*, p. 58

8. Pearson, *Letters from Port Royal*, p. 222.

9. N. Y. *Times*, June 21, 1863.

10. Pearson, *Letters from Port Royal*, p. 233.

eral soldiers who bivouacked for a time in St. Mary's Parish, Louisiana, told the Negroes on one of the plantations that "Massa Lincoln" wanted to borrow all their gold and silver for three months until a high official came up the bayou; this officer would give their gold and silver back to them and also turn over to them the white people's houses and gardens. As guarantee of the fulfilment of their promises they gave the gullible laborers certificates in exchange for their money. These were nothing more than square pieces of tissue paper with a soapmaker's advertisement printed thereon. In this manner the Negroes were relieved of eight hundred dollars. They spent much time and energy washing white garments that they might be fitly clad to greet the emissary of Lincoln, "de high ossifer," as they termed him. But much to their perplexity, he never came.[11]

In spite of the Negroes' lack of familiarity with finance they soon learned to complain about the wages which they received and to demand increases. They were often coached to raise objections by well-meaning, but sometimes ill-advised, friends from the North. In a public address to a South Carolina group in January, 1864, a Mr. Hunn condoled the Negroes on the small pay which they received saying, "What's 30 cents a day in these times for a man who has to maintain himself and his family?" This observation caused a great commotion among the Negroes. They responded with mutterings of "that's so."[12] A few days later a group of women came to Philbrick complaining about

11. Duganne, *Twenty Months in the Department of the Gulf*, pp. 104 ff. General Saxton, "military governor" of South Carolina, wrote to Secretary Stanton in December, 1864, that the army of occupation was generally unfriendly to the blacks; that this feeling was manifested in "personal insult and abuse, in depredations on their plantations, stealing and destroying their crops and domestic animals, and robbing them of their money. The women were held as a legitimate prey of lust. . . . There was a general disposition among the soldiers and civilian speculators here to defraud the Negroes in their private traffic, to take the commodities . . . by force or to pay for them in worthless money. At one time, these practices were so frequent and notorious that the Negroes would not bring their produce to market for fear of being plundered." *O. R.*, Ser. 3, IV, 1029.

12. Pearson, *Letters from Port Royal*, p. 244.

their pay, though he had just recently raised the average daily wage for adults from about 50 cents to 60 cents.[13] Complaints were made intermittently throughout 1864. When the time came for beginning the new crops in 1865, some of the laborers demanded a rate of compensation more than twice as great as that which they had been receiving. When Philbrick remonstrated with them for the excessiveness of their demands, one of them said that he knew "very well they had been jamming the bills into that big iron cage [meaning Philbrick's safe] for six months, and there must be enough in it now to bust it." Philbrick refused to raise the pay of his laborers, being of the opinion that, after being idle for a few weeks to think about the matter and to hope for more, they would gradually go to work for the same wages which they had previously received.[14]

The Negroes greatly preferred money to a share of the crop as compensation for their labor. Early in 1865 when Philbrick's employees demanded a large increase in their pay he suggested to them that they accept an interest in the crop in lieu of wages; but they demurred, as they had noticed that more money was in evidence among the laborers who had worked for wages the previous year than among the laborers who had worked for a share of the crop.[15] The native planters were inclined to favor the share-crop system, not only because it involved less risk, but because it was less suggestive of a change in the Negroes' status than the payment of wages. In April, 1865, A. Franklin Pugh of Louisiana tried to get his Negroes to agree to accept one-eighth of the crop as compensation for their labor for the coming season. It seems that they had been working on some kind of share system the previous year as they had complained that "they did not know what they were working for and everybody else's folks had a plenty of money and they had none."[16] They refused to contract to work

13. Pearson, *Letters from Port Royal,* pp. 246, 250.
14. *Ibid.,* pp. 300–301, 304.   15. *Ibid.,* p. 295.
16. Diary of A. Franklin Pugh, entry of April 11, 1865. On Feb. 20, 1865, Pugh wrote: "I have settled with the Negroes today. As was expected they were very much dissatisfied with what they got if I had given

for an interest in the crop for 1865. Pugh wrote in his diary on April 14: "I have agreed with the Negroes today to pay them monthly wages. It was very distasteful to me, but I could do no better. Everybody else has agreed to pay the same and mine would listen to nothing else." Thereafter, Pugh made cash payments quarterly. Each time of settlement was the occasion of much grumbling and muttering of dissatisfaction on the part of the Negroes. By the end of the year Pugh was thoroughly exasperated. "Staid on New Hope plantation all day," he wrote, "preparing to settle with the Negroes. . . . I had almost as lief be shot as to do it, but it must be done."[17]

In 1865 several lessees near Vicksburg decided to experiment with various plans of compensation. On one plantation they agreed to furnish food and rations and to share the proceeds of the crop with the laborers; on another they paid wages at the rate of ten dollars a month, furnishing rations free and reserving one-half the wages until the end of the year; on a third place they paid each laborer one dollar at the end of the day's work and required him to buy his own rations. On the first place the Negroes were wasteful of their rations as they were not responsible for their costs; they were slothful in their labor since there was no prospect of immediate reward; and they felt little individual responsibility for the outcome of the crop. On the second they were more industrious. On the third they were much more frugal and worked with far more zeal than on the other two places.[18]

The treatment of the Negroes as to food and clothing was about as diverse as it was in the matter of wages. It

them the whole crop they would have been equally so. The fact is that they are like children and cannot be satisfied."

17. *Ibid.*, entry of Dec. 7, 1865.

18. Knox, *Camp-Fire and Cotton-Field*, p. 354. Some planters in the Mississippi Valley paid their Negroes by the pound for picking cotton in the fall of 1864 in lieu of the prescribed minimum monthly wage. This plan was generally adopted by planters in Arkansas. L. B. Eaton who inspected conditions in that state late in 1864 said that those who paid their pickers regularly and promptly every week accomplished a third more than those who paid irregularly. Eaton, *Report for 1864*, pp. 66–67.

was governed by practically the same principles. The government regulations for plantation labor usually required the employer to provide suitable food and comfortable clothing. In some cases a cash commutation was allowed for clothing, the planters being required to keep a stock on hand for sale to the Negroes at cost, or at a 10 to 15 per cent advance on wholesale prices. Planters who were possessed of a sense of fairness and justice interpreted these regulations as the government authorities intended and provided as well for their employees as circumstances would permit. Those whose sole motive was to make money evaded the requirements, fed their hands poorly, clothed them scantily, or sold them wearing apparel at exorbitant prices.

The laborers in the country along the Mississippi from Natchez northward seem to have suffered more from lack of proper food and clothing than did those of other localities. This was attributable in part to the frequence of guerrilla raids. Planters were reluctant to stock their plantations with supplies for fear they would be captured or destroyed. Then, the feeling of uncertainty as to the possibility of carrying the crop through to a profitable harvest tended to make employers parsimonious in providing for their laborers. Again, the disturbed condition of the country made it difficult for military authorities to exercise a close supervision over plantation affairs. The chief factor, however, seems to have been the character of the men who planted in this district. They were mostly lessees who had come to the South with the intention of making a quick fortune. James Yeatman, president of the Western Sanitary Commission, who made an inspection of conditions along the Mississippi late in 1863, said of these men: "The parties leasing plantations and leasing these Negroes do it from no motives either of loyalty or humanity. The desire of gain alone prompts them; and they care little whether they make it out of the blood of those they employ or from the soil."[19] The superintendent of freedmen at Natchez was

19. Yeatman, *Report*, p. 8.

bitter in the denunciation of these lessees, "the object of whose highest thought," he said, "is a greenback, whose god is a cotton bale and whose devil is a guerilla."[20]

As one would expect, Negroes working for these men were often hungry and destitute of clothing. A Negro on a plantation in the Vicksburg district told Yeatman that he had been without bread for days; that he was never allowed over four pounds of meat a week; that he had to buy his own flour and get corn where he could find it on abandoned plantations; and that though it was then late fall he had received no pay or clothing since April. Laborers from other plantations gave similar testimony. "None received molasses, rice, or beans, and hominy only when they choose to make it."[21]

Few of the lessees conformed to the intentions of the military authorities in providing garden plots for their employees. In cases where ground was allotted for this purpose some of the Negroes sought to supplement their meager rations by raising vegetables. This attempt "availed them little," according to Chaplain Fiske, "as the soldiers of the neighboring garrisons have been deterred, neither by discipline nor principle, from appropriating the entire product of their labor. The same impossibility has stood in the way of their raising poultry or pigs, privileges from

20. Joseph Warren, compiler, *Extracts from Reports of Superintendents of Freedmen*, First Series, May, 1864, p. 16. T. W. Knox, correspondent of the N. Y. *Herald*, who, with an associate, leased two plantations in Louisiana in 1864, and who seems to have been an exception to the general type, says of lessees of 1863: "The majority were unprincipled men who undertook the enterprise solely as a speculation. They had as little regard for the rights of the Negro as the most brutal slave-holder had ever shown. Very few of them paid the Negroes for their labor except in furnishing them small quantities of goods for which they charged five times the value. . . . Some of the lessees made open boasts of having swindled their Negroes out of their summer's wages by taking advantage of their ignorance. The experiment did not materially improve the condition of the Negro save in the matter of physical treatment. . . . The difference between working for nothing as a slave and working for the same wages under the Yankee was not always perceptible to the unsophisticated Negro." *Camp-Fire and Cotton-Field*, pp. 316–317.

21. Yeatman, *Report*, p. 7.

which in the olden time, they derived no small advantage."
He adds the statement, conservative in the abstract, but
significant when the strong anti-slavery feeling of the time
is considered, that "it is doubtful whether on the whole,
they have lived more bountifully than on well managed
plantations in the past."[22]

Unscrupulous planters frequently charged the laborers
exorbitant prices for clothing. Yeatman said that he saw
shoes which could be purchased at St. Louis for $1 a pair
sold to the Negroes at $2.50, and calicoes which could be
bought at 20 cents to 24 cents sold at 75 cents per yard.
Colonel Samuel Thomas, superintendent of freedmen in the
Vicksburg district, questioned one hundred planters as to
what profit they made on clothing which they sold to their
employees. According to their own testimony, "one-half
sold at cost and transportation; one-quarter at 15 per cent
profit; one-quarter at 25 per cent profit."[23]

Planters in all regions under Federal control, whether
men of principle or speculative adventurers, usually were
confronted with difficulties sufficient to tempt them to be
parsimonious in the treatment of their laborers. Those who
began operations in South Carolina in 1862 were handicapped by a lack of tools, most of which had been taken
away or destroyed by the fugitive owners or by the Negroes. The laborers were restless. They were averse to
planting cotton because it was associated in their minds
with slavery and Federal soldiers had advised them to plant
only food crops; the Negroes had even torn up the gins to
prevent a resumption of cotton culture. The smallpox broke
out early in the season and took a heavy toll from among
the laborers. Employers were unable to begin planting until late in the season. Cotton seed was inferior because no
selection had been made when the crop of the previous year
was sent North to be ginned. On some plantations a profit

22. Eaton, *Report for 1864*, p. 51. Fiske had made an inspection of
plantation conditions in the districts of Natchez, Vicksburg, and Helena
a short time before he made this statement.
23. *Ibid.*, pp. 9, 29.

was made, but, on the whole, the crop of 1862 was not sufficient to pay the year's expenses.[24] There was an improvement of conditions in 1863; but a new difficulty appeared in the conscription of able-bodied colored men for military service. In March when rumors came of General Hunter's order of enlistment, hardly a man slept in his bed for a full week on account of fear of being taken into the army. Negro men were even afraid to go to the superintendent's house to get their pay lest they be trapped.[25] Their fears were not without foundation. Black recruiters, with or without white officers, visited the plantations and forced colored men to go with them from their cabins at night. Those who resisted or tried to run away were sometimes shot. These practices were, of course, very injurious to the planting interests.[26] But in spite of this and other handicaps a fair crop was made in 1863, producing returns sufficient, probably, to pay the deficit of the previous year. In 1864 there were disturbances from "Rebel" raids in some localities but on the whole prospects were good in the summer. In September and October, however, the caterpillars visited the islands and so ravaged the fields as to leave in most localities "less than a 2/3 crop."[27]

In the Mississippi Valley the difficulties of the planters were even greater than those of South Carolina and other localities. This was especially true of the districts along the river from Natchez north. In 1863, the first year of operations under Federal control, planting was retarded because the leases were not made until late in the season. The ground was hastily plowed. Little care was given to the selection of the seed. The lessees, in their eagerness to make

24. Pearson, *Letters from Port Royal*, pp. 83, 99, and *passim;* W. C. Gannett, "The Freedmen at Port Royal," *North American Review*, CI (July, 1865), 17; Pierce, *The Freedmen of Port Royal*, p. 314 and *passim.*
25. Pearson, *Letters from Port Royal*, pp. 173–174.
26. Philbrick wrote of a visit of recruiters to his place during the ginning season of 1863. "This raid," he said, "will break up my ginning on this end of the Island and put it back at least two weeks for the men are so scared that they won't dare to go to work." *Ibid.*, p. 239.
27. Gannett, "The Freedmen at Port Royal," *North American Review*, CI (July, 1865), 18–19.

fortunes, frequently planted much more ground than they could properly cultivate. In the summer "Rebel" raids were frequent; many plantations were stripped of their mules and horses and the Negroes frightened. In some cases work was resumed; in others the crops went to waste. No lessee, according to T. W. Knox, made more than half an ordinary crop and "very few secured even this return."[28]

The early part of the season of 1864 was very dry; and as a result the planters did not get their crops in the ground until April. Bad seed necessitated replanting in a number of instances. Many difficulties grew out of the fact that most of the lessees were unaccustomed to cotton farming. There was much loss of time from sickness due in large measure to lack of proper food and clothing and a disregard of principles of sanitation. Guerrilla raids were even more frequent and destructive than the previous year on account of the withdrawal of many Federal garrisons and the penetration of planters into exposed localities. From 95 plantations which Chaplain Fiske inspected in the districts of Natchez, Vicksburg, and Helena, 2,134 head of stock and 967 Negroes were taken. Most of these losses were from plantations in the Vicksburg district.[29] Several lessees were murdered by the raiders.[30] Before the summer was over fully one-third of the land originally leased in the Vicksburg district was abandoned. About the first of September the army worm made its appearance and attacked the cotton crop with devastating results. The prospective yield in the Vicksburg district before the coming of the army worm was forty thousand bales; its ravages reduced the crop to eight thousand bales.[31]

Added to the difficulties attributable to the "Rebels" and to nature were the restrictions imposed upon the movement of cotton by the Treasury agents. There was a tre-

28. Knox, *Camp-Fire and Cotton-Field*, pp. 313–316.
29. Eaton, *Report for 1864*, p. 49.
30. Knox, *Camp-Fire and Cotton-Field*, pp. 448–449; Warren, *Extracts from Reports of Superintendents of Freedmen*, First Series, May, 1864, pp. 22–23.
31. Eaton, *Report for 1864*, p. 36.

mendous amount of red tape connected with shipment in
the form of affidavits of the fulfilment of contracts, proof
that the cotton to be shipped was grown in 1864 and on the
plantation of the shipper, and permits from various officials. All this involved expense. In some cases the whole
value of the cotton was consumed by fees before a sale could
be effected. T. W. Knox had a planter acquaintance "who
fell into the hands of the Philistines," as he termed the
Treasury officials, and before he completed the delivery and
sale of his cotton "he found himself a loser to the extent of
$300." Knox said that he knew of several other cases in
which the cotton did not cover the charges but left small
bills to be paid by the owner.[32]

In the latter part of 1864 one of the "Yankee" planters
of the Vicksburg area lifted up his voice in lamentation at
the combined impositions of nature, "Rebel" raiders, and
Treasury agents. In a letter to the *Wisconsin State Journal* he wrote, "Dear Journal: 'who hath woe, who hath sorrow?' He that raiseth a cotton crop on a Government plantation. Who hath much greenbacks and expecteth more?
The official that letteth the plantation, blocketh the game
[same?] during its cultivation, and putteth an embargo
on the crop when raised! Who hath honesty undefiled? He
that hath hair growing in the palm of his hand." Amid difficulties and at much expense, he continued, men from the
North came down, stocked the plantations, and started a
crop with the promise of military protection. "The thing
was going off 'beautiful,' when lo! the guerilla came and
swept off all those Yankee assets like a whirlwind." Many
lessees retired from the field in disgust. A few restocked
their plantations and began anew. Shortly thereafter mili-

32. Knox, *Camp-Fire and Cotton-Field,* p. 404. Knox, who was acquainted by experience with the difficulties incident to the shipment of
cotton, also said that "not a hundredth part of the official dishonesty at
New Orleans and other points along the Mississippi will ever be known.
Enough has been made public to condemn the whole system of permits
and Treasury restrictions . . . as they were managed during the last two
years of the war these agencies proved little less than schools of dishonesty." *Ibid.,* pp. 402–403.

tary orders were issued restricting the reception of plantation supplies. Then came Massachusetts recruiting officers
who "raided every plantation . . . enlisting to the credit
of the Old Bay State every able-bodied he-nigger in the
country.". The recruiters were followed in a short time by
other officers with orders to take the planters' horses and
mules.

"All these trials," according to the correspondent, "were
borne with commendable fortitude but unfortunately not a
Christian spirit. So Divine Providence took a hand . . .
and appointed the army worm as receiver of the crop."
The army worm, he explained, "is so called from its re-
semblance to the army officers who always appropriate to
their use at least 9/10 of all cotton that passes through
their hands." Little cotton was left by the caterpillars. As
the planters began to pick this the officials went to work
inventing regulations and they could "beat the planters
two to one." This proved the *coup de grâce*, and, concludes
the correspondent, "so mote it be."[33]

There was doubtless a general improvement in the physical treatment of the Negroes after they passed under Federal control. The regulations issued by the government authorities usually interdicted the use of the lash and other
cruel modes of punishment. Planters were ordered to turn
recalcitrant and insubordinate blacks over to the provost
marshals to be punished in some manner suitable to the offense, such as imprisonment in darkness on a bread and
water ration or being put to work for the government without pay. There is abundant evidence, however, of the use
of considerable roughness in the handling of Negroes on the
plantations after the coming of the "Yankees." Even the
whip was not altogether obsolete. Its most frequent use was
in the outlying districts where the visits of the provost
marshal were infrequent.[34] A Louisianan named Pugh dis-

33. Quoted by the New Orleans *Daily Picayune,* Nov. 10, 1864.
34. "Reports of the Assistant Commissioners of the Freedmen's Bureau," *Sen. Ex. Docs.,* 39th Cong., 1st Sess., II, no. 27, 64. James Walkinshaw, an overseer in the Lafourche district of Louisiana during a tem-

covered a case of "thieving" on his plantation in 1865. The Negroes involved, according to Pugh, preferred his settling the matter to taking it before the provost marshal. He whipped one of them but let the other off on the plea of "the ladies." Three days later, however, he took the Negroes to the provost marshal who gave them a very light punishment. The officer may not have known of Pugh's having previously made use of the whip. There is no indication in the planter's diary of his having received reproof therefor.[35] James McKaye, one of the members of the Freedmen's Inquiry Commission, reported that on many plantations in the lower Mississippi Valley whipping was permitted by the provost marshals.[36]

Chaplain Fiske, who questioned the Negroes on ninety-five plantations along the Mississippi River in 1864 as to their treatment, said that no complaint was made on forty-eight places. On the remaining forty-seven "there was complaint of rough, or profane, or obscene, or insulting usage, while blows and kicks have been not infrequently administered on some." The blows and kicks, he added, were most common on plantations superintended by native Southern overseers.[37] Some of the Northern lessees in the Mississippi Valley, much to Fiske's disapproval, had hired these overseers, in the belief that experience was necessary in the handling of Negroes; and, all too frequently, they had shown "a thorough itching after an uncomfortable tend-

porary reoccupation of the territory by Confederates, upbraided a Negro in the field for permitting another laborer to do twice as much plowing as he. The Negro contradicted him. The overseer was reported to have said, "Don't contradict me. I don't allow anybody white or black to do that; if you contradict me again, I'll cut your heart out; the Yankees have spoiled you Niggers but I'll be even with you." In the course of the continuation of the altercation Walkinshaw drew his dagger and stabbed the Negro in the breast. On the return of the Federals later, the overseer was arrested, tried, and sentenced to six months' imprisonment in the parish prison. *Daily Picayune,* Aug. 6, 1863.

35. Diary of A. Franklin Pugh, entries of Aug. 30, Sept. 1, and Sept. 2, 1865.

36. McKaye, *The Emancipated Slave Face to Face with His Old Master,* p. 26.

37. Eaton, *Report for 1864,* p. 45.

ency toward the old system."[38] That peace was not the general order on the plantation is indicated by Fiske's testimony that "during the year now closing, the provost marshals have been too few. . . . The complaints arising between planter and laborer are endless. The laborer is accused as lazy, as vicious, as impudent, as thievish or a liar, as quarrelsome, as a breeder of discontent. The planter is accused of keeping false time, over-charging for goods, giving short rations, refusing to feed dependents, neglecting the sick, severity, insults, and blows."[39]

The proscription of the usual modes of punishment did not have a salutary effect on the general conduct of the plantation Negroes. Lying, theft, quarreling, fighting, and destruction of property were all accentuated in the early days of freedom. A Louisiana planter wrote in 1864 that his outbuildings not in use were torn to pieces and gradually destroyed. "In fact," he said, "a spirit of destruction and semi-barbarism seems to pervade a country once noted for . . . the tidiness of its buildings and fencing." "A few days since," he added, "I commenced gathering corn, and much to my surprise, I found one of the squares near the quarters minus about one-half. This corn had been gathered by the basketful to feed their hogs and save their own for market." A few days later another Louisianan complained that in his locality stealing had become "the order of the day."[40] Still another "Old Planter" wrote that the Negroes would "take horses or mules at will, and travel all night. . . . There is no police, no watch, no guards to arrest them and proprietors or employers are powerless." "The usual safeguards of locks, houses, fences, are as nothing," he added. "I have lost during the last twelve months over one thousand dollars worth of copper taken from the evaporating pans in my sugar houses. . . . New plows, as well as old, and harrows, saws, axes, and indeed every implement of value, have been taken and sold." "They have

38. Eaton, *Report for 1864,* p. 53.   39. *Ibid.,* p. 54.
40. New Orleans *Times,* Oct. 13 and 21, 1864.

taken from one sugar house alone," he said, "as much as fourteen hogshead of sugar, leaving the empty casks standing in their places to prevent a vacancy being observed. At another, any number of barrels of sugar and molasses, and these in some instances sold openly, and in others secretly. . . . I had a fine stock of hogs and sheep—every hog is gone, and I have but two sheep left. . . . The consumption of fuel is enormous."[41]

The testimony of old planters may need to be taken *cum grano salis* in view of the fact that they were chafing under a system forced upon them by the "iniquitous Yankees." But their depictions are substantially true. Planters and others from the North were impressed with the Negroes' propensity toward lying and theft. The fact that they generally attributed these faults to the blighting effects of slavery caused them, at first, to adopt a very tolerant attitude.[42] But those who remained in close association with the Negroes for a considerable period of time lost much of their patience, especially when these short-comings seemed to grow worse rather than to improve under "Yankee" instruction and supervision. A Massachusetts superintendent of a plantation in South Carolina wrote in August, 1863: "On the whole the people have been growing more lawless this year." He added that courts had been established for the Negroes and he hoped an improvement would result.[43] One of his Northern associates wrote a few months later, however, that men and boys who bore witness in the

41. *Ibid.,* Nov. 2, 1864. Caroline E. Merrick wrote to her daughter in November, 1865: "You know I have never locked up anything. Now I am a slave to my keys. I am robbed daily. Spoons, cups and all the utensils from the kitchen have been carried off. I am now paying little black Joe to steal some of them back for me as he says he knows where they are. I cannot even set the bread to rise without some of it being taken. . . . It is astonishing that those we have considered most reliable are engaged in the universal dishonesty. I understand they call it, 'spilin' de Gypshuns.'" Caroline E. Merrick, *Old Times in Dixie Land,* p. 78.

42. J. Miller McKim, *The Freemen of South Carolina,* p. 30; Nordhoff, *The Freedmen of South Carolina,* p. 24; Preliminary Report of Freedmen's Inquiry Commission, in *O. R.,* Ser. 3, III, 431.

43. Pearson, *Letters from Port Royal,* p. 210.

courts "took the oath one after another and then lied as if they had sworn to do so." Another of the Massachusetts group of superintendents complained in December, 1865, that he did "not get more than one-fifth of the . . . seed cotton" after it was ginned, and that it was probable that "they steal the balance." Still another wrote a few days later that the Negroes were "stealing cotton at a fearful rate."[44]

Of all the missionary-superintendents who came to South Carolina during the war, none seemed to suffer greater disillusionment than "C. P. W." He assumed his duties on a sea island plantation in July, 1862, "fresh from Harvard," and full of enthusiasm for the improvement of the "degraded" blacks. After more than two years' work among them he wrote: "The untrustworthiness of these people is more apparent and troublesome than ever. . . . Their skill in lying, . . . their habit of shielding one another (generally by silence), their invariable habit of taking a rod when you . . . have been induced to grant an inch, their assumed ignorance and innocence of the simplest rules of *meum* and *tuum* joined with amazing impudence in making claims—these are the traits which try us continually in our dealings with them and sometimes make us almost despair of their improvement—at least in the present generation. It is certain that their freedom has been too easy for them —they have not had a hard enough time of it. In many cases they have been fair spoiled."[45]

When all factors in the treatment of Negroes are taken into consideration—food, clothing, compensation, and discipline—the laborers on plantations operated by the "old planters" were better off than those on places run by Northern lessees. The former were less influenced than the latter by the get-rich-quick motive, they were more concerned with the permanent tenure of their property and with making a living for their families and employees until the return of peace and civil government. The "old plant-

44. Pearson, *Letters from Port Royal*, pp. 269, 320, 322.
45. *Ibid.*, p. 287.

ers" felt more solicitude for the Negroes because of past association with them and because of the realization of a dependence on their labor in the future. Thomas W. Conway, superintendent of Negro labor for the Department of the Gulf, himself a Northern anti-slavery man, said in his report to General Hurlbut for 1864: "Of the men who are known as the 'old planters' of this country, so far as dealing fairly with the freedmen is concerned in the matter of wages, I have to inform you, that, as a rule, they have paid them more promptly, more justly, and apparently with more willingness than have the new lessees from other parts of the country."[46]

Getting the Negroes to work satisfactorily under the free-labor system was a problem for native planters and Northern lessees alike. In the case of the former, the treatment which had been accorded the Negroes in the years preceding the arrival of the "Yankees" was a considerable factor. Planters who had treated their Negroes kindly as slaves generally obtained better work from the blacks after Federal occupation than those masters who had dealt harshly or indifferently with the workers under the old régime. A Northern plantation superintendent wrote from South Carolina in the fall of 1863 that there was "as much difference between the plantations adjoining this on the North and those adjoining on the South as between Boston, Massachusetts and Yellville, Arkansas. At Reynold's the people are industrious, courteous, and gratified. At Capers' . . . outrageously lazy and impudent." "This contrast," he added, "is caused by the difference in their masters. The kinder the master, the greater we find the industry of the people."[47]

The best laborers were usually those who remained

---

46. *O. R.*, Ser. 1, XLVIII, pt. 1, 707. L. B. Eaton who inspected plantation conditions in Arkansas late in 1864 makes a comparison more favorable to the lessees. But his testimony as to the general character of the latter is not in harmony with Fiske, Thomas, Yeatman, and others. Eaton, *Report for 1864,* p. 65.

47. *Williams [College] Quarterly,* XI (1863), 75.

quietly on their places after Federal occupation, continuing work there on a compensation basis. Those who abandoned the old plantations, and wandered about from camp to camp, suffering great hardships in the form of destitution and disease, and, acquiring perhaps a spirit of restlessness and an increased tendency to roam, were much less efficient workers as a result of their peregrinations.

Remoteness from army camps was another factor conducive to industry on the plantations. The Federal soldiers sometimes did great damage by premeditated or careless remarks to the Negroes about the relief from hard work which the state of freedom offered; and the soldiers did not frequently prove enviable examples of industry, steadiness, and sobriety. The higher wages which were sometimes paid for military work and the novelty of camp life often made it difficult for planters to keep the Negro men in the fields.[48]

A feeling of security from guerrilla and Confederate raids tended to promote consistent labor. In some of the more exposed localities the Negroes were in constant dread of attack. Chaplain Fiske said that as he rode up to the Negro quarters on his tour of inspection he would frequently catch sight of the blacks "scattering to the weeds like frightened hares" thinking that his approach might signify another "Rebel" raid.[49]

The assignment of definite tasks, frequent check-ups on their performances, and the prompt payment of wages were effective in improving the Negroes' industry. In some cases those who had been unable to work for years on account of some indefinite bodily infirmity were restored to soundness as if by a miracle after the coming of freedom and the introduction of the wage system.[50]

48. Pearson, *Letters from Port Royal*, p. 13.
49. Eaton, *Report for 1864*, p. 53.
50. Frederick A. Eustis of South Carolina said in 1863 that he knew at least twenty Negroes "who were considered worn out and too old to work under the slave system who are now working cotton, as well as their two acres of provisions; and their crops look very well." *O. R.*, Ser. 3, III, 435.

When T. W. Knox put his employees to work picking cotton in 1863 he did not weigh the amount picked by each one for the first few days. The Negroes, however, would confidently estimate the weight of their respective baskets at two hundred pounds. One night Knox surprised them by bringing the scales to the fields and weighing the pickings of the individual laborers. There was much apparent disappointment when the amounts so unhesitatingly estimated at two hundred pounds proved by weight to be not more than fifty pounds. Thereafter the "tell-tale," as the Negroes sometimes called the scales, was brought regularly to the field contributing much to the improvement of industry.[51] After the cotton was harvested and a new crop begun, several of the Negroes who were now working for wages by the month began to feign sickness. For a while Knox was in a quandary as to how to handle this problem. Finally the idea of a ticket system was suggested to him. A number of red, yellow, and white tickets were procured for issuance by the overseer at the end of each day. The red ones were for a full day's work, the yellow for a half-day, and the white for a quarter-day. These were collected every Saturday night and due credit was given for the amount of labor performed by each hand during the week. "The day after the adoption of our ticket system," said Knox, "our number of sick was reduced one-half and we had no further trouble with pretended patients."[52]

Other employers adopted plans of giving presents or extra provisions to stimulate labor.[53] E. S. Philbrick promised a yard of cloth "for every task of cotton hoed in July" in order to get the Negroes to give the crop a "last hoeing." The Negroes who failed to do this final hoeing looked "rather glum" when the cloth was issued in September to their exultant neighbors. Philbrick had considerable diffi-

51. Knox, *Camp-Fire and Cotton-Field*, p. 349.
52. *Ibid.*, p. 426.
53. Major Sargent, superintendent of freedmen for the Arkansas district said in 1864: "The wiser planters held out extra inducements by way of rewarding industry, by promising a bale of cotton, or a suit of clothes, etc." Eaton, *Report for 1864*, p. 36.

culty in getting his Negroes to work on Saturday. In May, 1862, he adopted the policy of withholding the bacon ration from Saturday loafers. A year later he sought to promote general industry by giving extra rations of molasses and bacon. The little Negroes were especially gladdened by the "poke and sweetnin'," greeting with dancing eyes the piggins of molasses on the heads of their mothers as they brought them home for the first time.[54] When the sable urchins were allowed to carry the jugs from the big house they would steal a lick at the "stopper" en route to the cabins.[55]

The question of whether or not the Negroes worked better for Northerners or Southerners is a very difficult one on account of the nature of the evidence. The former were so strongly convinced that the free-labor system was superior in every respect to slavery that they were inclined to notice and emphasize cases of industry and to overlook and minimize instances of laziness and slothfulness. The latter were inclined to reverse the process on account of their disbelief in and detestation of the "Yankee innovation." As far as overseers are concerned it is probable that the Negroes worked better under the newcomers from the North than under those who had directed them in slavery. Toward the latter they sometimes took the opportunity offered by the coming of the Federals to vent their hatred, refusing to work for them and even driving them off the plantation.[56] Knox says that many of the residents around Vicksburg tried to get Northern men as partners after Federal occupation of their territory because they were confident "a fine cotton crop could be made 'if there was some Northern man to manage the niggers.' " "It was the general

54. Pearson, *Letters from Port Royal*, pp. 48, 88, 191, 208.
55. "Journal of Miss Susan Walker," *Quarterly Publication* of the Historical and Philosophical Society of Ohio, VII, no. 1, 43.
56. George H. Hepworth, *The Whip, Hoe and Sword, passim*. Some of the overseers left of their own accord on account of fear of violence from the Negroes after the Federals came. A Louisiana overseer named McKaye was murdered by freedmen in October, 1862. New Orleans *Daily Picayune*, Nov. 22, 1862. Another Louisiana overseer was attacked and severely beaten. *Ibid.*, Dec. 19, 1863.

complaint with the people who lived in that region," he added, "that with few exceptions, no Southern man could induce the Negroes to continue at work."[57]

It is quite possible that in the early days of Federal occupation the proneness of the Negroes to regard the Northerners as their deliverers and their desire to prove by the fruits of their labor that they were worthy of freedom— this was a point much stressed by the Federals—had a salutary effect on their work for "Yankee masters." Likewise their inclination—sometimes at the suggestion of the Northerners—to regard their late owners as instruments of oppression who desired to secure their reënslavement had a deleterious influence on their labor for the old masters.[58] But Northerners were not universally successful in getting the Negroes to work. General T. W. Sherman wrote the War Department from South Carolina in December, 1861, that his soldiers were having to perform all the necessary military labor. The Negroes, he said, "are disinclined to labor and will evidently not work to our satisfaction without those aids to which they have ever been accustomed, viz. the driver and the lash."[59] The Reverend Horace James, superintendent of Negro affairs in North Carolina, said in 1864 that he had observed that the Negroes were *"slow and shiftless workers.* Seldom does one of them do a good days work when laboring for another party. . . . It almost gives one the backache to witness their labor. . . . Their habit is to strike a few blows, and then lean against a fence in the sun, and the last as much as the first."[60] Colonel Samuel Thomas, superintendent of freedmen for the Vicksburg district, reported in 1864 that the Negroes generally worked "as well as was expected," but added that their old slave habits, "so slow and shiftless

---

57. Knox, *Camp-Fire and Cotton-Field*, p. 325.
58. Knox said that during the earlier part of his stay in the environs of Vicksburg he was surprised at the readiness with which Negroes obeyed men from the North and believed they would fulfill their promises while they looked with distrust on all Southern white men. *Ibid.,* p. 375.
59. *O. R.,* Ser. 2, I, 785.
60. James, *Annual Report of the Superintendent of Negro Affairs in North Carolina* (1864), p. 45.

often antagonize with the quick, active blood of the new Yankee planters."[61]

The experiences of E. S. Philbrick and his associates in South Carolina, as recorded in their letters, indicate that the Negroes showed a tendency after working for several months under "Yankee" masters to take advantage of their leniency in dealing with them. "W. C. G." wrote on January 4, 1863, that the Negroes were "very wayward— now they work and then they stop—and some stop before they begin." Philbrick himself was dissatisfied with the Negroes' work; on one occasion he wrote that the Port Royal project could "afford to lose some of the Methodism now bestowed upon it." Toward the end of his experiences in South Carolina he wrote: "Now to tell the truth I don't believe myself that the present generation of Negroes will work as they were formerly obliged to. . . . It will take many years to make an economical and thrifty man out of the freedman."[62]

The almost unanimous testimony of the native planters was that the Negroes worked very poorly under the free-labor system—a system defined by one of them as a "scheme in which there is a good deal of the free and but little of the labor."[63] In the fall of 1864 General Banks invited comment from the planters on the workings of his arrangements with a view to making helpful changes for the coming year. Several of the old planters took advantage of this invitation to give their experiences under Federal occupation; and for the first time since Butler's arrival on the scene, a New Orleans paper published open criticisms of the new régime. One of these articles—the experience of an "Old Planter"—is particularly valuable on account of its moderate tone and the evident desire of the author to be fair.[64] For thirty-seven years this correspondent had been engaged in raising sugar and cotton on the same

61. Eaton, *Report for 1864,* p. 30.
62. Pearson, *Letters from Port Royal,* pp. 221, 287.
63. New Orleans *Times,* Oct. 13, 1864.
64. *Ibid.,* Oct. 21, 1864.

estate. He had seventy-five good field hands, all except five or six of whom remained with him after the Federal occupation. His average crop before the war was from 600 to 1,100 hogsheads of sugar and from 1,200 to 2,200 barrels of molasses, with sufficient corn for the use of the plantation. In October, 1862, the Federals invaded the country and General Butler prescribed a wage system for labor which he adopted. He went to work to save his sugar crop, paying his hands a dollar a day during the harvesting season. But "with the incentives in the way of money and moral suasion in every way, together with the assistance of the military to keep order," he finished the crop with less than 100 hogsheads of sugar.

"The crop of 1863," he said, "was begun with the most promising auspices in everything but the quality of the labor by which it was to be worked." At the commencement of the harvesting season "the standing crop of cane was considered good for 800 hogsheads of sugar." But with all possible "energy and perseverence," and with the "hiring of near 40 white men and buying near $2,000 worth of wood" he was "at last fortunate enough in saving about 40 hogsheads of sugar." This was the result of the first year's work under General Banks's system.

In 1864 he began operations under Banks's new regulations which were calculated to stimulate the laborer to increased exertion. But they proved ineffective. "In truth," he added, "the nature of the Negro cannot be changed by the offer of more or less money—all he desires is to eat, drink, and sleep and perform the least possible amount of labor. . . . I am safe to say that I do not receive more than half of what would be considered by any impartial judge as fair labor from the laborers I have employed." "The ordinary laborers engaged on my plantation before the war," he continued, "kept it in perfect repair and in good working order but under the present order of things not a ditch has been dug, . . . the fences are all rotting down, the buildings are decaying and going to ruin with no means of preventing or remedying the evils. . . .

Wherever you look, the eye rests on nothing but the relics of former things fast passing to destruction."

Another planter in relating his experiences for 1864 said that on January 12 he commenced work with thirty-one men and twenty-one women. Between that time and October 1 the men lost an average of thirty-five and one-half days each from a working period comprising two hundred eight and one-half days—or nearly one-sixth of the time—"not to mention other losses during the day by delays in going to work or by killing time in various ways." During the same period the women lost seventy-six days each, a fraction over one-third of the time.[65]

A third contributor testified that in the last season under the old régime, 1861, he had made twelve hundred hogsheads of sugar. In the first under the new order, 1862, though he lost few of his Negroes he made only ninety hogsheads. The universal testimony of the planters in his district, he said, was that some compulsory process was necessary on each sugar plantation to make the Negroes behave and work. Unless this compulsion was permitted, sugar raising in Louisiana was doomed.[66]

At a meeting of planters held in New Orleans in November, 1864, a speaker drew a vivid picture of the Negroes' labor on the plantation under the new régime. They started out, he said, at seven o'clock in the morning and before one o'clock every one of them came back. On the weekly visit of the provost marshal all hands would work faithfully as long as he was in sight. They always seemed to know when he was coming. But after he left they relapsed into their habits of idleness.[67]

The Negroes on "Mooreland," the plantation of Governor Thomas O. Moore of Louisiana, caused their employer a great amount of worry and concern on account of their indolence and idleness under the free-labor system. In the back of the plantation account-book covering the period 1860–1867 there is a section captioned "General

65. New Orleans *Times*, Oct. 13, 1864.
66. *Ibid.*, Oct. 26, Nov. 2, 1864.   67. *Ibid.*, Nov. 22, 1864.

Conduct of the Freedmen and Women Employed, 1866,"
entered by the owner or someone representing him. An entry dated January 24 contains a complaint against Julia
as being "lazy, indolent and insolent . . . on one occasion
when . . . asked when the hands would finish a certain cut
[Julia] replied when they were done, they would be finished, that has been the character of replies from her. . . .
The nursing her infant and the advantage it affords her
to take to lose time, makes her only a *half* hand." From
February 28 to April 24 there are a number of complaints
against Dallas who seems to have been a particularly bad
case. "[March] 5, while sitting where the plowers were,
Dallas stopped as to obey a call of nature, went into the
woods and remained 15½ minutes, that night I sent for
him to give him a private talk on the impropriety of such
a long stay and other conduct of his to correspond with the
same, he was aware of it, but said he was fixing his breeches
—[March] 6. Yesterday the same was repeated in presence of [the] Ag[en]t and when spoken to, replied he had
tried to please and now did not care a G—d d—n—such
language is used in presence of the Agt. frequently and
often in mine and the plowing by this boy is not half done.
. . . [March] 8 . . . Mr. Wiley remarked to him 'he
would not let the others gain a round [in plowing] before
breakfast'—he replied if he did, there was nobody to whip
him for it. . . . April 24 Whipping his mule and his plowing done so badly I had to make Sandy follow after him
and do it over. I showed his work to him and asked him
and asked him [*sic*] a half dozen times if he thought he
could do it worse, he made no reply but stuck his mouth
out contemptuously and drove off." On one page there is
an undated blanket complaint given after this fashion:

	Without any complaint being made to me by
Tony	by [*sic*] those freedmen and women 9½ o'clock
John	W[ednesday] they took out their teams from the
Romeo	plow and came home saying, "it was too bad to
	plow"—The land is black, stiff, sticky prairie

Peter
Ben
Warren
Dallas
Jordan
George I
Eliza
Amanda
Ann
Jenny

land, that always plows badly, you can't work it dry and bad to do so wet but what I complain of—if my Agt. did not in *their opinion* do his duty and remove them to some other point, *why did they not come to me and make the statement above!* Their conduct is *disobedient,* defiant, disrespectful, and shows in the extreme a disregard for my interest, and I require the infliction of some severe punishment or penalty. I go but seldom where they are at work, from the fact that the conduct of several is so disobedient and disrespectful and annoying, that I am forced to try and to do all through my Agt.[68]

Three years after the war had ended the following notice, signed "B," Butler, Georgia, appeared in a Southern agricultural journal:

$50 REWARD

Is offered for information that will enable me to make a living, and make the ends meet on my farm by the use of Negro labor. I have a good farm and all the necessary appliances, and have been trying to do the above up-hill task for three mortal years of freedom but haven't done it—have exhausted all my theories and those of my neighbors, and am about giving the matter up for good.

The subscriber added that he would not give the reward for a theory but that an actual experience must be presented.[69]

The testimony of this Georgian, though not given until 1868, has a tone strikingly similar to that given by Louisianans and Mississippians in 1864 and 1865. Experiences of planters throughout the Federal-controlled portions of the South, whether they were natives or Northerners, af-

68. Mooreland Plantation Account Book (MS. in the archives of the University of Texas at Austin).
69. *Southern Cultivator* (Athens, Ga.), XXVI (1868), 207.

ford convincing evidence that, despite the attraction of wages, bounties, and other inducements, the work of the Negroes during the early years of the free-labor régime was most unsatisfactory.

XIV

GOING TO SCHOOL

THE education of Negroes under Federal control had its beginning in Virginia. Lewis Tappan, treasurer of the American Missionary Association, wrote General Butler in the summer of 1861 suggesting that the organization which he represented would be willing to aid in the care of contrabands collected at Hampton and Fortress Monroe. When Butler replied on August 10 that he would welcome any aid from the association, that body commissioned the Reverend L. C. Lockwood as a missionary to Virginia. He reached Hampton early in September and General Wool, who had succeeded Butler, gave him authority to enter upon his work immediately. Lockwood opened a Sunday school for Negroes on September 15 in the home of ex-President Tyler. Two days later in a small brown house near the old female "Seminary" he established "the first day-school for the freedmen." The first teacher of this school was Mary S. Peake, a mulatto, her mother being a "very light" free woman of color and her father a white man, "an Englishman of rank and culture."[1]

In the months which followed, other schools were founded by the American Missionary Association at Fortress Monroe, Norfolk, Portsmouth, Newport News, and on plantations in the vicinity of these towns.[2] The mansion of ex-Governor Wise was used for a time as a colored school. Other societies joined the American Missionary Association in the promotion of Negro education in Virginia in 1862, 1863, and 1864. The most active of these were the New England Freedmen's Aid Society, the Pennsylvania

1. *History of the American Missionary Association,* pp. 11–12.
2. *Ibid.,* pp. 11–15.

Freedmen's Relief Association, the National Freedmen's Relief Association of New York, and the Friends Association for the Aid and Education of Freedmen.[3] In April, 1864, reports revealed that there were over 3,000 pupils enrolled in Negro schools in Virginia, the number of teachers reported was fifty-two, at least five of whom were colored.[4]

As a general rule, teachers for the Negro schools—in Virginia and elsewhere—were commissioned and paid by benevolent associations; the government furnished subsistence, usually in the form of army rations, and transportation. The benevolent organizations also rendered material aid to education by providing clothing and food for destitute pupils and equipment in the form of books, slates, and maps. The schools were usually housed in buildings abandoned by "Rebels," but sometimes new edifices were erected.

Several schools were established for the refugees who flocked to Washington during the course of the war. The Philadelphia Friends erected a schoolhouse on Nineteenth Street in Washington, a substantial frame building forty by sixty feet, with a large schoolroom on the first floor and lodging rooms for the teachers above; the teachers were sent by the Boston and Philadelphia Freedmen's Relief Associations. Another school was built in the Capitol City by the Scotch Covenanters. The Trustees of Colored Schools of Washington established one institution for the refugees; the teachers were paid by the New England Freedmen's Aid Society.[5]

The earliest efforts for the education of freedmen in North Carolina seem to have been made by the chaplains of Northern regiments serving under Burnside's command. Notable among these chaplains were Woodworth, Stone,

3. See the reports of these organizations.
4. *Second Annual Report of the New England Freedmen's Aid Society,* pp. 31–32.
5. *Report to the Executive Committee of the New England Yearly Meeting of Friends upon the Condition and Needs of the Freed People of Color in Washington and Virginia,* pp. 3–4.

Hall, and Horace James. Evening schools were held for
the contrabands located in the vicinity of the regimental
camps. The first instruction given to the freedmen of Plymouth, North Carolina, was in the spring of 1862 by the
chaplain of the Twenty-fifth Massachusetts Regiment.

When the Reverend Horace James was made superintendent of Negro affairs in the early part of 1863 one of
the first things which received his attention was the establishment of freedmen's schools to be taught by "cultured
females" from the North. The first day-schools for colored
children in North Carolina were opened in July of that year
in two Negro churches. Others were established at Beaufort, Washington, Plymouth, and Morehead. In January,
1864, the number of pupils in all the schools was 1,500.
Attendance steadily increased until July, the aggregate
reaching nearly 3,000. Sixty-six teachers were commissioned for this territory by the different benevolent associations, most of them being sent by the Boston and New
York societies and by the American Missionary Association. For the children who could not attend the day-ses-
sions, and for adults, evening schools were organized. The
teachers not only directed the activities of these two sessions, but they devoted considerable time outside of school
hours to the distribution of clothing and provisions to the
needy.

During the period of James's supervision of Negro affairs the Reverend William T. Briggs was appointed superintendent of education for the district of North Carolina. He made regular visits to the schools and the teachers
submitted monthly reports to him, giving the statistics and
the general condition of the schools. Copies of these reports were forwarded to the societies supporting the
teachers.[6]

Educational activities in North Carolina were greatly
hindered by serious epidemics of smallpox in the early part

6. James, *Annual Report of the Superintendent of Negro Affairs in
North Carolina* (1864), pp. 35–40.

of 1864 and of yellow fever in the following autumn. Thousands of Negroes were victims of the former plague. Whites suffered worse from the fever. Many of the teachers who went North at the end of the terms in the summer did not return until December, after the epidemic had passed. Several who remained or returned were stricken and one died.[7]

General Butler, who assumed command of the military Department of Virginia and North Carolina in the latter part of 1863, did much to promote the educational interest of freedmen. By his order the city of Norfolk was divided into districts and teachers appointed "as in the New England free school system." At Hampton he provided for the erection of a large schoolhouse sufficient to accommodate from six hundred to eight hundred pupils.[8]

The education of the freedmen in South Carolina was begun under the auspices of the New England Freedmen's Aid Society, organized under the name of the Educational Commission, as the result of an appeal issued in the form of a general order on February 9, 1862, from Hilton Head by General T. W. Sherman. In this order Sherman said that he was dividing the territory under Federal control in South Carolina into districts, and that one or more instructors were needed for each of these divisions whose duty it should be to teach "both old and young the rudiments of civilization and Christianity."[9]

A few weeks after this appeal was made, the first party of representatives of the New England society—thirty-one in number, twenty-seven men and four women—sailed for South Carolina. On their arrival it was discovered that the most immediate need was for superintendents of labor, and some of the party who had intended to teach were assigned to the duty of directing the work of the blacks. The

7. *Ibid.*, pp. 16–17.
8. *Report to the Executive Committee of the New England Yearly Meeting of Friends upon the Condition and Needs of the Freed People of Color in Washington and Virginia*, pp. 6–7.
9. *O. R.*, Ser. 2, I, 805–806.

four women, however, and two or three of the men immediately assumed the duties of teaching. Schools were established on a few of the larger plantations.[10] During the months following the arrival of these first teachers they were joined by additional representatives of their own organization and by those of other societies, including the National Freedmen's Relief Association, the Pennsylvania Freedmen's Relief Association, and the American Missionary Association. Returns made in June, 1863, showed an aggregate of 1,911 persons receiving instruction in town and plantation schools, 600 in the former and 1,311 in the latter. These returns were not complete. According to estimates, the aggregate enrollment was around 5,000.[11]

Throughout the remainder of the war the great majority of the Negroes receiving instruction in the military Department of the South were taught on the plantations, though schools were established at Beaufort, Fernandina, and St. Augustine. After the fall of Charleston steps were taken to provide instruction for the colored residents of that city and for those who flocked in from the surrounding country, but little was accomplished before the end of the year. The plantation schools generally opened at noon and closed at three o'clock in order to permit the children to have the best part of the day for work in the fields. In South Carolina, as elsewhere, evening schools were held for the benefit of the adults.[12]

The education of Negroes in the Department of the Gulf did not have as auspicious a beginning as in the East. Some instruction was begun in a quiet way by private individuals shortly after the Federal occupation of New Or-

10. *First Annual Report of the Educational Commission for Freedmen with Extracts from Letters of Teachers and Superintendents*, pp. 9–11.

11. *Second Annual Report of the New England Freedmen's Aid Society*, p. 13.

12. Pierce, "The Freedmen at Port Royal," *Atlantic Monthly*, XII (1863), 304; *First Annual Report of the Educational Commission for Freedmen with Extracts from Letters of Teachers and Superintendents*, p. 26.

leans in May, 1862. Benevolent societies did not enter the
field immediately. Their hesitation was due, in part, to the
fear that the establishment of colored schools would arouse
the antagonism of the loyal white population. The first
real impetus given to Negro education was the issuance of
General Order Number 64, dated August 29, 1863, by
General Banks. By this order a Commission of Enrollment
consisting of three persons was appointed to regulate enrollment, recruiting, employment, and education of persons of color in the Department of the Gulf.[13] Under the
direction of this commission several schools were established
in New Orleans and vicinity. A few schools were also started
by benevolent associations.

With the issuance of General Order Number 23 by
Banks on February 3, 1864, a system of public Negro
education was launched in the Department of the Gulf. By
the provisions of this order the provost marshal general
was to divide the different parishes into police and school
districts of convenient size; schools sufficient in number for
the instruction of children under twelve years of age were
to be established, at least one in each district. The schools
so established were to be placed under the direction of a
superintendent of education; each planter who employed
colored laborers was required to make provision for the instruction of their children.[14]

To carry out these provisions, Banks issued another order, Number 38, on March 22, creating a Board of Education for Freedmen consisting of three members, to assume general direction of educational activities in the department. Among the duties and powers conferred upon
this board were the following: 1. The establishment of one
or more schools in each district as defined by the parish
provost marshals. 2. The acquisition by purchase, or by
other means, of sites of land suitable for school purposes
and the erection of proper buildings thereon. 3. The selec-

13. *O. R.*, Ser. 1, XXVI, pt. 1, 704.
14. *Ibid.*, XXXIV, pt. 2, 228.

tion of teachers "as far as practicable from the loyal inhabitants of Louisiana." 4. The purchase of the necessary books, stationery, and apparatus for the use of these schools. 5. The regulation of the course of study, discipline, and hours of instruction for children on week-days, and adults on Sunday. 6. The levy of a school tax upon real and personal property, including crops of plantations, in every district, sufficient to defray the expenses of education for the period of one year. 7. The coöperation, as far as practicable, with the recently elected superintendent of public education, Lieutenant W. B. Stickney. This order also fixed the date of the current school year as February 1, 1864, to February 1, 1865, and appointed to membership on the board Colonel H. N. Frisbee, Lieutenant E. M. Wheelock, and Isaac G. Hubbs.[15]

The tax levy provided in this order had not been made when the board issued its report in February, 1865.[16] But the educational program had been carried forward by funds advanced by the government through the quartermaster's department. The average monthly expense of instructing each pupil was estimated at $1.50. A one-and-a-half-mill tax, netting about $150,000 for the department, was estimated as necessary to cover the expense of education for the first school year under the Board of Education.

Soon after the creation of the board, the management of the schools which had been established and conducted under the Commission of Enrollment was turned over to that

15. Frisbee was relieved soon after his appointment and Major B. Rush Plumly was designated to fill the vacancy. Hubbs, a native of New Orleans, was subsequently expelled from the department, after which time the work of the board was carried on by two members. *Report of the Board of Education for Freedmen, Department of the Gulf, for the Year 1864.* Plumly, who acted as chairman, served without pay. The secretary, Wheelock, received a lieutenant's salary. New Orleans *Times,* Feb. 23. 1865.

16. This report indicated that the levy was to be made "as soon as possible." That it was made later in the year is indicated by an entry of a Louisiana planter in his diary in October that he had "inquired about the negro school tax and found that my tax would amount to over 130 dollars." Diary of A. Franklin Pugh, entry of Oct. 31, 1865.

body. The direction of the small number of institutions which had been operating under the auspices of the benevolent societies was also gradually assumed by the board. At the end of 1864, 95 schools with 162 teachers and 9,571 pupils were in operation in the department. During the nine months of the board's supervision there had been an average monthly increase of 10 schools, 15 teachers, and 850 pupils. One hundred and thirty of the 162 teachers were Southerners. It was the expressed aim of the board "to select the most capable and worthy," but according to the *Report*, it was "not unmindful of those whose loyal antecedents and consequent suffering from the rebellion entitle them to sympathy and aid." Salaries ranged from fifty to eighty dollars a month. Some of the teachers were colored.[17] There were in addition to the day-students given above over 2,000 adults receiving instruction in high schools and Sunday schools conducted under the board's auspices. On February 1, 1865, the estimated number of children of school age (five to twelve) in the department was about 20,000; of these over 11,000 were in school.[18]

The educational system was much better developed in New Orleans and vicinity than it was in the remote rural sections of the Department of the Gulf. Weekly inspections were made of schools in all except the latter sections; these were inspected but once a month. The Board of Education set up the following rules to be observed in all the schools: 1. Each school was to be kept in session every week day, except Saturday, from 8:45 to 2:30 with a half-hour recess at noon. 2. The teacher was to arrive at the schoolhouse not later than 8:30. 3. Roll was to be taken at 8:45 and the first exercise was to be either the singing of an appropriate melody, the repeating of the Lord's Prayer, or the reading of a selection from the Bible. 4. A regular order of exercise was to be posted in the schoolroom and duplicate copies to be furnished the Board of Education. No

17. *Second Annual Report of the New England Freedmen's Aid Society*, p. 48.
18. *Ibid.*

class period was to exceed thirty minutes. 5. Pupils not engaged in reading were to be kept busy by suitable memory, slate, or other exercises. 6. The students were to pass in and out of the school in military order. 7. The teacher was to make monthly account to the board for all books, charts, and other equipment received, and failure to comply with this rule would cause the value of unreported equipment to be deducted from the teacher's salary. 8. The teacher was also to "render faithfully" to the board a weekly report of attendance, and "the exact hour, to the minute of opening and closing school each day." 9. Plantation laborers over twelve years of age were not to be admitted to the school without written consent of their employers. 10. The modes of punishment were not to differ in any respect from those employed in white schools.[19]

With the opening up of the country along the Mississippi from Cairo to Natchez the services of benevolent societies were offered for the education of the blacks. These offers were usually accepted and the teachers encouraged by the military authorities, especially by John Eaton, superintendent of the Freedmen's Department and his assistants. The government ordered that all teachers duly accredited by the various societies should be furnished as far as practicable with transportation, quarters, rations, and places in which to conduct schools. Teachers who first assumed their duties in this territory were representatives of the American Missionary Association, the Western Freedmen's Aid Commission, the Western Sanitary Commission, and the Society of Friends. After the surrender of Vicksburg many more came from these and other organizations, including the Northwestern Freedmen's Aid Commission, the National Freedmen's Relief Association, the Board of Missions of the United Presbyterian Church, the Reformed Presbyterians, and the United Brethren in Christ.[20]

19. *Second Annual Report of the New England Freedmen's Aid Society,* p. 25 (Appendix C).
20. Eaton, *Report for 1864,* p. 81; Yeatman, *Report,* Dec. 17, 1863, *passim.*

In the early months of their operation the schools established by the benevolent agencies suffered from lack of a central supervision and unified direction. Each society chose its own area of operations, establishing schools and conducting them wherever and however it thought best. The teachers had to have the approval of the local officers of the Freedmen's Department in order to draw rations; but otherwise this department had no control over their activities, though it did give advice as to the location and distribution of schools.

To secure a greater degree of uniformity in the activities of the different societies, Adjutant General Lorenzo Thomas issued an order on September 26, 1864, placing educational affairs under the general supervision of John Eaton. By this order Eaton was required to appoint superintendents of colored schools through whom he should direct the location of all schools, the occupation of houses, and other details pertaining to Negro education. In compliance with these instructions the Reverend L. H. Cobb was appointed superintendent of colored schools in the District of Memphis, the Reverend James A. Hawley in the District of Vicksburg, the Reverend Joel Grant in the District of Arkansas, and J. L. Roberts at Columbus, Kentucky.[21]

In his General Order Number 9, issued in March, 1864, Adjutant General Thomas had specified that provision was to be made for at least one school in each police district in the country along the Mississippi included in the Department of the Tennessee and the State of Arkansas for the education of colored children under twelve years of age. This order was never carried out in the rural sections, largely on account of the disturbed state of the country and the apathy or opposition of the planters. An investigation of plantations in the Vicksburg district in the fall of 1864 revealed that no schools had been provided by the employers, with the exception of a few Sunday schools. The

21. Eaton, *Report for 1864,* pp. 84–86.

same situation was found to be generally true on plantations in other sections.[22] In the cities and freedmen's camps
the educational facilities were much better than on the
plantations because of the greater security from "Rebel"
raids and the greater ease of procuring teachers and equipment.[23]

The work of providing educational facilities for the
freedmen in the Department of the Cumberland seems to
have been initiated by Major G. L. Stearns. His specified
duties were confined to the recruiting and organization of
colored troops, but soon after establishing his headquarters at Nashville in September, 1863, he began to procure
teachers for colored schools in the vicinity. Through his
exertions money was raised for the establishment of a Negro girls' school within the city. Several benevolent organizations responded to his appeals for aid. The one most
active in this department, however, was the Pennsylvania
Freedmen's Aid Association. W. F. Mitchells, one of its
representatives, was appointed to superintend the establishment of colored schools in middle and eastern Tennessee and in northern Georgia and Alabama.[24]

Everywhere the work of educating the Negroes who came
within the Federal lines was encompassed by many difficulties. One of the most embarrassing of these was the lack of
suitable buildings and equipment. In many instances
churches which had come into disuse because of the exodus
of the majority of the white inhabitants were appropriated for use as schoolhouses. While these provided good
shelter, they were far from satisfactory in other respects.
In the first place, there was no provision for separating the
various classes other than by assembling them in different
parts of the room. In some cases, as many as three and four
classes recited at one time in the same room.[25] This complicated the problems of both discipline and instruction. The
pews of the churches were ill-adapted to writing. Some of

22. Eaton, *Report for 1864*, pp. 32, 52, 58.
23. *Ibid.*, p. 32.   24. *O. R.*, Ser. 3, IV, 771.
25. *Freedmen's Record*, I (June, 1865), 96, 98.

them were so high as to obscure the little Negroes from the teachers' view.

Many of the teachers, however, would have considered themselves fortunate to have had the use of a church for schools. In some sections of the Mississippi Valley the only buildings available for school use were dilapidated sheds and cabins. This situation was especially true of portions of Louisiana where new houses could not be built for lack of funds, and where the desire to avoid arousing the antagonism of the loyal population tended to make the military authorities reluctant to seize good buildings for educational uses. As a consequence, only third-rate buildings were appropriated. These were roughly repaired, each fitted with a cheap stove, a window or two cut for light and air, and school was begun.[26] Elizabeth Bond, a teacher at Young's Point, Louisiana, wrote on April 3, 1864: "I opened school here in a rough log house, thirty feet square and so open that the crevices admitted light sufficient without the aid of windows. The furniture consisted of undressed plank benches without backs, from ten to twelve feet long, and in the center of the room stood an old steamboat stove about four feet long which had been taken out of the river."[27] A teacher in another parish reported a situation even more discouraging: "Arrived, found a place to live a mile and a half from the school shed. Dreadful people, dirty and vulgar, but the best I can do. . . . Did well enough till it rained, since then I have walked three miles a day ankle deep in thick black mud that pulls off my shoes. Nothing to eat but strong pork and sour bread. . . . The school shed has no floor and the rains sweep clean across it, through the places where the windows should be. I have to huddle the children first in one corner and then in another to keep them from drowning or swamping."[28]

26. *Report of the Board of Education for Freedmen, Department of the Gulf, for the Year 1864*, p. 7.

27. *Report of the Executive Board of Friends Association for the Aid and Elevation of the Freedmen* (May 11, 1864), p. 11.

28. *Report of the Board of Education for Freedmen, Department of the Gulf, for the Year 1864*, p. 8.

Very few of the teachers had a sufficiency of suitable equipment in the way of books, charts, and slates. A Louisiana teacher began school with only a few inferior charts which she had picked up in an army camp as aids for the imparting of knowledge to her dusky charges. She taught for five weeks before books and slates arrived.[29] A school was established at the "rope-walk," a place for the reception of refugees at Norfolk, in a rough room at one end of the building, which had neither floor, doors, nor windows. The teachers taught the Negroes their letters from cards pinned upon the walls, using their umbrellas as pointers.[30]

Some schools were fairly flooded with the publications of Northern tract societies and the miscellanies from New England attics. But fortunate indeed was that teacher who could equip an entire class with books of the same author, or even of the same grade. In his *Report* of December 17, 1863, Yeatman said that he visited a school in Louisiana the pupils of which were "using books of every kind and description." Some were using scraps of paper. One Negro was learning his letters from a volume of Tennyson's poems.[31] Bibles and Testaments were used in the teaching of reading in a number of schools. There was a general shortage of spellers in all sections, probably because these were more widely used than other books. Most of the books and other articles of equipment were furnished by benevolent organizations. In a few schools the teachers required students who were able to buy books to do so. One teacher expressed the opinion that the pupils studied better from books which they bought than from the ones which were given them.[32]

The crowded condition of most of the schools complicated the problem of providing ample desks and benches.

29. *Report of the Executive Board of Friends Association for the Aid and Elevation of the Freedmen*, p. 11.

30. *Extracts from Letters of Teachers and Superintendents of the New England Freedmen's Aid Society*, Fifth Series, p. 9.

31. Yeatman, *Report*, p. 11.

32. *Third Report of a Committee of the Representatives of the New Yearly Meeting of Friends upon the Condition and Wants of the Colored Refugees*, p. 10.

It was not unusual for surplus pupils to sit about the walls and in the aisles on the floor.[33]

Another great difficulty which was encountered by those engaged in educating the Negroes was prejudice. Some of the Southern whites were bitterly opposed to the education of the blacks; others merely contemptuous. This attitude was encouraged in some instances by the circulation of reports that the "nigger teachers" were the "scum" of Northern society and of questionable reputation.[34] The teachers were frequently the objects of local white hatred and contempt. A "Yankee" woman who began a colored school in the African Church in Richmond in April, 1865, said that white people would gather at the windows during the day and sneer and laugh, and "top their heads and say, 'the idea of a darkey's going to school!' " One of the male observers was heard to say: "Well, I would not mind their going to school so much if they had nigger teachers; but to see white folks teaching 'em, that's awful!"[35] A member of the Louisiana legislature, on riding by a colored school yard with a Northern friend, stopped and looked intently and then earnestly inquired, "Is *this* a school?" On receiving an affirmative answer he threw up his hands and said: "What! Of niggers? . . . *well, well!* I have seen many an absurdity, in my lifetime but *this is the climax of absurdities*."[36]

But the expression of opposition frequently exceeded contemptuous remarks. In Louisiana the teachers found great difficulty in getting credit at the stores; as their pay was frequently in arrears, the inability to buy on account worked a distinct hardship on them.[37] The inhabitants, even those classed as loyal, were so averse to boarding the "nig-

33. For an example see *Extracts from Letters of Teachers and Superintendents of the New England Freedmen's Aid Society,* Fifth Series, p. 7.

34. Katherine Smedley, The Northern Teacher on the South Carolina Sea Islands, p. 36 (M. A. thesis, University of North Carolina).

35. *Freedmen's Record,* I (June, 1865), 98.

36. *Sen. Ex. Docs.,* 39th Cong., 1st Sess., II, nos. 27, 112.

37. *Report of the Board of Education for Freedmen, Department of the Gulf, for the Year 1864,* p. 8.

ger teachers," that the commanding general of the Department of the Gulf had to issue a special order in the summer of 1864 calling upon planters to provide accommodations for the teachers and threatening to remove from the department those who failed to comply.[38] This order caused an improvement in the situation; but there remained a number of teachers who, being unable to secure lodging, had to take up residence in some "weather-proof shelter" and board themselves, or stay with colored families.[39]

In one locality where the efforts of some teachers to procure lodging at any price proved futile, the military authorities compelled a "loyal planter" to receive them. He had to comply with the order; in a short time he conceived a plan to get rid of his enforced guests. He sent his family away on a visit, invited a group of his friends in and "turned his home into a sort of bawdy-house that presented scenes which these ladies could not witness and in which they were invited to participate." In this way the house was rendered uninhabitable for the dispensers of knowledge and they felt compelled to leave.[40]

In a number of instances the prejudice of the whites against the Negro schools led to acts of violence, sometimes on the part of loyal citizens. Colored pupils were stoned on their way to and from school.[41] Bricks and missiles were thrown through the windows while schools were in session imperiling the safety of teacher and pupils. In Thibodaux, Louisiana, a schoolhouse was broken open on successive nights for months, "the furniture defaced, the books destroyed, and the house made untenable by nuisance."[42] At Columbia, Tennessee, a white "nigger teacher" was publicly whipped; another was visited by a group of young men who ordered him to leave the country in five minutes

38. *Report of the Board of Education for Freedmen, Department of the Gulf, for the Year 1864*, p. 26.

39. *Ibid.*, p. 7; *Sen. Ex. Docs.*, 40th Cong., 3rd Sess., III, pt. 1, 161.

40. New Orleans *Tribune*, Sept. 13, 1864.

41. *Sen. Ex. Docs.*, 39th Cong., 2nd Sess., I, nos. 6, 58.

42. *Report of the Board of Education for Freedmen, Department of the Gulf, for the Year 1864*, p. 9.

at the peril of his life, saying that "no d—— Yankee or Northern man should stay in that place and teach niggers."[43] Several colored families at Huntsville, Alabama, were turned out of their houses for permitting their children to go to school.[44] A schoolhouse in the vicinity of Beaufort, North Carolina, was burned by a small band of guerrillas a short time after opening. The teacher, Mrs. Croome, who stayed nearby, was called from her room and threatened with violence if she ever again attempted to "teach niggers to read."[45]

Educational enterprises did not always have the active support of Northerners. Those who leased plantations in the Mississippi Valley were very apathetic in the matter of providing schooling facilities for their employees. Chaplain Fiske testified that their cultivation of plantations was a "mere temporary speculative venture," and that the whole spirit of such operations was "fatally opposed to these plans for the culture and elevation of the laborer."[46] Military officers were sometimes loath to coöperate with the teachers. After the Federals occupied New Orleans, General Emory admonished Thomas Conway not to advocate publicly the establishment of schools for colored children "as it would be very dangerous."[47] Edwin Stanley, military governor of North Carolina, opposed the opening of a school for Negroes at Newbern in 1862.[48] A provost marshal in Louisiana refused to aid a teacher in the establishment of a school saying that he didn't believe in "nigger teachers" and that he didn't enlist to help them.[49]

43. *House Ex. Docs.*, 40th Cong., 3rd Sess., III, pt. 1, 161.

44. *Report of the Executive Board of Friends Association for the Aid and Elevation of the Freedmen*, p. 14.

45. James, *Annual Report of the Superintendent of Negro Affairs in North Carolina* (1864), p. 21.

46. Eaton, *Report for 1864*, p. 52.

47. *Report of the Board of Education for Freedmen, Department of the Gulf, for the Year 1864*, pp. 4–5.

48. *O. R.*, Ser. 1, IX, 400–402.

49. *Report of the Board of Education for Freedmen, Department of the Gulf, for the Year 1864*, p. 8.

Irregularity in attendance of Negroes was a serious hindrance to their educational progress. One reason for absences was that during the cultivating and planting season the service of all except the very young ones was needed in the fields. Planters were required to send children under twelve years of age to school; this requirement was often ignored, or evaded, by claiming that those whose ages might be in question were over twelve. Another cause of interruptions in attendance was the transiency of the colored population, especially in areas near the Confederate lines where fugitives were frequently arriving and laborers leaving for work on plantations or in the army. There were also noticeable increases in the number of absentees on wash days and during revival-meeting seasons.[50]

Figures on attendance for extensive areas are not available on account of the lack of uniform policy in keeping records. In some localities the records were so fragmentary as to be hardly worthy of the name. The teacher who attempted to keep them was confronted with many perplexities. A North Carolina teacher reported that the name "Bill" or "Tom" had sometimes remained upon his book for several days waiting for the owner thereof to decide upon a surname.[51] The average attendance of the pupils in South Carolina was estimated as between three-fifths and two-thirds of the enrollment.[52] The records of the school at Newbern, North Carolina, for September, 1864, showed an average monthly attendance of 128 out of an enrollment of 200. During the month 23 pupils left to attend other schools and 17 left to find employment.[53] In May, 1864, the Friends' school at Alexandria, Virginia, had 275 names

50. Smedley, The Northern Teacher on the South Carolina Sea Islands, p. 59.

51. *Extracts from Letters of Teachers and Superintendents of the New England Educational Commission for Freedmen,* Fourth Series, p. 8.

52. *Second Annual Report of the New England Freedmen's Aid Society,* p. 13.

53. *Extracts from Letters of Teachers and Superintendents of the New England Educational Commission for Freedmen,* Fourth Series, p. 8.

on the roll; the average daily attendance was 160.[54] Attendance was best in large cities like New Orleans and Memphis; it was worst in the rural sections. A teacher from a country district near Norfolk wrote in 1864 that the people engaged in working on the farms came in small parties to school throughout the day with greater numbers coming in the evening.[55]

Some teachers who worked in plantation areas sought to solve the problem of irregular attendance by literally carrying the schools to the pupils, going from place to place during the day to hold classes. Two sisters near Portsmouth, Virginia, served eighteen plantations in this manner, making the rounds in an "uncertain tumble-down carriage." They carried with them clothing, books, block letters with a ground frame in which to build sentences, and slates. At each place they called the Negroes together, dressed the destitute, taught the young and very old, and encouraged them to study until their next visit.[56]

Another factor which handicapped the promotion of Negro education was the shortage of teachers. The response of the people at the North to both the physical and the intellectual needs of their ebon-hued charges was generous. But the burden of supplying these multitudinous needs was exceedingly heavy for private benevolence. The number of teachers in the South, including both Northerners and Southerners supported by private and public means, was never adequate to provide instruction for the masses of freedmen.[57]

In order to meet the deficiency of white teachers, native

54. See *Third Report of a Committee of the Representatives of the New York Yearly Meeting of Friends upon the Condition and Wants of the Colored Refugees*, p. 7.

55. *Extracts from Letters of Teachers and Superintendents of the New England Freedmen's Aid Society*, Fifth Series, p. 7.

56. *Ibid.*, p. 8.

57. Although great care was exercised in most cases in the selection of teachers to be sent South, some of these proved incompetent or maladjusted after a short period and returned home. McKim, *The Freedmen of South Carolina*, p. 17.

blacks were frequently called upon to assist in instruction. Some of these assistants were chosen from among those who had learned to read during the slave era, of which there were a considerable number in the South.[58] Many teachers adopted the policy of choosing certain older and more advanced students, after the school had been in operation for several weeks, to assist in teaching the younger and more backward pupils what they themselves had learned. A Beaufort, South Carolina, instructor had several colored assistants to whom she devoted one hour in the afternoon to very careful instruction to prepare them for the next day's program. These assistants were paid from the returns of a weekly five-cent levy on each pupil, their aggregate compensation averaging about three dollars a week.[59] A teacher who had charge of a district on St. Helena Island appointed a committee on education composed of colored representatives from each plantation. The duties of this body were to visit the district school once a month in order to mark the progress of the pupils, to act upon any subject which might be brought before them pertaining to the proper regulation of the school, and to do their best to secure the attendance of all children of school age. This scheme was a source of much satisfaction to the Negroes.[60]

In several instances Negroes undertook the education of their fellows on their own initiative. In Natchez, Mississippi, three schools were established, each by a colored woman. All charged tuition; one at the rate of two dollars a month and the other two at one dollar a month.[61] When a group of freedmen was transferred from Edisto to St. He-

58. See Carter G. Woodson, *The Education of the Negro in the South Prior to 1860*, p. 205 and *passim*.
59. *First Annual Report of the Educational Commission for Freedmen with Extracts from Letters of Teachers and Superintendents*, pp. 26–27.
60. *Ibid.*, p. 34.
61. Yeatman, *Report*, Dec. 17, 1863, p. 14. One of these teachers was said to have operated a secret night school for Natchez slaves for years before the outbreak of the war. Laura S. Haviland, *A Woman's Life Work*, p. 300.

lena Island in July, 1862, two Negro men, one about forty years of age and the other seventy, gathered about one hundred and fifty of the newcomers into two schools and taught them for five months until white teachers were provided by benevolent societies.[62]

Immediately after the Federal occupation of Savannah the Negroes established two large schools in buildings located in the colored section of the city. An examination was held at which five men and ten women, all colored, qualified as teachers. The more advanced of the two institutions was placed under the superintendence of a Negro by the name of Porter, who, in spite of the prohibitory legislation on the subject had, during the period of slavery, acquired considerable experience in teaching. The teachers received salaries ranging from thirty-five dollars a month for the two principals to fifteen dollars a month for the female instructors; they received rations from the government. The schools were under the direction of a colored school board —the executive body of the "Savannah Educational Society"—some of the members of which were represented as being men of "real ability and intelligence." The American Missionary Association and the New England Freedmen's Aid Society gave the two Negro-controlled schools some assistance in the form of equipment and money.[63]

The Negroes who entered the schools established by "Yankee" benefactors in various parts of the South were of all ages, sizes, hues, and conditions. Mother, child, and grandchild sometimes came hand-in-hand to the schoolroom.[64] Of 160 pupils in a Newbern, North Carolina, school in 1863, 50 were between six and twelve years of age, 95 were between twelve and forty-five, and 15 were over forty-

62. Pierce, "The Freedmen at Port Royal," *Atlantic Monthly,* XII (1863), 305. The Freedmen's Inquiry Commission observed similar instances in Virginia. *O. R.,* Ser. 3, III, 432.

63. *Freedmen's Record,* I (June, 1865), 92–93.

64. *Third Report of a Committee of the Representatives of the New York Yearly Meeting of Friends upon the Condition and Wants of the Colored Refugees,* p. 17.

five.[65] A Louisiana teacher commenced school with 130 pupils "varying in age from four to forty years, and of every shade, from coal black to almost white, with light hair and blue eyes."[66] The students came to school in all kinds of clothing varying from the handed-down finery of their ex-masters to miscellanies of rags pinned together with nails and thorns. A "Yankee" captain met a boy going to school in South Carolina "clad in a shirt of Brussels and a pair of trousers of ingrain carpet."[67] Some of the older pupils seemed to take a great pride in cleanliness and neatness; most of the younger ones had to be sent to the well to wash their hands and faces at the beginning of each school day. A Young's Point, Louisiana, teacher described her new charges as "wild, very destitute of clothing, and, in personal appearance, extremely filthy."[68] Another teacher spoke of her pupils as being "dirty, ragged, lousy, and neglected."[69]

There was one point of homogeneity among the students both old and young in the first days of colored education: this was their eagerness to go to school and to learn to read. To them reading and schools were symbols of freedom and a guarantee against the return of slavery. Immediately after the occupation of Wilmington, North Carolina, by the Federals, a teacher announced that he would meet the colored children at nine o'clock on a certain morning at the church to enroll them. Very early in the morning of the appointed day Negroes began to appear at the church ground. By seven o'clock the yard was full and the street was blocked. Anxious parents would come pushing their way through the crowd with their dusky charges in train

65. *Extracts from Letters of Teachers and Superintendents of the New England Educational Commission for Freedmen*, Fourth Series, p. 8.
66. *Report of the Executive Board of Friends Association for the Aid and Elevation of the Freedmen*, p. 11.
67. Nordhoff, *The Freedmen of South Carolina*, p. 9.
68. *Report of the Executive Board of Friends Association for the Aid and Elevation of the Freedmen*, p. 11.
69. *Report of the Board of Managers of the Indiana Freedmen's Aid Commission*, Sept. 7, 1864, p. 21.

saying to the teacher that they wanted "dese yer four children's names tooken," or, "Please, Sir, put down dese yer," or, "I wants dis gal of mine to jine."[70] A South Carolina mother told a teacher that she would do her daughter's required work in the fields if the girl were permitted to go to school.[71]

Both children and adults apparently made very zealous students for a time after the schools opened. A North Carolina teacher reported that the children had "repeatedly and unanimously" voted on the approach of holidays that they "preferred school to play."[72] The superintendent of freedmen at Newbern said that the children frequently carried their books home with them. In passing through the camps he was often "assailed by little urchins holding out their slates and asking, 'Please, Sir, set me a copy' "; it was no uncommon thing, he added for those " 'just let loose' from school to gather in groups and go through with a spelling exercise in fine style and close off with 'Hail Columbia!' "[73] The adults usually attended school in the evenings or in the afternoons after their day's work was done. They often took their spellers and readers to the fields with them to study at intervals of rest;[74] labor superintendents making their regular rounds of inspection were sometimes plied with questions by workers in the fields as to the identification of letters of the alphabet and the pronunciation of words. A South Carolina superintendent reported that

70. *Nineteenth Annual Report of the American Missionary Association,* 1865, p. 23.

71. *First Annual Report of the Educational Commission for Freedmen with Extracts from Letters of Teachers and Superintendents,* p. 25.

72. *Second Annual Report of the New England Freedmen's Aid Society,* p. 33.

73. *Nineteenth Annual Report of the American Missionary Association,* p. 23.

74. "M. H. C.," writing from Norfolk, June 10, 1864, said concerning adults: "Their books in many cases were worn as constantly as their clothes . . . and while for a moment resting themselves, or their poor worn-out animals, the book was sure to be on duty." *Extracts from Letters of Teachers and Superintendents of the New England Freedmen's Aid Society,* Fifth Series, p. 7.

some of the laborers in the field studied more than they worked; he threatened to take their books away from them if they did not perform their required tasks.[75] After a few weeks of school most of the adults began to lose their zeal for education. This was attributable partly to the fact that going to school lost its novelty, and partly to the difficulty which they had in learning.[76]

According to the testimony of teachers, the behavior of the colored children in school was generally of such a nature as to give little cause for worry. In weighing this testimony, however, allowance must be made for the fact that most of the teachers were from anti-slavery circles of the North and therefore inclined to observe and report only the virtues of their charges. Doubtless the conduct of the colored pupils was enviable in some respects. The Negro children had been taught by their parents and their masters to have great respect for white authority, and this training was often utilized to advantage by their Northern teachers. Then, too, they had usually been taught to have a wholesome regard for the property of others. Concerning the manifestations of this characteristic among the pupils, the Board of Education of the Department of the Gulf reported: "Another habitude of these colored children is their care of books and school furniture. There is an absence of that Young American lawlessness so common on Caucasian play grounds. The walls and fences about the colored schools are not defaced, either by violence or vulgar scratching. They do not whittle or ply the jack-knife at the expense of desks and benches." The board also noted with approval that "the imagination of these juveniles is generally incorrupt" and that "from the two most prevailing and disgusting vices of school children, profanity and obscenity," they were "singularly free."[77]

75. First Annual Report of the Educational Commission for Freedmen with Extracts from Letters of Teachers and Superintendents, p. 26.

76. Pierce, The Freedmen of Port Royal, p. 322; Gannett, "The Freedmen at Port Royal," North American Review, CI (1865), 4.

77. Report of the Board of Education for Freedmen, Department of the Gulf, for the Year 1864, p. 14.

The characteristic of the pupils which gave the teachers the greatest concern was their propensity toward fighting and quarreling. A teacher in Charleston reported that on one occasion she was "horror-stricken to see two big boys rush at each other and before the sentinel at the door could interfere, one had received a fearful cut in the face with a knife."[78] Another teacher wrote from Baton Rouge that when she first opened her school "not a day passed without two or three fights among the pupils when at their play and these were often severe and bloody." She added that as the school continued there was a marked subsidence in their pugnacity. A young Massachusetts woman who went to the Sea Island district of South Carolina in 1862 to teach noticed that there was a "great deal of tyrannizing over each other" among her pupils. "Mind now, Min', run quick" they would say, or "I knock you," or "I kill you dead." "Cursing," she said, "as they call calling names, etc., is one of the hardest things I have to contend with in school, they are so quick to interpret any look or act into an offense and resent it on the spot with word or blow." Later she wrote that she had recently "had a long talk with some of my big girls who had been very noisy and fighting—they do 'knock' each other most unmercifully, and I can't instill any better notions into them. 'Anybody hurt you, you 'bleeged to knock 'em' is the universal response."[79]

Restlessness, moving about, talking, eating and drinking in school—many of them brought bottles of water and lunches with them—and studying aloud also gave the teachers considerable trouble.[80] The pupils were not accustomed to confinement as close as that required in the schoolroom, and it was with much difficulty that they made the adjustment. According to a Charleston teacher, "they had no idea of school life and found sitting still and mental

78. Elizabeth G. Rice, "A Yankee Teacher in the South, An Experience in the Early Days of Reconstruction." *Century Magazine*, LXII (May, 1901), 153.

79. Pearson, *Letters from Port Royal*, pp. 214–215.

80. *Freedmen's Journal*, I (1865), 4, 114.

application the most laborious task they had ever been set to do. They wanted to talk, or to get up and walk around the room and they fell asleep in their seats, even falling upon the floor as easily as babes."[81] This instructor found it impossible to enforce authority without resort to punishment. Effective methods were to make the offenders sit on the floor in the front of the room "with legs kept straight and feet turned up," and to have them stand and toe a line. "They seemed to dislike having attention drawn to their feet, which were usually bare." Josiah and Tony, two students of this Charleston teacher, occasionally had to be whipped. Though the rod was lightly applied their evident familiarity with such punishment would cause them to scream and writhe as if in great agony and to beg for mercy, even before the first blow was struck. Their piteous cries, however, had a salutary effect on the behavior of the others. This gave rise to a joke among the teachers "that when visitors of apparent consequence were seen coming, the outer sentinel would send the brief message, 'whip Josiah' as he, being the older and more practiced in his howling made consequently a larger impression on the school." If the message was simply, " 'whip Tony,' it was presumed that in the sentinel's estimation the visitors were of minor consequence."[82]

When the confinement of the schoolroom became too irksome, pupils would sometimes go to their teacher with a request for permission to go home on account of a stomach-ache. This ailment became so "remarkably prevalent" that one teacher decided to investigate; she found according to her own statement that stomach-ache "was a generic term for every kind of ailment from head to foot."[83]

When the pupils first came to school the stock of knowledge of both old and young was very limited. Superstitions were innumerable, especially in isolated sections where con-

81. Rice, "A Yankee Teacher in the South," *Century Magazine,* LXII (May, 1901), 152.
82. *Ibid.,* p. 153.   83. *Ibid.*

tact with whites had been limited. Among peculiar ideas prevalent in the Sea Island district of South Carolina was the belief that hags were evil spirits; that there was a kind of witchcraft which only certain persons could cure; that when a sleeping child was picked up and moved, its spirit must be recalled or it would cry on awaking until it was taken back to the same place and its spirit invoked; that turning an alligator on its back would bring rain; and that talking about a person while in a boat might bring a storm.[84] Very few of the pupils anywhere knew anything "about the government, the President, or the laws of the land." Their conceptions of the months and of time were very imperfect.[85] The "dial" of South Carolina pupils was said to be as follows: "When the first fowl crow—at the crack o'day—w'en de sun stan' straight oberhead—at frog peep—when fust star shine—at flood tide, or ebb tide, or young flood—on las' moon, or new moon."[86] The teachers sought to remove the deficiencies of their pupils in these fields of practical knowledge as well as to instruct them in the "three R's."

In the spring of 1865 smallpox broke out in the vicinity of Beaufort, South Carolina. The commanding military officer ordered that all children be vaccinated. One morning a physician came to the school taught by Elizabeth Botume to inoculate the children. Miss Botume, desirous of avoiding a commotion, quietly called the largest girl in the room to her desk and rolled up her sleeve, the other students looking on closely, their large, rolling eyes giving unmistakable evidence of suppressed alarm. The doctor took hold of the girl's hand, giving her a reassuring smile, but when he raised his lancet restraint broke loose. The intended victim "uttered a shriek exclaiming, 'O Jesus save

84. Pierce, "The Freedmen at Port Royal," *Atlantic Monthly,* XII (1863), 303.

85. *Report of the Executive Board of Friends Association for the Aid and Elevation of the Freedmen,* p. 13.

86. Botume, *First Days Amongst the Contrabands,* p. 128.

me!' and snatching away her hand, she darted out of the room" with the other pupils close behind. There was no more school that day.[87]

The answers which the pupils gave to some of the questions asked them were amusing. An adult student of Jackson, Mississippi, when asked who made her, replied, "I don't know 'xactly, sir. I heard once who it was, but I done forgot de gentmun's name."[88] A little North Carolina girl when asked the meaning of the word "wool" answered, "It is hair," at the same time placing her hand on the top of her woolly head. Another pupil, with mischievous inclinations, was asked the meaning of "hide"; her prompt response was "To hide a switch from mammy."[89] Other answers were reflective of practices and tendencies characteristic of the Negroes. When a South Carolina teacher asked her class what the ears were for, a little girl quickly responded, "to put ring in." Even more suggestive was the statement made by a Virginia pupil when the teacher asked the difference between rational and irrational: "Why its rational," he said, "when we draw rations and irrational when we don't." Another boy when asked his father's business said, "Father does not do anything, but mother draws rations."[90] Upon the reception of a large outline map in a North Carolina school, one pupil wanted the teacher to point out President Lincoln's state to him. Another wanted to know the location of the Union army; "Oh, I know, I see the camps," interjected another, pointing to the tent-like figures used to represent mountains. The inquiry as to whether or not General Washington lived in Virginia prompted one curious pupil to ask, "was he secesh?"

The Massachusetts origin of a great number of the teachers was not without classroom reflection. The following catechism overheard by E. L. Pierce in a South Caro-

---

87. Botume, *First Days Amongst the Contrabands*, p. 44.
88. William Wells Brown, *The Negro in the American Rebellion*, p. 280.
89. *Freedmen's Record*, I (June, 1865), 96.
90. *The Freedman*, I (1865), 5.

lina school taught by a resident of Massachusetts indicates the emphasis upon points considered vital:

Q. Where were slaves brought to this country?
A. Virginia.
Q. When?
A. 1620.
Q. Who brought them?
A. Dutchmen.
Q. Who came the same year to Plymouth, Massachusetts?
A. Pilgrims.
Q. Did they bring slaves?
A. No.[91]

A teacher at Hilton Head, South Carolina, asked in the course of an oral review quiz: "Where was our Savior born?" One of the boys immediately shouted "Boston," to the obvious satisfaction of all. Another teacher noticed surprise and disappointment on the faces of her pupils when she showed them the comparatively small space occupied on a United States map by Massachusetts. The students were considerably relieved and reassured by the explanation offered by one of their number: "It looks small on de map, but its mighty big when you gits dere."[92]

The government and military authorities came in for their share of recognition in the schoolrooms. To the question, who wrote the Ten Commandments, a South Carolina pupil replied "General Saxby"—a commonly-used perversion of "General Saxton," commander of the Department of the South, whom the Negroes held in great esteem; another ventured the answer, "Uncle Sam," and, still another, "Columbus." A religiously-inclined visitor in a Sea Island school asked, "Children, who is Jesus Christ?" After a period of embarrassing silence a small boy yelled out, "General Saxby, Sar"; whereupon an older boy

91. Pierce, "The Freedmen at Port Royal," *Atlantic Monthly*, XII (1863), 305.
92. *Freedmen's Record*, II (1866), 6, 27.

jumped up and exclaimed, "Not so, boy, Him's Massa Linkum."[93]

During the slave era the colored children usually had only one name, the praenomen. To facilitate distinction in the classes and on the rolls, and also to encourage the impression that slavery was a thing of the past, teachers insisted that the pupils adopt the use of surnames, or "titles" as the South Carolina Negroes called them. The children fell in with the idea readily; the result was ,a surprising miscellany of combinations, made up by joining indiscriminately such names as "Pumpkin," "Squash," "Cornhouse," "Honey," "Baby," "Missy," "Abraham Linkum," and "George Washington" to such imposing "titles," in South Carolina, as Rhett, Barnwell, Middleton, Stuart, and Elliot. An unhappy consequence of this free choice of names was the tendency of the children to change them according to their whims, much to the confusion of the teachers whose rolls of the same pupils often showed striking dissimilarity from one day to another.[94]

The subjects receiving greatest attention in the schools were reading, spelling, writing, and arithmetic. History and geography were taught in some of the advanced classes. Textbooks commonly used were Hilliard's *First* and *Second Readers*, the *Bible Reader*, Cowly's *Speller*, and the *New York Speller*. The New Testament was widely used for the teaching of both reading and spelling. A preference was sometimes shown for large reading books, the pupils supposing that they learned faster from them.[95] The alphabet and the multiplication table were sung. Sewing was taught to girls and women in some of the schools. Students in Richmond were reported as going through a series of "graceful gymnastics."[96] A Cambridge, Massachusetts,

93. Botume, *First Days Amongst the Contrabands,* pp. 102, 109.
94. *Ibid.,* pp. 46–47.
95. *Extracts from Letters of Teachers and Superintendents of the New England Educational Commission for Freedmen,* Fourth Series, p. 10.
96. *Freedmen's Record,* I (June, 1865), 99.

teacher who had a school on St. Helena Island drilled "a class in elocution, requiring the same sentence to be repeated with different tones and inflections."[97]

The schools were affected by the prevalent military and patriotic spirit of the times.[98] A colored assistant to a white teacher in South Carolina acquired an army cap and took it upon himself to go around the village every morning, collect the male students, and march them to school in military style, he walking backward in front of the company shouting out orders as if he were a drill sergeant. A favorite pastime of pupils was to get together outside of school hours for spelling exercises; the boy chosen to hold the book and give out the words was designated as "the officer of the day" and he enjoyed great prestige among his juvenile associates.[99] Programs were given from time to time at the schoolhouses on which occasions "Yankee" songs were sung and patriotic recitations given by the pupils. At exercises held at "Uncle Sam's School," in Arlington, Virginia, the following verse was sung "with a perfect gusto":

> So come bring your books and slates,
> And don't be a fool
> For Uncle Sam is rich enough
> To send us all to school.[100]

The following items appeared on a program given by the colored schools of New Orleans on the anniversary of Washington's birthday in 1868: Declamation—Union; tableau—The Dawn of Liberty (this represented a group

97. Pierce, "The Freedmen at Port Royal," *Atlantic Monthly*, XII (1863), 305.

98. A Charleston teacher wrote in April, 1865, that the "great desire" of her pupils was "to be good Yankees and do as the Yankee boys do." *Freedmen's Record*, I (June, 1865), 95.

99. *Extracts from Letters of Teachers and Superintendents of the New England Educational Commission for Freedmen*, Fourth Series, p. 8.

100. *Freedmen's Record*, I (Oct., 1865), 161.

of freedmen bowed down before the Goddess of Liberty) ; song—Good Time Coming; tableau—The Fruits of Liberty (a schoolroom scene with each pupil studying) ; recitation—The American Flag; essay—Darkness of the Past, Brightness of the Present; concluding song—No Slave Beneath the Flag.[101]

Religion was greatly emphasized in the teaching of the blacks. This was attributable largely to the fact that most of the teachers were missionary representatives of benevolent and religious organizations. The "otherworldliness" with which these representatives sometimes regarded their missions was reflected in the conversation of two teachers in South Carolina. On espying a dirty little Negro trudging along, one said, "A little lower than the angels"; the other replied, "Of such is the Kingdom of Heaven."[102] As a rule, school each day was opened or closed—and sometimes both—by an exercise consisting of scripture readings, prayers, and songs. In their prayers the Negroes called down all manner of blessings on the teachers; nor were they forgetful of "Mr. Linkum" and his associates.[103]

Favorite songs were "America," "Sound the Loud Timbrel," "Our Flag is There," "John Brown,"[104] "I Would Not Let You Go, My Lord," "Wrestling Jacob," "Down in the Lonesome Valley," "Roll, Jordan, Roll," "Heaven Shall Be My Home," and "Tell My Jesus Huddy Oh

101. New Orleans *Daily True Delta,* Feb. 23, 1865.

102. Smedley, The Northern Teacher on the South Carolina Sea Islands, p. 31.

103. One venerable Negro prayed as follows: "Grant O Lord that not a feather be lacking in the wing of the North. Indulgent father, we tank thee that thou didst ever make a Linkum. O spare his life and bless our Union army. May one man put a thousand to flight and ten chase ten thousand." *Extracts from Letters of Teachers and Superintendents of the New England Educational Commission for Freedmen,* Fourth Series, p. 11. A woman prayed, "Oh may we get safely over on the other side of Jordan, out of gunshot of the Devil." *Ibid.,* p. 14.

104. The "Yankee" soldiers were very much amused at hearing the children sing this song, especially when they came out emphatically on the words, "We'll hang Jeff Davis on a sour apple tree." Pierce, "The Freedmen at Port Royal," *Atlantic Monthly,* XII (1863), 304.

[Howd'y' Do]." The words of this last song are particularly interesting:

> In de mornin' when I rise,
>   Tell my Jesus, Huddy Oh?
> In de mornin' when I rise,
>   Tell my Jesus, Huddy Oh?
>
> I wash my hands in de mornin' glory,
>   Tell my Jesus, Huddy Oh?
> I wash my hands in de mornin' glory,
>   Tell my Jesus, Huddy Oh?
>
> Pray, Tony, pray boy, you got de order,
>   Tell my Jesus, Huddy Oh?
> Pray, Tony, pray boy, you got de order,
>   Tell my Jesus, Huddy Oh?[105]

The poet Whittier wrote a song especially for a school
on St. Helena Island. The closing stanzas were as follows:

> The very oaks are greener clad,
>   The waters brightly smile;
> Oh, never shone a day so glad,
>   On sweet St. Helena's Isle!
>
> For none in all the world before
>   Were ever glad as we,—
> We're free on Carolina's shore,
>   We're all at home and free![106]

Bible stories were told and read to the pupils by their
teachers. The account of David's encounter with Goliath
was one of the favorites. When inquiry was made of a Virginia group as to who could repeat this story which had
been told by the teacher a considerable time previously, a
boy volunteered the following: "David was a boy that
minded his father's sheep, and Goliah was *a mighty strong*

105. *Ibid.*   106. *Ibid.*

man, who had on an iron cap and brass pantaloons, and Goliah wanted to fight David, Goliah had a big sword and spear, but David had a slungshot and he picked up five little rocks and put them into his *haversack* and went out to fight Goliah. The big man was so mad he cussed and swore awfully, and David took his slungshot and chucked him in de head wid a rock, and den chopped his head off, and if de Lord hadn't helped him, he couldn't never have done it."[107] In view of the strength of the religious note in the teaching of the colored children, it is not surprising that a South Carolina pupil when asked the three requirements of a good school answered in all solemnity, "Father, Son, and Holy Ghost."[108]

The determination of the progress made by the Negroes in their school work is about as difficult as settling the question of their behavior, the complicating factor in both cases being the tendency of the anti-slavery teachers to exaggerate in the pupils' favor. This tendency was noticed and commented on by a Northerner after three years' residence on the islands of South Carolina. Early in 1865 he wrote: "Many friends of the Port Royal movement have a very exaggerated notion of the extent of the education already accomplished there. . . . Perhaps the teachers, for want of material to form definite reports, were obliged to make general statements at first, and may have colored them too warmly . . . none can read with perfect confidence, few without frequent hesitation."[109]

The subjects in which the most rapid advancement was observed were those involving a maximum of memory and a minimum of reasoning. "The memory," wrote E. L. Pierce, "is very susceptible in them, too much so, perhaps, as it is ahead of the reasoning faculty."[110] This was also the opinion of the members of the Board of Education of

107. *The Freedman,* I (1865), 7.
108. Pearson, *Letters from Port Royal,* p. 32.
109. Gannett, "The Freedmen at Port Royal," *North American Review,* CI (1865), 3.
110. Pierce, "The Freedmen at Port Royal," *Atlantic Monthly,* XII (1863), 307.

the Department of the Gulf. In their report for 1864 they said: "They are quick-witted, excelling in those branches that exercise the perceptive and imitative powers and the memory while they are slower in arithmetic and in studies that tax the reasoning powers."[111] Thus more rapid progress was made in reading and spelling than in arithmetic. Writing was very difficult for most students, both old and young; in the case of the latter, clumsiness was doubtless an inhibitive factor. A South Carolina teacher said in January, 1863, that she had a blackboard with numerals and figures on it, all of which the oldest pupils knew "tolerably," but she added, "They make sorry work trying to copy figures on their slates. I let them use them every day now, however, for they must learn by gradually growing familiar with the use of the pencil not to use it like a hoe. There are furrows in the slates made by their digging, in which you might plant benny-seed if not cotton."[112]

Much of the progress made in subjects such as reading and spelling was only apparent. A northern labor superintendent amused himself and two of the teachers on one occasion in South Carolina by having some of the pupils read to him with their books turned upside down. This they did "as readily as the right way," according to one of the teachers.[113] A Charleston teacher said: "Singing and marching were the general exercises they liked best; all others were usually failures. For instance, I would say to the school, 'Today is Wednesday. What day will tomorrow be?' and when someone had the right answer, I would have them repeat it several times in concert; yet, the chances were that in a few minutes the same question would call forth the same series of guesses. Still, because they had an instinctive ear for rhythm, they would . . . count to ten together, or partly get through the . . . alphabet. Yet if I would ask suddenly, 'What number comes after seven?' or

111. *Report of the Board of Education for Freedmen, Department of the Gulf, for the Year 1864,* p. 14.
112. Pearson, *Letters from Port Royal,* p. 149.
113. *Ibid.,* p. 180.

any such question, the whole list would be guessed over again."[114]

But despite the poor showing made by the Negroes in their studies, and despite numerous other difficulties confronted by the teachers of freedmen such as opposition of prejudiced whites, inadequacy of equipment, shortage of funds, and lack of coöperation by some of the military authorities, the education of Negroes under Federal control made substantial progress from its inception in Virginia in 1861 to the end of the war in 1865.

114. Rice, "A Yankee Teacher in the South," *Century Magazine,* LXII (May, 1901), 153.

XV

FIGHTING FOR FREEDOM

THE decision on the part of the North to make soldiers of Negroes came only after a long period of vacillation and controversy. Until the time of the issuance of the Emancipation Proclamation Lincoln seemed to have no definite policy in regard to this or any other phase of the vexatious Negro problem except that included in his general aim of preserving the Union.

Within a few days after the fall of Fort Sumter, the War Department was forced to consider the question of receiving Negroes into the army. Jacob Dodson, a colored man employed in the United States Senate Chamber, who had been "three times across the Rocky Mountains in the service of the country with Fremont and others," wrote Secretary Cameron that he knew of some three hundred reliable free colored citizens of the city of Washington who desired to enter the military service for the defense of the city, presumably under his command. Cameron replied on April 29 that "this Department has no intention at present to call into the service of the Government any colored soldiers."[1] The Department seemed to waver from this position in the fall of 1861. Instructions given to General T. W. Sherman on his departure for operations on the South Carolina coast suggest that the government was playing with the idea of receiving fugitives and abandoned slaves into the army. The general was informed by the acting Secretary of War that in the disposition of the contrabands he was to be governed in general by the instructions which had been given to Butler in Virginia a few months earlier; i.e., to refrain from returning fugitives, to put the able-bodied ones to work, and to charge against their la-

1. *O. R.*, Ser. 3, I, 106, 133.

bor the upkeep of those unable to work. But Sherman was also told that much was left to his discretion; that he should employ the contrabands "in such services as they may be fitted for—either as ordinary employees, or if special circumstances seem to require it, in any other capacity, with such organization (in squads, companies, or otherwise) as you may deem most beneficial to the service; this, however, not being a general arming of them for the service."[2]

Within two weeks after these instructions were given, word came to G. P. Miller, a colored physician of Battle Creek, Michigan, that the War Department had authorized Sherman to enroll Negroes in the army. Miller immediately wrote to Cameron asking permission to raise a brigade of colored men to serve in any capacity, but preferably as sharp-shooters. The acting Secretary of War replied on November 8, 1861, that "the orders to General Sherman . . . authorize the arming of colored persons only in cases of great emergency, and not under regular enrollment for military purposes. . . . Upon reflection you will perceive that there are sufficient reasons for continuing the course thus far pursued."[3]

General Sherman, whether from inability to interpret his ambiguous instructions, or other reasons, took no steps toward making soldiers out of the South Carolina Negroes. It was left to his bold abolitionist successor, General David Hunter, who assumed command of the Department of the South in May, 1862, to test the meaning of the orders. The new commander was of the opinion that some of the able-bodied contrabands within his lines ought to be enlisted as soldiers. Consequently, he detailed Sergeant C. T. Trowbridge to begin recruiting activities. Within a short time a regiment was filled, armed, and uniformed. It was designated as the First South Carolina Volunteers. Hunter's action provoked both favorable and unfavorable comment throughout the Union. A large portion of the

2. *O. R.*, Ser. 1, VI, 176.   3. *Ibid.*, Ser. 3, I, 609, 626.

press condemned him. The incident served, at least, to project the question of arming the Negroes before the country.

On June 9, 1862, Wickliffe of Kentucky introduced a resolution in the House calling upon the Secretary of War to inquire if Hunter had organized a regiment of slaves; if he had been authorized to do so; if he had been furnished with clothing, uniforms, and provisions for such a force; and if he had been supplied with arms for that purpose.[4] On June 14, Secretary Stanton replied to Wickliffe's inquiry that the War Department was not aware that any regiment of Negroes had been organized by General Hunter; that he had not been instructed to muster into the army of the United States the fugitives or captive slaves; that he had been furnished with clothing and arms for the force under his command without instructions as to how they should be used; and that General Hunter had not been furnished by order of the War Department with arms to be placed in the hands of those slaves.[5]

In the meantime, Wickliffe's inquiry had been forwarded to Hunter. The latter is reported to have been much delighted at the receipt of the request for information.[6] He immediately forwarded an answer to the Secretary of War who endorsed it and dispatched it to the House. There the letter was read on July 3, 1862. Hunter said that he had organized no regiment of "fugitive slaves," but that he did have "a fine regiment of loyal persons whose late masters are fugitive rebels"; that the late Secretary Cameron had

4. *Cong. Globe*, 37th Cong., 2nd Sess., pp. 2620–2621.
5. Charles G. Halpine, writing under the *nom de plume* "Private Miles O'Reilly," says that Hunter had forwarded reports of his steps in detail to the War Department, had asked for pay, clothing, etc., but the department had remained silent. J. T. Wilson, *The Black Phalanx*, p. 148. E. L. Pierce, special agent of the Treasury Department in South Carolina in 1862, said that Secretary Stanton did furnish "muskets and red trousers to General Hunter's Regiment," but did not think his authority sufficient to justify paying the Negroes. It seems unlikely that Stanton was ignorant of Hunter's Negro regiment. Pierce, "The Freedmen at Port Royal," *Atlantic Monthly*, XII (1863), 312.
6. "O'Reilly" says that Hunter broke out in loud laughter on receipt of the inquiry. Wilson, *Black Phalanx*, p. 151.

authorized Brigadier General T. W. Sherman to employ
all loyal persons offering their services in defense of the
Union in any manner that he might see fit, and that these
instructions had been transmitted to him on his succession
to Sherman's post; that since these instructions made no
distinction as to character or color or the nature of employment, he deemed them sufficient authority for the arming of the loyal Negroes whose masters had fled; that he
hoped to be able "to organize and present to the present
government from forty-eight thousand to fifty thousand
of these hardy and devoted soldiers."[7]

The piquant tone of this letter caused an uproar in the
House. Wickliffe was enraged. Dunlap offered a resolution
to the effect that the sentiments of Hunter's letter "are an
indignity to the American Congress, an insult to the
American people and our brave soldiers in arms." The
House as a whole seemed to enjoy the situation. The discomfiture of the gentleman from Kentucky was the source
of particular enjoyment to some of the Republican members. Lovejoy suggested that since Wickliffe was absent
during the reading of the first part of the letter it should
be read again for his benefit. Wickliffe replied that he did
not want to hear it. Mallory of Kentucky thought that the
boisterous manifestation of approbation by the Republican
members was regrettable. The entire affair was to him a
scene "disgraceful to the American Congress."[8]

Though Hunter's letter provided a boisterous occasion
for Congress, the policy adopted by the general in South
Carolina was evidently not in accord with the prevailing
sentiment of the time and did not receive the support of
the administration.[9] "Hunter's Regiment" was kept at drill
until the first week in August, then disbanded, with the exception of one company.

7. *O. R.*, Ser. 3, II, 196–198.
8. *Cong. Globe,* 37th Cong., 2nd Sess., pp. 3102, 3109, 3125.
9. *O. R.*, Ser. 3, II, 314. Buckingham, Assistant Attorney General, wrote
to the governor of Wisconsin August 6, 1862: "The President declines to
receive Indians or Negroes as troops." The governor had written the
President offering the services of some Negroes and Indians as soldiers.

The matter of arming the Negro came up for serious debate in Congress shortly after the Hunter episode. This discussion is interesting for the light which it throws on the general attitude of the country toward the matter. On July 9, 1862, a motion was presented in the Senate to amend the act of February 28, 1795, authorizing the President to call out the militia to suppress insurrection.[10] Grimes of Iowa moved to amend the motion by adding that there should be no exemption under any of the militia laws for military service on account of lineage and color, but "that all loyal able-bodied male persons between the ages now fixed by the laws of the United States shall be called to the defense of the country."[11] This proposal met with various objections, mostly from the borderstate members. King of New York offered a substitute to the effect that the President be authorized to receive into the service of the United States, "for the purpose of constructing intrenchments, or performing camp service or any labor or any war service for which he may be found competent persons of African descent"; and that the mother, wife, and children of a person rendering such service be free. A lengthy debate ensued and several amendments were proposed. The bill as finally approved on July 17 embodied the provisions of King's substitute but applied only to the slaves of disloyal owners.

There is a vast difference in the bill as it was originally presented and the substitute which was adopted. The original proposed to give the Negro everywhere an equal status with the white in the militia, to make him a full-fledged soldier. Negroes might be brought into the service as soldiers under the clause "or any military service," but the debate on the bill indicates that the emphasis was on the clause the "constructing of intrenchments or the performing of camp service." Senator Sherman of Ohio argued that "we must

10. The act of 1795 made the term of the militia in the national service only three months.
11. For this motion and succeeding debate, see *Cong. Globe*, 37th Cong., 2nd Sess., pp. 3198 ff.

employ these Negroes, not probably as soldiers, but as laborers, as servants. In the South the Negroes do the labors of the camp. They do all the hard work. Why shall we not avail ourselves of their services to perform the same class of duties for us." Senator Fessenden said that "the white soldiers resented the fact that they, who had volunteered to fight the battles of their country should be employed in digging ditches and throwing up entrenchments . . . when there were numbers . . . acclimated who were ready to volunteer their services." Senator Wilson was of the opinion that "the shovel and the ax had ruined thousands of young men of the country. We could have employed thousands of colored men at low rates of wages to do that ditching and thus saved the health, the strength and the lives of our brave soldiers."[12]

Although the desire for Negroes as soldiers was secondary to that of securing their services as laborers, a majority of Senators was unwilling to limit the use of the blacks to labor functions by this bill. Davis of Kentucky moved to strike out the words, "or any war service." His motion was defeated.

That the administration did not construe the militia act of July 17, 1862, as authorizing a general arming of the Negroes is indicated by an incident which occurred shortly after its passage. On August 6, 1862, General James H. Lane issued a general order authorizing the enlistment of two regiments of blacks in Kansas. On the same day he notified Secretary Stanton that he was receiving Negroes into the service, giving as authority for his action "the late act of Congress." Stanton informed the impetuous general on August 23 that his colored regiment could not be accepted; that according to the law of July 17 such troops could be raised "only upon express and special authority of the President" and that he had not given such authority in Kansas.[13]

The weight of public opinion as reflected in the argu-

---

12. *Cong. Globe*, 37th Cong., 2nd Sess., pp. 3198 ff.
13. *O. R.*, Ser. 3, II, 294, 311–312, 445.

ments in Congress and the statement of the press in 1862 was unfavorable to a general arming of the former Negro slaves. One of the leading arguments advanced was that such a policy would incur foreign disrespect and disapproval. Senator Davis of Kentucky said that it was "an inglorious, ignoble, and cowardly admission that there is any such stress of necessity as that. Why, Sir, do you not perceive that the Englishman, the Frenchman, and the Spaniard are already beginning to contemn and spit upon you."[14]

Another reason brought forward in opposition to arming the Negroes was the fear of stirring up a servile insurrection in the border slave states and even the "Rebel" states. Senator Sherman of Ohio said that "ordinarily to arm Negroes would be shocking to our sense of humanity for the reason that from the history of slave insurrections we associate Negro warfare with the burning of houses and all the scenes of desolation attendant upon savage warfare." Davis of Kentucky recounted the Nat Turner and Santo Domingo uprisings in their terrible details in his argument against the proposal to arm the Negroes.

A third reason offered against the enlistment of Negroes was that they would not fight, or that they were inferior as fighters. T. J. Morgan, colonel of the Fourteenth United States Colored Infantry, said that the Negro was considered unfit to be a soldier "because he belonged to a degraded, inferior race, wanting in soldierly qualities; that his long bondage had crushed out whatever of manliness he might naturally possess; that he was too grossly ignorant to perform intelligently the duties of the soldier."[15] The editor of the New York *Times* early in 1863 spoke of the doubt in the minds of the people as to the Negro's fighting ability, but added cautiously, that he saw no way of testing the question except by trying the experiment.[16] General W. T. Sherman wrote to his wife, January 15, 1865,

14. *Cong. Globe*, 37th Cong., 2nd Sess., pt. 4, p. 3206.
15. Wilson, *Black Phalanx*, p. 290.
16. New York *Times*, Feb. 16, 1863.

"I want soldiers made of the best bone and muscle in the land and wont attempt military feats with doubtful materials. . . . I am right and wont change."[17] At an earlier date he had written: "I cannot bring myself to trust Negroes with arms in positions of danger and trust."[18]

A fourth argument against the use of the Negroes as soldiers was that the white troops would not fight in company with black ones. General W. T. Sherman thought it "unjust to the brave soldiers and volunteers" to place them on a par with Negro recruits.[19] Senator Davis said that he knew the soldiery of the Northwest and that they wanted no auxiliaries. They would "feel themselves degraded" fighting by the side of Negroes.[20]

The chief argument advanced in favor of the use of the Southern Negroes as soldiers was necessity. The Union army was apparently in hard straits in July, 1862, when the proposal to arm the blacks was being debated.[21] Fessenden said in the Senate on July 9, that the governors of the various states had asked the President to call out 300,-000 men a few days before. Let the people know, he added, that the reason we are calling on the blacks is our great need.[22] Senator Rice said that at one time he was not in favor of employing Negroes, "but now we have not enough men on the Potomac to authorize an advance. . . . I would . . . resort to all the means that are known in civilized warfare."[23] The general tone of the debate in Congress was

17. Howe, ed., *Home Letters of General Sherman*, p. 328. Chase and others had written to Sherman to try to get him to change his attitude toward the Negro.

18. *Ibid.*, p. 253.

19. Moore, *Rebellion Record*, XI, 188.

20. *Cong. Globe*, 37th Cong., 2nd Sess., p. 3204, July 9, 1862.

21. On July 11, 1862, McClellan was replaced by Halleck because of his failure to go on to Richmond. Morgan's famous Kentucky raid was in progress, July 4–28. Forrest captured Murfreesboro, Tenn., and a Union garrison July 13. "Miles O'Reilly" voiced a popular sentiment, according to T. J. Morgan, when he said: "The right to be killed I'll divide with the nayger, and give him the largest half." Wilson, *Black Phalanx*, p. 290.

22. *Cong. Globe*, 37th Cong., 2nd Sess., p. 3201.

23. *Ibid.*, p. 3202.

that the war was dragging on at a burdensome expense of men and money and that every possible means should be employed to bring it to a speedy end.

Advocates of a colored soldiery also contended that the recruiting of Negroes at the South would not only add to the strength of the Union, but would weaken the Confederacy. The slaves were used in the fields to support the white soldiers in the army. The people at the North should undermine this supporting power by enlisting the Negroes in the Union army. Adjutant General Thomas told the soldiers of the Department of the Gulf at Lake Providence, Louisiana, April 8, 1863, that "the Administration has determined to take from the rebels this source of supply—to take their Negroes and compel them to send back a portion of their whites to cultivate their deserted plantations. . . . They must do this or their armies will starve."[24]

Another argument in favor of arming the Negro was the salutary effect that military life would have on him. It would "inspire the bondsman of the South with a truer sense of his worth and capacity." It would create respect for the Negro among the whites. The respect of the nation for its "brave defenders" would, in turn, teach the Negro self-respect.[25]

The open avowal of the administration in the Emancipation Proclamation that the freeing of the slaves was one of the incidents, if not one of the aims of the war, was followed in a short time by official pronouncements on the question of receiving Negroes into military service. In the same address to the army at Lake Providence, April 8, 1863, Adjutant General Thomas said concerning fugitives: "They are to be encouraged to come to us; they are to be received with open arms; they are to be fed and clothed; they are to be armed . . . I am here to say that I am authorized to raise as many regiments of blacks as

24. Williams, *History of Negro Troops in the War of the Rebellion*, p. 109.
25. *Continental Monthly*, VI (1864), 198.

I can. . . . I have the fullest authority to dismiss from the Army any man, be his rank what it may, whom I find maltreating the freedmen."[26]

These and other positive administrative utterances were given wide publicity by the press and they doubtlessly caused a considerable flow of public sentiment in favor of a Negro soldiery for the Union.

The first Federal authorization for the recruiting of Negro soldiers was given on August 25, 1862, to General Saxton, successor to Hunter as commander of the Department of the South. The order, accompanied by the suggestive remark that "this must never see daylight because it is so much in advance of public opinion," authorized the enlistment of laborers not exceeding fifty thousand and soldiers not exceeding five thousand.[27] Saxton began the work of organizing the First South Carolina Volunteers immediately, with Hunter's abortive regiment, which in August had dwindled to one company, as a nucleus. In January, 1863, the organization of this first authorized regiment was completed.[28] During the war five Negro regiments were organized in South Carolina and Florida, the last being formed at Hilton Head in April, 1865.

Louisiana proved a fertile field for the recruiting of Negroes both slave and free. Many of the free Negroes who had been serving under the Confederates "surrendered" when the Union troops arrived at New Orleans.[29] After the capitulation of the city to the Federals, great numbers of fugitives thronged to its borders. Phelps asked Butler for authority to organize some of the refugee Negroes for military purposes. Butler, who at this time had a very low opinion of the soldierly qualities of the fugitives, refused the request in July, 1862, suggesting instead that Phelps

26. *Annual Cyclopedia* for 1863, p. 26.
27. Wilson, *Rise and Fall of the Slave Power*, III, 370.
28. Wilson, *Black Phalanx*, p. 469.
29. *Ibid.*, p. 183; Wilson says that the "Creole" commanding the Negro brigade deliberately delivered his command into Federal hands.

employ them in cutting down trees.[30] But having appealed to his superior in vain for reënforcements, Butler decided to receive some of the Negroes into the military service. On August 22, he issued an order authorizing the enlistment of the free Negroes of Louisiana including those who had served under the Confederacy.[31] In two weeks one thousand Negroes were organized into a regiment known as the First Regiment, Louisiana Native Guards.[32] Before the end of the year two other regiments were mustered in by Butler.

Early in 1863 the government entered boldly and vigorously into the work of recruiting an army of colored soldiers. In May of that year Adjutant General Thomas was dispatched to the Mississippi Valley with orders to raise as many Negro regiments as he could. He expressed publicly the hope of recruiting twenty such units.[33] On the same day that Thomas was sent to the West, Daniel Ullmann was ordered to Louisiana to recruit a brigade of colored troops. General Banks, who had succeeded Butler, was instructed to coöperate with Ullmann as the War Department desired that "a large military force from the colored population of Louisiana should be raised at once." The day following the issuance of the above orders to Thomas and Ullmann, Lincoln wrote to Andrew Johnson, military governor of Tennessee, that he had heard that Johnson was thinking of raising a Negro military force. The President said that, in his opinion, the country needed no specific thing so much as a man of Johnson's position and ability to undertake such a project. "The bare sight of 50,000 armed and

---

30. *Ibid.*, pp. 192 ff.; *O. R.*, Ser. 1, XV, 534 ff.

31. No authorization for Butler's order could be found. He probably sensed the change taking place in the administration's attitude. Only three days after its issuance, authorization was given Saxton to enlist Negroes in South Carolina.

32. G. W. Williams, *History of the Negro Race in America*, II, 287. J. T. Wilson says that half of these "free" Negroes were former slaves, or slaves who swore that they were free.

33. *Annual Cyclopedia* for 1863, p. 26.

drilled black soldiers, upon the banks of the Mississippi," he added, "would end the rebellion at once. If you have been thinking of it, please do not dismiss the thought."[34] A short time later, E. A. Wild was sent to North Carolina to raise a brigade of colored troops.[35]

To facilitate the work of recruiting, the War Department in May, 1863, created a Bureau of Colored Troops. While the general purpose of the bureau was to coördinate enrolling activities throughout the country, it devoted most attention to recruiting in the middle and eastern states, areas which had hitherto been neglected.

In its efforts to get Negroes into the ranks, the government received abundant, though not always welcome, aid from substitute brokers and "state agents." The former were a group of "professional recruiters" brought into existence by a provision in the enrollment act of March 3, 1863, permitting a drafted man to send a substitute to serve in his stead. Following the first call for men under this measure, there was a shameful scramble to secure substitutes at the least possible cost. Brokers, acting in the interest of those who sought thus to evade service, combed the Federal-controlled portions of the South buying up ignorant and needy Negroes at a cheap rate to serve as substitutes, lining their own pockets in the process with fat commissions. This practice became so notorious that the War Department issued an order in the latter part of July, 1863, in compliance with instructions from the President, that men of African descent should be accepted only as substitutes for other blacks.[36]

The "state agents" were by-products of the Act of Congress of July 4, 1864, which permitted the recruiting of men in the "Rebel" states and the crediting of recruits thus secured to the quotas of the loyal states. Between the time of the enactment of this provision and its repeal in March, 1865, 1,405 agents were sent by Northern state

34. *O. R.*, Ser. 3, III, 100–103. 35. *Ibid.*, Ser. 1, XVIII, 723.
36. *Ibid.*, Ser. 3, V, 632–633.

governors into the South. The total number of recruits credited through these agents was only 5,052. Local bounties, according to the provost marshal general, were "lavishly provided" by the loyal states in order to induce enlistment. Bounty-brokers were enriched, military officers corrupted, and Negroes defrauded. The commander of the military district of North Carolina complained, in September, 1864, that men and officers at the outposts had been resorting to the practice of sending fugitive slaves who came to them for protection "to *particular* agents," receiving from these agents pecuniary reward, instead of sending the fugitives to the provost marshals as ordered.[37]

The combined activities of regular recruiting organizations, substitute brokers, and "state agents" failed to bring into the ranks the desired number of Negroes by voluntary methods. The Negroes, much to the perplexity of a considerable portion of the Northern population, did not always show alacrity to seize the opportunity to fight for the cause of freedom; in many cases they revealed a distinct aversion to enlistment, offers of freedom to themselves and their families, bounties, and encomiums on the dignifying and elevating influence of army service notwithstanding. Compulsory enrollment was provided by the conscription acts of March 3, 1863, and February 24, 1864;[38] but the application of these acts was limited to the states in the Union. In the portions of "Rebeldom" under Federal control, force was applied by the military commanders in varying degrees and by various methods to secure the enlistment of the blacks. One practice, used very effectively, was to send male fugitives directly to recruiting headquarters when they came into the lines. There, the gullible Negroes fresh from slavery were "persuaded" into uniforms with comparative ease. A Virginia Negro gave the writer an en-

37. *North Carolina Times* (Newbern), Sept. 6, 1864.
38. The act of March 3, 1863, did not mention the Negro, but the War Department held that he was subject to its provisions. The act of Feb. 24, 1864, provided for the enrollment of "all able-bodied colored persons between the ages of twenty and forty-five years." *O. R.*, Ser. 3, V, 654 ff.

lightening account of his entrance into the United States army. One moonlight night in March, 1864, after having escaped from his master's premises, he cautiously approached the Federal lines. "All at once someone said, 'Halt! Who comes there?' I said, 'a fren',' very faintly. De sentry called for de corporal o' de guard. De corporal o' de guard come ridin' out with five men all armed with rifles, the bayonets glistenin' in de moonlight. Dey asked me whar I come from. I told 'em Lawrenceville. I thought dat my time was come. I was praying hard all de time. Dey was United States Colored Troops but I thought dey might kill me; I was green and ignorant." Brown said that the soldiers took him into camp and gave him some hardtack to eat; after eating he went to sleep. "De next morning," he continued, "a white recruiting officer, came around to whar I was with a great big book and said, 'My man, don't you want to be a soldier?' I said, 'No Sar.' But de colored soldiers gathered round me and said, 'Aw come on an' be a soldier wid we boys.' I finally said, 'All right.' Dey took my name down in de book an' asked me a lot of questions. Dey den took me and kept me in de guard house all day. Next morning dey took me to de recruitin' office and read de Bible to me. Den dey read out of a little blue book about obeying superior officers, about killing a soldier for going to sleep, and a lot o' rules. Dey den made me take de oath of 'legiance wid my hand raised up, an' den I had to kiss de Bible. Den I went to camp."[39]

Another effective method of getting the Negroes into the ranks was to put them at hard work such as digging ditches and throwing up breastworks, and then extend to them the privilege of becoming soldiers. In July, 1863, Secretary Stanton wired Major Foster at Fort Monroe, Virginia, asking his coöperation in the recruitment of Negroes. Foster replied immediately that he would gladly coöperate. "I propose," he said, "to make a levy for five

<hr/>

39. Statement to the author in 1933 of Anderson Brown, Petersburg, Virginia.

days work on the defenses on all unemployed Negroes in
and around Norfolk and Portsmouth and in the meantime
to bring up General Wild's recruiting officers to induce
them to enter his brigade."[40]

In the military departments of the South, the Gulf, and
the West Mississippi, the commanding generals ultimately
resorted to an open conscription of all able-bodied Negro
men within specified age limits.[41] Under authority of these
conscription orders, and in many instances without the authority of such orders, recruiting squads scoured the country forcing Negroes into the army. Hunter resorted to
such practices to fill the ranks of his abortive regiment of
South Carolina "Volunteers" in 1862.[42] When General
Saxton succeeded Hunter he gave "earnest and repeated
assurances" that forced enlistments would not again be
used. But when General Foster assumed command of the
Department of the South in 1863, he ignored Saxton's assurances and ordered an indiscriminate draft. This order,
according to Saxton who entered a vigorous protest against
it, "spread universal confusion and terror. The Negroes
fled to the woods and swamps, visiting their cabins only by
stealth and in darkness. They were hunted to their hiding
places by armed parties of their own people and . . . compelled to enlist." Three boys, he added, "one only fourteen
years of age, were seized in a field when they were at work"
and sent to a distant regiment. One man "was shot dead
and left where he fell" because of his failure to obey the
orders of one of these recruiting companies.[43] So great did
the fear of the Negroes become, that according to the report of a Northern plantation superintendent in South
Carolina, "a strange white face drives them from the field
into the woods like so many quail." Church services were
likewise broken up, the male worshippers seeking egress

40. *O. R.*, Ser. 1, XXVII, pt. 3, 732.
41. *Ibid.*, XIV, 1020; the New Orleans *Era*, Aug. 9, 1864.
42. Holland, ed., *Letters and Diary of Laura M. Towne*, p. 50.
43. *O. R.*, Ser. 3, IV, 1028, report of Saxton to Stanton, Dec. 30, 1864.

through the windows.[44] According to another superintendent the "larger part of the native regiments" were "filled by wholesale conscription . . . carried out by hunting, and in several instances shooting down the fugitives."[45]

These practices were not confined to South Carolina. In New Orleans, "squads of Negro soldiery . . . scoured the city in quest of recruits to their force. With the audacity of a posse in search of a criminal they visited private houses to drag therefrom the servants of its occupants."[46] In Kentucky use of rough tactics to compel the enlistment of Negroes became so notorious that it was called to the attention of President Lincoln. In February, 1865, he wrote to an officer at Henderson: "Complaint is made to me that you are forcing Negroes into the military service, and even torturing them—riding them on rails and the like to extort their consent. . . . The like must not be done. . . . Answer me on this."[47]

It is impossible to ascertain the exact number of Negro soldiers in the Union army. The files in the Adjutant General's office show a total of 186,017.[48] There were probably more than this number actually enlisted. According to J. T. Wilson quite a few mulattoes served in white regiments.[49] Wilson also says that the practice prevailed in some sections of putting a live Negro in a dead one's place and having him answer to the dead man's name. He estimated the total number of Negroes enlisted in the ranks of the Union army as about 220,000.[50]

The majority of the soldiers of color in the Union army

44. Pearson, *Letters from Port Royal*, pp. 173–174.

45. Gannett, "The Freedmen at Port Royal," *North American Review,* CI (1865), 27.

46. *Daily True Delta,* Sept. 2, 1863. The New Orleans *Daily Tribune* reported the killing of a Negro who ran from one of these squads; see issues of Aug. 14, Aug. 19, and Oct. 11, 1863.

47. *O. R.,* Ser. 1, XLIX, pt. 1, 668.

48. Williams, *History of the Negro Race in America,* II, 301; *O. R.,* Ser. 3, V, 662.

49. Wilson, *Black Phalanx,* p. 179.

50. *Ibid.,* p. 123.

were from the slave states. The Adjutant General's files give the number of troops furnished from the different states as follows:[51]

Seceded States		Border Slave States	
Alabama	4,969	Kentucky	23,703
Arkansas	5,526	Maryland	8,718
Florida	1,044	Missouri	8,344
Georgia	3,486		
Louisiana	24,052	Total	40,765
Mississippi	17,869		
North Carolina	5,035		
South Carolina	5,462		
Tennessee	20,133		
Texas	47		
Virginia	5,723		
Total	93,346		

Thus, out of a total of 186,017 troops reported by the Adjutant General's office, 134,111 are listed as being from the slave states. Most of these were slaves or former slaves.[52]

The matter of securing capable officers to command the Negro troops was a difficult problem. A white officer directing Negro troops was subject to stigmatization and ostracism by his white companions. This was especially true during the first two years of the war. Colonel Dietzler of the Kansas Volunteers, in August, 1862, requested that a member of his regiment who was "full two-thirds 'nigger' " be transferred to "Jim Lane's nigger brigade" or mustered out of service.[53] General Hunter found great difficulty in getting white officers to command the units of his regiment. "Private Miles O'Reilly" said that the reply Hunter received from almost every competent young lieutenant or captain whom he approached on the subject was, "What! Command Niggers?" General Weitzel refused to

51. *O. R.*, Ser. 3, V, 662.
52. Wilson, *Rise and Fall of the Slave Power*, III, 403.
53. *Ibid.*, p. 288.

command the Negro troops raised by Butler in New Orleans.[54] Ullmann, an officer of Negro troops at Port Hudson, said in an address delivered shortly after the termination of the war: "Officers of the Ullmann Brigade will ever have occasion to remember with bitter feelings the contemptuous treatment they received at the siege of Port Hudson, from General and other officers who had heaped indignities upon 'Nigger Officers' as they were wont courteously to style us."[55]

54. Wilson, *Black Phalanx*, pp. 196 ff. Wilson says that there was a strong prejudice among West Point officers against Negro troops.

55. Daniel Ullmann, *Organization of Colored Troops and the Regeneration of the South*, p. 3. White officers of Negro troops were objects of particular contempt and hatred in the Confederacy. The Savannah *Republican* denounced Hunter, the initiator of the scheme of arming the Negroes, as "the cold-blooded abolition miscreant who, from his headquarters at Hilton Head is engaged in executing the bloody and savage behest of the imperial gorilla who, from his throne of human bones at Washington, rules, reigns and riots over the brutish and degraded north." Quoted by Wilson, *Black Phalanx*, p. 154. President Davis wrote to the Union Government inquiring whether Hunter was authorized to raise his regiment of emancipated slaves or whether he was acting on his own authority. Although no response was received from the authorities at Washington, the Confederate War Department issued a general order stating that Hunter or any other commissioned officer engaged in preparing slaves for armed service should, if captured, "be not regarded as a prisoner of war but held in close confinement for execution as a felon" on the President's order. *General Orders* Confederate States Army, no. 60, April 21, 1862. The Confederate Congress, on January 12, 1863, passed a series of resolutions in which it was resolved that "every white person being a commissioned officer or acting as such, who during the present war shall command negroes, or mulattoes, in arms against the Confederate States . . . shall be deemed as inciting servile insurrection and shall, if captured, be put to death or otherwise punished at the discretion of the court." Wilson, *Black Phalanx*, p. 318. No evidence could be found that this order was carried out in any instance. President Lincoln issued a retaliatory proclamation July 30, 1863, in which he ordered that for every soldier of the United States killed in violation of the laws of war, a "Rebel" soldier should be executed. *Ibid.*, p. 320. Some of the officers of Negro troops who were captured at Petersburg, when asked what regiments they were attached to, gave the numbers of certain white ones for fear that they would be molested. One of them, more courageous than the rest, answered, "Lemuel D. Dobbs, Nineteenth Negroes, By G–d." His frankness won for him more consideration than that received by his associate officers. *Per-*

The change in the attitude of the administration toward
the enlistment of Negroes facilitated the securing of officers. Adjutant General Thomas in his address in April,
1863, said that he had authority to dismiss from the army
any man, whatever his rank, whom he found maltreating
the freedmen. There are instances of officers being dismissed for open disrespect to white soldiers commanding
Negro troops. T. J. Morgan, a white officer in the Fourteenth United States Colored Infantry, chanced to meet a
former acquaintance in Nashville, in 1864, at a social gathering. When he offered his hand his old friend, now a colonel, ignored it and made a cool bow. As Morgan turned
away, the colonel remarked to those about him that he "did
not recognize these nigger officers." A short time afterwards
the colonel was dismissed from the army.[56]

As a rule, the commissioned officers of Negro regiments
were whites. There were some colored men commissioned by
the State of Massachusetts. Two regiments of the Corps
d'Afrique, raised by Butler in Louisiana, were almost entirely officered by blacks.[57] The noncommissioned officers
were, in many cases, colored men.

The life of the Negro soldiers in the Union army was replete with difficulties and hardships. But considerable relief from the numerous burdens incident to military service
was found in religious exercises. When the sable recruits
gathered around the campfire at night, it was not an unusual thing for a song to break out. The singing might
lead shortly to a "shout-meetin' " with the dancing and
hand-clapping characteristic of this phenomenon. On the
march and in the camps the dusky soldiers frequently
found comfort and inspiration in the chanting of spir-

sonal Narratives, Soldiers and Sailors Historical Society of Rhode Island,
Fifth Series, no. 1, p. 29. See also Jones, Rebel War Clerk's Diary, II,
26.

56. Wilson, Black Phalanx, p. 295.

57. Williams, History of Negro Troops in the War of the Rebellion,
p. 141.

ituals of which they had an abundant store. The following were among the favorites:

WRESTLING JACOB

O wrestlin' Jacob, Jacob, day's a breakin';
 I will not let thee go!
O wrestlin' Jacob, Jacob, day's a breakin';
 He will not let me go!
O I hold my brudder wid a tremblin' hand;
 I would not let him go!
I hold my sister wid a tremblin' hand;
 I would not let her go!

THE DRIVER

O, de ole nigger-driver,
 O gwine away;
Fust ting my mammy tell me,
 O gwine away;
Tell me 'bout de nigger-driver,
 O gwine away.

Nigger-driver second devil,
 O gwine away;
Best ting for do he driver,
 O gwine away;
Knock he down and spoil he labor,
 O gwine away.[58]

Prayer and preaching services were held frequently.[59] Sometimes these were conducted by white soldiers or chaplains; on other occasions by Negroes. Some of the colored exhorters had confused ideas of the Scripture. A Negro

---

58. T. W. Higginson, *Army Life in a Black Regiment*, pp. 209–219.

59. The Reverend John G. Fee, founder of Berea College, engaged for a time in instructing colored soldiers at Camp Nelson, Kentucky, said: "At night the camps of these colored men were scenes of continual prayer and praise, with frequent preaching." *History of the American Missionary Association*, p. 16.

corporal addressing his soldiers said that "If each one of us was a praying man, it appears to me that we could fight as well with prayers as with bullets—for the Lord has said that if you have faith even as a grain of mustard-seed cut into four parts, you can say to the sycamore tree, 'Arise and it will come up!' "[60] Another exhorter proclaimed, "Paul may plant and may polish wid water but it wont do."[61]

But despite erroneous ideas concerning the scripture and an undue emphasis of emotionalism the religious zeal of the Negro soldiers generally tended to strengthen their courage and to make them more dutiful in the performance of their military services.[62]

In general, the conduct and behavior of the Negro soldiers compared favorably with that of their white comrades. They were less given to intemperance and the use of profane and obscene language. They seem to have had a greater respect for the orders of their superiors and for the rules and regulations governing army life. They were not, however, the avatars of good behavior which their officers and others interested in creating a good opinion of them sometimes depicted them to be. Lying, stealing, shamming sickness, and quarreling were not uncommon among them. The reports of the proceedings of the provost court in the New Orleans newspapers reveal a fondness of the colored soldiery for the chicken roosts of that city and its environs. On one occasion two members of a Negro regiment were brought before the court on the charge of "foraging among the chickens and cabbages of the vicinity." A white officer who appeared in their defense said that he thought it an impossibility for the accused Negroes to have gotten out of the barracks to commit the offense.

60. Higginson, *Army Life in a Black Regiment*, p. 255.

61. *Ibid.*, p. 27. This was a perversion of the Apostle Paul's statement in First Corinthians 3. 6: "I have planted, Apollos watered; but God gave the increase."

62. *Preliminary Report of Freedmen's Inquiry Commission to the Secretary of War*, p. 17.

The judge replied that he thought "all things possible to a nigger when he felt inclined to steal."[63]

Corporal William Crawford and Private Alf Ward of the Second Louisiana Colored Regiment sought to appease their hunger for domestic fowls under cloak of military authority. They went to a house near Algiers, Louisiana, and told the owner, an old man, that they had an order to seize all the chickens, geese, and ducks about the place. The ruse was brought to naught by the resistance of the owner and a neighbor who came to his assistance and disarmed the corporal. During the mêlée the corporal drew his bayonet on the old man and shot a duck with his pistol. When he was disarmed, the private swore to shoot the man who had dared to make his corporal a prisoner. But all this was to no avail. Both Negroes were sentenced to a year's residence on Tortugas Island.[64]

The propensity of the colored soldiers toward displaying authoritativeness, and the readiness of the whites to interpret any irregularity of conduct as " 'niggers' putting on airs," frequently brought the two racial elements into conflict in New Orleans. A common cause of friction was the attempt of the blacks to ride in the cars designated for the exclusive use of the white people.[65] The pompousness of the colored soldiery was sometimes exasperating to Negro civilians.[66] An old colored woman in New Orleans had the audacity to call colored Private Molliere a "nigger." She was rewarded for her boldness by a punch on the head.[67]

Instances of flagrant insubordination on the part of

---

63. *Daily Picayune,* Dec. 9, 1862.   64. *Ibid.,* Feb. 21, 1864.

65. New Orleans *Times,* May 13, 1864; *Daily Picayune,* Oct. 17, 1862. Butler ordered the admission of "decent colored people into white cars," but after his departure from the city, the order was not enforced. New Orleans *Tribune,* Jan. 13, 1865.

66. General W. T. Sherman wrote to General McPherson in 1863 that the Negro soldiers at Blake's Plantation, Mississippi, were wandering about the country doing "infinite mischief." They "naturally cluster about the old Negro inmates of abandoned plantations and put on the majestic air of soldiers." *O. R.,* Ser. 1, XXX, pt. 3, 277.

67. *Daily Picayune,* Sept. 26, 1863.

colored troops were rare. The most serious case was the mutiny of a portion of the Fourth Regiment, Corps d'Afrique, at Fort Jackson, Louisiana, on December 9, 1863. The uprising was precipitated by the whipping of two members of the regiment with a cart whip by the lieutenant colonel, Benedict. A short time after the punishment had been inflicted, about half of the regiment came rushing out upon the parade discharging their guns into the air and shouting threats, most of which were directed at Benedict. The colonel of the regiment, Charles Drew, testified at the trial of those arrested as ringleaders of the revolt, that the angry soldiers cried out, "Give us Colonel Benedict; we did not come here to be whipped by him. Kill Colonel Benedict. Shoot him." Major William E. Nye said that they shouted, " 'Kill the son-of-a ———' and other words of like meaning." One black soldier cried out, "Kill all the damned Yankees." At a general court-martial, at which no Negroes were permitted to testify, seven of the colored soldiers were found guilty of mutiny. Five of these were sentenced to periods of imprisonment or hard labor or both. Two received death sentences, but these were later suspended until "further orders." Lieutenant Colonel Benedict was found guilty of inflicting "cruel and unusual punishment," and dismissed from the service.[68]

The ordinary punishment for infractions of camp regulations consisted of confinement in the guardhouse, "bucking and gagging," suspension by the thumbs with only the toes touching the ground, and carrying ball and chain.[69] A common punishment for minor aberrations was a ride on the "wooden horse." This device consisted of a small log about twelve feet in length laid across the top of two upright supports placed at each end. It was about fifteen feet from the ground. Offending soldiers were required to

---

68. *O. R.,* Ser. 1, XXVI, pt. 1, 456 ff.

69. *Ibid.,* p. 466. Statement of Nat Black, Pulaski, Tennessee, to the writer in 1933. Professor Frederick Albert Shannon in his *Organization and Administration of the Union Army,* I, 226, says that bucking and gagging and hanging by the thumbs were used as punishments for white troops.

sit on this "horse" for periods of time varying with the gravity of their infringements. Sometimes eight or ten Negroes would ride the "horse" at one time. A guard was stationed on the ground below to prevent unduly rough riding or dismounting.[70]

The testimony in the trial of the participants in the Fort Jackson mutiny of December 9, 1863, revealed that at least in the Fourth Regiment, Corps d'Afrique, kicking and cuffing were not uncommon methods of correction. Captain William K. Knapp testified that he had frequently seen Lieutenant Colonel Benedict "strike men in the face with his fist and kick them because their brasses were not bright or their boots not polished." He was said to have struck one man in the face with a sword for not being dressed properly. Another punishment resorted to by Benedict on at least two occasions—once when the offense was the theft of corn for roasting—was to remove the shoes and stockings from the men, tie them down on the ground with arms and legs stretched out, and to cover their faces, hands, and feet with molasses and to leave them in that condition all day.[71] Little wonder is it that the men mutinied; the remarkable thing is that they postponed the revolt until floggings were administered.

Severe disciplinary measures had to be employed in the case of desertion. Higginson is inclined to see everything good and nothing evil in the Negro, but he admits that on his arrival in Beaufort in 1862 to take charge of a Negro regiment he found "a good deal of anxiety among the officers as to the increase of desertions, that being the rock upon which the Hunter Regiment split." He goes on to say that after his arrival the evil was almost completely stopped. One of the Negroes who had escaped from the guardhouse was "half-accidentally" shot. He later died. Higginson says that this half-accidental shooting was one of the very best things that could have happened.[72]

70. Wilson, *Black Phalanx*, p. 248, illustration.
71. *O. R.*, Ser. 1, XXVI, pt. 1, 456 ff.
72. Higginson, *Army Life in a Black Regiment*, p. 43.

The fundamentals of military drill and training were acquired by the Negro with comparative ease. His "readiness of ear and imitation" were helpful attributes. According to Higginson, "to learn the drill one does not want a set of college professors; one wants a squad of eager, active, pliant school boys, and the more childlike the pupils are, the better." The ex-slaves were abundantly endowed with childlikeness.

The Negroes evidenced much pleasure at marching to music. In the absence of a band, a few drummers would suffice. They frequently marched to the music of their own singing. Among their favorite marching songs were "John Brown," "What Make Old Satan Follow Me So," "Marching Along," "Hold Your Light on Canaan's Shore," and "When This War Is Over."[73] But a "Brass-band" could lift the marching soldiers to the heights of ecstasy. A colored sergeant described its effects on him as follows: " 'And when dat band wheel in before us and march on— My God! I quit dis world altogeder.' "[74]

Despite the assuaging influence of spiritual exercises, there were a number of factors which tended to make army life more unpleasant for Negroes than for whites. Not the least among these was the disposition of commanding officers to overburden the blacks with the less desirable duties incident to the conduct of the war. True it is that Negro soldiers had occasional tastes of the more dignified military pursuits. They were used rather extensively as raiders and recruiters in the areas bordering on the Confederacy. Squads of them under white officers were frequently sent into "Rebeldom" to destroy salt-works and supply stores, to bring out cotton and lumber—commodities much in demand in the North—and to procure able-bodied slaves for the army. Their knowledge of the country, the erstwhile home of many of them, made them particularly valuable as foragers and raiders. Then, too, the persuasive influence which the ebon soldiers, clad in flashy blue uniforms with

73. *Ibid.*, p. 133.   74. *Ibid.*, p. 59.

brass buttons shining in the sun, had on the civilian men of color enhanced their effectiveness as recruiters. Negro soldiers were often called on to perform scout service.[75] They knew the country. They were helped from place to place by those of their own color who were friendly toward the "Yankees." Their effectiveness in this type of service was diminished considerably by their proneness to over-estimate the numbers of "Rebel" troops and their suscepti-bility to suggestion. According to Charles Nordhoff, a Northerner who had the opportunity of a close observation of the freedmen of South Carolina, "one of these blacks fresh from slavery will most adroitly tell you precisely what you want to hear. . . . Ask if the enemy had 50,000 men and he will be sure that they had at least that many; express your belief that they had not 5,000 and he will laugh at the idea of their having more than 4,500."[76] Some of the most valuable aid rendered to the Federals by the Negroes was in the capacity of guides and pilots. A colored sergeant served as a pilot in the movement of the Union fleet against Charleston in 1863. Native Negro guides were especially helpful in the operations along the wind-ing creeks and sinuous channels near Port Royal and Sa-vannah.

The roster of United States colored troops classifies some companies as artillery, others as engineers, and still others as cavalry. That the duties of these organizations were not always up to the level of their names is indicated by the fact that two cavalry regiments in Mississippi and Louisiana were mounted on mules, and used, in some cases at least, to drive in cattle, and that engineer troops in Louisiana, according to a communication from Adjutant General Thomas to Secretary Stanton were "designed to work on fortifications, but are armed with muskets."[77]

Upon the Negro soldiers fell the tedious work of garrison-

75. Vincent Colyer, *Brief Report of the Services Rendered by the Freed People to the United States Army in North Carolina*, p. 9.
76. Nordhoff, *The Freedmen of South Carolina*, pp. 24–25.
77. *O. R.*, Ser. 1, XV, 706; Ser. 3, III, 770, 1191.

ing many of the Federal forts along the Mississippi and the Tennessee rivers and in the coastal regions under Union control. They were also used to guard contraband camps and to provide protection for "Yankee-operated" plantations in Louisiana, Mississippi, and Arkansas.[78] Negro troops were used extensively in the erection of fortifications around Nashville, Chattanooga, Memphis, Vicksburg, Port Hudson, Washington, and Fort Monroe. Several regiments in Tennessee were detailed to work on the Louisville and Nashville and the Northwestern railroads. They supplied the labor for some of the heaviest and most dangerous projects undertaken by the Federal engineers. They planted the "Swamp Angel" and other heavy artillery in the marshy districts around Charleston. They dug Butler's famous Dutch Gap Canal, working often under the fire of Confederate batteries. During Butler's Louisiana sojourn, he used one of his regiments of Louisiana Native Guards "for many weeks" in cutting and planting sugar cane and in "preserving sweet potatoes and corn for the next year's planting."[79]

Occasionally colored soldiers were called upon to act as body servants to white Federal officers.[80] In South Carolina black troops were detailed to clean the quarters of their white comrades. This practice became so notorious that General Gillmore issued general orders in September and November, 1863, expressly forbidding such assignments.[81]

Officers of the Negro regiments made frequent protests against the impositions upon their troops. Colonel T. J. Morgan of the Fourteenth United States Colored Infantry complained to his superiors in December, 1863, that he felt that it was "degrading to single out Colored Troops for fatigue duty while white soldiers stand idly by." He

78. *Ibid.*, XLIX, pt. 1, 594; XXX, pt. 4, 27; Ser. 3, IV, 708–709, 764; Eaton, *Grant, Lincoln, and the Freedmen, passim.*

79. *Daily Picayune,* May 27, 1863.   80. *Ibid.*, July 21, 1863.

81. Williams, *History of Negro Troops in the War of the Rebellion,* p. 165.

also said that he did not feel that it was just "to require Colored Regiments to perform fatigue duty for other troops"; that he would rather carry his rifle in the ranks of fighting men than hold any position as "overseer of black laborers."[82] Brigadier General Daniel Ullmann wrote Senator Henry Wilson about the same time that the policy being pursued in reference to Negro troops in Louisiana was such as to confine them to "diggers and drudges." So much time was required for fatigue work, he added, that there was little opportunity for drill; "Months have passed at times without the possibility of any drill at all."[83] At Chattanooga members of the Fourteenth Colored Infantry worked from six to seven hours every day on fortifications "and on returning to camp had to prepare for dress parade which was held daily, except Sunday."[84]

In 1864 Adjutant General Thomas, influenced no doubt by the complaints of the officers of the colored troops and a portion of the Northern press friendly to the Negroes, notably Greeley's *Tribune*, issued a general order aimed at impositions upon the Negroes. This order declared that "the practice which has hitherto prevailed, no doubt from necessity, of requiring these troops to perform most of the labor on fortifications and the labor and fatigue duties of permanent stations and camps, will cease, and they will be only required to take their fair share of fatigue duty with white troops. This is necessary to prepare them for the higher duties of conflicts with the enemies."[85]

The burdensome tasks imposed on the black soldiers might have been less irksome had they received the same pay as the white troops. The militia act of July 17, 1862, the first official authorization of the enlistment of Negroes, made a clear discrimination against them. White persons enrolled under the act were to receive the full compensa-

82. Williams, *History of Negro Troops in the War of the Rebellion*, pp. 162–163.

83. *O. R.*, Ser. 3, III, 1126.

84. Henry Romeyn, "With Colored Troops in the Army of the Cumberland," *War Papers of the Commandery of the District of Columbia, Military Order of the Loyal Legion of the U. S.*, no. 5, p. 12.

85. Williams, *History of Negro Troops in the War of the Rebellion*, pp. 164–165.

tion allowed by law to soldiers; i.e., $13 a month with a
$3.50 allowance for clothing. "Persons of African de-
scent," however, were to receive only $7 with a $3 allowance for clothing. This unequal situation continued until
the summer of 1864 in spite of the bitter protests of the
Negroes and their friends. Colored soldiers from Massachusetts on duty in South Carolina served for a year without pay rather than accept the discriminating wages. The
Fifty-fourth Massachusetts Regiment went into battle at
Olustee, Florida, in February, 1864, with the cry, "Three
cheers for Massachusetts and seven dollars a month." Sergeant Walker of the Third South Carolina Volunteers
persuaded his company to register their protest by stack-
ing their arms and refusing to continue service. For this
mutinous act he paid the death penalty.[86]

In February and March, 1864, a long debate took pla⊾
in Congress on the question of the payment of colored
troops. There was apparently much reluctance to place
the blacks on the same basis as the whites. Both Conness ⊿ℓ
California and Lane of Kansas, the latter an erstwhile
zealot for recruiting colored soldiers, were opposed to any
retroactive action on the question. Lane made the statement that "no man in his sober senses will say that their
services are worth as much, or that they are as good soldiers."[87] Congress as a whole, in the opinion of John Mur-
ray Forbes, acted "like the devil" in regard to the "Negro pay bill,"[88] but after much delay the measure was
passed in June, 1864. By its provisions colored troops
were declared to be on the same basis as whites after January 1, 1864, and were to be paid accordingly.[89]

The fact that there was virtually no chance of promotion beyond the non-commissioned officer level was also the
source of much resentment for the black soldiers. Butler
permitted colored commissioned officers in the Louisiana

86. Brown, *The Negro in the American Rebellion*, pp. 223, 251–252.
87. *Cong. Globe*, 38th Cong., 1st Sess., p. 564.
88. Sarah Forbes Hughes, ed., *Letters and Recollections of John Mur-
ray Forbes*, II, 83.
89. *O. R.*, Ser. 3, V, 657–658.

Native Guards when those regiments were first organized, but when Banks assumed command of the Department of the Gulf he discontinued this policy on the grounds that it caused demoralizing friction between the Negroes and whites.[90] The sensitiveness of the colored people, especially the mulattoes of New Orleans, to this discrimination is indicated by the fact that on the third day of the State Convention of Colored People of Louisiana held in January, 1865, a motion was adopted creating a committee "to inquire why we are commanded and cannot command."[91]

The life of the Negro soldiers was also made disagreeable by the realization that the white troops regarded them as unwelcome allies. Manifestations of prejudice against them were numerous. A captain of an East Tennessee regiment was so angered by the sight of a company of Negroes marching by that he tore off his shoulder straps and threw them in the gutter.[92] Two Connecticut soldiers evidently deemed it more expedient to take out their resentment on the clothing of the Negroes. On accosting a colored soldier clad in a lustrous new outfit on Jackson Square in New Orleans they ordered him to undress. When he refused to comply they proceeded to tear his coat off. His complete disrobement was prevented by the timely arrival of a friendly white sergeant. It was not a strange thing to see a Negro soldier returning to the barracks at night à la Adam.[93] A resident of New Orleans became so irked at the sight of Negroes being taken into the army that he entered a colored recruiting office, seized the book kept for the signatures of the recruits, wrote indecent words therein, and then attacked the recruiting officer with his fists.[94] Soldiers in McClellan's army refused to serve as teamsters in the same wagon train with Negroes.[95]

90. *O. R.*, Ser. 1, XXVI, pt. 1, 688–689; Ser. 3, III, 46.
91. New Orleans *Tribune*, Jan. 12, 1865.
92. New Orleans *Daily True Delta*, Oct. 21, 1863.
93. Wilson, *Black Phalanx*, p. 132.
94. *Daily Picayune*, Nov. 7, 1862.
95. "North and South, The Controversy in a Colloquy," by "A White Republican," *Fraser's Magazine*, LXVI (1862), 311.

In the summer of 1862 an unusually dark-complexioned man succeeded in getting into a Kansas company. A short time thereafter thirty-six members of the company petitioned their colonel requesting the transfer of the newcomer, giving as their reasons "firstly we believe him to be a 'nigger'; secondly, that he was never properly assigned to our company, but after being refused in several other companies." They added that they had no objection to giving their services to their country, "but to have one of the company . . . pointed out as a 'nigger' while on dress parade or guard is more than we like to be called upon to bear."[96] Other Western soldiers threatened to desert when they heard that Negroes were being recruited.[97]

At Ship Island, Mississippi, the Federal gunboat *Jackson* was called upon to support three colored companies. Instead of training its guns upon the Confederates, it directed shots into the midst of the Negroes when they retreated. Some of the gunboat's crew had been killed a short time before in an altercation with a colored sentry.[98]

While Southern Negro soldiers had comparatively little part in the fighting done by Northern troops, there were several minor engagements in which the Negroes played conspicuous rôles. The first of these was the battle of Port Hudson, May 27, 1863. Port Hudson, a Confederate stronghold located on a bend in the Mississippi River about fifteen miles above Baton Rouge, was a point of considerable importance. The "Rebel" batteries were so situated as to make it impractical for a Federal boat to try to pass up the river. The Union authorities were very anxious to silence those batteries in order to get control of the two hundred miles of the Mississippi between Port Hudson and Vicksburg. The reduction of the fort would make possible the rendering of aid to Grant in his siege operations and the cutting of communications between the eastern and western parts of the Confederacy.[99] General Banks, com-

96. *Annual Cyclopedia* for 1862, p. 753.
97. Wilson, *Black Phalanx*, p. 294.   98. *Ibid.*, p. 208.
99. James Ford Rhodes, *History of the Civil War*, p. 248.

mander of the Department of the Gulf, essayed a general assault on Port Hudson on the morning of May 27. His effective force on the day of the attack was 13,000 men; that of the Confederates was approximately 6,000.[100] Included among Banks's troops were two colored regiments, the First and Third Louisiana Native Guards. The First Regiment was made up almost entirely of the free Negro population of New Orleans. Many of its members were men of culture and wealth, with a considerable admixture of white blood.[101] Most of the members of the Third Regiment were freedmen.

Banks placed the Native Guards, consisting of a total of 1,080 Negroes, on the right of the white regiments directly in front of two large forts. The assault scheduled for seven o'clock was supposed to be simultaneous all along the line, but through delay and misunderstanding, the right was not ordered forward until ten o'clock and the left did not get under way until two o'clock in the afternoon.

The black regiments when ordered forward at ten o'clock charged at double quick in four lines. At four hundred yards the Confederate batteries opened with a withering fire on the left. The first line fell back in some confusion and the second line went forward. It could not long endure the deadly fire. As it fell back the reorganized first line went forward again. The fight went on until four o'clock in the afternoon. The Negro troops made six distinct charges during the day over difficult ground. But the Confederate position proved too strong for the attacking forces. Port Hudson remained in Confederate hands until after the fall of Vicksburg.[102]

100. *O. R.*, Ser. 1, XXVI, pt. 1, 44. Banks in his report shortly after the battle estimated the Confederate force at 8,000; but when the garrison surrendered on July 9, he took only 5,500 prisoners. During the siege the Confederates, according to their report, had lost 400 men—200 killed and 200 from sickness. *Ibid.*, pp. 55, 144.

101. New York *Times*, June 11, 1863, letter of a white officer who participated in the battle. Brown, *The Negro in the American Rebellion*, pp. 168–170. Brown had heard it said of the members of the First Regiment that "not one of them was worth less than $25,000."

102. This account is based largely on the report of the New York *Times*

The Negro troops received special commendation from General Banks for the service which they rendered in the assault on Port Hudson.[103] Several instances of individual daring were reported by press correspondents. These were received with enthusiasm by friends of the Negroes throughout the country and cited as proof that "Negroes will fight." The color sergeant of the First Louisiana, Anselmas Planciancois, on receiving the colors from his colonel before leaving New Orleans had said, "Colonel, I will bring back these colors in honor or report to God the reason why." A correspondent of the New York *Times*, an eye witness of the Port Hudson battle, reported that when this sergeant fell mortally wounded in a charge upon the Confederate works, he "hugged the colors to his breast." A struggle ensued between the two color corporals on either side of him for the honor of carrying the standard forward; the contention was settled by one of them receiving a serious wound. A black lieutenant was said to have mounted the Confederate works three or four times. Captain Calloux of the First Louisiana, a man of culture and attainment, "so black that he actually prided himself on his blackness, died the death of a hero leading on his men in the thickest of the fight." One colored man "was observed with a rebel soldier in his grasp tearing the flesh from his face with his teeth, other weapons having failed him."[104]

The losses of the colored regiment in this encounter, according to the New York *Times* correspondent, were 37 killed, 155 wounded, and 116 missing. If these figures are accurate, the Negroes suffered proportionately heavier losses than the whites. Banks's official report showed casualties as follows: killed 293; wounded 1,545; missing 157. The Negroes, comprising one-twelfth of the troops en-

correspondent in the issue of June 13, 1863, and Banks's official report to Halleck, *O. R.*, Ser. 1, XXVI, pt. 1, 44–45.

103. *O. R.*, Ser. 1, XXVI, pt. 1, 44–45.

104. New York *Times*, June 13, 1863; Roy, "Our Indebtedness to the Negroes for their Conduct during the War," *New Englander*, LI (1889), 357–358; Brown, *The Negro in the American Rebellion*, pp. 168–171; Cincinnati *Daily Gazette*, June 9, 1863, quoting New York *Herald*.

gaged, bore one-eighth of the loss in numbers killed, one-tenth in wounded, and three-fourths in missing.[105]

The next engagement in which Negro soldiers had an important rôle was the battle of Milliken's Bend, June 7, 1863. The scene of this encounter was a small town on the Mississippi, about twenty-five miles, as the river runs, above Vicksburg. In anticipation of an attack on Vicksburg, Grant had withdrawn most of the Federal forces from the vicinity, leaving the garrison at Milliken's Bend in charge of about 1,100 men, most of whom were Negroes from Louisiana and Mississippi, with little experience in the use of arms. Very early in the morning of June 7 a force of about 1,500 Texans under General H. E. McCulloch advanced upon the Federals who were drawn up behind a levee. The Confederates, in preparing for the attack, had collected a large number of mules, and these they drove before them as they advanced against the Federal position. These movable breastworks were soon dissipated by bullets and fright but the Confederate troops marched on over the rough ground and mounted the levee. There a heated hand-to-hand struggle ensued, gun-butts and bayonets being used freely by both sides. The Negroes fell back behind the river bank, the Texans following close behind them with the disposition, if not the cry, to grant "no quarter."[106] The fierce fighting continued on the river's edge until the directly descending rays of the scorching summer sun—the thermometer, according to General Taylor, registered ninety degrees in the shade—indicated the ap-

105. New York *Times*, June 13, 1863; *O. R.*, Ser. 1, XXVI, pt. 1, 47. The *Times* does not give total casualties; Banks does not report losses of Negro regiments. Discrepancies between the two reports would change the ratios.

106. Several Federal accounts state that the "Rebels" cried "no quarter" and killed the wounded. This charge is not uncommon in the reports of the Negro engagements. It is given considerable credence here, however, by the statement of General Taylor in his report that he had ordered McCulloch to "drive the enemy into the river so as to permit no time for escape," and that *unfortunately* some 50 [Negroes] with . . . their white officers were captured." Italics mine. *O. R.*, Ser. 1, XXIV, pt. 2, 459.

proach of noon. At this juncture the Federal gunboats *Lexington* and *Choctaw* came up, by order of Admiral Porter who had been informed of the Confederate attack, and began to drop shells in the midst of the Texans. They immediately withdrew, with the Negroes in close pursuit, to a point beyond the range of the Federal guns. The attack was not renewed.[107]

The fierceness with which this fight was conducted is indicated by the fact that Federals who walked over the field afterwards found "Yankee" Negroes and "Rebel" whites lying side by side, each pierced by the bayonet of the other, and the skulls of several Confederates smashed in by the butts of the Negroes' rifles.[108] Captain M. M. Miller, who left Yale College in his senior year to command a Negro company, wrote to his aunt three days after the battle that his regiment went into the fight with 300 men and came out with 50 killed and 80 wounded, and that he had "six broken bayonets to show how bravely my men fought." "It was a horrible fight," he added.[109] General McCulloch in his report of the battle said that of the wounds received by his men, "More are severe and fewer slight than I have ever witnessed among the same number in my former military experience."[110] The total Union loss in this battle was reported as 101 killed, 285 wounded, and 264 captured or missing. McCulloch reported the Confederate casualties as 44 killed, 130 wounded, and 10 missing.[111]

Negro soldiers also had a part in the battle of the Crater, near Petersburg, Virginia, July 30, 1864. After the Federal authorities decided to make a breach in the Confederate works by setting off a mine beneath them, Burn-

107. This account is based largely on the reports of Admiral Porter of the Federal forces, Generals Taylor and McCulloch of the Confederate Army, *ibid.*, XXVI, pt. 2, 457–465, 467–470, and dispatches to the Cincinnati *Daily Gazette*, June 13, 16, 17, 18, 19, and the New York *Times*, June 13, 14, 1863.

108. Cincinnati *Daily Gazette*, June 16, 1863.

109. *O. R.*, Ser. 3, III, 452–453.

110. *Ibid.*, Ser. 1, XXIV, pt. 2, 469.

111. *Ibid.*, pp. 448, 469.

side selected the Fourth Division of his corps to open the attack when the explosion should take place. This division was composed of eight regiments, all colored, three of which were from Maryland, one from Virginia, and the others from Northern states. Burnside's avowed reason for choosing the Negro troops to lead the attack was that they were fresh, having never before been under fire, and would consequently be more likely to dash forward with the recklessness and impetuosity necessary to gain the crest beyond the Confederate lines than the whites whose constant exposure to desultory Confederate fire for weeks past would tend to make them seek shelter. He planned to send his white troops in afterwards to hold the position gained by the Negroes.

In accordance with this plan the blacks were carefully drilled for some days in preparation for their part in the movement. But on July 29, the day before the assault, Burnside's superior, General Meade, notified him that he did not approve the scheme. He ordered Burnside to send his white troops in first and to use the Negroes as a supporting force. Meade gave as reasons for demanding the change in plans his conviction that the initial movement was of too great importance to be entrusted to unseasoned blacks and the belief that such a step would cause criticism in the North as evidence of an inclination to "put the niggers in front!" Burnside objected to the change so strenuously that Meade referred the matter to Grant; the latter supported the position taken by Meade.

When the mine exploded early on the morning of July 30, Burnside's three divisions of white troops began to advance, the First Division under Ledlie in the center, and the Second and Third Divisions under Wilcox and Potter on the right and left sides. They were repulsed, some of the men taking cover in rifle pits vacated by the Confederates, and others in the huge crater made by the explosion. The colored division under Ferrero was then ordered forward in two lines—each brigade composed a line—over the center route taken by the First Division to take the crest beyond the mine. When the Negroes came to the crater they found their path blocked by Ledlie's men. Some of the Negroes got through, however, and others went around. Negroes of the leading brigade engaged the Confederates at a short distance beyond the crater and succeeded in taking two stands of colors and some two hundred prisoners. They could not withstand the galling fire which was concentrated on them, however, and fell back shortly in confusion. After considerable difficulty in rallying and reforming the broken lines, the officers led the blacks in a second advance toward the crest. Again they met a withering fire. The leading regiments became panic stricken. The demoralization quickly spread to the others and all retreated in great disorder, sweeping some of the white troops before them to the rear. Many of the Negroes scrambled into the yawning crater, already choked with dead, wounded, and dying, and others sought cover farther in the rear. In vain did the surviving officers attempt to rally their demoralized and scattered colored forces. After noon Burnside, in accordance with instructions from Meade, gave the order for all the troops to fall back to a position beyond the reach of the Confederate batteries.[112]

The colored division suffered far more heavily in this affair than did the white divisions, with total losses more than half again as large as those of any other.[113] The

112. This narrative is based chiefly on the official reports of Burnside, Ferrero, and the leaders of the Negro brigades, and the testimony given before the Court of Inquiry on the Mine Explosion, *O. R.*, Ser. 1, XL, pt. 1, 42–167, 521–599; also the accounts given in the New York *Times*, Aug. 2, 1864, and the New York *Herald*, Aug. 2, 3, 1864.

113. The casualties of the four divisions in this attack were as follows:

	Killed	Wounded	Captured or Missing	Aggregate
First division	65	239	350	654
Second division	92	354	386	832
Third division	106	354	199	659
Fourth division (colored)	209	697	421	1,327

O. R., Ser. 1, XL, pt. 1, 246–248.

Fourth Division lost 55 officers, killed and wounded, while the First lost 36; the Second, 48; and the Third, 35. Officers of the colored troops exposed themselves with great daring in the effort to urge their men forward. Colonel John A. Bross seized the standard of his regiment after five color-bearers had fallen in quick succession before him, rushed impetuously to the top of an eminence, planted the flag upon the parapet, drew his saber with one hand, removed his hat with the other and fell mortally wounded crying, "Rally, my brave boys, rally."[114] Major James C. Leeke of the Thirtieth Regiment stood on the ramparts shouting encouragement to the troops with blood from a chest wound gushing from his mouth after his colonel, Delevan Bates, had fallen to the ground at the head of the regiment with a wound in his face.[115] In unhappy contrast to this gallantry was the conduct of the division commander, General Ferrero, whom the Court of Inquiry on the Mine Explosion found guilty of "being in a bombproof habitually" during the attack.[116]

The last major encounter in which considerable numbers of Southern black troops were actively engaged was the battle of Nashville, December 15–16, 1864. The colored soldiers participating were in two brigades, the First under Colonel Thomas J. Morgan, consisting of the Fourteenth, Seventeenth, Eighteenth, and Forty-fourth Regiments, United States Colored Troops, and the Second under Colonel C. R. Thompson, consisting of the Twelfth, Thirteenth, and the One Hundredth Regiments. These brigades were attached to the command of General J. B. Steedman. Most of the troops composing them were from the country around Nashville.

On the first day of the battle the colored brigades, which were placed on the extreme left of the Union forces, were called upon to make a demonstration against the Confederate right in order to divert attention from the main as-

114. Roy, "Our Indebtedness to the Negroes for their Conduct during the War," *New Englander*, LI (1889), 359–360.
115. *O. R.*, Ser. 1, XL, pt. 1, 597.   116. *Ibid.*, p. 128.

sault against the left by Smith's Corps. The Negro regiments executed the part assigned to them with success, and the Confederates were driven back along the entire front. During the night the Confederates re-formed their lines in a stronger position, occupying on their right a fortified place on an eminence about six miles south of Nashville known as Overton Hill. On the second day General Wood, holding the Union center, ordered Colonel Post of his corps to make an assault on this stronghold. General Steedman ordered Thompson's colored brigade to participate in the movement and told Morgan to protect Thompson's flank. In the forward movement Thompson's men became separated and somewhat disorganized. Thompson led the Twelfth Regiment aside under the protection of a small hill to re-form it. The One Hundredth Regiment moved forward with Post's men, and fell back with them after the gallant Post fell seriously wounded. The Thirteenth Regiment, operating almost independently of the others, advanced to a point near the Confederate works, some of the men even mounting the parapet, according to Colonel Thompson; but being unable to hold this advanced position in the face of the murderous fire poured upon them, the men fell back. As the broken lines were being repaired for a second assault, exultant shouts were heard on the right. It soon became apparent that the troops in that quarter, taking advantage of the diversion created by the charge on the hill had broken through the Confederate lines. Steedman's and Wood's troops immediately joined in the forward movement and swept the Confederates from the hill with little resistance.[117]

A fair appraisal of the general conduct of Southern Ne-

117. *Ibid.*, XLV, pt. 1, 37–39, 504–548, 698–705; T. J. Morgan, "Reminiscences of Services with Colored Troops in the Army of the Cumberland, 1863–1865," *Personal Narratives, Soldiers and Sailors Historical Society of Rhode Island*, 3rd Series, no. 13, pp. 41–48; New York *Herald*, Dec. 22, 1864; New York *Times*, Dec. 19, 24, 1864; Romeyn, "With Colored Troops in the Army of the Cumberland," *War Papers of the Commandery of the District of Columbia, Military Order of the Loyal Legion of the U. S.*, no. 51, pp. 23–26.

gro soldiers under fire is rendered extremely difficult by the
nature of the available testimony on the subject. Most of
this testimony is that of persons who were interested in
creating a good impression of the Negro soldiers—officers
who commanded them, and correspondents of newspapers
friendly to the Negroes, or to the administration's policy
of arming them. It is unfortunate for history that the enlistment of Negro soldiers became such an issue politically.
 Those who criticised the performance of the Negroes in battle were wont to be styled "copperheads"; friends of the
administration were inclined toward extravagant praise of
their conduct to prove the wisdom of the President's policy
of enlisting them. Historians who have given the subject
any considerable attention seem to have been unduly influenced by the laudatory nature of the evidence; this is especially true of the colored writers whose treatments of the
Negro soldiers' conduct in battle are eulogiums of their
courage and bravery.

Testimony of those who fought against the Negro soldiers is comparatively rare. The attitude of the average
Confederate soldier toward his sable opponents was that of
splendid indifference; to take cognizance of the Negroes'
presence as a factor in the opposing ranks was a conde-
scension he was loath to make. Such testimony as does ex-
ist is as extreme in character as that of the Northern Ne-
grophiles.

The divergence between the two extreme types of evidence is well illustrated by two accounts of the Negroes'
part in the assault of Port Hudson placed in juxtaposi-
tion. The first, that of a white Federal officer is as follows:

On their extreme right the two Negro regiments advanced
over the bayou . . . toward the enemy's works. . . . A fire
of musketry opened from the top of the bluff, and from the
rifle-pits all the way down. The fire was supported by their
batteries. . . . They stood up nobly, but it was impossible to
cross the bayou. . . . Slowly they fell back, the enemy not
daring to follow them. Hearing our heavy fire, another

charge was made, and another, and a fourth with a like result. . . . A fifth charge was made. . . . They stood like veterans and were mown down, and finally a retreat was ordered which was made as if by old soldiers. . . . I find that many sneerers are very polite to Colonel Nelson of the Third Louisiana. . . . No regiment behaved better than they did. They never staggered under a fire from a superior force and batteries of the largest guns known to warfare. . . . They fought with great desperation and carried all before them. They had to be restrained for fear they would get too far in unsupported. They have shown that they can and will fight well. I hope the Copperheads will now stop their abuse.[118]

The second account is that of a Confederate officer who participated in the fight. After praising the gallantry of the white Union troops he said of the Negroes as if an afterthought:

This was the battle of the 27th of May. A demonstration had indeed been made upon our extreme left, but it did not amount to a charge. A couple of Negro regiments with a line of white troops behind them came up through a growth of young willow trees to the edge of the clearing, a distance of between six and seven hundred feet from a rifle pit we had dug along the bluff which came out at that place. They were fired into by a small party of skirmishers in the woods on their flank, and from the thinly-lined rifle pit in their front, with a couple of small mountain howitzers which we had there. They broke at our fire and clustered behind the willow trees, apparently too panic-stricken either to advance or run. Our shots tore the fragile willows into fragments and the splinters were probably as dangerous as our fire, so that they were stricken down with great havoc. On account of the line of white troops behind them they probably had some difficulty in getting away, but in fifteen minutes after they first appeared, none of them was to be seen except the dead and those who were too badly wounded to crawl off. . . . The nearest of their dead to our rifle pits were two hundred

118. New York *Times*, June 11, 1863.

yards distant. This was the last we saw of Negro troops at Port Hudson.[119]

It is not in accord with reason to believe that men fresh from slavery and almost wholly inexperienced in the handling of arms should have been as valorous and as consistently devoid of wavering, skulking, and other evidences of fear usually characteristic of novitiates in arms as the friends of Negro soldiers have usually represented them to be. There are extenuating circumstances and Northern testimony to the contrary. General Banks in his commendation of the conduct of the Negro troops at Port Hudson —which commendation has been widely used as evidence of the Negroes' valor—made decided reservations. "The history of this day, proves conclusively," he said, "that the Government will find in this class of troops effective *supporters and defenders*. . . . They require only *good officers*, commands of limited numbers and *careful discipline* to make them excellent soldiers."[120] Colonel Greenleaf of a white Massachusetts regiment in the battle described the conduct of the Negroes as "an exhibition of cowardice on the part of the entire gang instead of that courageous and valiant spirit of which so much has been written."[121] This statement must be taken *cum grano salis* because Greenleaf was apparently opposed to the use of Negroes in the army in any except labor pursuits. In appraising the conduct of the colored troops at Port Hudson it should be remembered that fully one-half of them were free-born; that most of them had been under military organization since 1861; and that many of them were members of the influential mulatto element of New Orleans.

Milliken's Bend was the first engagement in which colored troops outnumbered the whites; it was also the first

119. New Orleans *Daily True Delta*, Aug. 9, 1863.
120. *O. R.*, Ser. 1, XXVI, pt. 1, 45. Italics mine. By "good officers" Banks means whites. He was opposed to the use of colored officers. *Ibid.*, pp. 688–689.
121. New Orleans *Daily Picayune*, Aug. 19, 1863, quoting correspondent of Chicago *Times*.

instance where most of the Negroes participating were ex-slaves. The Federal force consisting of about 800 Negroes and 300 whites fought behind breastworks. They were driven from their protected position to the edge of the Mississippi by a Confederate force of 1,500. The tide was turned by the timely arrival of two Federal gunboats. Admiral Porter of the Federal fleet gave most of the credit for the ultimate repulse of the Confederate assault to the gunboats and the white troops. In his report to General Grant he said: "Last night or early this morning the rebels . . . attacked Milliken's Bend and nearly gobbled up the whole party. Fortunately I heard of it in time to get the Choctaw and Lexington up there just as the attack commenced. . . . Our troops (mostly Negroes) retreated behind the banks near the waters edge, and the gunboats opened so rapidly on the enemy that they scampered off, the shells chasing them as far as the woods. . . . There are about 300 troops here in all not counting the blacks. . . . The 29th Iowa (I think it was) behaved well today [i.e., the white regiment; it was the 23rd Iowa instead of the 29th]. It stood its ground against great odds and kept the enemy out of the camps until the men could form and get into some kind of order."[122]

About half of the Negroes engaged at the Crater affair were from Virginia and Maryland. The almost universal testimony of those who were in position to observe their conduct is that they ran when their charge on the crest was repulsed. Their commander, General Ferrero, testified before the committee investigating the battle that "they retreated in great disorder and confusion." H. G. Thompson, colonel of the Nineteenth Regiment United States Colored Troops, said, in answer to a question as to how the

122. *O. R.*, Ser. 1, XXIV, pt. 2, 453–454. In an earlier dispatch he said that the retreating Negroes became infuriated when they saw their wounded comrades being slain, turned upon the Confederates, "slaughtered them like sheep and captured 200 prisoners." He was evidently misinformed about the prisoners because McCulloch reported only ten men missing. In Porter's second dispatch he does not make special mention of the Negroes.

Negroes behaved: "They went up as well as I ever saw
troops go up. . . . They came back on a run, every man
for himself."[123] Officers of some of the Union white troops
testified that their men were demoralized and pushed back
by the panicky Negroes.[124] A Northern white soldier who
took part in the fight and who was sympathetic toward the
Negroes said in a letter written two days after the battle:
"Worse still, the 13th Indiana white . . . deliberately shot
down many of the retreating soldiers. When I say there is
a fearful mortality among the dusky heroes you will readily
understand how it happened."[125] The New York *Herald*
correspondent reported that after their repulse the Negroes "ran, a terror-stricken, disordered mass of fugitives,
to the rear of the white troops. In vain their officers en-
deavored to rally them with all the persuasion of tongue,
sabre and pistol."[126]

The colored troops engaged in the charges upon Overton Hill during the battle of Nashville were mostly ex-
slaves. They had a comparatively insignificant part in this
affair, but Northern testimony indicates that they made a
better showing in this battle than the same class of troops
had previously made. Colonel Thompson, the commanding
officer of the colored brigade actively engaged admits, however, that about half of his force became so disorganized
during the assault as to require withdrawal for re-forma-
tion before the other troops were repulsed. General Wood,
whose corps Thompson's troops supported in the assault,
does not mention the assistance given by the Negroes in his
report of the movement; neither do any of his subordinates.

While the colored soldiers were not as efficient fighters
as their Northern eulogists represented them, it is just as
true that they were not the inconsequential cowards depicted by Southern disparagers. They made several successive charges over very difficult ground and under gall-

123. *O. R.*, Ser. 1, XL, pt. 1, 93, 106.
124. *Ibid.*, pp. 78, 100.
125. New York *Times*, Aug. 7, 1864.
126. New York *Herald*, Aug. 2, 1864.

ing fire at Port Hudson. Their unhappy showing at the Crater may be attributed in part to the adversity of circumstances. They had been drilled for days to lead the assault, only to have their rôle changed on the eve of the battle. When they went into the engagement the white troops who had preceded them had suffered a repulse; some of these had set a bad example for their sable comrades by skulking under cover and refusing to obey orders to advance. The colored soldiers had to march through the ranks of the more or less demoralized whites in order to charge the crest. In the advanced position they encountered the concentrated fire of infuriated Confederates. They lost most of their officers. Their division commander was absent in a bombproof. At the charge on Overton Hill some members of one colored regiment advanced through a hail of bullets to within a few feet of the Confederate works.

There is evidence in Confederate testimony that the colored soldiers deserved more credit than was generally given them by Southerners. General McCulloch in his official report of the battle at Milliken's Bend said that the Confederate charge upon the first Federal position "was resisted by the Negro portion of the enemy's force with considerable obstinacy, while the white or true Yankee portion ran like whipped curs almost as soon as the charge was ordered."[127] Confederate Major General Clayton, who occupied a position on Overton Hill assaulted by the Negroes, said that a color-bearer carrying a flag with the following inscription "Eighteenth Regiment U. S. Colored Infantry; presented by the Colored Ladies of Murfreesborough," was shot down *"in a few steps"* of the "Rebel" works.[128] A Confederate artilleryman told of three successive charges made by Negroes under a severe fire in a minor engagement in South Carolina. "I never saw such disregard of danger and certain death as these Negroes displayed," he

127. *O. R.*, Ser. 1, XXIV, pt. 2, 467.
128. *Ibid.*, XLV, pt. 1, 698. Italics mine. The proximity of this or another color-bearer of a Negro regiment to the "Rebel" works is mentioned in the report of Brigadier General Holtzclaw, *ibid.*, p. 705.

added. His explanation of this demonstration of courage, so surprising to him, was: "We heard afterwards that they had been fed up on liquor until they were crazy drunk."[129] The Richmond *Daily Dispatch* offered a similar explanation—"bad whiskey"—for the advance made by the Negroes at the Crater.[130]

Southerners hooted the enlistment of Negroes by the North early in the war; their attitude is reflected in the comment of a Confederate soldier: "Oh let them come by all means; we will soon turn their swords into ploughshares and their spears into reaping hooks";[131] and the statement of a "Rebel" soldier that "if every Negro in the South was in the Yankee army it would make very little difference with the fighting strength of the enemy."[132] People of the South also ridiculed the conduct of the colored troops in the early battles, a newspaper correspondent reporting that at Port Hudson, "what did not get killed or wounded made good use of their long heels and this was the last seen of them."[133] They attributed apparent gallantries of Negroes to bayonet prodding *en derrière* by white soldiers, or to the terrifying threats of the officers.[134] But in striking inconsistency with this deprecation and ridicule was the adoption of an act in the eventide of the Confederacy providing for the enlistment of 300,000 Negro soldiers to fight for Southern independence.

Generally speaking, the conduct of the Negroes in the war did not prove them good or bad fighters. It did show them capable of performing acts of reckless courage; it manifested their ability to go forward in impetuous charges

129. Confidential source of information.
130. Issue of Aug. 2, 1864.
131. *Weekly Confederation* (Montgomery), May 17, 1861.
132. *Genealogical Notes on the Family of Mays and Reminiscences of the War between the States from Notes Written around the Campfires by Samuel Elias Mays*, p. 164.
133. Charleston *Daily Courier*, Aug. 7, 1863, quoting Montgomery *Advertiser*.
134. Ford, *Life in the Confederate Army*, p. 40; Girard, *Les États Confédérés*, p. 12.

under galling fire. Their dependability in standing up against stubborn and sustained resistance was left for future determination.

In addition to the Negroes actually enrolled as soldiers, there were a great many who were attached to the army in an accessory capacity as laborers and servants. In some cases the attachment was more or less permanent, the laborers being organized into squads, and even included on the army muster roll; but they were not permitted to wear soldiers' uniforms.[135] As a general rule, however, the connection was only temporary, the workers being hired for definite tasks. It is impossible to determine the number engaged in this accessory capacity. According to the only available estimates the number was not less than that of the regularly enlisted soldiers; i.e., about 200,000.[136]

Almost all the Negroes engaged in this type of service were from the South. Their most important work was the digging of intrenchments and canals, the erection of fortifications, and the building and repair of railways and military roads. They also served extensively as teamsters, cooks —every regiment according to one authority had ten to twenty Negroes along with it to do the cooking and take care of the teams—hostlers, cattle-drivers, butchers, porters, dockhands, boat hands, mechanics, wheelwrights, coopers, and carpenters.[137] Federal officers frequently employed contrabands as body servants.[138] Negro women were sometimes employed as laundresses and as hospital nurses. An extensive use of colored females around the camps was discouraged by the authorities because of the demoralizing

135. *O. R.,* Ser. 1, XVII, pt. 2, 158–159.

136. Paul T. Arnold, "Negro Soldiers in the United States Army," *Magazine of History,* XI (1910), 4, 10; Williams, *History of the Negro Race in America,* II, 262.

137. *O. R.,* Ser. 1, XII, pt. 1, 53; XVI, pt. 1, 816, pt. 2, 227, 291, 437; XVII, pt. 2, 56, 113, 149, 158, 159; XXIII, pt. 2, 17–18; Ser. 3, II, 807; Colyer, *Brief Report of the Services Rendered by the Freed People to the United States Army in North Carolina,* p. 9; New Orleans *Times,* Aug. 27, 1864; *Daily Picayune,* Dec. 9, 1862.

138. *O. R.,* Ser. 1, VIII, 584; Ser. 3, III, 840. Eaton, *Report for 1864,* p. 20.

influences resulting therefrom.[139] "Prostitution," observed one officer, "is worse than slavery."[140] In the Department of the Gulf four captains and two lieutenants were dishonorably discharged from the service for forcing an entrance into the quarters occupied by colored laundresses at Fort Jackson.[141]

The life of the military laborers was a hard one. The hours were long and the labor frequently heavy. The Negroes were sometimes compelled to work in positions exposed to Confederate batteries. Eight colored men and an overseer engaged in digging a countermine during the siege of Vicksburg were killed when the "Rebels" exploded a mine beneath them.[142] Early in the war many of the Negroes worked for only clothing and subsistence. The wages authorized by the government usually ranged from five to eight dollars a month and rations. A considerable part of this was not infrequently withheld for clothing, or for the support of non-laborers; in Virginia for a time in 1861, all of the wages were appropriated for these purposes.[143] The pay authorized was very commonly in arrears. An investigating commission appointed by the Secretary of War in June, 1864, reported that of a total of 2,768 men employed by one engineer between the summer of 1862 and April, 1864, only 310 had been paid. The aggregate receipts were only $13,648 out of the $85,858.50 due. Some of the men had not received pay for the work done in 1862; their chances of receiving it in 1864 were considerably diminished by the fact that the paymasters required that they be identified by the foremen under whom they had labored two years before. The total amount due colored workers on fortifications in the vicinity of Nashville, in August, 1864, was, according to the commission's report,

139. O. R., Ser. 1, XXIII, pt. 2, 17–18.
140. Ibid., XXXIV, pt. 4, 93.
141. New Orleans Times, March 23, 1864.
142. O. R., Ser. 1, XXIV, pt. 2, 416.
143. "Report of Major General John E. Wool on the Number, Age, and Condition of the Africans in the Department of Virginia," House Ex. Docs., 37th Cong., 2nd Sess., VII, no. 85, 2–7.

$112,292.17.[144] Colored men who did nine months' work on a defense project at Franklin, Tennessee, at the promised rate of ten dollars a month, received only ten dollars each at the end of the period. White laborers who worked with them were paid in full. Many of the colored men were enlisted in the army after their labor on the defense was completed without being given anything to show for their previous work. The quartermaster had them receipt the pay rolls; these he kept in his possession, probably to his future enrichment.[145]

The colored laborers were also defrauded in respect to clothing and food. In spite of the fact that generous amounts of money were withheld for clothing, the Negroes were frequently compelled to work in scanty, ragged attire. An officer in Virginia who had charge of feeding a squad of Negro laborers appropriated a part of the daily ration prescribed for each hand and sold the food thus pilfered to sutlers.[146]

Delinquent or refractory laborers were punished. Men guilty of minor offenses were sometimes made to stand on a barrel; women were confined in dark rooms.[147] More brutal treatment, however, was not uncommon.[148]

It is not to be wondered that Negroes had an aversion to military labor. Rarely did an officer secure a sufficiency of volunteer workers. Impressments, authorized and unauthorized, were resorted to throughout the Federal-controlled portions of the South.[149] "Able-bodied Negroes," according to the superintendent of Negro affairs in North Carolina, "were offered employment at the best wages, and

144. "Report of Thomas Hood and S. W. Bostick, Special Commissioners upon the Condition and Treatment of Colored Refugees in Kentucky, Tennessee and Alabama," *Sen. Ex. Docs.*, 38th Cong., 2nd Sess., no. 28, pp. 12–15.

145. *Ibid.*

146. *House Ex. Docs.*, 37th Cong., 2nd Sess., VII, no. 85, 2–7.

147. Pierce, *The Freedmen of Port Royal*, p. 313.

148. *O. R.*, Ser. 3, III, 840.

149. *Ibid.*, Ser. 1, VIII, 464; XVI, pt. 2, 227, 291, 437; XVII, pt. 2, 56, 154; XXXII, pt. 2, 479; XLII, pt. 2, 590, 653; Ser. 3, III, 684, 840.

whosoever hesitated was persuaded to work by the solicitation of the bayonet."[150]

The inconsiderate and discriminatory treatment accorded Negroes in Federal military pursuits, whether as laborers or as full-fledged soldiers, is a regrettable episode in the transition of the colored race in America from slavery to freedom. In fact, the entire experience of Southern Negroes during the War of Secession was discouraging and disillusioning. The outbreak of the war and the coming of the "Yankees" fired the hope and enthusiasm of the blacks throughout the South. To many of them in peripheral portions of the Confederacy freedom was not long in coming, as a result of Federal advances in 1861 and 1862. Others in remoter regions chafed under continuing bondage, while feigning contentment and happiness to their unsuspecting masters, till 1864 and 1865. But whether release from slavery came early or late, it was always accompanied by unexpected hardship. Those Negroes who were assembled in contraband camps died by the thousands; those who were employed on plantations received treatment little better than that which they had received under the old régime; those who entered military pursuits were dealt with in a manner more becoming to slaves than to freedmen. In the light of all these unhappy experiences, it must have been apparent to Southern Negroes when the triumph of the North in 1865 assured the final end of slavery that the fight for real freedom had just begun.

150. James, *Annual Report of the Superintendent of Negro Affairs in North Carolina* (1864), p. 56.

BIBLIOGRAPHICAL NOTE

THE following discussion includes only the more important materials used in this study. No attempt is made to list every item cited in the footnotes.

PART I. NEGROES IN THE CONFEDERACY

MANUSCRIPTS

MANUSCRIPT materials consist chiefly of plantation records, diaries, and correspondence. The records of Greenwood Plantation (1858–1864) near McPhersonville, South Carolina, and Shirley Plantation (1816–1872) on the James River, both in the Library of Congress, deserve special mention. The records of Magnolia Plantation (1859–1863) below New Orleans, in the custody of J. de Roulhac Hamilton of the University of North Carolina, are very valuable for the light which they throw upon the effect of Federal invasion on the Negroes; frequent mention is made of affairs on neighboring places. The R. F. W. Allston Papers (in private possession), containing many letters and reports of overseers on the Allston plantations of South Carolina, include the war period; they contain a wealth of information concerning the labor and conduct of slaves. The diary of J. B. Moore, in the possession of Judge Stone Devours of Laurel, Mississippi, tells of the troubles experienced by a planter-lawyer of North Alabama during Federal raids. The diaries of John N. Waddell, Presbyterian minister and small slave-owner of La Grange, Tennessee, and Betty Herndon Maury of Fredericksburg, Virginia, both in the Library of Congress, are helpful. The Clay Papers in the Duke University Library tell of the troubles which members of the family of Senator C. C. Clay had with the care and control of slaves on a plantation in an invaded area; the most useful material in this collection consists of the letters written by Senator Clay's mother. The Pettigrew Papers in the Library of the University of North Carolina contain a wealth of varied material on Negroes during the war. This family had wide and influential connections in North and South Carolina and carried on a voluminous correspondence. The collection is particularly valuable for the light which it throws on the removal of slaves before Federal invasion. The University of Texas has perhaps the largest manuscript and transcript collection of ante-bellum Southern history material in the South. Papers which had particular bearing upon this study were those of the Massie family of Virginia and those of W. H. Neblett of Texas. In the use of the latter, allowance must be made for the morbid pessimism of Mrs. Neblett.

The journal of Samuel P. Boyer, surgeon on a ship of the South Atlantic Blockading Squadron, has a number of valuable references to the reception of fugitives from the coast regions of Georgia and South Carolina. This journal is on deposit in the Library of Congress. Letters written to the governors of Mississippi, Alabama, and Texas, in the respective state archives, contain much information concerning the conduct of slaves. The same is doubtless true of the letters written to the governors of other Southern states, but I have not used them.

A great number of letters and other manuscripts in private possession in various parts of the country were consulted in the preparation of this work. While individual mention cannot be made of all items and collections of this class, special attention should be called to the journal of the Reverend James A. Lyon in possession of Dr. Robert H. White of Nashville, Tennessee; papers of the Abernathy family of Giles County, Tennessee, in possession of Miss Sue Rogers, of Pulaski, Tennessee; and the Mulberry Hill Plantation Letters in the library of the late Ulrich B. Phillips. These manuscripts, generously made available for use in this study by their custodians, threw valuable light on obscure points.

NEWSPAPERS

THE *Confederate States Almanac* for 1863 says of the newspapers of the time, "they are all sizes and colors"—"short enough for a pocket handkerchief one day and big enough for a table cloth another." But, in spite of their variations and defects, the newspapers and contemporary periodicals are the most valuable of the source materials for the study of the Negro in the Confederacy. The Charleston Library Society has almost complete files of the Charleston *Daily Courier* and the Charleston *Mercury*. The Confederate Museum and the Virginia State Library have fairly complete files of the *Daily Richmond Examiner*, the Richmond *Enquirer*, the *Daily Dispatch*, the Richmond *Whig*, and less complete files of the *Sentinel*. In one or both of these libraries there are partial files of a number of papers which contain valuable information concerning the religious life of the slaves; among them are the *Southern Churchman* (Richmond, Protestant Episcopal), the Richmond *Christian Advocate* (Methodist Episcopal), and the *Southern Presbyterian* (Columbia and Augusta). The State Library at Montgomery has a good collection of Alabama papers including the Montgomery *Weekly Advertiser* (files of this paper are also available at the office of the Montgomery *Advertiser*), the Montgomery *Weekly Mail,* the Mobile *Daily Advertiser and Register,* and the *Southwestern Baptist* (Tuskegee). The Georgia State Library has almost complete files of the *Southern Recorder* (weekly, Milledgeville). The Carnegie Library of Atlanta has nearly all the issues of the *Southern Confederacy* (daily, Atlanta), through May, 1863. Duke University Library has a good collection of North Carolina papers, almost complete files of the *Southern Field and Fireside* (weekly, Augusta), and scattered issues of other Confederate periodicals.

The State Library at Austin has an excellent collection of Texas newspapers. Good files of Louisiana papers for the Confederate period are available in the Louisiana State University at Baton Rouge, the Howard Memorial Library, the *Picayune* Office, and the City Hall Archives of New Orleans. Of particular interest is the Civil War file of the Opelousas *Courier* in the Louisiana State University Library printed on double sheets of wall paper, one sheet being in English and the other in French.

OFFICIAL DOCUMENTS

OF documentary sources in print, the *Official Records of the Union and Confederate Armies* published by the United States Government (1880–1901) in 128 volumes, are most valuable. Much of the material is official only in the sense that it is included in the government's collection. The Fourth Series is devoted exclusively to Confederate matters. The acts of the state legislatures and the *Journals of the Confederate Congress* (Washington, 1904–1905) contain relevant material.

PRINTED JOURNALS AND MEMOIRS

PRINTED diaries and memoirs are of uneven value. There are several which deserve mention as being particularly helpful. The

Chronicles of Chicora Wood (New York, 1923) by Elizabeth W.
Allston Pringle, daughter of R. F. W. Allston, is a valuable supplement to the Allston Papers mentioned above. The book is
largely devoid of the rhapsodic tone which characterizes many
recollections. Elizabeth Allen Coxe, *Memories of a South Carolina Plantation during the War* (privately printed, 1912), based
on a diary kept by the author, is attractively written and seemingly reliable. Parthenia Hague, *A Blockaded Family* (Boston,
1888), and Victoria Clayton, *White and Black under the Old
Regime* (Milwaukee, 1899), describe conditions on plantations in
Southern Alabama. The tone of these accounts is somewhat ro-
seate. The same criticism applies to Mary Gay, *Life in Dixie during the War* (Atlanta, 1892); Mrs. Irby Morgan, *How It Was*
(Nashville, 1892); and Susan D. Smedes, *A Southern Planter*
(New York, 1900).

Dolly Sumner Lunt, *A Woman's War-Time Journal* (New
York, 1918), is a valuable though brief record, kept by a native
of Maine who became the wife of a Georgia planter long before
the war. Mary B. Chesnut's spicy *Diary from Dixie* (New York,
1905), has several allusions to the conduct of slaves. J. B. Jones,
Rebel War Clerk's Diary (Philadelphia, 1866), contains occasional comments on the Richmond slave market and on political
phases of the Negro question. *Two Diaries,* journals of Misses
Susan R. Jervey and Charlotte St. J. Ravenel (published by the
St. John's Hunting Club, South Carolina, 1921), are valuable for
the light which they throw on the conduct of "low country" South
Carolina slaves during the Federal raids. "The Westover Journal
of John A. Selden, Esquire, 1858–1862," edited by John Spencer
Bassett (*Smith College Studies in History,* VI, no. 4, Northamp-
ton, Mass., 1921), tells of difficulties on a Virginia plantation resulting from Federal invasion.

The observations of Europeans who visited the Confederacy
are valuable. Arthur J. Fremantle, *Three Months in the Southern
States* (New York, 1864), is particularly helpful because of the
extent of the author's travels and the attention which he gives to
various phases of slavery. Other works of this class worthy of
mention are C. Gerard, *Les Etats Confédérés Visites en 1863*
(Paris, 1864); the Reverend W. W. Malet, *Errand to the South
in the Summer of 1862* (London, 1863); and *Two Months in the
Confederate States* (London, 1863), by an English Merchant.
The fact that these visitors were generally friendly to the South

and to slavery must be taken into consideration in the use of their accounts.

SECONDARY AUTHORITIES

ULRICH B. PHILLIPS, *American Negro Slavery* (New York, 1918), and *Life and Labor in the Old South* (Boston, 1929), while devoted primarily to the ante-bellum period, are indispensable as a background to a proper understanding of the institution of slavery during the war.

Though monographs are not very fruitful sources of information concerning the war-time Negro, the following contain some enlightening materials: W. L. Fleming, *Civil War and Reconstruction in Alabama* (New York, 1905); W. W. Davis, *Civil War and Reconstruction in Florida* (New York, 1913); F. L. Owsley, *State Rights in the Confederacy* (Chicago, 1925); J. C. Schwab, *The Confederate States of America* (New York, 1901); and Charles H. Wesley, *Negro Labor in the United States, 1850–1925* (New York, 1927).

Histories of the United States covering the war period say practically nothing about the Southern Negro outside of his relation to political and military questions. The statements of Confederate historians are confined largely to general commendations of the Negro's industry and faithfulness.

PART II. NEGROES UNDER FEDERAL CONTROL

MANUSCRIPTS

PLANTATION records, diaries, and manuscripts of a similar nature which throw light on the day-by-day activities of the Negro laborers under Federal control are exceedingly rare. The Library of Louisiana State University has two very valuable items of this class; namely, the Plantation Record Books of Pleasant Hill Plantation in southwest Mississippi for a twenty-year period, 1846–1866, and the Plantation Diary of A. Franklin Pugh, covering a period of seven years, including four years of the war era. The Account Book of Mooreland Plantation, 1860–1868, evidently the property of Governor Thomas O. Moore of Louisiana, in the University of Texas Archives, has a very valuable comment on the work of Negroes under the free-labor system. The William Law Papers, 1761–1890, in the Duke University Library contain several interesting accounts and contracts with freedom on a South Carolina plantation.

NEWSPAPERS

MOST of the newspaper material consulted deals with political and military aspects of the Negro question. However, the New York *Times, Herald,* and *Tribune* contain occasional reports and comments on labor on leased plantations and the conditions in contraband camps. As a general rule, the *Tribune* assumed an attitude friendly to the Negro on controversial points, the *Herald* held the opposite extreme, and the *Times* took a position between the two. The New Orleans papers, good files of which are available in the Howard Memorial Library, the City Hall Archives, and the *Picayune* office, contain material on many phases of the Negroes' activities. The New Orleans *Times* and the *Picayune* revealed a greater tendency than the other papers to be critical of the policies of the Federal military authorities, the latter being suspended by Banks for a time in 1864. The *Era* was prejudiced in favor of those in authority; it claimed to be the official paper of the National Government in New Orleans for the publication of military orders and other official items. The New Orleans *Tribune* was the organ of the free colored element.

OFFICIAL DOCUMENTS

DOCUMENTS of particular value, in addition to the *Official Records,* include the "Report of Major General John E. Wool on the Number, Age, and Condition of the Africans in the Department of Virginia," *House Executive Documents,* 37th Cong., 2nd Sess., no. 28; *Report of the Board of Education for Freedmen, Department of the Gulf, for the Year 1864* (New Orleans, 1865); and Edwin L. Pierce, *The Freedmen of Port Royal* (New York, 1863), an official report of an agent of the Treasury Department who had charge of Negro affairs in South Carolina for a time in 1862.

PAMPHLETS, JOURNALS, CORRESPONDENCE

THE most helpful material on this phase of the study was found in the flood of pamphlets which emanated from the press during the war or shortly thereafter; of these, the periodic reports of benevolent societies which include frequently letters written by representatives telling of their experiences with the ex-slaves, were most useful; those of the New England Freedmen's Aid Commission, the New York and the New England Yearly Meeting of Friends, the National Freedmen's Relief Association, and the American Missionary Association deserve special mention. The reports of the superintendents of freedmen contain an abundance of material on all phases of the Negroes' activities; particularly relevant are the John Eaton, *Report of the General Superintendent of Freedmen, Department of the Tennessee and State of Arkansas for 1864* (Memphis, 1865); the *Annual Report of Thomas W. Conway, Superintendent, Bureau of Free Labor, Department of the Gulf, to Major General Hurlbut, for the year 1864* (New Orleans, 1864); Reverend Horace James, the *Annual Report of the Superintendent of Negro Affairs in North Carolina* for 1864 (Boston, 1865); and Reverend Joseph Warren, *Extracts from the Reports of Superintendents of Freedmen Compiled from Records in the Office of Colonel John Eaton, Jr. General Superintendent of Freedmen, Department of the Tennessee and State of Arkansas* (Vicksburg, 1864). Other valuable items in this class of material are *A Report on the Condition of the Freedmen of the Mississippi, Presented to the Western Sanitary Commission,* Dec. 17, 1862 (St. Louis, 1864), by James E. Yeatman; "Reminiscences of Service with Colored Troops in the Army of the Cumberland, 1863–1865," by Thomas J. Morgan, published in *Personal Narratives of the Soldiers and Sailors Historical Society of Rhode Island,* Third Series (Providence, 1885); and "The Freedmen of South Carolina: Some Account of their Appearance, Character, Condition, and Peculiar Customs," by Charles Nordhoff, in *Papers of the Day,* collected and arranged by Frank Moore (New York, 1863).

Memoirs, diaries, and letters of those who worked among the ex-slaves were published in great numbers. But the value of these, like much of the other material issuing from the pen of Northerners, is greatly diminished by the tendency of the authors to see much good and little evil in those who had so recently been released from the "curse of slavery." This fact must be kept in mind constantly in the use of these materials. Perhaps the most useful of works of this class is John Eaton's *Grant, Lincoln, and the Freedmen* (New York, 1907), which tells in detail of the experiences of the author as superintendent of Negro affairs in the

Valley of the Mississippi and also throws much light on the attitude of high military officials and the administration toward the question of the disposition of contrabands. Thomas W. Knox, *Camp-Fire and Cotton-Field* (New York, 1865), contains a vivid account of the difficulties of a "Yankee" newspaper correspondent who attempted unsuccessfully to make a crop with free labor in Louisiana. *First Days Amongst the Contrabands* (Boston, 1893) by Elizabeth Hyde Botume tells of the activities of an Easterner who taught Negroes in South Carolina. The author's Negrophilism is alleviated somewhat by her sense of humor. *The Letters and Diary of Laura M. Towne* (Cambridge, 1912), edited by Rupert Sargent Holland, gives the experiences of another "Yankee" school teacher in South Carolina; *Letters from Port Royal Written at the Time of the Civil War* (Boston, 1906), edited by Elizabeth Ware Pearson, is the correspondence of a group of Eastern philanthropists who worked in South Carolina as plantation superintendents and teachers during the war. These letters constitute a valuable source on many phases of the contrabands' activities.

Thomas Wentworth Higginson, *Army Life in a Black Regiment* (Boston, 1870), is an interesting, though biased, account of the experiences of an anti-slavery Easterner who commanded a pioneer regiment of Negro troops.

INDEX

ABANDONED plantations, leasing of, in Mississippi Valley, 185–186, 188–189; sale of, by Federal Government, 199–200

See also Freedmen; Treasury Department; War Department

Agriculture, diversification in Confederacy, 25–29, 44–48

See also Cotton; Sugar; Wheat; Labor of freedmen; Labor of slaves

Alabama, movement of slaves in, at invasion, 5; slave code of, modified, 35; restriction of cotton acreage in, 44–45; extension of iron industry in, 60–61; expansion of coal mining in, 61; trial of slaves in, 170

Alexandria, Va., contraband camp in, 202

Algiers, La., concentration of freedmen in, 214

Allen, Gov. H. W., letter of, to body servant, 144

Allston, R. F. W., difficulty of clothing slaves on plantation of, 29; plantations supervised by Negro driver, 51; deterioration of machinery on plantations of, 53; engages in salt-making, 61–62; misconduct of slaves on plantations of, 79–80; religious life of slaves of, 103; slaves of, as military laborers, 132

American Missionary Association, work of, among freedmen, 260, 262, 264, 268

See also Freedmen's aid societies

Andrew, Gov. J. A., opposes sending of freedmen to North, 202

Andrews, Eliza, on negro songs, 103–104

Anthony, Lt. Col., insubordination of, 182

Antietam, Battle of, 196

Arkansas, slave code of, modified, 34–35; restriction of cotton acreage in, 45; education of freedmen in, 269; recruiting of freedmen in, 311

Arming of slaves, in colonial South Carolina, 146–147; in Revolution, 147; considered early in war, 148–149; advocated by Cleburne, 150; attitude of Jefferson Davis toward, 150–151, 158–159; considered by Confederate Congress, 151–152; arguments supporting, 152–154; opposition to, 152, 154–157; results of, 159–162; reported in North, 191

Army, Confederate. *See* Soldiers, Confederate

Army, United States. *See* Soldiers, Federal; War Department

Army worm, destruction wrought by, 242–243

Augusta, Ga., slave prices in, 88–89

BANKS, N. P., supervision of freedmen's affairs by, 189, 210–222, 254–255; labor system adopted for Mississippi Valley, 226; invites comment of planters on free labor system, 254; promotes education of freedmen, 264–268; attacks Port Hudson, 325–326; on conduct of Negro soldiers under fire, 327, 336

Barbecues, enjoyment by slaves, 42–43

Barksdale, Senator, corresponds with Lee on arming slaves, 158

Bates, Delevan, conduct at Battle of Crater, 332

Baton Rouge, concentration of freedmen in, 211, 214